Suing the Gun Industry

A Battle at the Crossroads of Gun Control and Mass Torts

Timothy D. Lytton, Editor

University of Michigan Press
Ann Arbor

2008   2007   2006   2005   4   3   2   1

A CIP catalog record for this book is available from the British Library.

Library of Congress Cataloging-in-Publication Data

Suing the gun industry : a battle at the crossroads of gun control and
mass torts / edited by Timothy D. Lytton.
p.   cm.
Includes bibliographical references and index.
ISBN 0-472-11510-3 (cloth : alk. paper)
1. Firearms—Law and legislation—United States.   2. Torts—United
States.   3. Class actions (Civil procedure)—United States.
I. Lytton, Timothy D., 1965–
KF3941.S85   2005
346.7303'8—dc22   2004030731

CONTENTS

ACKNOWLEDGMENTS

This project was made possible by the encouragement of my faculty colleagues at Albany Law School and the generous financial support of Dean Tom Guernsey, who funded both my own research and a conference for contributing authors in the fall of 2003. Associate Dean Bob Begg and his library staff, in particular Bob Emery and Mary Wood, fielded a steady flow of research requests. Lucas Mihuta, Seth Zoracki, and Alexandra Harrington provided essential research assistance. Alexandra Harrington, Theresa Colbert, and Tammy Weinman helped organize the conference. Beyond this, Alexandra Harrington coordinated the editing process among all of the authors and kept the project on schedule. I am grateful for all of her many efforts.

I am especially indebted to Peter Schuck for encouraging me to undertake editing a book on gun litigation in the first place and coaching me throughout the process. When I was a law student in the late 1980s, Peter introduced me to the field of mass torts, and he both inspired me to pursue a career in the legal academy and helped me secure a position. I am very proud to be among Peter's many students, and the more I develop my own ideas about law, the more I realize just how deeply indebted to him I am.

Austin Sarat tutored me in how to write a book proposal and how to edit a volume of independent essays. Steve Wasby read the entire manuscript and offered sage advice about organization of the chapters. Jim Reische at the University of Michigan Press has shepherded the book from proposal to publication, while Kevin Rennells provided valuable assistance coordinating the editing stages.

The greatest reward of working on this project has been the opportunity to work closely with the contributing authors. It has been an honor to work among such thoughtful and talented scholars, and I am grateful for their individual and collective mentoring.

My parents, Bernard and Norma Lytton, and my sister, Jennifer, have supported me enthusiastically in this project, as they have in so many others throughout my life. My wife, Rachel Anisfeld, continues to be my toughest scholarly critic and my most ardent supporter. This volume is dedicated to our children, Medad and Margalit, in the hope that by means of honest debate about the regulation of firearms the world they inherit will suffer less from government restrictions on liberty and the carnage of gun violence.

INTRODUCTION

*An Overview of Lawsuits
against the Gun Industry*

TIMOTHY D. LYTTON

Since the early 1980s, a growing number of gun violence victims have turned to the tort system seeking compensation for their injuries. These victims have filed claims not only against their assailants but also against gun sellers and manufacturers. By suing sellers and manufacturers, who have deeper pockets than the assailants, victims seek to improve their chances of receiving compensation. Victims also view successful tort claims as a way to promote safer firearm designs, to deter future sales to criminals, and to place part of the blame for gun violence on the industry. In addition to claims by individual victims, over thirty municipalities and the State of New York have filed lawsuits against the industry, seeking to recover the costs of law enforcement and emergency medical services related to gun violence. Several of these government lawsuits also demand injunctions that would force the industry to incorporate safety features into firearms and to restrict sales in ways aimed at reducing gun violence. In response, the industry and its allies have lobbied state legislatures and Congress to grant them statutory immunity. Proponents of the suits claim that this litigation will reform the industry in ways that will reduce gun violence. Opponents argue that the suits represent an end run around the legislative process and that the costs of defending these suits, even if the courts ultimately reject them, will wreak financial ruin on the industry.

    This book examines lawsuits against the gun industry within the context of two larger controversies at the top of the nation's domestic political agenda: gun control and tort reform. Throughout, discussion of the litigation is framed by two questions. The first, central to the debate over gun control, is whether regulating the firearms industry can reduce gun violence. The second, underlying the disagreement about tort reform, is what role, if any, courts should play in the creation of public policies such as gun control.

It may be helpful at the outset to clarify the relationship between gun litigation and gun control policy. Many lawsuits against gun manufacturers demand only money damages for injuries suffered by victims of gun violence or, in the case of suits brought by municipalities, for the costs of police and emergency services occasioned by gun violence. While the principal aim of these claims is compensation, they have regulatory implications insofar as they discourage manufacturers from engaging in the types of conduct that gave rise to the claims in the first place. Some lawsuits against manufacturers aim more directly at regulatory outcomes, demanding injunctive relief in the form of restrictions on the way gun manufacturers do business. Thus, whether by implication or by design, gun litigation has the power, and often the purpose, to regulate the firearms industry.

Lawsuits against the gun industry promote two types of regulations—the imposition of safety standards in the design of firearms and restrictions on the ways guns are marketed. Disagreement about the efficacy of these types of regulations has fueled many decades of legislative controversy over gun control. Stiff resistance to firearms regulation by the National Rifle Association (NRA) has defeated or significantly scaled back most congressional attempts to impose design standards and sales restrictions. Gun control proponents have filed lawsuits against the gun industry as a way to shift the struggle over gun control from legislatures to courts, where NRA lobbying power is not effective. They have argued that the NRA's fierce lobbying tactics and its use of campaign contributions to reelect its allies and defeat its enemies distort the legislative process and that litigation is a legitimate way to overcome the NRA's undue political influence. The NRA and the industry have fired back accusations that courts have no business deciding the gun control policy issues raised by plaintiffs' claims and that these issues should be decided by democratically elected legislatures, not unelected judges. The NRA has denounced the suits as an attempt to achieve through litigation the very same reforms rejected by federal, state, and local legislatures. This argument has held sway with many judges and legislatures.

Judges have dismissed all but a few of the suits, many based on a reluctance to engage in judicial policy-making, to "legislate from the bench." For their part, legislatures in thirty-two states, lobbied heavily by the NRA, have passed legislation granting the industry immunity from suit. There is strong congressional support for similar nationwide immunity legislation. In turn, gun control proponents have pointed to immunity legislation as further evidence of the gun lobby's power to manipulate the legislative process.

The chapters that follow offer a variety of perspectives on gun violence, gun control, the gun industry, gun litigation, and the use of gun litigation as a regulatory tool. This book aims not to resolve the tensions between these different perspectives but rather to deepen appreciation of them and the ways in which they sometimes complement and sometimes clash with each other. Thus, by providing insight into the diversity of views driving the litigation, the book aims to advance discussion; it does not pretend to offer a solution. This introduction begins with an overview of gun litigation and then examines a number of themes that run throughout the book.

The Rise of Personal Injury Suits against Firearm Manufacturers and the Transformation of Gun Litigation into a Mass Tort

Throughout the 1980s and the first half of the 1990s, lawsuits by shooting victims against gun manufacturers took the form of individual plaintiffs seeking compensation from individual defendants. Plaintiffs portrayed their suits as traditional personal injury claims based on conventional theories such as negligence or strict product liability. Beginning in the mid-1990s, plaintiffs began to develop novel theories of liability and new litigation strategies. In 1998, two cities filed suit against the entire industry, seeking not only money damages but also injunctive relief in the form of design standards and marketing restrictions. Within a few years, gun litigation had been transformed from a relatively obscure collection of personal injury cases into one of the most notable legal trends of the decade. By 2000 gun litigation was regularly front-page news, and manufacturers faced potentially bankrupting industrywide liability exposure as a result of suits by dozens of individual victims, over thirty cities, and the State of New York.

The rise of lawsuits against the gun industry is part of a larger trend to reframe gun violence as a public health problem. In the 1960s and 1970s, injury prevention emerged as a field of inquiry within public health.[1] As this field developed, researchers turned their attention to violence as a source of injury and to gun violence in particular. Talking of a gun violence "epidemic," public health scholars sought to identify the causes and distribution of gun violence injury using epidemiological tools common in the study of disease.[2] Epidemiological interest in identifying the "disease agent" drew attention to firearms, which in turn spurred interest in safer gun designs.[3] A desire to isolate "environmental factors" that foster gun violence led researchers to examine the marketing and distribution of firearms, giving rise to proposals for greater restrictions on gun sales.[4] Increasing interest in firearm designs and marketing restrictions spurred by this public health approach has expanded the focus of attention from the individual perpetrators of gun violence to include manufacturers and dealers. As a result, there has been less emphasis on criminal sanctions as a response to gun violence and more interest in industry regulation as a way to prevent it.[5] Early lawsuits against the gun industry both were inspired by this focus on gun designs and marketing restrictions and helped to promote it.[6] And given legislative resistance to their proposed reforms, public health scholars expressed support for the litigation.[7]

The transformation of gun litigation from the early individual personal injury suits into a mass tort is part of a second trend. In the 1960s, injury victims, advocacy groups, and plaintiffs' attorneys began using tort litigation as a tool to address large-scale public health problems by suing industries that manufacture the products that cause them. This type of litigation is characterized by the aggregation of hundreds, thousands, or even, in some cases, millions of victim claims; the naming of most or all manufacturers as defendants; and the use of epidemiological studies linking the injuries of the victims to the conduct of the industry. Other features include a high level of organization among both the plaintiffs' and the defendants' bars, high-stakes global settlement negotiations that involve detailed regulatory terms, managerial judging, bankruptcy, and government involvement. Inspired by this type of mass tort litigation against the manufacturers of asbestos, Agent Orange, Bendectin, the Dalkon Shield, silicone breast implants, and, perhaps most of all, tobacco, plaintiffs' attorneys and gun control advocacy groups developed a new strategy for suing the gun industry. They organized litigation efforts, aggregated victim claims, compiled complex social science data linking gun makers to gun violence, mobilized state and local government cost-recoupment suits, and conducted settlement negotiations with an aim to force gun makers to accept design changes and marketing restrictions.[8] The reinvention of gun litigation as a mass tort has attracted enormous public attention, placing it in the center of both the gun control controversy and the debate over tort reform. At the same time, individual victims have continued to file old-style personal injury actions. Let us now turn to a survey of the liability theories behind the litigation.

Theories of Liability

As a preliminary matter, it will be helpful to distinguish four types of lawsuits against the gun industry. First, and least controversial, are product liability claims against manufacturers for injuries caused by guns that malfunction. Plaintiffs have prevailed in many of these cases.[9] Second are negligent entrustment claims against retail dealers who sell guns that are subsequently used in crimes. These cases have proven more controversial, and plaintiffs have prevailed in only a few instances.[10] Third are claims against wholesale distributors and manufacturers for injuries caused by misuse of a gun that could have been prevented by equipping the gun with a safety device. And fourth are claims against wholesale distributors and manufacturers for injuries caused by the criminal use of a gun that could have been prevented by more restrictive marketing and sales practices. It is these last two types of cases—involving design modification and marketing restriction claims—that are at the center of the controversy over gun litigation. For the most part, courts have been hostile to these claims. The great majority have been dismissed or abandoned prior to trial, and of the few favorable jury verdicts obtained by plaintiffs, all but one have been overturned on appeal.[11] A handful of claims have been settled prior to trial.[12]

My discussion of the doctrinal theories behind lawsuits against the gun industry will focus on design modification and marketing restriction claims. These cases involve a variety of different types of shootings. In some, the victim is shot by a criminal assailant as the target of an attack or as a bystander. In others, the victim is accidentally shot by another who does not intend to discharge the firearm. In a few cases, the victim shoots himself or herself, either by accident or in a suicide attempt. The plaintiffs in most of these cases are the victims themselves or, if the shooting was fatal, a relative or representative of the victim's estate. In some cases, the plaintiffs are municipal governments, and in one case, the plaintiff was the State of New York. The defendants are either individual distributors or manufacturers or, in some cases, the industry as a whole.

Strict Liability for Abnormally Dangerous Activities

Most jurisdictions adhere to the doctrine that "[o]ne who carries on an abnormally dangerous activity is subject to liability for harm to . . . another resulting from the activity, although he has exercised the utmost care to prevent the harm."[13] Gun litigation plaintiffs have asserted that the manufacture, distribution, and sale of firearms is an abnormally dangerous activity and that gun manufacturers, distributors, and retail sellers should be held strictly liable for injuries related to gun violence.[14] With one exception, courts have rejected this theory, holding that the manufacture and sale of firearms—approximately 4.5 million new guns each year—is a common activity that poses no abnormally high risk to the public.[15]

The exception, *Kelley v. R.G. Industries*, attracted much attention when it was decided in 1985 but has had little lasting doctrinal impact on gun litigation.[16] In that case, the Supreme Court of Maryland imposed strict liability on the manufacture, distribution, and sale of "Saturday Night Specials," which the court defined as cheap, easily concealable handguns "particularly attractive for criminal use and virtually useless for the legitimate purposes of law enforcement, sport, and protection." The manufacture, distribution, and sale of this class of weapon, the court held, posed an abnormally high risk of criminal misuse. Following the *Kelley* decision, the Maryland legislature passed a law overturning the doctrine of strict liability for the manufacture and sale of Saturday Night Specials and replacing it with a board of experts to identify and restrict the sale of handguns with a high risk of criminal misuse.[17] In the years following, courts in other states expressly rejected the *Kelley* doctrine. It is worth noting, however, that as a result of the case the defendant ceased production and sale of Saturday Night Specials.[18] As for the plaintiff, he abandoned the case, preferring to declare a legal victory rather than engage in a costly trial to obtain a judgment likely under six figures from a foreign parent corporation with no attachable assets in the United States.[19]

Defective Design

As a general rule, manufacturers are subject to liability for injuries caused by design defects in the products they produce.[20] Plaintiffs have argued that the failure of gun manufacturers to equip their firearms with safety features such as gun locks or personalization technology constitutes a design defect.[21] When it comes to firearms, however, the concept of a design defect is highly controversial. Under one widely accepted approach, a product design is defective when the risks associated with the design outweigh its utility.[22] Citing this doctrine, plaintiffs have argued that the risks associated with handguns—designed to be small and concealable, making them attractive to criminals—outweigh their utility.[23] Courts have rejected this theory, holding that liability for design defect applies only to products that are defective in the sense that they malfunction in some way. In the words of one court: "[w]ithout this essential predicate, that something is wrong with the product, the risk-utility balancing test does not even apply."[24]

According to another widely accepted approach, a product design is defective when the "foreseeable risks of harm posed by the product could have been reduced or avoided by the adoption of a reasonable alternative design . . . and the omission of the alternative design renders the product not reasonably safe."[25] Plaintiffs have alleged that the failure of manufacturers to incorporate safety features into guns constitutes a design defect. Some cases have focused on safety features such as a chamber-loaded indicator that would alert the bearer of a gun to the presence of a live round in the firing chamber.[26] This type of safety feature would prevent accidental shootings that occur when the possessor of a gun mistakenly believes it to be unloaded. Other cases have focused on safety features such as locking devices or personalization technology that would render guns inoperable in the hands of unauthorized users.[27]

Gun manufacturers have responded to these claims in a number of ways. They argue that the accidental discharge of firearms results from improper and unintended use of the weapon, in some cases by children, and that liability should rest with gun owners who fail to secure their weapons or to supervise their proper use.[28] Gun manufacturers have also asserted that mechanical locking devices might defeat the usefulness of a gun in situations where an authorized user might not have time to unlock the gun. They allege similarly that personalization technology may be subject to electronic failure when the gun is needed for self-defense.[29]

Claims against gun manufacturers based on reasonable alternative design theories have fared better in the courts than those based on risk-utility theories. Two alternative design cases have made it to juries, and one resulted in a verdict for the plaintiff.[30] Other cases are currently pending. The fate of these cases, and of design defect claims against gun manufacturers in general, is still unclear.

Negligent Marketing

According to generally accepted tort doctrine, one may be subject to liability for negligence if one fails to exercise reasonable care and, as a result, injures another. Plaintiffs have asserted that gun manufacturers are negligent in failing to take reasonable precautions that would prevent their guns from being acquired by individuals likely to use them for criminal purposes. These precautions include a number of voluntary marketing restrictions, for example, refusing to supply firearms to retail dealers who sell a disproportionate number of guns used in crimes.[31] The failure to take these precautions, allege plaintiffs, is a cause of gun violence. Manufacturers have responded that such precautions would do no good, since those bent on acquiring guns for criminal purposes could easily evade sales restrictions or purchase guns on the black market. Moreover, manufacturers assert, even if voluntary marketing restrictions could reduce gun violence, regulating gun sales is the job of government, not the industry.[32]

For the most part, one has a duty to exercise reasonable care only to prevent foreseeable injuries. In addition, one is generally under no duty to prevent even foreseeable injuries where the risk of injury arises out of the conduct of a third party. For example, if an individual learns of a stranger's intention to harm another, the individual is normally under no duty to restrain the stranger or to protect the victim, even if it would be reasonable to do so. Courts do, however, impose such duties where there exists a special relationship between the individual and the injurer or between the individual and the victim.[33] Such special relationships are characterized by the individual's unique capacity to control the risk of harm posed by third parties, for example, a parent's capacity to restrain a violent child or a landlord's capacity to protect tenants from intruders.[34]

Manufacturers have argued that they owe no duty to gun violence victims to exercise control over retail sales since the misuse of guns is not a foreseeable consequence of marketing guns to the general public.[35] In addition, they assert that they owe no duty to prevent injury to victims by third parties who misuse guns.[36] Plaintiffs respond that gun violence is a highly foreseeable risk of marketing guns and, furthermore, that manufacturers are uniquely situated to supervise the sales of retail dealers whom they supply. On this basis, plaintiffs argue, courts should recognize that gun manufacturers have a duty to exercise reasonable care in marketing firearms and that they should be held liable when their breach of this duty results in injury.

Whether there exist specific marketing restrictions short of a total gun ban that would reduce gun violence is the central question at the heart of these negligent marketing cases. Only if marketing restrictions would reduce gun violence can it be said that manufacturers have a unique capacity, and therefore a duty, to take reasonable precautions to prevent injuries due to gun violence. And only if these marketing restrictions are modest enough to appear reasonable in the eyes of a jury can it be said that the failure to adopt them is unreasonable and therefore a breach of the duty to exercise reasonable care. And, finally, only if these modest marketing restrictions are effective can it be said that the failure to adopt them causes injury. Plaintiffs in negligent marketing suits present a variety of different marketing restrictions and offer often complex social science analysis to establish the potential effectiveness of these restrictions in reducing gun violence. Let us examine briefly three leading theories of negligent marketing.

OVERSUPPLY

In *Hamilton v. Beretta*, plaintiffs alleged that gun manufacturers knowingly oversupplied handguns to dealers in states with weak gun controls and that this oversupply resulted in the sale and resale of those guns to individuals in states with strict gun controls, where the guns were subsequently used in crimes.[37] For example, plaintiffs asserted that defendant gun makers oversupplied handguns to dealers in Florida knowing that many of those guns would be smuggled to New York for use in crime. In support of this theory, plaintiffs presented federal law enforcement statistics indicating that 40 percent of handguns used in crimes in New York between 1989 and 1997 were originally sold in five Southern states with weak gun control laws. They also commissioned a study suggesting that manufacturers were supplying guns to retail dealers in those states far beyond the estimated demand for new guns among residents. And, finally, they cited data showing that a significant number of guns used in crime had been purchased within the previous three years, which they interpreted as indicating that these guns were purchased, not stolen, by the criminals who used them. All of this evidence, according to the plaintiffs, added up to proof that the oversupply of guns to Southern markets was a significant cause of gun crime in the North, and in New York in particular, where the plaintiffs were injured.[38] Defendants countered that oversupply is a normal by-product of legitimate competition between firms for market share and that the industrywide cooperation that would be required to prevent it would likely run afoul of antitrust laws. A Brooklyn jury found three of the twenty-five defendants liable.[39] The New York Court of Appeals subsequently overturned the verdict, rejecting the theory of oversupply as overbroad. "Without a showing that specific groups of dealers play a disproportionate role in supplying the illegal gun market," the court held, "the sweep of plaintiffs' duty theory is far wider than the danger it seeks to avert." Allowing liability based on oversupply, the court explained, "would have the unavoidable effect of eliminating a significant number of lawful sales to 'responsible' buyers by 'responsible' Federal firearms licensees (FFLs) who would be cut out of the distribution chain" by manufacturers seeking to reduce their liability exposure. While the court rejected the theory of oversupply, it left open the possibility that a duty to exercise reasonable care in marketing firearms might be acceptable on some narrower basis.

OVERPROMOTION

In *Merrill v. Navegar*, plaintiffs alleged that the manufacturer of a semiautomatic pistol designed for close combat-style assaults should have limited promotion and sale of the gun to the military and law enforcement, the only consumers who might have legitimate use for such a weapon.[40] In arguing that the manufacturer's promotion of the weapon to the general public was negligent, plaintiffs pointed to the combination of design features and advertising. The Tec-DC9 (so named because its maker designed it to circumvent the Washington, D.C., ban of its predecessor—the Tec-9—which was banned also in California, where *Merrill* was filed) was capable with modification of delivering fully automatic spray fire, was easily concealed, and could be fitted with silencers and flash suppressors. Promotional materials emphasized the paramilitary appearance of the gun, boasted its "excellent resistance to fingerprints," and assured dealers that it was as "tough as your toughest customers."[41] The manufacturer responded that it owed no duty to refrain from selling a legal product to the public and that the suit was barred by the California Civil Code's prohibition on product liability actions against gun manufacturers based on assertions that the risks of a weapon outweigh its benefits. The California Supreme Court, relying on the Civil Code provision, affirmed the trial court's grant of summary judgment in favor of the defendants. In response, the California legislature revised the relevant Civil Code section to allow for product liability claims against gun makers, opening the door to future suits of this kind.[42]

FAILURE TO SUPERVISE RETAIL DEALERS

Plaintiffs in several cases have alleged that manufacturers are negligent in failing to train and monitor retail dealers in order to prevent illegal sales.[43] Plaintiffs argue that dealer training on how to comply with gun laws, to keep better track of store inventory, and to spot fraudulent buyers would reduce access to guns by criminals. Moreover, using data available from the Federal Bureau of Alcohol, Tobacco, Firearms and Explosives (BATFE), plaintiffs maintain that manufacturers could identify and refuse to supply dealers who have a record of illegal sales or to whom large numbers of crime guns are traced. Defendants have responded that such training would be ineffective and that attempts to police retail sales would interfere with law enforcement efforts to uncover and prosecute rogue dealers. Courts in several jurisdictions have rejected this theory, although several cases are currently pending.[44]

Public Nuisance

The details of public nuisance doctrine vary significantly from jurisdiction to jurisdiction. Most courts, however, agree on the general definition of a public nuisance as "an unreasonable interference with a right common to the general public."[45] Plaintiffs have alleged that the extensive illegal secondary market in firearms constitutes a public nuisance for which the gun industry is responsible. These claims rely on many of the same allegations as negligent marketing suits. For example, a lawsuit brought by the City of Chicago alleged that gun manufacturers oversupply suburban retail dealers, who sell handguns to residents of the city, where handgun possession is illegal. The suit further asserted that manufacturers design and advertise weapons in ways attractive to criminals and that they fail to discipline irresponsible dealers. Oversupply, overpromotion, and the failure to supervise retail dealers, according to the city, are all unreasonable interferences with the public right of Chicago residents to be free from the human and material costs of gun violence. The Illinois Supreme Court rejected the city's claim, holding that manufacturers and wholesale distributors owe no duty to the public at large to guard against the criminal misuse of guns.[46]

Courts in several jurisdictions have rejected similar public nuisance claims on two additional grounds: first, that the industry marketing practices in question are legal, and second, that plaintiffs cannot establish a direct connection between industry marketing practices and illegal gun sales. For example, the U.S. Court of Appeals for the Third Circuit rejected a suit by the City of Philadelphia, holding that the sale of "lawful products that are lawfully placed in the stream of commerce" cannot be the basis of a public nuisance claim.[47] A New York state appellate court, in affirming the dismissal of New York State's public nuisance claim against the gun industry, held that "the harm plaintiff alleges is too remote from defendants' otherwise lawful commercial activity."[48]

By contrast, other courts have specifically held that the legality of the industry's marketing practices does not insulate it from liability and that plaintiffs have at least alleged a close enough connection between particular industry practices and illegal gun sales to avoid dismissal of their claims. The Supreme Court of Indiana, reinstating a suit by the City of Gary, held that "a nuisance claim may be predicated on a lawful activity conducted in such a manner that it imposes costs on others" and that allegations concerning the industry's refusal to crack down on illegal sales by retail dealers, if proven true, would be sufficient to support liability for public nuisance.[49] Moreover, there is some question as to whether considerations of remoteness are even relevant in actions where plaintiffs are seeking merely abatement of the nuisance, as opposed to money damages.[50]

When public nuisance claims are brought by private parties, plaintiffs must additionally show that they suffered "special injury"—harm different from that experienced by the general public. A public nuisance claim brought by the National Association for the Advancement of Colored People (NAACP) against the gun industry foundered on just this element. After a six-week trial, the Federal District Court in Brooklyn dismissed the case. In an unusual 261-page memorandum, the court concluded that

> The evidence presented at trial demonstrated that defendants are responsible for the creation of a public nuisance and could—voluntarily and through easily implemented changes in marketing and more discriminating control of the sales practices of those to whom they sell their guns—substantially reduce the harm occasioned by the diversion of guns to the illegal market and by the criminal possession and use of those guns. Because, however, plaintiff has failed to demonstrate, as required by New York law, that it has suffered harm different in kind from that suffered by the public at large in the State of New York, the case is dismissed.[51]

The memorandum offers a highly detailed analysis—accompanied by illustrative charts—in support of its finding of industry responsibility for illegal gun markets. While ostensibly a document justifying dismissal of the case, the memorandum reads like a blueprint for bringing a successful public nuisance claim against the industry. It is worth mentioning that the judge who wrote this memorandum was Jack B. Weinstein, who also presided over *Halberstam v. Daniel*, the first negligent marketing case to reach a jury, and the *Hamilton* case, the first negligent marketing case to obtain a jury verdict favorable to plaintiffs (later overturned on appeal). Judge Weinstein currently presides over a public nuisance suit, which he refused to dismiss, brought by the City of New York.[52] In another public nuisance case brought by private plaintiffs, *Ileto v. Glock*, the victims and survivors of a shooting spree by Buford Furrow, who shot several children at a Southern California Jewish community center and a U.S. postal worker, filed a public nuisance claim against a group of industry defendants.[53] The U.S. Court of Appeals for the Ninth Circuit reversed a trial court's dismissal of the claim, which is now likely to reach trial.

Deceptive Trade Practices

Lawsuits brought by municipalities have alleged that manufacturers' advertising claims contain intentional misrepresentations in violation of state laws prohibiting deceptive trade practices.[54] Municipal plaintiffs have disputed industry assertions that keeping a gun at home increases safety. These assertions, they argue, contradict public health studies showing that the presence of a gun in the house increases the risk of gun-related injuries to family members. Defendants have countered that these studies fail to take seriously the self-defense benefits of gun ownership. While most courts have rejected these claims, in at least two cases courts have refused to dismiss them.[55]

Defenses

There are two common defenses raised by gun manufacturers in addition to those already mentioned. The two often appear together and, as a result, are frequently confused with one another. They are, however, quite distinct.

REMOTENESS

Defendants have argued that the injuries of gun violence victims are too remote from the alleged wrongdoing by gun manufacturers to support liability.[56] In one version of this defense, gun manufacturers assert that the plaintiffs lack standing to bring suit against them in the first place. For example, in dismissing the City of Bridgeport's suit against the gun industry, the court held that the city's claimed losses in responding to gun violence were entirely derivative of harms suffered by the victims themselves and that "a plaintiff who complains of harm resulting from misfortune visited upon a third person is generally held to stand at too remote a distance to recover[;] . . . standing requires a colorable claim of direct injury to the complaining party."[57] Municipal plaintiffs have responded to this argument by asserting that many of the costs of responding to gun violence—for example, the costs of security patrols or metal detectors in public buildings—are independent of harms to any particular gun violence victim.

In another version of the remoteness defense, gun manufacturers argue that their alleged wrongdoing is not a proximate cause of harm to the plaintiff.[58] According to well-settled tort doctrine, a defendant is not liable for negligence unless his failure to exercise reasonable care is a proximate cause of harm to the plaintiff. Depending upon the situation, proximity may be defined by the directness of the connection between the defendant's wrongdoing and the plaintiff's harm, the foreseeability of the defendant's wrongdoing resulting in harm to the plaintiff, or the public policy implications of holding the defendant liable.[59] Whether the defendant's negligence is a proximate cause of harm to the plaintiff is normally a matter of fact for a jury to decide. Occasionally, judges will make this determination themselves if they believe that there is no room for reasonable disagreement. (By contrast, the issue of standing is always decided by the judge.) Courts have dismissed a number of lawsuits against the gun industry for lack of proximate cause.[60]

THE FREE PUBLIC SERVICES DOCTRINE

A common defense raised by gun manufacturers against municipal plaintiffs is the free public services doctrine, also known as the municipal cost recovery rule.[61] According to this doctrine, a government entity may not recover from a tortfeasor the costs of public services occasioned by the tortfeasor's wrongdoing. Curiously, while some courts have accepted this doctrine as a well-established principle of common law, others have dismissed it as without precedent. A handful of courts have relied on the doctrine in dismissing municipal claims.[62]

The Social Science Underpinnings of Gun Litigation

Both plaintiffs and defendants in gun litigation rely heavily on social science findings from the fields of public health, criminology, and economics. These findings provide a foundation for claims and defenses in individual cases. They also undergird competing arguments about the potential effectiveness of proposed remedies such as design modification and marketing restrictions. Beyond the realm of gun litigation, social science findings also play a prominent role in legislative battles and the broader public debate about gun control. Indeed, in the war over gun control, scholarly debate among social scientists is itself a significant battleground, exhibiting the same highly polarized, and often nasty, exchanges typical of ad campaigns and public debates. Scholars on both sides disagree vociferously not only about each other's findings but also about each other's integrity. Charges of fabricating data and skewing results have become increasingly common in recent years.

Personal attacks aside, some of the disagreement among scholars is due to differences in the disciplines within which they work. These distinct disciplines influence the way scholars define problems and the types of solutions on which they focus. For example, public health scholars bring an epidemiological perspective to the study of gun violence: they focus on morbidity and mortality rates and advocate environmental changes and alterations in the agent of injury (i.e., guns) that do not rely heavily on behavior modification. Thus, the public health literature on gun violence tends to emphasize the magnitude of injury and death from gun violence, including not only assaults but also accidents and suicides, and to call for changes in how guns are marketed and designed. Public heath scholarship places little faith in behavior modification as a response to gun violence, whether in the form of crime deterrence or gun safety courses. By contrast, criminologists view gun violence as primarily an issue of criminal behavior: they focus on crime rates and advocate crime-deterrence strategies. Thus, the criminological literature focuses primarily on the more limited problem of gun injury and death resulting from assault and discusses gun-crime deterrence strategies such as criminal prosecution, police searches for illegal weapons, and private gun ownership for self-defense. To be fair, there is less uniformity of orientation and opinion among criminologists than among public health scholars, and there is increasing interdisciplinary overlap between the two fields. Nevertheless, it is not unfair to say that a significant source of disagreement between public health scholars and many prominent criminologists arguing over gun control stems from differences in the way that these two disciplines frame issues and the types of solutions on which they focus. Thus, they argue over not only how big the problem is but *what* the problem is, and they debate not only the efficacy of a proposed solution but the relevance of it. This battle of experts is further complicated by the additional participation of economists, historians, sociologists, and legal scholars.

Chapters 1 and 2 offer an introduction to the public health and criminological literature on gun violence and gun control. In chapter 1, Julie Samia Mair, Stephen Teret, and Shannon Frattaroli survey public health findings that gun violence is a significant source of death and injury, and they argue that policies directed at modifying gun designs and restricting gun marketing offer promise of reducing gun-related mortality and morbidity rates. In chapter 2, Don Kates offers an overview of criminological studies suggesting that narrowly tailored government restrictions on gun ownership and sales effect only marginal decreases in gun violence rates and that broad restrictions may even cause an increase in gun violence rates by depriving private citizens of an effective means of self-defense. In characteristic fashion, the public health and criminology perspectives presented in these two chapters talk past one another. The public health chapter defines the problem of gun violence to include assaults, accidents, and suicides (this last category accounting for over half of gun deaths); emphasizes the magnitude of this problem in terms of injury, death, and economic cost; and focuses on nonbehavioral solutions such as incorporation of safety features in guns and increased marketing restrictions. By contrast, the criminology chapter is more concerned with murder rates than with injuries, accidents, or suicides; stresses the high cost of enforcing gun control laws; and advocates private gun ownership for self-defense as the most effective means of addressing gun assaults.

The two chapters do, however, join issue on one significant point: the relation between widespread private gun ownership and gun violence rates. Whereas chapter 1 concludes that "[t]he weight of public health research finds that the high prevalence of guns in the United States is associated with this country's high gun death rate," a central claim of chapter 2 is that "criminological research does not support claims that gun availability to ordinary people promotes violence." Kates goes so far as to denounce the link between gun ownership and gun violence rates as "an erroneous mantra" of the public health community. To be fair, Mair, Teret, and Frattaroli do not claim that widespread private gun ownership *causes* gun violence; they are careful to insist only upon an association between the two. Of course, a mere association provides a much weaker foundation upon which to argue that a reduction in gun ownership would result in lower gun violence rates. This argument is most speculative—indeed, Kates argues that it is just plain wrong— when applied to murder and assault rates. It is stronger, however, when applied to accident rates: less gun ownership presents less opportunity for accidental shootings with guns—an argument largely unaddressed by criminologists. Professors Franklin Zimring and Gordon Hawkins, in contrast to Kates and the scholars upon whom he relies, are criminologists who assert a causal link between widespread private gun ownership and gun violence rates. In their book, *Crime Is Not the Problem: Lethal Violence in America,* they argue that the prevalence of guns in America, while not associated with higher crime rates, is associated with higher rates of lethal violence. A significant aim of their study is to encourage criminologists, and the public at large, to consider the problem of gun violence from the perspective that public health scholars have been advocating all along—"to shift the subject from crime to life-threatening violence."[63] Chapters 1 and 2 thus introduce the tension between public health and criminological perspectives on gun violence, especially where they miss each other and where they disagree. When reading, one should keep in mind, however—as the work of Zimring and Hawkins shows, along with other recent work by scholars in both fields—that the disciplinary battle lines are neither clear nor fixed.

Aside from the relationship between public health and criminology scholarship, chapters 1 and 2 also offer insight into some limitations of the findings offered by social science. For example, Mair, Teret, and Frattaroli explain that national "[v]ital statistics data provide no useful information about the guns used to kill and do not include information about perpetrators of gun homicides or, when applicable, unintentional gun deaths." While there are small-scale studies that compile such information for specific localities, they "fall short of providing nationwide, comprehensive data."[64] Such data are essential to evaluating the remedies to gun violence advocated by the public health community. More comprehensive data on whether certain types of guns are more prevalent in gun deaths are essential to determining the efficacy of "an outright ban" on the sale of those guns; data on the perpetrators of gun homicides are necessary in evaluating the effectiveness of additional barriers to purchasing guns; and data on the circumstances of accidents are required in determining the usefulness of additional safety features. Kates, for his part, admits up front that "[c]arefully tailored gun controls can marginally reduce gun violence rates," although his chapter goes on to condemn the "futility" of gun marketing restrictions and the "failure" of stiff penalties for illegal possession or use of guns due to lax enforcement and inadequate resources. One should be careful not to belittle the value of marginal reductions in gun violence. Indeed, marginal reduction is a mark of success for most, if not all, public policies aimed at addressing social problems. That passenger-side air bags offer marginal reductions in highway fatalities is hardly an insignificant achievement. Furthermore, safety features or sales restrictions, while not shown to have any impact on murder rates, might reduce accidents. Whether the reduction in accident rates is worth any losses in self-defense against assaults (due to reduced effectiveness or availability of guns) remains unclear. At the present time, social science simply cannot answer this question.

In addressing questions about gun design and marketing at the heart of gun litigation or more general discussions about gun violence, it is helpful to examine the gun industry. In chapter 3, Tom Diaz argues that the structure of the gun industry produces a tendency over time to design and sell weapons of increasing "lethality" and that this trend causes an increase in gun violence rates. Perhaps the most illuminating insight of Diaz's discussion is that the increasing killing power of guns is not based on any secret conspiracy among gun makers to supply weapons to street gangs and illegal paramilitary groups but rather is simply the result of market forces not unlike those in any other consumer-product industry. Just like the automobile industry, gun makers need to continuously produce new models in order to maintain sales. In the words of a gun industry analyst quoted by Diaz, "[w]ithout new models that have major technical changes, you eventually exhaust your market."[65]

Diaz's claim that this "deliberate enhancement of lethality contributes directly to the criminal use of firearms and to death and injury resulting from firearms use" features prominently in many lawsuits against the gun industry. Plaintiffs have claimed that the marketing of easily concealed guns is an abnormally dangerous activity, that manufacturers are negligent in marketing guns with increased firepower, and that especially lethal guns are defectively designed. The link, however, between lethality and gun violence rates is difficult to prove, since, as Diaz himself admits, "uniform national data on firearm injury is not available. There is simply no resource from which one can obtain such useful data as types of handguns, caliber, and number of rounds taking effect in shootings." In support of the link between lethality and gun violence, he does cite "a national survey of anecdotal medical evidence," a "study of shootings in Philadelphia," comments from "law enforcement officials," and a recent study by a gun control advocacy group on 211 fatal shootings of police officers. Furthermore, Diaz argues, aside from any effect on gun violence rates, increased lethality results in more damage to shooting victims in the form of multiple and larger wounds. While Diaz's assertions that the industry's gun designs and marketing practices are responsible for gun violence have yet to be definitively proven, his analysis of lethality is nevertheless essential to understanding how the gun industry operates.

The prevailing view among social scientists is that collecting more data on guns and gun violence will promote consensus and ultimately lead to a resolution of the gun control controversy. In chapter 4, Dan Kahan, Donald Braman, and John Gastil challenge this view. They argue that people's positions on gun rights and gun control are determined not by social science but by culture. Indeed, Kahan, Braman, and Gastil argue that disputes about social science findings are nothing more than a proxy for cultural differences. One's cultural commitments determine which studies one finds convincing: "Culture not only *matters* to citizens in the gun debate; but it *determines* how they evaluate and even what they believe about the consequences of gun control."

Culture determines individuals' views on gun control, according to Kahan, Braman, and Gastil, because culture affects risk perception, and one's views on gun control are ultimately about the type of risks one fears most. The fear of some risks and the disregard of others, they explain, both "reflect and reinforce" an individual's values and worldview. For example, those with a more "egalitarian" cultural orientation will be more "sensitive to environmental and industrial risks, the minimization of which reinforces their demand for the regulation of commercial activities productive of disparities in wealth and status." By contrast, those with a more "individualist" cultural orientation tend to fear "the dangers of social deviance, the risks of foreign invasion, or the fragility of economic institutions," all of which they perceive as serious potential threats to individual liberty. Kahan, Braman, and Gastil cite empirical evidence that

these "cultural orientations . . . more powerfully predict individual attitudes toward risk than myriad other influences, including education, personality type, and political orientation." The gun control debate is framed
by social science scholarship as a contest "between *two* competing risk
claims: that insufficient gun control will expose too many innocent persons to deliberate or accidental shootings and that excessive gun control
will render too many law-abiding citizens vulnerable to violent predation." Egalitarians fear the first risk more and therefore support gun control, while individualists fear the second risk more and consequently
oppose gun control. Both sides readily cite social science findings that support their risk perceptions, and they distrust findings that contradict them.

Kahan, Braman, and Gastil dismiss gun litigation—with its intense
focus on competing social science claims—as "culturally obtuse." Litigants exacerbate the misplaced obsession with statistics by plying juries
with complex data analyses concerning the impact of gun designs and
marketing on gun violence rates. Juries, in evaluating this evidence, are
likely to split along the same cultural divide that underlies the broader
gun debate. To the extent that juries do reach verdicts in these cases, they
will merely offer an endorsement of one side or the other, adding to the
polarization that has made the controversy so intractable. "Gun litigation won't work," conclude Kahan, Braman, and Gastil, "because it
doesn't do anything to extricate the gun issue from the conflict between
competing cultural styles in American life."

If Kahan, Braman, and Gastil are right—that views about gun control
are ultimately rooted in culture—then the work of social scientists like
Mair, Teret, Frattaroli, and Kates is not only irrelevant but actually
counterproductive in advancing the debate over gun policy. And if the
primary function of gun litigation is to put the social science on trial,
then gun litigation will do more to entrench the current stalemate than to
alleviate it.

Kahan, Braman, and Gastil's cultural critique of gun litigation focuses
primarily on jury verdicts. Later chapters suggest, however, that other
parts of the litigation process—such as filing, discovery, and
settlement—may have far greater impact on the gun control debate than
jury verdicts. In chapter 6, I suggest that these aspects of gun litigation
may have an impact on the cultural dimension of gun control politics.
Insofar as gun litigation has reframed the gun control debate—from
merely a contest between public safety and individual gun ownership

rights to also a contest between individual rights to recovery in tort and crime reduction through self-defense—it complicates the easy identification of gun control with egalitarianism and gun rights with individualism. This new complexity could prompt people to reconsider their views on gun control. Indeed, it might even be a sign that gun litigation has potential to generate the kind of "constructive cultural deliberation" that Kahan, Braman, and Gastil promote as a solution to the current standoff.

Even gun litigation jury verdicts themselves may be viewed as culturally relevant. Where Kahan, Braman, and Gastil see polarization and incoherence, one might instead perceive a tendency toward compromise and accommodation that has enabled both sides to declare victory. For example, in the *Halberstam* case, the jury found that the defendants were negligent in selling gun kits but that their negligence was not a proximate cause of the plaintiff's harm, validating part of each side's case. In the *Hamilton* case, the jury found fifteen of the twenty-five defendant manufacturers negligent, nine to be the proximate causes of injury to the plaintiffs, and three liable for specified amounts of damages—an outcome that might be characterized as both moderate and the product of compromise. By avoiding a clear endorsement of either party's position, these verdicts allowed both sides in the gun debate to view them as significant victories and vindication of their views. While clearly these verdicts have not produced a resolution to the gun debate, they may be evidence that the litigation process offers more in the way of dialogue and deliberation, or at least moderation and compromise, than Kahan, Braman, and Gastil's cultural critique admits.

Kahan, Braman, and Gastil's trenchant cultural critique raises the question of just how the gun debate found its way into litigation in the first place. It is to this question that we now turn.

Reasons for the Rise of Gun Litigation

Aside from the desire of individual plaintiffs to obtain compensation for their losses and to hold the gun industry accountable, there are a number of larger social and political forces that account for the rise of gun litigation. Viewed from one perspective, gun litigation is fueled less by shooting victims than by their lawyers, who have designed and coordinated the litigation. From a second perspective, gun litigation might be viewed as a new front in the ongoing political battle between gun control and gun rights advocates. From yet a third perspective, one could consider it the result of larger ideological and institutional trends, such as an ascendant vision of the tort system as a regulatory tool. Finally, commentators commonly cast gun litigation as a logical, and perhaps even inevitable, outgrowth of tobacco litigation. The chapters in Part II address these different perspectives on gun litigation.

The rise of gun litigation is commonly attributed to trial lawyers run amok, in particular to well-heeled antitobacco lawyers looking for another unpopular industry with which to do battle. In chapter 5, Howard Erichson moves beyond this overly simplistic account, exposing how a unique alliance among three distinct groups of players on the plaintiffs' side—activists, politicians, and trial lawyers—gave rise to municipal gun litigation. Erichson shows how, on the one hand, cooperation among these three groups made the municipal litigation possible while, on the other hand, divergent interests among the groups gave rise to significant differences between the resulting lawsuits. He uses the New Orleans and Chicago suits, filed within two weeks of one another, as illustrations.

The New Orleans suit was designed by a group of antitobacco trial lawyers working with activist lawyers from the Legal Action Project of the Brady Center to Prevent Gun Violence. The Chicago suit grew out of a collaboration between an activist law professor concerned about inner-city crime and a city attorney who was formerly a federal prosecutor. For the New Orleans trial lawyers, Erichson explains, gun litigation was not only a just cause but also, importantly, an investment opportunity; for the Chicago team, the litigation was primarily a law enforcement strategy. This difference is reflected in the legal theories behind each suit. The mind-set and background of the trial lawyers in the New Orleans suit resulted in a lawsuit based on design defect theory and modeled on mass tort product liability litigation. By contrast, the Chicago suit was based on a novel theory of public nuisance and resembled a government public safety action. Thus, according to Erichson, "[t]he gun litigation is a story of mixed motives—moral, political, and financial—by diverse actors on the plaintiffs' side."

One should be careful in reading Erichson's illuminating account of the municipal litigation not to ignore the important role of lawsuits against gun makers filed by individual plaintiffs. These suits predate municipal litigation by more than fifteen years, and, as later chapters will argue, they hold out as much, if not more, promise of gun industry reform. As an analysis of the individual actors behind municipal gun litigation, however, Erichson's account offers a depth and subtlety missing in previous accounts.

Beyond a clearer understanding of the role of plaintiffs' lawyers in shaping gun litigation, there is much to be learned by examining the broader political context within which gun litigation has arisen. In chapter 6, I argue that many big-city mayors and gun control advocates have filed lawsuits against the gun industry as a way to pursue gun control policies that they have failed to achieve through the political process. They blame this failure on NRA corruption of the legislative process. In turn, the gun industry, with help from the NRA, has turned to state legislatures and Congress for protection in the form of statutory immunity from the lawsuits. Thus, while gun control advocates are using tort litigation to circumvent the legislative process, the industry and the gun lobby are calling on legislatures to usurp the judicial role by deciding lawsuits.

I assert that this situation is bad for both gun violence policy and the institutional integrity of legislatures and courts. On the one hand, using litigation as a means to elude the NRA's lobbying power may ultimately prove self-defeating, since the gun lobby can easily shift its resources from legislative politics to judicial elections. Furthermore, this approach to litigation is likely to further politicize the judiciary, increasing the influence of interest groups on judicial decision making. This is not, however, to reject all lawsuits against the gun industry or to deny that suits based on viable common law claims may have a legitimate impact on the legislative process. On the other hand, broad immunity legislation undermines the integrity of the judicial process by resolving lawsuits on the basis of political power rather than legal principle, and it impairs the capacity of courts to play a supportive role in refining and enforcing the legislature's own regulatory policies. In contrast to broad grants of immunity, I examine and defend more focused legislative responses to the perceived excesses of gun litigation.

While my analysis of gun litigation as an extension of interest-group politics places it within the broader context of gun control politics, it is worth considering also larger ideological and institutional trends beyond the gun control debate. In chapter 7, Richard Nagareda examines gun litigation as a new form of mass tort litigation that aims, in addition to securing compensation for accident victims, at specific regulatory outcomes. According to Nagareda, this new form of litigation—"social policy tort litigation"—results from a confluence of two specific trends, one in tort theory and the other in regulatory practice. On the one hand, during the past hundred years, scholars have successfully promoted an "instrumental conception of tort law" as a regulatory tool well suited to risk management and loss spreading. On the other hand, the past twenty-five years, starting with the Reagan revolution in the early 1980s, have witnessed a steady retreat away from the large-scale centralized government regulation that characterized the New Deal and the Great Society. Thus, according to Nagareda, "the ascendance of regulatory theories of tort law and the emergence of a political landscape inhospitable to demands for government regulation have . . . created a hospitable intellectual and political environment for the development of social policy tort litigation." The regulatory power of social policy tort regulation, explains Nagareda, lies not only, and perhaps not even primarily, in "definitive judicial rulings but through the dynamics of [mass] tort litigation itself—through settlements that would implement prospective changes in defendants' practices in the face of doctrinal uncertainty." Unfortunately, Nagareda points out, much social policy tort litigation (and gun litigation is no exception) "seeks to implement its regulatory program in a manner strikingly unmindful of the lessons learned about conventional regulation in the public sphere," lessons such as the importance of regulatory cost-benefit analysis and interagency coordination.

Nagareda's account of gun litigation is based on a compelling analysis of developments in tort law and changes in the regulatory environment that encouraged the litigation. His critique of the litigation rests on a claim about the inferiority of gun litigation as a regulatory tool compared to legislative and agency regulation. The crux of this claim is that gun litigation lacks essential features for effective regulation—namely, cost-benefit analysis and interagency coordination. The current regulatory regime governing guns, however, is plagued by a dearth of cost-benefit analysis all around. Moreover, there may be more policy coordination between gun litigation and government regulatory efforts than Nagareda's critique suggests. The reason for the paucity of cost-benefit analysis in gun regulation—whether by the federal or state legislatures, BATFE, or the tort system—is the difficulty in measuring the marginal benefits of gun controls in terms of crime, accident, and suicide prevention and the marginal costs in terms of diminished self-defense. As the chapters in Part I illustrate, current social science findings do not reliably support this sort of precise cost-benefit analysis of current or proposed policies. As for policy coordination, Erichson's account reveals that municipal litigation has often been brought by teams of private, public interest, and government lawyers working together. Furthermore, as I argue in chapter 10, many lawsuits against the gun industry complement, rather than compete with, the regulatory efforts of legislatures and agencies by filling gaps in legislation, uncovering important regulatory information, and enhancing agency enforcement resources.

A theme common to many different perspectives on gun litigation is the link between lawsuits against the gun industry and lawsuits against the tobacco industry. As Erichson's chapter shows, antitobacco lawyers played a prominent role in the rise of municipal gun litigation. In chapter 8, Stephen Sugarman examines the similarities between tobacco litigation and gun litigation as public health strategies. Sugarman explores the potential of gun litigation to change positive social attitudes about gun ownership—"to convince ordinary folks that keeping a firearm for self-defense reasons is unwise or inappropriate"—and to encourage gun makers to equip their weapons with safety features such as child-proof locks and personalization technology. While Sugarman offers a public health perspective, unlike Mair, Teret, and Frattaroli, he emphasizes the potential of behavior modification as well as marketing and design restrictions. And while he stresses the importance of behavior modification, unlike Kahan, Braman, and Gastil, he does not consider gun litigation culturally obtuse—he sees it instead, like tobacco litigation, as highly attentive to the cultural dimensions of regulation. In the end, however, Sugarman concludes that tobacco litigation has made at best modest contributions to tobacco control policy and that gun litigation is unlikely to be much more effective.

The limitations of social science findings about gun violence make any claims about the potential public health benefits of gun litigation speculative, and, as a result, Sugarman's analysis is tentative and his conclusions cautious. Given this uncertainty, perhaps the most important contribution that gun litigation could make is that of generating information about the link between gun industry marketing practices and gun designs, on the one hand, and gun violence, on the other. A number of the chapters in Part III explore this potential benefit of the litigation. Unsurprisingly, they reach different conclusions. And, of course, there is always the view of Kahan, Braman, and Gastil, who suggest that more information, no matter how accurate, will not address the real differences of opinion, which are rooted in cultural attitudes.

Litigation as a Means of Regulating the Gun Industry

Whether viewed from the perspective of individual plaintiffs and their lawyers or in the broader contexts of gun control politics and mass torts, gun litigation is a regulatory response to gun violence. Evaluating the regulatory merits of gun litigation rests on one's views not only about gun control but also about the institutional competence of the tort system to make public policy. The chapters in Part III offer a variety of different ways by which to evaluate whether litigation is an effective and legitimate way to make gun control policy.

One way to evaluate the regulatory competence of the tort system is to compare it to other regulatory institutions such as legislatures and administrative agencies. In chapter 9, Peter Schuck offers just such a "comparative institutional analysis," weighing "the relative advantages and disadvantages of undertaking gun control through common law litigation versus other forms of social policy-making and implementation." Schuck argues that tort litigation is inferior to legislative and agency risk regulation in six ways. First, litigation does not produce as much or as reliable "technocratic information" about gun-related risks, and this type of information is essential for effective policy-making. Moreover, the threat of litigation actually discourages manufacturers from developing this information on their own, for fear that it might be used against them in lawsuits. Second, policy-making judges are insulated from "political information" concerning what types of regulation the public and different interest groups favor, making any resulting policies unresponsive to voter preferences. Third, common law courts, limited in most cases to awarding money damages, lack effective "policy instruments" for crafting and enforcing nuanced policies. Fourth, courts lack the capacity for "social learning"—the ability to "obtain feedback on their policies' real-world effects" and to adjust them accordingly. Fifth, tort rules lack "predictability"—they are generally "much less determinate and transparent than regulations." Sixth, judicial policy-making carries with it the risk of failure, followed by public disappointment and a lowering of public esteem for the legitimacy of the courts.

Schuck's assessment is not all negative. He does admit that, to date, gun litigation has generated some "new policy-relevant information about gun-related violence" and "captur[ed] the industry's undivided attention," forcing it to examine its own role in the problem of gun violence. Yet even in conceding these points, he questions whether these results would not have been eventually produced without litigation by a regulatory agency. As for the future of the litigation, however, he is unequivocal, concluding that "[a]t this point . . . it amounts to a costly and institutionally inappropriate distraction from the real political and policy tasks before us."

Schuck's six-pronged comparative institutional analysis offers a powerful tool for assessing the suitability of gun litigation as a regulatory tool. The high level of generality at which Schuck applies his analysis to gun litigation may, however, lead him to underestimate its regulatory value. Throughout, he admittedly "finesse[s] the substantive issues of gun control policy," characterizing his role as "that of an Olympian designer of an optimal regime for controlling gun-related risks, one who compares the litigation option as it now exists to the regulatory option that would become viable were the gun control movement to achieve greater political success in the future." To ignore the political realities of gun control politics—in particular, NRA dominance of the legislative process and chronic underfunding of BATFE—obscures some of the regulatory value of gun litigation. Gun litigation is responsible not merely for uncovering new policy-relevant information about gun designs and industry marketing practices but for focusing public attention on these regulatory strategies in the first place and keeping it there. Persistent public concern for designing safer guns and questioning some marketing strategies has the potential to embolden both legislatures and agencies to explore these policy options despite NRA opposition. Public awareness may also create a market for the development of safety technologies. Furthermore, as I argue in chapter 10, the ongoing threat of liability enhances legislative and agency regulation by providing gun makers with incentives to avoid marketing schemes designed to circumvent statutory regulations and by supplementing scarce enforcement resources.

Addressing complex social problems often requires the involvement of multiple regulatory institutions. In many, if not most, areas of public policy, legislatures, agencies, and courts work together in making, refining, and enforcing policy. In chapter 10, I argue that tort litigation plays a "complementary role" in regulating the gun industry. While legislatures and agencies should take the lead in making gun violence policy, courts should embrace a secondary role that supports their efforts. I offer specific examples of lawsuits against the gun industry that illustrate four ways in which gun litigation complements the efforts of legislatures and courts to regulate the industry. First, the civil discovery process generates information relevant to regulating gun designs and industry marketing practices. Second, tort liability fills gaps in statutory rules and agency regulations, deterring gun makers from seeking technically legal ways around the law. Third, the threat of tort liability supplements scarce BATFE enforcement resources by encouraging self-regulation and voluntary compliance among gun makers, distributors, and retail dealers. And fourth, gun litigation offers opportunities for a decentralized, federalist approach to gun industry regulation.

My defense of a complementary role of tort litigation in regulating the gun industry is not, however, a blanket endorsement. I criticize those suits that employ mass tort aggregation strategies designed to pressure manufacturers into settlement and those that pursue policies already rejected by the legislative process. In both of these types of cases, plaintiffs are attempting to use tort litigation as an alternative, rather than as a complement, to legislative and agency regulation.

The line between complementary judicial policy-making and overreaching is hard to define with any precision. Defining the limits of the judicial policy-making role, I explain, depends more on "a sensibility rather than a set of determinate rules." While this approach has the virtue of being sensitive to context and avoiding oversimplification, it leaves my evaluation of gun litigation open to charges of being too subjective. Furthermore, while my account offers more detail about gun control and gun litigation than Schuck's, the differences may be more a matter of tone than substance. In many cases, his tentative admissions concerning the regulatory value of gun litigation cite the same facts as my qualified endorsements.

Schuck's comparative institutional analysis suggests that the information about gun designs and marketing practices uncovered by gun litigation would eventually have come to light absent lawsuits against the industry. In chapter 11, Wendy Wagner challenges this view, citing the comparative superiority of litigation in obtaining hard-to-get, or "stubborn," information. She criticizes comparative institutional analyses that emphasize the superiority of legislatures and agencies in using regulatory information without accounting for their capacity to obtain it. While commentators like Schuck assert that legislatures and agencies are better suited to address complex regulatory issues like gun control based on arguments about competency and representative capacity, Wagner argues that they fail to assess the capacities of these institutions to extract "the information needed for informed and reasoned debate" from often highly secretive industries like the gun industry. "If political institutions are incapable of generating information needed for competent problem solving," she observes, "then their superior capacities in resolving the problems once the information is produced are beside the point. Analysts must account for stubborn information problems or run the risk that their institutional comparisons will be incomplete." Wagner contends that tort litigation in general and gun litigation in particular have been effective means of extracting information that legislatures, agencies, and markets have failed to uncover.

According to Wagner, the information-extracting capacity of tort litigation benefits not only the tort system. It also enhances prospects for reconciling policy differences within legislatures, agencies, and the public at large. Polarization within the gun control debate is due in part, she asserts, to lack of information: "Without information, interest group leaders [may be] emboldened to advocate extreme positions." Thus, more information is likely to lead to more moderation. Wagner shares with social scientists like Mair, Teret, Frattaroli, and Kates the belief that, at bottom, the gun control controversy persists because of inadequate information. But if Kahan, Braman, and Gastil are right—that the fight is really about competing cultural views—then the extraction of more information by gun litigation is just another diversion from the honest cultural confrontation that is needed to advance the gun control debate. In response, Wagner suggests that "credible information . . .

endorsed by trusted experts on both sides of the gun debate" would narrow the cultural divide by promoting a shared sense of what policy options are even feasible and, if feasible, worth the costs.

Even assuming that more information would advance the gun control debate, comparative institutional analysis suggests reasons to doubt Wagner's endorsement of tort litigation as the best way to extract it. Tort litigation not only has a capacity to extract information; it also has a tendency to hide it. While the discovery process empowers plaintiffs to extract stubborn information, the settlement process often provides defendants an opportunity to seal that information using confidentiality clauses. Indeed, the threat of future litigation may encourage the industry to hide more information in secret settlements than it otherwise would have. To be fair, however, given the history and politics of gun industry regulation, it is doubtful that, absent litigation, the industry would have shared or surrendered this information to legislative or agency regulators or that government officials would have even asked for it in the first place. Moreover, in municipal suits, publicly accountable government plaintiffs are less likely to enter into sealed settlements.

In the end, Wagner concludes that the theoretical promise of gun litigation in terms of extracting stubborn information is not matched by practical results. Gun litigation, she argues, has discovered little new information, and "the . . . information that has been produced through discovery has not been transformative," painting a picture more of "corporate inattention" to gun violence risks than industry malfeasance. As the most notable accomplishment of the litigation, she cites greater industry and public attention to safer gun designs and distribution practices. Wagner's conclusions do not address an important question prompted by Nagareda's analysis: are the modest regulatory benefits of gun litigation in terms of information and internal industry reform worth the costs? This question may be impossible to answer, but this lack of cost-benefit accountability is the very reason that Nagareda questions the use of gun litigation as a regulatory tool in the first place.

Institutional analysis of tort litigation often ignores the primary mechanism by which the tort system effects risk regulation: insurance. In chapter 12, Tom Baker and Thomas Farrish examine the extent to which commercial insurance carriers deter, manage, and spread gun-related risks by imposing conditions—such as proper storage and sales practices—on the liability insurance policies that they offer to gun manufac-

turers, distributors, and retail dealers. Their findings are largely negative, that "there is very little regulation by insurance of gun-related
activities." Their study reveals that, by means of selective exclusion of
risks arising out of intentional harm, product liability, and mass torts,
insurance policies provide few incentives to gun makers and sellers to
take precautions that might eliminate or reduce the risks of gun violence.
This situation, they lament, amounts to a missed opportunity, since
"leaving gun violence outside the liability insurance umbrella may in fact
promote gun violence by depriving the gun arena of a potentially powerful institutional force for the prevention of harm." They explain that a
liability insurance industry responsible for paying millions of dollars in
gun-related claims in any given year would have an incentive to learn
more about gun violence and, if it determined that there were cost-effective prevention measures, to impose those prevention measures on
insureds either through the underwriting process or through engagement with public regulators. In addition, depending on what the research
revealed, owning a gun could lead to a premium surcharge, which could
remove some guns from circulation. "Moreover . . . insurance-funded
researchers could function as the 'honest brokers' in the debates over the
safety and costs of guns, much as they have in the field of auto and fire
safety."

Thus, in theory, liability insurance markets could provide market
incentives to reduce gun violence risks, to generate reliable regulatory
information, and to recommend proven risk-reduction policies to public
regulators. In practice, however, the insurance industry has largely
opted out of gun regulation.

As tort litigation increasingly plays a role in public regulation, it is
bound to bump up against constitutional limitations that restrain government regulators. In chapter 13, Brannon Denning examines two constitutional limitations that are especially relevant to gun litigation: the
Second Amendment and the dormant Commerce Clause. He first examines whether the Second Amendment's guarantee of the right to keep
and bear arms—which he interprets as guaranteeing an individual
right—might restrict tort claims against the gun industry. The argument
in favor of a Second Amendment restriction on gun litigation is based on
an analogy to the First Amendment's free speech protection as a limit on
defamation suits by public figures or by private parties concerning matters of public concern. After careful analysis, Denning rejects this anal-

ogy, concluding that gun litigation does not pose the kind of governmental threat to individual liberty that motivates First Amendment restrictions on defamation suits.

Denning next questions whether gun litigation has regulatory implications that would violate the dormant Commerce Clause doctrine (DCCD). In interpreting the DCCD, the U.S. Supreme Court has held that a state may not regulate "extraterritorially." That means, Denning explains, "a state may not 'project' its legislation into another state or seek to effectively regulate economic activity that takes place beyond its borders." The gun industry has argued that municipal suits demanding changes in marketing practices violate this aspect of the DCCD, since they call for judgments based on state tort law that would regulate commercial activity beyond the borders of the state. The Supreme Court of Indiana recently rejected such a DCCD challenge to a suit brought by the City of Gary, pointing out that states are free to promulgate their own product liability standards through tort law and declaring that it saw no principled distinction between the imposition of money damages under state product liability law and injunctive relief for negligent marketing and nuisance based on an industry's marketing practices. Far from eliminating DCCD concerns, points out Denning, this observation "merely raise[s] further questions about state tort law and whether constitutional doctrines have anything to say about its regulatory effects on products with national markets."

In a somewhat more cautious tone, Denning admits that "limiting the tort law of the fifty states through DCCD would be nothing short of revolutionary." Perhaps it would be more accurate to call it *counterrevolutionary*, given the revolutionary nature of developments in product liability and mass tort over the past fifty years. Denning's analysis raises the possibility that, aside from legislative reactions, potent constraints on regulatory tort litigation could eventually be imposed by the Constitution.

The Persistence of Disagreement over Gun Litigation

So where do all these different perspectives on gun violence, gun control, and gun litigation leave us? The aim of this book is not to reconcile these different perspectives but rather to put them next to each other in order to highlight issues that remain unresolved and to offer insight into why these issues are so hard to resolve. Indeed, what emerges is that the difference in perspective itself accounts for much of the difficulty in resolving the controversy over gun litigation. For example, the lack of consensus about whether gun design or marketing affects gun violence rates is itself partly rooted in differences between the disciplines of public health, with its broad focus on all gun-related death and injury, criminology, which focuses more narrowly on crime rates, and sociology, which considers the question itself merely a diversion from an underlying cultural divide. So, too, the debate about whether tort litigation is an appropriate tool for generating more information about the link between the gun industry and gun violence (or for confronting the underlying cultural divide) depends largely on the alternatives to which one compares it. Gun litigation appears less appropriate when one compares it to general standards of regulatory accountability such as cost-benefit analysis or interagency coordination, as Nagareda does, or to "the regulatory option that would become viable were the gun control movement to achieve greater political success in the future," as Schuck does, than when one takes into account the political reality of NRA domination of the political process, as I do, or the regulatory system's failure to uncover stubborn information, as Wagner does.

Besides information, another unresolved issue is enforcement. Is it possible to effectively enforce regulations concerning gun design and marketing, and, if so, at what cost? And is tort litigation an appropriate enforcement mechanism? Again, different answers emerge depending upon whether one approaches these issues from the perspective of public health policy (Mair, Teret, and Frattaroli, and Sugarman), crime control (Kates), commercial liability insurance (Baker and Farrish), or constitutional law (Denning).

Thus, the controversy over gun litigation is attributable not only to inadequate information but also to different perspectives that focus on different questions or take different approaches to the same questions. This insight is important for the study of other policy disputes. A good grasp on policy disputes requires understanding why it is so hard—at times impossible—to resolve them. Indeed, understanding the irreconcilability or noncomparability of different views is as important as finding common ground, since we need not only to resolve policy differences when we can but to live together even when we cannot. The ability to live peacefully alongside those with whom we disagree based on deeply held convictions is an essential skill—a core virtue—of a liberal society. In the end, will a clearer picture of the disagreement really help policymakers resolve the controversy over gun control? Perhaps not. But the contributors to this volume all share the conviction that, by increasing mutual understanding, it can promote peaceful coexistence and, perhaps, even dialogue.

As this book goes to press, the New York City and Gary, Indiana, lawsuits are in discovery and individual suits across the country are headed for trial. Simultaneously, there is widespread support in Congress for legislation that would grant the gun industry broad immunity, putting an end to gun litigation. But regardless of the outcomes of these latest developments, the lessons of gun litigation will add to our understanding of the role of guns, tort litigation, and, most important, controversy in our society.

PART I

Perspectives on Gun Violence,
Gun Control, & the Gun Industry

CHAPTER 1

A Public Health Perspective on Gun Violence Prevention

JULIE SAMIA MAIR, STEPHEN TERET,

& SHANNON FRATTAROLI

Gun violence is a public health problem. Each year in the United States, tens of thousands of people are killed by gunfire and many more are seriously injured with resulting disabilities.[1] Among the victims of gun violence are curious young children who encounter loaded guns and do not understand the damage they can cause; depressed teenagers who commit suicide; victims of domestic abuse; and the casualties of many other violent crimes. For some population groups, death by gunfire is the number one cause of death. It has been estimated that the lifetime medical costs of gun violence that occurred in the single year of 1994 was approximately $2.3 billion,[2] a huge sum of money that could be better spent on solving other societal ills. Whether measured by mortality or morbidity statistics, by cost to society, or by sheer grief and disruption to the population, the toll of gun violence is too high, and it places the public's safety at unacceptable levels of risk. Interventions are needed to address this public health problem.

Although guns and gun violence have long been a part of American life,[3] it is only in the past few decades that guns and gun-related injuries have come to be seen as a public health issue. In the past, gun-related homicides were viewed as a problem to be solved by law enforcement and the criminal justice system. Gun-related suicides were problems belonging to the discipline of mental health. The comparatively small numbers of unintended gun deaths were seen as within the province of hunter safety courses or other educational programs for accident prevention.

With the blossoming of the field of injury prevention within the discipline of public health, a field that only came into general recognition in the 1970s, researchers, practitioners, and advocates began to recognize the toll that guns take on the public's health. Instead of having a fractionated view of gun deaths by separately considering homicides, suicides, and unintended gun deaths, articles began to appear in health journals that aggregated all gun deaths.[4] When gun deaths were combined, based on the reasoning that all of the deaths involve the same vehicle (i.e., a gun), it was realized that guns form the second leading cause of injury death in the United States, surpassed only by motor vehicle–related deaths.[5] As previously noted, for some segments of the population such as young African American males, gun-related deaths are the leading cause of deaths overall.[6]

The aggregation of all gun deaths, simple as that sounds, is an idea that is quintessential to the public health method of thought and therefore an idea that was dormant until those in the field of public health addressed their attention to guns as a health problem. Public health has a tradition of looking beyond the individuals inflicted with injury or disease. The physical and social environments in which human damage occurs, and, importantly, the vehicles or vectors that deliver the agents of injury or disease, are all considered part of the causation of morbidity and mortality and therefore possibly part of the solution to reducing the incidence of morbidity and mortality.

Public health researchers and practitioners recognize that changing the behaviors of people involved in the causation of injury and disease is a potentially effective approach but one that is difficult to achieve. Changing the man-made products that are associated with injury and disease can sometimes be more easily accomplished than changing the behaviors of those who use the products. This has been the case with automobiles. After many years of trying to raise the skills of the driving public, it was realized that cars and highways could be redesigned so that, when the foreseeable crash occurs, the vehicle occupants do not have to suffer fatal injuries. Seatbelts, energy-absorbing steering columns, air bags, and breakaway road signs have all helped to save hundreds of thousands of lives that otherwise would have been lost in crashes.[7]

Similarly, although gun injuries are often the result of troublesome behaviors involving rage, depression, and carelessness, and are compounded by social ills such as poverty and discrimination, there may be interventions available to reduce gun-related deaths that do not focus solely on modifying individuals' behaviors. But most gun policies prior to the past two decades addressed individuals' behaviors, and often those individuals were already in possession of guns, resulting in reactive rather than preventive policy strategies. The initial recognition that guns were involved in a great many deaths in the United States fell short of the formulation of sound prevention policies to address this public health risk.

In 1980, an article was published in the *Journal of Public Health Policy* that suggested for the first time that gun policy might be more effective if it focused less on the behaviors of shooters and more on the product itself.[8] The article (and other articles following it)[9] postulated setting policy priorities categorized according to a fictional life span of a gun. The suggestion was made that the manufacture of a gun is analogous to its birth and that other milestones in the life span of the gun include its sale, possession, and use. Most policy was directed toward the end of this life span—the use of the gun. The suggestion was made that for policy to be most effective, with effectiveness being defined as producing a reduction in the incidence of gun-related deaths and injuries, the focus of policy should be shifted backward in time along this fictional life span. The most effective policies might be those that regulate the design and marketing of guns.

This public health perspective on gun violence prevention achieved rapid and widespread acceptance within the health and medical communities. *Healthy People*, the U.S. surgeon general's report on the nation's ten-year health goals to be achieved by 1990, recognized that firearms were claiming tens of thousands of lives each year. In discussing health protection strategies, the report stated: "Measures that could reduce the risk of firearm deaths and injuries range from encouraging safer storage and use to a ban on private ownership."[10] The public health literature on the epidemiology of gun violence and the policies to reduce it blossomed in such leading medical journals as the *Journal of the American Medical Association* and the *New England Journal of Medicine*. The descriptive epidemiology of gun violence was fully explored, and some hypothesis-testing research on topics such as the risks of gun ownership was reported. Additionally, the new literature began to include scientific evaluations of policies designed to reduce the incidence of gun violence.

By 1988, James Mercy and Vernon Houk of the federal Centers for

Disease Control and Prevention (CDC), in a call for continued scientific investigation of firearms as a public health problem, delineated four steps needed "for further research and the development of effective strategies to prevent firearm injuries."[11] These steps involved the determination of the size, characteristics, and cost of the problem; the determination of the number, type, and distribution of firearms in the United States; the further development of hypothesis-testing epidemiologic research; and the rigorous evaluation of regulations and other interventions that affect the risk of firearm injury. More studies followed these suggestions, and by the early 1990s a body of evidence existed indicating that firearms were a leading public health problem and that policies to address the problem were both needed and feasible.

Around the same time, however, a concerted attack against the public health community's efforts to reduce gun violence was mounted. In a 1995 article by Don Kates and colleagues, published in the *Tennessee Law Review*, it was suggested that the public health literature on gun violence was created by academics who "prostitute scholarship, systematically inventing, misinterpreting, selecting, or otherwise manipulating data to validate preordained political conclusions."[12] In addition, the National Rifle Association (NRA) was critical of efforts to frame gun violence as a public health issue and led the campaign to end gun violence prevention research funded by the CDC.[13] In 1992, Congress established the National Center for Injury Prevention and Control (NCIPC) in the CDC with the mission to reduce injury-related morbidity and mortality. Unhappy with the findings of firearms-related research funded by the NCIPC, in 1995, when Republicans controlled the House of Representatives, the NRA tried to influence the congressional agenda on funding of the NCIPC. The NRA claimed, among other things, that the NCIPC's injury prevention research was duplicative of that conducted by other federal agencies and driven by political goals. Although the NCIPC survived, in June 1996 the House Appropriations Committee approved an amendment that cut over two million dollars from the NCIPC's budget, the exact amount the CDC spent on gun violence prevention research. The Senate ultimately restored the cut funding, but the funding was earmarked for other injury research. The CDC was also prohibited, and continues to be prohibited, from using federal funds "to advocate or promote gun control." Clearly, the public health approach to gun violence had triggered a powerful, negative response by organizations and individuals traditionally viewed as pro-gun.

The public health perspective we describe in this chapter recognizes gun injury as a significant source of morbidity and mortality and promotes policy interventions aimed at gun design and marketing as the preferred strategy for reducing gun death and injury. In the first section of the chapter, we use federal data to define the scope of gun injury and death in the United States and describe gun death trends over time. A review of analyses that consider the societal cost of gun violence concludes this measurement section. In the second section we then examine several interventions that focus on gun design, sale, and possession and explain the preference for interventions aimed at the design and marketing levels. In the concluding section to this chapter we briefly discuss the public health tools available for realizing the design and marketing interventions previously described.

Measuring the Toll of Gun Injury and Death

Epidemiology of Firearm Death and Injury

The epidemiology of firearm-related morbidity and mortality provides a foundation on which to consider gun violence prevention strategies. Data in this section were obtained from the National Center for Injury Control and Prevention (WISCARS, see note 1). Understanding the nature and extent of a problem is the first step in the public health approach to problem solving. The extent of this understanding is determined by the quality and scope of available data about the issue. Vital statistics records provide information about the number of gun homicides, suicides, and unintentional gun deaths that occur in the United States. The CDC offers online access to these data in aggregate. Basic demographic information about the deceased is available on the CDC's web site. With few exceptions, these demographic data are complete, providing a reliable, basic description of the population killed by gunfire. Vital statistics data provide no useful information about the guns used to kill[14] and do not include information about perpetrators of gun homicides or, when applicable, unintentional gun deaths. National estimates of nonfatal gun injuries are available through the CDC web site beginning with the year 2000. The data are the result of a national injury surveillance system that collects information from a sample of hospital emergency departments. These data are also limited in that they do not include information about the gun.

In an effort to address the shortcomings of existing surveillance efforts, the National Violent Injury Statistics System (NVISS) was developed in 1999. This initiative currently includes a small number of pilot sites, and there are plans to implement the system nationally. Once in place, NVISS will provide detailed information about the weapons used to commit violent injuries and offer researchers and policymakers valuable information for prevention initiatives.

In the following examination of gun-related death and injury we review trend data for a twenty-year period (1981–2000) and highlight information available from the latest government statistics. We frame the trend analysis using the most recent twenty years of available data in part because the beginning of the time period roughly coincides with the history of public health's involvement in this issue.

Between 1981 and 2000, more than 675,000 people were killed by gunfire in the United States. Approximately 83,000 of the people who lost their lives were younger than twenty years old. More than half of the 675,000 gun deaths were suicides, 42 percent were homicides, and 4 percent were unintentionally inflicted. The unacceptable toll of 675,000 deaths exists even though by the year 2000 the gun death rate in this country declined to its lowest point in over twenty years.

People of all ages, races, and both genders are represented in these numbers. However, the burden associated with gun deaths and injuries falls disproportionately on certain subgroups within the population. In 2000, young adults between the ages of twenty and twenty-four were killed by gunfire at a rate of 21 per 100,000—the highest rate among the age groups and more than double the total population rate of 10 per 100,000. Gun death rates among African Americans that year were twice the rate for whites. In 2000, men were six times more likely to die by gunfire than were women.

That African Americans suffer disproportionately high firearm death rates is a well-established and often cited fact of gun-related death and injury in the United States. In 2000, just as in 1981, firearm death rates among African Americans exceeded the rates for all other Americans. Total population data for these two years suggest a difference between

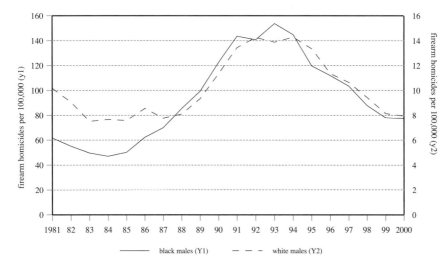

Fig. 1.   Firearm homicide among 15–24 year old males, United States (1981–2000). Please note the difference in scale on the two axes. The y1 axis depicting the black male rate is 10 times larger than the y2 axis depicting the white male rate. (Data from CDC/National Center for Injury Prevention and Control.)

the rate of firearm death in 1981 (15 per 100,000) and 2000 (10 per 100,000), but that difference does not reveal changes in certain subpopulation statistics that signal a troubling development in firearm violence and further strengthen the case for public health involvement in prevention efforts.

The most significant changes over the past twenty years have been the sharp increases and subsequent decreases in gun deaths among adolescent and young adult males. Between 1985 and 1993, the rate of gun deaths among fifteen- to nineteen-year-old males more than doubled and the rate among twenty- to twenty-four-year-old males increased from 35 to 59 deaths per 100,000. Most of this change is attributable to rapid increases in gun homicide; however, gun suicide within these age groups also rose. While the upward trend in gun homicide among male youth is evident in each racial category, the numbers are most pronounced among African Americans. Gun homicides increased 250 percent between 1985 and 1993 among fifteen- to nineteen-year-old African American males and 180 percent among those between the ages of twenty and twenty-four. In 1993, African American males between the ages of fifteen and nineteen were being killed by guns at a rate of 131 per 100,000; among white males of the same age the rate was 13.

The high rates of 1993 marked the peak of this gun homicide trend.

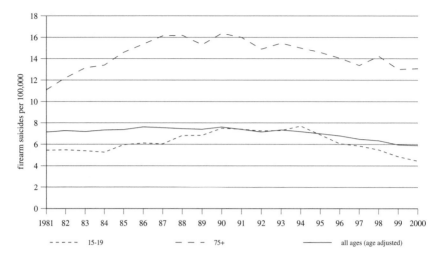

Fig. 2. Firearm suicide among select age groups, United States (1981–2000). (Data from CDC/National Center for Injury Prevention and Control.)

With these numbers, the realization that guns had become a threat to the lives of our youth began to take root, and the traditional public health commitment to vulnerable populations, such as youth, further strengthened the resolve of many public health professionals to commit resources to reversing this trend. In the years that followed the 1993 peak, gun homicide rates declined. While gun homicides rates remain lower in the current decade relative to the 1990s, 43 percent of all young African American males who died in 2000 were victims of gun homicide. Among young white males, 7 percent of all deaths in 2000 were the result of a firearm homicide.[15]

Other trends in gun mortality over the past twenty years are less well publicized. While suicide is often associated with teens, the highest rates of gun suicide in this country occur among our population's oldest. Between 1981 and 1990, gun suicide among those age seventy-five and older rose 46 percent. This increase was driven by the white male rate, which in 2000 numbered 36 per 100,000. By comparison, the gun suicide rate for the whole U.S. population was 6 per 100,000 that year. The rate of unintentional gun death over the past twenty years has steadily decreased. In 1981 the rate of unintentional gun death was 0.8 per 100,000; by 2000 the rate had declined to almost one-third of that number. Unintentional gun deaths, like gun homicides, are most numerous among young males.

Nonfatal gunshot wounds treated in emergency departments, another important component of the epidemiologic data, were estimated to number 75,000 in 2000. For every gun homicide, an estimated four people are shot during nonfatal gun assaults; for every five people who commit suicide with a gun, one person attempts suicide with a gun and survives; and for every unintentional gun death, another thirty people are estimated to survive unintentional gun shootings.

An argument is sometimes made with respect to gun suicides and homicides that, if the gun had not been available, a different weapon or method would have been used with the same result. The research, though, does not support this position, and, in fact, strong evidence exists indicating that the choice of weapon affects the outcome of both self-inflicted and intentional violence.[16] Suicidal persons choose a method that is both acceptable to them and available. If the method of choice is not available, substitution of another means of killing themselves sometimes, but not always, occurs, but the substituted method may be less likely to result in a completed suicide.[17] Attempted suicide by a firearm has a very high case fatality rate, meaning that most attempts will result in death, whereas attempts of suicide by other means have a substantially lower case fatality rate.[18] For example, ingestion of poison may leave time for lifesaving medical intervention, but a gunshot to the head is often immediately fatal. With respect to homicides, guns also make it easier to kill, turning, for example, what might have been a fistfight between angry youth into a homicide irrespective of intent to kill.[19]

The previous accounting of the death and injury associated with firearms provides insight into the cost of an armed society. The toll of gunfire highlights the need for the complementary problem-solving

TABLE 1.   Gun Deaths and Nonfatal Gun Injuries in the United States, 2000

	Gun Deaths	Nonfatal Gun Injuries
Assault	11,071	49,431
Self-inflicted	16,586	3,016
Unintentional	776	23,237

tools and preventive orientation of public health in order to realize a future where guns are far less prominent vehicles of human suffering.

Economic Costs of Gun Violence

The economic burden of gun violence entails far more than the cost of victims' medical expenses or lost productivity, which represent only a fraction of the total societal cost.[20] The true burden of gun violence also reflects the public and private expenditures taken to reduce the risk of gun injury and death and includes the fear of victimization that remains even after risk-reducing efforts have been made. Society as a whole pays through a reduced standard of living for everyone.

The most obvious expenditure to reduce the risk of gun injury and death is tax increases to prevent gun-related crime. Taxes pay for enhanced security—such as metal detectors and security personnel—at schools, airports, and other public places, amounting to hundreds of millions of dollars per year. Taxes pay to protect law enforcement, including as much as one hundred million dollars each year on bulletproof vests alone. Taxes also pay for prosecuting and punishing criminal offenders. Assaults in which a gun is used tend to be more deadly than other assaults, and homicides are more expensive to investigate, prosecute, and punish than robberies and assaults. It has been estimated that gun violence increases the costs of administrating the criminal justice system by over two billion dollars a year.

Gun violence also affects where people choose to live, work, attend school, and travel. Urban flight has been shown to be sensitive to homicide rates, and guns increase the likelihood that a violent crime will turn deadly. Many people would rather live in a safe neighborhood than enjoy an easy commute or access to urban cultural amenities. Those who cannot afford to move may take precautions such as sleeping on the floor to avoid bullets coming through windows or spending as little time as possible outside, further reducing their quality of life.

One way to translate the reduction in the standard of living caused by the threat of gun injury and death into specific dollar estimates is through the "willingness-to-pay" approach. Specifically, what would people in the United States be willing to pay to reduce the risk of gun-related injury? The willingness-to-pay approach has been used in public health to evaluate a variety of public health initiatives. Compared with the cost-of-injury approach, which looks at the traditional costs to victims of gun violence such as medical expenses and lost productivity, the willingness-to-pay approach looks at more difficult-to-measure societal costs from the threat of gun violence and the expenditures to reduce the risk of gun-related injury.

Willingness-to-pay can be estimated through the contingent valuation (CV) method, which infers what people are willing to pay for goods not bought and sold on the market (e.g., improved health and safety) using hypothetical market scenarios. Using the CV method, as part of a 1998 nationally representative telephone survey of 1,204 adults, respondents were asked if they would be willing to pay an additional fifty, one hundred, or two hundred dollars in taxes each year for a program that would make it more difficult for criminals and delinquents to obtain guns if that program would reduce gun injuries by 30 percent. Because the amount of the tax increase presented to each respondent was determined randomly, about one-third of the sample provided answers for each of the three dollar amounts. Depending on whether the response to this question was positive or negative, a follow-up question was asked, either doubling or halving (respectively) the initial dollar amount.

Analyzing the results, Cook and Ludwig found that 76 percent of respondents would pay an additional fifty dollars of taxes for a program to reduce crime-related gunshot injuries by 30 percent, 69 percent an additional one hundred dollars, and 64 percent an additional two hundred dollars. By extrapolating the data to all U.S. households, the researchers determined that people would be willing to pay more than twenty billion dollars in increased taxes to reduce crime-related gun injuries by 30 percent.

A Public Health Perspective on Strategies to Reduce Gun Injury

We suggested earlier that, from a public health perspective, the most effective strategies to reduce gun injury and death are those that target the design and marketing of a gun—at the birth of the fictional life span. This next section explores that proposition in more detail, raising some of the main issues that arise along the different stages of a gun's life.

Issues regarding Design

Two of the principles that help define the discipline of public health are as follows: (1) preventing damage to humans by injury and disease is preferable to repairing damage after it has occurred; and (2) prevention is best accomplished by protection that is provided automatically on a population basis and does not require each individual to always act carefully. This is why we fluoridate water supplies to reduce the incidence of dental caries rather than ask each individual to remember to consume a certain amount of fluorine each day. We regulate the design of products for safety, such as specifying certain dimensions for baby cribs to reduce the risk to infants of strangulation rather than asking parents to choose their cribs carefully and always to monitor their sleeping babies. Applying this approach to the area of gun violence, it is considered more effective and therefore preferable to address the design of guns before they get into the hands of millions of people rather than rely upon our ability to control the behaviors of those millions so that they always act prudently once the guns are in their hands.

Safe design can be mandated by government regulations. For most consumer products, the nation's Consumer Product Safety Commission (CPSC) has the responsibility to protect the public from unsafe designs. But regarding guns, the CPSC has been expressly forbidden by Congress to regulate design safety.[21] In fact, no federal agency comprehensively regulates the safe design of firearms, despite the fact that guns are the second leading cause of injury deaths in the United States. Guns, and particularly handguns, could be designed more safely by the use of existing, inexpensive technologies, resulting in a saving of lives. Gun manufacturers have been reluctant to use some of these technologies and have been adamant in their opposition to any regulations that would require safer guns.[22]

Two examples of existing technologies that would likely save lives if they were used uniformly on all handguns are loaded chamber indicators and magazine safety devices.[23] A loaded chamber indicator lets the person holding a gun know whether there is a bullet in the chamber, just like a camera lets the user know if it is loaded with film. Its purpose is to help prevent an unintentional discharge of the gun, which has been known to result in death. A magazine safety prevents a pistol from being fired if the magazine or clip, in which the ammunition is stored, has been removed from the pistol. Again, deaths have resulted from people believing a gun was unloaded and then pulling the trigger. A magazine safety is important because some people think that, once they remove the magazine, all of the ammunition has been removed; however, often a bullet remains in the chamber of the gun, and if the trigger is pulled on a pistol without a magazine safety, that bullet will be discharged. In a 1997 nationally representative survey, over one-third of respondents either erroneously believed that a pistol could not be fired with its ammunition magazine removed (20.3 percent) or did not know (14.5 percent). Of this one-third, 28 percent lived in homes with guns.[24]

The technologies for loaded chamber indicators and magazine safeties have existed since the early twentieth century, and the cost of these safety devices is minimal.[25] But the vast majority of pistol models presently being sold do not include these safety devices.[26] Some manufacturers provide the safety devices on some of their models but not others. This is akin to a car manufacturer offering seatbelts on some models but not others—a behavior that would be illegal, due to federal safety regulations for motor vehicles.

Another important design feature that would materially enhance the safety of guns is the use of technology that discriminates between authorized users of a gun and unauthorized users.[27] Every year, many die from homicides, suicides, or unintended deaths when a gun is operated by an unauthorized user. This could be a criminal who stole a gun or bought a stolen gun from another, a depressed teenager using the gun for suicide, or a curious young child who does not understand the dangers presented by guns. Many of these deaths could be averted if the gun was made so that it was personalized or operable only by certain authorized users. Personalization of guns can be accomplished by the use of locks built into the gun itself or by technologies that recognize the biometrics of the authorized users.[28] A few gun makers, such as Taurus, now offer some forms of personalization based on internal locking devices,[29] but most newly made handguns are as easily operated by a thief or young child as by the owner.

Cook and Ludwig analyzed the cost-effectiveness of personalized technology and found that the benefits associated with requiring personalized technology on new guns should more than outweigh the costs.[30]

Issues regarding Sales

While the preferred intervention from a public health perspective is to produce a safer product, interventions aimed further along the life span of a gun—such as at the point of sale—can also help to reduce injuries and death from gunfire. To understand the potential of interventions at this level, it is first important to understand a little about the market for guns.

In the mid-1990s, it was estimated that 200 million guns were privately owned in the United States, including more than 60 million handguns. Each year, about 4.5 million new guns and about the same number of used guns are sold, and about five hundred thousand guns are stolen. The gun market involves sales through federally licensed dealers (primary market) or through largely unregulated transactions between private individuals (secondary market). About 60 percent of all transactions (including new and used guns) are conducted through the primary market.[31]

In 2001, there were almost sixty-four thousand federally licensed gun dealers.[32] The license allows the dealer to buy an unlimited number of guns from manufacturers, distributors, and dealers in other states. Licensed gun dealers must keep records of gun sales, conduct background checks on prospective buyers, and allow inspections by the Bureau of Alcohol, Tobacco, Firearms and Explosives (ATF).[33]

Licensed dealers are an important source of guns for criminals and youth.[34] One study that looked at the willingness of gun dealers to participate in illegal straw purchases (i.e., a transaction where the gun dealer sells a gun to an authorized buyer knowing that the buyer intends to immediately transfer the gun to a prohibited user) found that more than half of the gun dealers were willing to sell a handgun under a straw purchase scheme.[35] Although other studies looking at crime gun traces suggest that the majority of dealers are law abiding,[36] only a few corrupt dealers can divert large numbers of guns through off-the-record sales to gun traffickers.[37] Even law-abiding dealers can unwittingly help prohibited users obtain guns if they unknowingly engage in a straw purchase.

In the secondary market, guns are sold and traded between unlicensed individuals. These transactions can be legal or illegal and may involve family members, friends, drug dealers, or gun traffickers. Most criminals and youth obtain their guns in the secondary market because, under federal law, unlicensed sellers and private individuals do not have to conduct background checks or keep records of the transaction. Although some states do regulate the secondary market, enforcement of these laws is believed to be minimal.

EFFECTIVENESS OF CONTROLLING SALES BY LICENSED DEALERS

The most far-reaching intervention at the dealer level is to establish an outright ban on the sale of a particular type of gun, usually those that are considered the most dangerous and with the least utility. One study found that Maryland's ban of so-called Saturday Night Special handguns reduced gun homicide rates by 6.8 percent to 11.5 percent, amounting to forty fewer homicides per year than would have been expected without the ban.[38] The short-term effect of the 1994 federal law banning certain assault weapons and large-capacity magazines may have slightly reduced gun homicides even though the potential effect of the ban is limited because assault weapons are used in relatively few crimes.[39]

More commonly, however, the goal at the dealer level is to prevent guns from ending up in the hands of criminals, youths, and other prohibited users. But there is no assurance that once a gun is sold to an authorized user it will remain in legitimate hands. For example, the most common and most lethal method for adolescents in the United States to commit suicide is shooting themselves with a gun, and often the source of those guns is the victim's home or the home of a relative or friend.[40] Many guns are also stolen from residences. In a 2001 nationally representative survey, 12 percent of the respondents who personally owned a gun had at least one gun stolen from them.[41] Government studies also show that theft from retail outlets as well as from residences is an important source of guns for criminals.[42] Thus, even if all guns were sold only to authorized users, there would still be gun injury and death related to those sales, although the level of gun violence under such a scenario would presumably be lower than current rates.

Despite these limitations, controlling the sale of guns at the dealer level can make it more difficult for criminals and other prohibited users to obtain guns, potentially reducing gun injury and death. One way to curtail the flow of guns to prohibited users is to limit the number of guns a potential buyer can purchase. Three states (California, Maryland, and

Virginia) prohibit individuals from purchasing more than one handgun and/or other gun within a thirty-day period. Without these so-called one-gun-a-month laws, a corrupt buyer could legally purchase from a gun dealer an unlimited amount of guns and illegally resell them to prohibited users. In an evaluation of Virginia's one-gun-a-month law, Weil and Knox documented that, relative to other southeastern states, guns first sold in Virginia were less likely to be recovered in crimes following the law's effective date, suggesting that the restriction disrupted the illegal interstate transfer of guns.[43]

Another way to analyze the potential of interventions aimed at the dealer level is to measure the association between the denial of handgun purchases and the risk of subsequent criminal activity. A California study comparing handgun purchasers who had a felony arrest with those who were denied a purchase because of a felony conviction found that those who were allowed to purchase a gun were at a greater risk for subsequent criminal offenses involving a gun or violence.[44] A similar study found that denial of a handgun purchase to potential buyers with a violent misdemeanor conviction was also associated with a reduced risk of subsequent arrest for a violent or gun-related crime.[45]

More generally, restraints on sales from licensed dealers should also increase prices in the secondary market, deterring some criminals and youth from buying guns in the secondary market as well.[46]

CHALLENGES TO REDUCING GUN VIOLENCE THROUGH SALES LEVEL INTERVENTIONS

Although interventions aimed at retail sales are promising, there are several challenges that limit their potential. The major challenge is the thriving and largely unregulated secondary market. A prospective buyer who cannot buy a gun from a licensed dealer can look to many other potential sources.

Certain federal laws can also limit the effectiveness of interventions on the dealer level. Licensing and registration have been suggested as interventions that could reduce gun injury and death, although some disagree with this approach.[47] In general, licensing requires that the prospective gun buyer obtain a license before purchasing a gun. Licensing can entail background checks, gun safety training, and other requirements, potentially weeding out high-risk individuals. Registration generally requires a gun owner to provide his or her name and contact information, the serial number of the gun, and the gun's description to a central authority that stores the information. Registration makes tracing the ownership of guns recovered in crimes easier, potentially dissuading some legitimate owners from transferring their weapons to prohibited users. An analysis of the relationship between state licensing and/or registration laws and guns recovered in crime suggests that the combination of licensing and registration makes it more difficult for criminals and youths to obtain guns.[48] Only a few states have both laws, and because the Firearms Owners' Protection Act of 1986 prohibits a national gun registry,[49] this intervention cannot be implemented on a national level without a change in current law.

The Firearms Owners' Protection Act also undermines the federal government's ability to assure dealer compliance with federal gun laws by limiting warrantless inspections of a dealer to one per year, by weakening the penalties for most recording-keeping offenses from felonies to misdemeanors, and by establishing high standards of proof for suspected violations of federal gun law.

Another challenge is implementation. In fiscal year 1998, there were approximately two hundred full-time equivalent field inspectors for tens of thousands of Federal Firearms Licensees (FFLs). Using 1998 data and assuming a licensee population of one hundred thousand, the ATF estimated that it would take twenty-six hundred full-time inspectors to make one annual inspection of all licensed retail dealers. In 2000 and 2001, the percent of FFLs inspected was less than 4 percent (3.5 percent and 3.6 percent, respectively). Thus, even if federal law allowed the ATF more than one warrantless search per year, the ATF does not even have the personnel to conduct one search of every FFL each year because of too few ATF field inspectors. Another example of an implementation problem concerns the Brady Handgun Violence Prevention Act of 1993 (the Brady Act). A government review found that the National Instant Criminal Background Check System Index database used for conducting background checks has relatively few records for most of the categories that would disqualify prospective gun purchasers (e.g., mentally incompetent adjudications, fugitive status, restraining orders), thus undermining the law's potential effectiveness.

None of these challenges are insurmountable—for example, all sales on the secondary market could be regulated, federal law could be changed to allow ATF more flexibility, and Congress could allocate sufficient resources to ensure that existing laws can be fully implemented.

A PUBLIC HEALTH APPROACH TO CONTROLLING SALES: FOCUSING ON MANUFACTURERS

If preventing the retail sale of guns to prohibited users can limit the availability of guns to criminals and youths and reduce gun injury and death, the question arises of what are the best ways to accomplish that goal. From a public health perspective, an intervention aimed at tens of thousands of dealers is more difficult to implement than an intervention aimed at the relatively few manufacturers. Gun manufacturers could be required to engage in practices that would make it nearly impossible or extremely difficult for corrupt or irresponsible dealers to stay in business—such as not selling their products to dealers who fail to implement adequate security measures to prevent theft or weed out corrupt employees or who conduct business at gun shows where background checks are not performed on all sales. Manufacturers in other industries follow their products throughout the distribution chain to the point of sale.[50] There is no reason why gun manufacturers could not do the same.

Issues regarding Possession

Often the most difficult place to intervene to reduce injuries caused by a consumer product from the standpoint of effectiveness is with the user of the product—at the end of the product's life span. Teaching millions of individuals to use a product safely tends to be far less effective than designing a safer product. Over time, the benefits of educational programs aimed at changing behavior tend to wane and people return to prior unsafe behavior. But once a product is designed safely, barring manufacturer defects, it should remain safe for the duration of its use. A safe design also protects the user from a momentary lapse in attention, whether while driving a car or handling a product like a gun. Because guns are so lethal, safe design becomes even more important. The fact that it is difficult to change people's behavior does not mean it cannot be done or that it is not an important component of public health initiatives. For example, child access prevention laws that carry felony penalties may encourage some people to store their guns safely.[51] But public health seeks to advance the interventions that are most effective, and the most effective way to reduce injury caused by consumer products is to produce a safe product.

STORAGE PRACTICES

A gun in the home should be stored locked and unloaded, with the ammunition stored separately in a different locked location, making the gun inaccessible to children, suicidal adolescents, burglars, and other prohibited users. But survey findings consistently demonstrate that many gun owners store their guns unsafely, often both loaded and unlocked and accessible to children. An estimated one in three handguns—over 20 million—as well as one in six long guns are stored loaded and unlocked.[52] National survey data reveal that, among homes with children and guns, 9 percent kept guns both loaded and unlocked and 4 percent kept guns unloaded, unlocked, and stored with ammunition.[53] Thus, 13 percent of these homes—about 1.4 million homes where 2.6 million children resided—stored guns unsafely. There is reason to suspect that the number of guns stored unsafely may be even higher because the household member who responds to the survey may not be the gun owner.[54]

Several studies suggest that firearms training is not necessarily associated with safe storage practices and may be associated with unsafe practices.[55] More favorable results were reported in a study evaluating a community-based program that used a high-profile, multimedia, public education campaign; individually tailored gun safety counseling; and a gun lock distribution component.[56] The findings suggest, though, that gun safety training alone does not promote safer storage practices and that little is known about the long-term effect of the intervention or whether this program would show similar results in a different population.

MISCONCEPTIONS OF RISK

Many gun owners—especially handgun owners—report that they own a gun for protection. This concern for protection may account for unsafe storage practices because some people may want easy access to their weapon.[57] But rather than offering protection as some have claimed, several studies evaluating the protective effect of home ownership found that keeping a gun in the home increases the risk of gun-related homicide, suicide, and fatal unintentional injury. For example, using a matched case-control design, Wiebe found that having a gun in the home almost quadrupled the risk of a fatal unintentional shooting,[58] increased the risk of gun suicide by nearly seventeen times, and raised the risk of gun homicide by 72 percent.[59] Wiebe's findings support previous research that suggests that, instead of providing protection, a gun in the home increases the risk of death[60] and support other studies finding an association between handgun purchases and an increased risk of dying from violence.[61]

Many parents, including those who own guns, assume that their child will behave safely with guns. Webster and colleagues found that, in a convenience sample from three pediatric practices in Maryland, almost half of the gun owners (46 percent) believed that children age six or younger could distinguish between a real and toy gun compared to 10 percent of non–gun owners.[62] Fourteen percent of gun owners also believed that children under twelve years old could be trusted with a loaded gun compared to 3 percent of non–gun owners. In a survey of parents of children between the ages of four and twelve at selected pediatric ambulatory care centers in Atlanta, Farah, Simon, and Kellermann found that 74 percent of gun-owning parents and 52 percent of non-gun-owning parents believed that their child could distinguish between a real and toy gun.[63] A large percentage of parents trusted their child with a loaded gun, including 35 percent of the parents who kept at least one gun loaded, 23 percent of gun-owning parents, and 14 percent of non-gun-owning parents. A significant portion of parents (14 percent of gun owners and 10 percent of non–gun owners) trusted their child between the age of four and seven with a loaded gun.

BEHAVIORAL APPROACHES

Although some parents may believe that telling their child not to play with guns will prevent injury,[64] educational approaches do not appear to be effective. Hardy and colleagues found that, in a matched case-control study of four- to six-year-olds in two urban daycare centers, an intervention that included a thirty-minute presentation and instruction from a police officer had no effect on modifying the children's gun-playing behavior.[65] In a later randomized control study of four- to seven-year-olds involving a more intensive five-day gun safety program, Hardy also found that the intervention did not affect the likelihood that a child would play with a gun.[66] Another study evaluating the effectiveness of two gun safety programs—the NRA's Eddie Eagle GunSafe Program (mainly educational) and a behavioral skills training program (BTM) (instruction, modeling, rehearsal, and praise/corrective feedback)—found that, while both programs effectively taught the four- and five-year-old participants to reproduce verbally gun-safety skills, neither program effectively taught the children to use those skills in a simulated situation.[67] With respect to the children exposed to the Eddie Eagle GunSafe Program, they also could not demonstrate the gun-safety skills in a role-play scenario, leading the authors to conclude that education alone does not ensure that the child can actually perform the skills. Even gun safety instruction targeting older children may not work. In a study to determine how boys between the ages of eight and twelve reacted when they discovered a real handgun while playing, more than 90 percent of the boys who handled the gun or pulled the trigger had received some form of gun safety instruction.[68]

With the apparent misconception about the risks of keeping a gun in the home and the effectiveness of behavior-oriented approaches, it is not surprising that each year a large number of unintentional shootings occur. Most occur when someone—including a child—has been "playing" with a gun or has been involved in routine activities such as cleaning, loading, and handling the gun. For example, in a California study of fatal unintentional shootings among children, the most common circumstance surrounding the shooting was when a child had been playing with a gun.[69] In another study examining both fatal and nonfatal unintentional shootings of youth (ages zero to nineteen) over a six-year period, where the circumstances of the injury were known, the victim had been playing with a gun 57 percent of the time.[70] And in a national study of people treated in U.S. hospital emergency departments, where data were available, about half of the injuries involved routine gun-related activities and an additional 8 percent occurred when someone was playing with a gun.[71]

The research is no more encouraging with respect to adolescent suicides. Several case-control studies have found a significant association between the presence of a gun in the home and the risk of adolescent suicide.[72] Because of this risk, experts recommend that guns be removed from the homes of suicidal adolescents.[73] Yet, one study found that, even after a suicide attempt, 23 percent of the families kept a firearm with ammunition in the home.[74] In other studies, even some parents of suicidal adolescents and adolescents at risk of suicide, who were counseled to remove guns from their homes or to lock them up, did not do so.[75]

Conclusion

The commitment of public health is to determine, through scientific investigation, the risks to the public's well-being and the best ways to reduce those risks. Once the risks and the effective prevention strategies are identified, public health seeks to implement those strategies through policies, educational programs, and advocacy. Some risks are easier to identify than others. For example, it took substantial efforts over a long period of time to prove the causal connections between tobacco products and certain diseases such as lung cancer. With guns, the causal connection between being shot and being at risk of death is readily apparent. The design interventions discussed in this chapter address the undisputed causal connection between guns (a manufactured product designed to inflict injury) and gun injury independent of a relationship between population level availability and violence. An individual with a bullet wound suffers that injury, on the most basic level, as a result of a gun having been successfully discharged. Similarly, distribution strategies are designed to limit gun access to agreed-upon high-risk users, such as convicted felons and youth, irrespective of general availability. The proper intervention for reducing the nation's toll of gun-related deaths, however, is a subject of considerable controversy. There are some (generally not working in the field of public health) who argue that more guns would mean fewer gun-related deaths.[76] Although beyond the scope of this chapter, this assertion has been met with substantial criticism, mostly regarding the research methodology used in reaching this conclusion.[77] The weight of public health research finds that the high prevalence of guns in the United States is associated with this country's high gun death rate[78] and that changing the current practices of gun design and distribution could likely reduce the gun violence problems we face.

How can the current practices of gun design and distribution be changed? Here too the discipline of public health can provide lessons of success. Several decades ago, it was recognized that changes in motor vehicle design would decrease the unacceptable number of highway fatalities occurring in the United States. Specifically, the introduction of air bags into cars was believed to be able to reduce the number of car crash deaths by thousands per year. But the effort to get air bags in cars through legislation and regulation was unsuccessful. Car makers fought government mandates for air bags so fiercely that in 1983 the U.S. Supreme Court stated, "For nearly a decade, the automobile industry waged the regulatory equivalent of war against the airbag."[79]

Ultimately, litigation played a strong role in introducing air bags into cars. Public health advocates urged trial lawyers to sue car makers for their failure to offer existing, lifesaving technology to the public. In response to this call for action, a lawsuit was brought against Ford Motor Company for its failure to offer an air bag as an option to a young woman who was seriously injured in a frontal crash. Ten days into the trial of the case, Ford settled it by the payment of $1.8 million.[80] Many air bag lawsuits followed, and then Ford began to offer air bags in its new cars as an option.

Whereas the strong automotive industry had been able to thwart legislation and regulation to protect the public's health, it could not so easily do so regarding litigation. Similarly, the pro-gun-lobbying forces have been able to control, to a great extent, gun legislation and regulation at the federal and state levels. It is for this reason that public health practitioners and advocates turned to litigation as a tool for reducing the toll of gun violence on this nation's well-being.

CHAPTER 2

The Limited Importance of Gun Control from a Criminological Perspective

DON B. KATES

An Erroneous Mantra

Carefully tailored gun controls can marginally reduce gun violence rates. But criminological research does not support claims that gun availability to ordinary people promotes violence. The oft-heard mantra "more guns equal more death, fewer guns equal less" cannot be squared with U.S. experience since 1946 (the earliest time for which reliable figures on murder and gunstock rates exist). That year those rates were 34,430 guns and 6 murders per 100,000 population. As of 2000 the gunstock rate had swelled to 95,500 but the murder rate was only 6.1 per 100,000.[1] Though murder rates varied greatly over the intervening years, those variations bear no apparent relation to the vast increase in guns.

> The per capita accumulated stock of guns (the total of firearms manufactured or imported into the United States, less imports) has increased in recent decades, yet there has been no correspondingly consistent increase in either total or gun violence. . . . About half of the time gun stock increases have been accompanied by violence decreases, and about half the time [they have been] accompanied by violence increases, *just what one would expect if gun levels had no net impact on violence rates.*[2]

The total gunstock quintupled from almost 48.5 million in 1946 to almost 260 million in 2000.[3] Yet, the murder rates for 1946 and 2000 were almost identical. This noncorrelation helps support the general criminological conclusion that violence rates reflect basic sociocultural and economic factors, not the mere availability of any particular form of weapon.

A half-century of evaluations of gun controls has yielded four largely negative findings: (1) gun availability does not *cause* ordinary law-abiding adults to kill, though guns facilitate violence by criminals; (2) victim gun ownership deters crime and allows self-defense; (3) though reasonable, gun bans to criminals and the irresponsible are very difficult to enforce; and (4) without guns, people intent on crime or suicide make do with other means.[4] Indeed, a 2003 study by the vehemently anti-gun Centers for Disease Control and Prevention concluded that no gun control had so far been shown to reduce violence.[5]

Basic U.S. Gun Statistics

By 2003 the United States had about 272 million civilian-owned firearms, with handguns estimated at almost 100 million. If new gun sales continue to increase at the 4–5 million per year rate of the last few decades, by 2005 the civilian gunstock will exceed 280 million, roughly 105 million being handguns.[6]

These figures reflect raw production and import-export data but take no account of factors that both increase and decrease gunstock by unknown amounts. Unknown numbers of guns were destroyed over the years by poor maintenance or after police confiscation. Conversely, unknown numbers of guns were added to the total gunstock through unrecorded imports (e.g., war souvenirs) or sale to civilians of old police and military weapons.

Gun ownership can be estimated from survey data, but these are even less reliable than production data, for large numbers of owners won't admit they own guns.[7] Nevertheless 40–45 percent of households admit they have guns, with an average of four owned per household. About 25 percent admit having handguns.[8]

Every category of gun death sharply declined during the 1990s. Gun murder declined from 17,746 in 1991 to 10,801 in 2000 (down from 7 deaths per 100,000 population to 3.9); gun suicide from 18,526 to 16,586; and fatal gun accidents from 1,441 to 776.[9]

The murder decline may be partly attributable to criminal attacks being deterred by increased victim access to guns (see later discussion). But gun suicide and fatal accidents also declined. This obviously cannot be attributable to increases in defensive gun ownership. What is clear is that the 1990s data do not support the "more guns equal more death" mantra. During that decade, the addition of 47 million new guns (and the enhanced availability of guns due to the issuance of 3.5 million concealed carry licenses) coincided with a more than 25 percent decline in overall gun death.

International Comparisons

Murder rates are much lower in Europe. Comparisons of the United States to a few low gun ownership European nations are routinely advanced as supporting the mantra. But when broad, nonselective comparisons are made, nations with more guns do not seem to have more murder. Norway has Western Europe's highest gun ownership (32 percent of households) yet its lowest murder rate. Norway's cross-Baltic neighbor Holland has the lowest European gun ownership (1.9 percent) but a 50 percent higher murder rate. Completing the pattern of noncorrelation, Sweden, with gun ownership midway between Norway and Holland (15.1), has a higher murder rate than Holland and a much higher rate than gun-laden Norway. In turn, Sweden's murder rate is lower than its cross-Baltic neighbor Germany, although Sweden has twice the gun ownership. Spain, with twelve times more ownership than Poland, has a 50 percent lower murder rate. Finland, with fourteen times more gun ownership than neighbor Estonia, still has the lower murder rate. (The bases for these comparisons—and countless similar ones—are the data set out in tables 2 and 3.)

The mantra is often supported by claims that the United States has the developed world's highest gun ownership (true) and its highest murder rates (false). This mistake came from the USSR's embarrassed falsification of Russian murder rates. Recent revelation of thirty-five years of accurate Russian rates shows they consistently exceeded those of America, despite Russia's decades of banning handguns and severely restricting other guns—with enforcement so drastic that few Russian civilians have guns and murders rarely involve them. As of 1998–2001 murders per capita in the former Soviet Europe (Lithuania, Latvia, Ukraine, etc.) are two to three times higher than in the United States, while in Russia they are four times higher.[10]

Broadscale comparisons among developed nations do not show those with higher gun ownership rates having distinctively higher murder rates. Using "homicide and suicide mortality data for thirty-six nations (including the United States) for the period 1990–1995," compared to gun ownership rates, there was "no significant (at the 5 percent level) association between gun ownership and the total homicide rate." In a later study of twenty-one nations, "no significant correlations [of guns] with total suicide or homicide rates were found." This is also internally: high gun ownership regions in Switzerland, Canada, England, and the United States do *not* have higher murder rates than low ownership areas.[11]

Advancing a Red Herring

In lieu of evidence that more guns equal more murder, the mantra's supporters assert that "More Firearms = More *Firearms* Violence."[12] Even this is not consistently true (see table 3). More important, it is irrelevant. The point of gun bans is to reduce death. Proving it works requires showing fewer deaths *overall*, not just that gun deaths fell while other kinds of violent deaths rose with no net difference.

Murderers seem able to find guns even in nations where gun ownership is low. Or they kill just as well with other weapons. As for suicide, in nations where guns are less available, comparable or greater numbers of suicides occur by other means.[13] Many European nations celebrated for banning guns have double or more the U.S. suicide rate. Gunless Russia's suicide rate is four times higher than that of the United States, just as is its murder rate. The thirty-six- and twenty-one-nation comparative studies show that lesser gun availability does not mean less murder or suicide. At most it means only fewer such deaths with guns. The consistent noncorrelation to gun ownership shows once again that high murder or suicide rates are attributable to basic sociocultural and economic factors, not mere availability of some particular weapon.

Failure of Foreign Gun Laws

Though it is often assumed that Western Europe's low murder rates stem from strict gun control, this is not true. The rates were far lower yet before World War II, when Europe had virtually no gun laws. Stringent laws appeared in the turbulent post–World War I era—aimed not against ordinary crime but against political violence. They failed to stem either. From World War I on, violent crime has plagued all Western nations regardless of their gun policies.[14] The following summary comes from a recent history of guns, gun laws, and violence in the United Kingdom.

> When it had no firearms restrictions England had little violent crime, while the present extraordinarily stringent gun controls have not stopped the increase in violence or even the increase in armed violence. . . . Armed crime, never a problem in England, has now become one. Handguns are banned but the kingdom has millions of illegal firearms. Criminals have no trouble finding them and exhibit a new willingness to use them. In the decade after 1957 the use of guns in serious crime increased a hundredfold [and it has continued to increase ever since].[15]

In the 1990s England, Scotland, Australia, and Canada topped decades of increasingly stringent controls by outlawing many popular types of firearms and confiscating them from hundreds of thousands of owners law abiding enough to surrender them. Far from violence abating, it so intensified that by 2000 Australia, Canada, England, and Scotland ranked as four of the five industrialized nations highest in violence. Despite much lower gun ownership, their violence rates were 100 percent or more above those of the United States and two other high gun ownership nations, Belgium and Spain.[16]

Zimring and Hawkins still espouse the mantra stressing that English murder rates remain far below ours.[17] More important, however, is that English murder rates started out far lower still—both absolutely and as compared to the United States—when England had no gun controls. The large increase of English murder over decades of ever more controls emphasizes the role of socioeconomic and cultural factors and the unimportance of the availability of any particular type of weaponry.

Australia is also experiencing severely increasing violence. Noting that murder had declined, its prime minister attributed that to a vast reduction in gun ownership. But the murder decline began more than fifteen years before the gun bans and did not accelerate with the massive confiscations of guns. Indeed, 2002 saw a reversal: an unprecedented increase in murder, with other deadly weapons being used rather than guns.[18]

Guns or No Guns, Ordinary People Do Not Murder

The "more guns equal more death" mantra appears plausible if one thinks murders are mostly committed by ordinary people where a gun was available in a moment of rage. But that is untrue of most murders, or many murders, or virtually any murders.[19] Homicide studies uniformly show that "virtually all individuals who become involved in life-threatening violent crime have prior involvement in many types of minor (and not so minor) offenses."[20] Far from being ordinary, they are extreme social deviants with life histories of crime, violence, substance abuse, and/or psychopathology. So consistently do homicide studies find this to be the case that these things "have now become criminological axioms" of the "basic characteristics of homicide"—for the great majority of murderers and most victims too.[21]

While only 15 percent of Americans have criminal records, about 90 percent of adult murderers have adult criminal records, averaging four major felonies over a six-year adult period. That is also largely true of juvenile killers (and victims) insofar as juvenile criminal records are available. Studies of juvenile killers also find that 80–100 percent are psychotic or have psychotic symptoms.[22]

Amazingly, the only fact ever cited to support the "ordinary people murder" mythology is that many murders occur in homes or involve acquaintances—as if violent deviants don't have fights or acquaintances or homes. National data on gun murders occurring among acquaintances and in homes show that "the most common victim-offender relationship" is "where both parties knew one another because of prior illegal transactions."[23] There are also many "family murders," but these are not ordinary families, nor are the killers ordinary, decent people: "[t]he day-to-day reality is that most family murders are preceded by a long history of assaults" by the killer upon his mate and/or children.[24]

For instance, of Massachusetts domestic murders in 1991–95, 75 percent of perpetrators had a prior criminal history and 23.6 percent were under an active restraining order at the time of the homicide. Forty percent of perpetrators had a history of having been under a restraining order at some time prior to the homicide, taken out either by the victim or some other person.[25]

In short, if laws could disarm potential murderers, current federal and state laws—which generally ban guns to juveniles, drug addicts, mental incompetents, and persons convicted of a felony or of a domestic misdemeanor—should suffice.[26]

Self-Defense with Guns

Not only is it pointless to disarm ordinary people (because they do not kill), it is counterproductive, both individually and socially, in minimizing the crime-reductive potential of self-defense. Contrast U.S. massacres in situations where only the killers were armed to Israel, where terrorists are often shot by intended victims because Israeli policy encourages civilians to carry guns so there will be armed defenders in all public places. Indeed, recent enactment of laws in some American states allowing qualified applicants to carry concealed handguns has resulted in U.S. incidents of massacres being ended by armed victims.[27]

Opponents of gun ownership declare self-defense both immoral ("lethal violence in self-defense only engenders more lethal violence")[28] and ineffective, asserting that guns can rarely be used in self-defense and that people who defend themselves *in any way* are much more likely to suffer severe injury; for victims of rape or robbery, "the best defense against injury is to put up no defense—*give them what they want* or run."[29]

However, all available data show that victims who defend with a gun are *less* likely to be injured than those who submit—and, of course, are far less likely to be robbed or raped.[30] In the great majority of gun defense cases, the victim's gun is not even fired; 80 percent or more of attackers flee when a victim just displays a gun.

How often are guns used in self-defense? Based on nineteen different population surveys, the criminologist

Gary Kleck found that Americans defend themselves with guns 2.5 million times per year by warding off threats to their persons and property. Phil Cook and Jens Ludwig put the number of defensive gun uses at 1.3 million per year. Hemenway and Azrael's national survey, sponsored by the National Institute of Justice, found 1.5 million defensive gun uses per year. All these surveys reveal a great deal of self-defensive gun use of firearms; in fact, more defensive gun uses than crimes committed with firearms.[31]

Kleck's findings were ruefully but praisingly hailed by the dean of American criminologists, Marvin Wolfgang, despite his vehement personal feelings ("I hate guns").[32] Concomitantly, Hemenway and Azrael and Cook and Ludwig deeply oppose defensive gun ownership and rejected Kleck's survey evidence as wrong—until their own survey results confirmed his. At that point they switched over to denying that surveys provide a reliable method for enumerating gun defense events.[33] They think survey respondents may be falsely claiming to have used guns for self-defense because that validates their decision to own a gun. Even as Hemenway and colleagues accept this *possibility*, they blithely reject the possibility that as many or more survey respondents falsely denied defensive gun use for fear of attracting police attention to an unreported gun incident. And even as Hemenway and colleagues reject the great majority of responses claiming gun self-defense, they accept as true the reports of respondents who say they were injured while resisting with a gun. Hemenway and colleagues hail this as proof of how foolish it is to resist rapists, robbers, and so forth, instead of "giv[ing them] what they want."[34]

To justify rejecting their own survey results showing vast numbers of gun defense uses, Cook and Ludwig emphasize that, taken at face value, those results would imply that 322,000 armed women routed rapists that year. This Cook and Ludwig ridicule because a different survey suggests there were only 316,000 rapes that year. But that other survey has been shown to underestimate the incidence of rape by as much as thirty-three times because so many victims will not disclose they were raped.[35] Conservatively assuming the second survey is off by a factor of only twenty, the actual number of rapes that year was over 6 million. So it is not at all implausible that another 322,000 attempted rapes were repelled when victims pulled guns.

Critics of defensive gun use ignore a point of surpassing import. A gun is the only mechanism that gives a weaker victim parity with an attacker (even if the attacker also has a gun). The next best alternative, a chemical spray, is ineffective against precisely those who are most likely to engage in violent attacks: people who are under the influence of drugs or alcohol or who are extremely angry.[36]

Widespread Legal Gun Carrying as a Deterrent to Violence

Carry concealed weapon (CCW) laws are based on the theory that violent crime is deterred if criminals fear that any given potential victim may be armed. The laws, which had been adopted in thirty-five states as of 2003, require that all law-abiding, responsible, trained adult applicants be issued a CCW license. National Institute of Justice surveys among prison inmates find that large percentages report that their fear that a victim might be armed deterred them from confrontation crimes. "[T]he felons most frightened 'about confronting an armed victim' were those from states with the greatest relative number of privately owned firearms." Conversely, robbery is highest in states that most restrict gun ownership.[37]

While it is clear that fear of armed victims does deter violence, the question remains of how important this deterrent is. Based on twenty-five years of data from all U.S. counties, the economist John Lott found that thousands of murders and other violent crimes did *not* occur in states that adopted such CCW laws. Anti-gun lobbying groups responded by falsely claiming that Lott's work had been financed by the gun lobby.[38] An ad hoc group of academics opposed to Lott's work took the unusual step of contradicting it in letters to the editor sent to every newspaper in America that had reported the finding.

One criticism was that the drops in violence were just too large to be attributed to the CCW laws, given that less than 5 percent of the populace actually obtained permits. This, however, is a non sequitur. The deterrent effect results not from victims actually shooting criminals but from criminals knowing that anyone they attack *may* be carrying a gun. The following are other criticisms of Lott's results.[39]

- The results are attributable to ordinary cyclical changes in the crime rate. To this Lott responds that his studies account for and exclude cyclical variation.

- As a technical matter, Lott has not accounted for variations between the time when certain CCW laws were enacted and when they were administratively implemented.
- While fear of armed victims caused violent crimes like robbery to drop, nonconfrontation crimes like burglary of unoccupied premises rose. Lott actually cites these facts as proving criminals are deterred from violent crime into nonviolent ones.
- Lott's focus on the entire twenty-five-year period rather than on the time periods in which various CCW laws went into effect magnifies the effect that only murder and robbery declined, but not aggravated assault and rape.
- Lott's findings cannot be trusted because the amount of crime decrease varied substantially between the different states that adopted the CCW laws.

Lott has replied to these and many other criticisms,[40] including a number of technical statistical objections raised by scholars not necessarily opposed to his findings on political grounds. Several such scholars have now replicated Lott's work using added or different data, additional control variables, or new or different statistical techniques they deem superior to those Lott used. Interestingly, the replications all confirm Lott's general conclusions; some even find that Lott *under*estimated the crime-reductive effects of allowing good citizens to carry concealed guns.[41] For what it is worth, Lott's book *The Bias against Guns*, which reiterates, extends, and defends his findings, is endorsed by three Nobel laureates.[42]

The Public Health Literature against Firearms

So far I have addressed criminological findings. Another entire literature on firearms emanates from the public health field. The following discussion derives from an extensive study of this literature I coauthored with a University of North Carolina biostatistician and three professors at Harvard and Columbia Medical Schools.[43] In 1979 the public health community adopted a goal to greatly reduce firearms ownership, a resolve it has formally and informally reiterated on many occasions.[44] This preexisting political goal closes medical and public health journals to ignore any other perspective. Public health journals and authors acknowledge—indeed proclaim!—that their purpose in discussing firearms is to "speak out for gun control." In the entire literature, consisting now of hundreds of public health publications, no more than five even question (much less reject) this perspective.[45]

This dedication to a predetermined political goal has a predictably adverse effect on the reliability and scholarship of this literature. Thus, a 2003 public health monograph asks, "Does a gun in the home increase the likelihood of being shot and killed, or does it confer protection against violent criminals?" Its purported answer consists of reciting the number of gun deaths (more than half of them suicides, incidentally) to prove the danger, while dismissing the protective value of guns without noting even one statistic or study to the contrary.[46] The monograph also asserts "the consistency" of all research with the "more guns equal more death" mantra. This consistency it manufactures by just not mentioning all the contrary research.[47]

Authors who are among the most prolific and influential in the public health literature assert that "limiting access to firearms could prevent many suicides." As if it supported that assertion, they cite a diametrically contrary research finding that if guns are unavailable people just commit suicide in other ways. The same authors also claim that "restricting access to handguns could substantially reduce our annual rate of homicide"—citing as support a Department of Justice–sponsored evaluation of firearms regulation that actually concluded that "[t]here is no persuasive evidence that supports this view."[48]

One of these authors, Dr. Arthur Kellermann, has written highly publicized "studies" but refused to disclose his underlying data to scholars wanting to check it; nor do the public health journals publishing him require him to do so.[49]

Probably the most widely referenced study in the public health literature compares Vancouver, Canada, to Seattle, claiming that (a) the latter had a distinctively higher rate of gun ownership, so (b) it had a distinctively higher murder rate. One problem is that (a) is false. The two cities' gun ownership rates are almost identical according to a survey apparently unknown to the authors, who also published an article blaming Seattle's supposedly higher gun ownership for its higher rate of suicide by young men. Far more important, however, is that comparison of two medium-sized cities is a wholly inadequate basis for concluding that higher gun ownership causes higher murder or suicide rates. It bears emphasis that the authors, and the *New England Journal of Medicine*, which published their article, were aware of research reaching opposite conclusions from a broad comparison of American states to Canadian provinces. The journal declined either to publish this research or to require the authors to refer to it and explain how their own results were valid despite their contradiction by a far larger, more meaningful data set.[50]

Indicative of the standards of the anti-gun public health literature is its repeated description of these Vancouver-Seattle comparison articles as "elegant."[51] In contrast, a Canadian social scientist cited them as exemplifying "studies [that] are an abuse of scholarship, inventing, selecting, or misinterpreting data in order to validate *a priori* conclusions."[52]

These faults characterize the entire public health literature. As a general rule it simply never mentions the vast corpus of criminological research that refutes or undercuts the "more guns equal more death" mantra.[53] Dubious or flatly false assertions made in editorials or by lobby groups are cited as if they were facts established by research.[54] (Failure to disclose when "facts" come from the anti-gun lobby is ironic since gun lobby criticism of inaccuracy in public health articles is shrugged off with "what do you expect from the gun lobby" responses.)[55]

Concluding eighty-some pages of such examples, my coauthors and I dismissed the entire anti-gun public health literature as "so biased and contain[ing] so many errors of fact, logic and procedure that it has no claim to contributing to a scholarly or scientific literature." We ended by quoting the sociologist James Wright's remarks on the public health literature's evocation of the simplistic "more guns equal more death" mantra in preference to addressing basic social, economic, and/or cultural factors that actually underlie murder and suicide. He begins by admitting that

> there is a sense in which violence is a public health problem. So let me illustrate the limitations of this line of reasoning with a public health analogy. After research disclosed that mosquitoes were the vector for transmission of yellow fever, the disease was not controlled by sending men in white coats to the swamps to remove the mouth parts from all the insects they could find. The only sensible, efficient way to stop the biting was to attack the environment where the mosquitoes bred. Guns are the mouth parts of the violence epidemic. The contemporary urban environment breeds violence no less than swamps breed mosquitoes. Attempting to control

the problem of violence by trying to disarm the perpetrators is as hopeless as trying to contain yellow fever through mandible control.[56]

Viability of Gun Laws

Disarming criminals, much less the general population, presents much more difficult problems than even enforcing narcotics laws. If narcotics are, as many think, harmful per se, reducing people's access to them even slightly is a benefit (though the costs to the criminal justice system may be inordinate). In contrast, since the great majority of gun owners never commit violence, disarming them would expend vast enforcement resources to no benefit. Laws designed to disarm criminals and the insane are obviously appropriate. But as will be seen, those whom it is most urgent to disarm are also the hardest to disarm.

The Futility of Supply-Side Measures

It is delusive, and a waste of resources, to hope that further regulation of the firearms industry can disarm violent felons. Probably less than 200,000 different guns are used in violent crimes annually, whereas just the number of guns stolen annually is upward of 750,000. Furthermore, federally sponsored prison surveys show most felons obtain guns not from theft or gun stores but from friends or on the black market (which doubtless recycles many stolen guns).[57]

Thus, criminals can obtain all the guns they need without ever visiting a gun store. Moreover the most important difference between gun and narcotics bans is that guns are not consumed by use. With proper care the life expectancy of a gun is virtually infinite.[58] So, even if felons could be deprived of all ways to get new guns, they need only keep the guns they already have.

Assuming supply-side controls ever produced a gun shortage among criminals, the result would just be to produce a market for organized crime to fill by importing guns or covertly manufacturing them.[59] Pot metal copies of modern handguns would actually sell for less than guns do now because they are much cheaper to produce and the black market is not burdened by taxes, record keeping, and safety standards.[60] Illustrative of the futility of supply-side control is the discovery by English police of a covert shipment of Croatian Mini-Uzi pistols *without serial numbers*. Some English drug gang or organized gun trafficker had the resources and connections in distant Croatia to either special-order thirty Mini-Uzis without serial numbers or have them stolen from the factory before serial numbers were stamped on them.[61]

In 1994 the head of Scotland Yard endorsed even more stringent gun laws lest England become like the United States, which foreign anti-gun advocates have long felt has such a gunstock as to make control efforts futile.[62] England responded to such sentiments by banning handguns, confiscating over 166,000 from owners law abiding enough to surrender them. But by the period 2000–2003 England's violence rate was among the highest in the developed world—twice the American rate[63]—and police were lamenting that though "Britain has some of the strictest gun laws in the world [i]t appears that anyone who wishes to obtain a firearm [illegally] will have little difficulty in doing so."[64]

In sum, there is scant reason to invest hope or resources in trying to reduce the overall supply of guns, especially by controls over the firearms industry.

The Failure of Demand-Side Strategy

A better alternative, at least theoretically, is demand-side control, that is, stiff penalties to frighten criminals into eschewing gun possession or misuse. But such laws are effectively nullified by the lack of the resources needed to make the threat credible. Twenty-five years ago, the premier study of gun law enforcement concluded the following:

> It is very possible that if gun laws do potentially reduce gun-related crime, the present laws are all that is needed if they are enforced. What good would stronger laws do when the courts have demonstrated that they will not enforce them?[65]

The last sentence oversimplifies the issues, lending spurious credibility to the gun lobby's "gun control" program (endorsed also by the other side) of laws supposedly mandating long prison terms for criminals misusing guns. Doubtless gun crime would be impacted if felons knew that severe sentences would be imposed on anyone possessing or carrying guns (or on anyone committing a robbery or other violent crime with a gun). But mandatory imprisonment laws are shams enacted to make politicians look good without the funding needed to ever implement them.

Prisons are already overflowing with felons who are far more dangerous than run-of-the-mill gun robbers, for example, rapists or robbers who have maimed victims. So what mandatory imprisonment laws irresponsibly enacted without funding would mean (if the criminal justice system took them seriously) is early release or lesser sentences for the most dangerous criminals in order to give longer sentences to felons who, at most, just pointed a gun at someone and took his money. Faced with this reality, prosecutors and judges find ways around supposedly mandatory sentencing for gun felons. Gun felons quickly discover they will not be severely punished for mere possession; even for gun robbery the penalty is often little more than for nongun robbery.[66] Given resource limitations it is understandable that judges and prosecutors ignore mandatory gun penalty laws in order to give longer sentences to more dangerous felons. But doing so deprives gun possession (or misuse) bans of their point, which is to disarm felons *before* they misuse guns. That does not work when real punishment comes only if they are caught in the very crimes the gun law was supposed to be preventing.

Strategies for Gun Law Enforcement

Pro- and anti-gun advocates have suggested differing, but not incompatible, strategies to effectuate gun controls. The program Project Exile involves highly publicized, concentrated federal prosecution of felons found with guns. It is claimed to have dramatically reduced illegal gun carrying when tried experimentally in Richmond, Virginia.[67] Strongly endorsed by the NRA, it is the Bush administration's primary approach to gun issues in contradistinction to the Clinton approach, which was to enact drastic laws but virtually never prosecute violators.

Project Exile's value might be maximized by combining it with what is called the Kansas City Program (so-named for where it was first tried). This program involves the concentrated targeting of violations of public

disorder and other minor laws rather than the disregard of such violations. This should not be confused with the "Broken Windows" theory,
which claims that enforcement of public disorder laws reverses visible
deterioration of neighborhoods that causes criminals to view them as
ripe for more serious crimes. The Kansas City Program uses the
enforcement of laws against littering, loitering, jaywalking, and so forth,
as an excuse for police to stop, arrest, and search violators.[68] Such a program of systematic searches may substantially deter criminals from routinely carrying guns.

Yet the limitations and costs of such still experimental programs must
also be understood. The main limitation is that they deter only *habitual*
gun carrying. This should reduce "crimes of opportunity" that were not
preplanned but occurred because a felon had a gun available when a
crime opportunity arose. But such programs will not affect gun carrying
for preplanned violent felonies like robbery of a store or bank or contract
killings. The chance of being caught with the gun is minimal when the
perpetrator carries it only to and from such a preplanned crime rather
than loitering on the streets waiting for an opportunity to misuse it.

Either program will also not work without (a) routinizing the creation
of excuses to search *and* (b) imposing serious penalties upon illegal gun
carriers and felons in possession. This means seriously increased costs
for prosecution and imprisonment. If those costs are not fully funded, the
result will be less capacity for long-term imprisonment of those guilty of
much more serious crimes.

A second cost is in civil liberties. Using minor crime as an excuse for
search is a strategy of pretextual evasion of the Fourth Amendment.
Moreover, it raises much the same specter of discriminatory enforcement
as does racial profiling. Police will not be cruising low-crime neighborhoods looking for excuses to stop, search, and arrest jaywalking white
housewives. The burden of pretextual searches will fall only on the disadvantaged and minority populations in high crime areas.

The question perhaps is not so much whether some types of gun crime
can be substantially reduced by such initiatives as whether the reduction
is worth the costs. Many would find the civil liberties costs unacceptable.
Others might deem the financial costs unacceptable. Among other things
the inevitable effect will be reduced resource availability for other criminal justice priorities and for social programs that may offer a chance to

alleviate the root causes of crime. It cannot be predicted whether Project Exile or the Kansas City Program will spread widely or be just two more briefly ballyhooed programs that are eventually dropped.

In closing I want to suggest three policy changes that could help disarm gun criminals, though not without appropriation of additional enforcement resources. The first change would be to reverse the policy by which federal gun laws are virtually never enforced. For instance, the Clinton administration claimed that the Brady Act background check stopped hundreds of thousands of convicted felons from buying guns. Yet there were less than fifteen prosecutions of such felons. Over 99.99 percent were never charged with violating federal law by trying to buy guns—and thereby left free to go out and buy guns on the street. Is it any wonder "statistical analysis [has] provided '*no evidence that implementation of the Brady Act was associated with a reduction in homicide rates*'"?[69]

Consider another question that is no less real for being rhetorical: Unless he spends his leisure hours reading the U.S. Code, how would the adult who sold a gun to the juveniles who used it in the Columbine school massacre know the sale violated federal law? Ordinary people learn the laws primarily from the publicity attendant to prosecutions under them. If, like many federal gun laws, violation is never prosecuted, how are people to know they are violating a law?

My second proposal would severely reduce the rights of violent felons against search and seizure. Under current state laws, crimes like robbery are theoretically subject to a prison term on the order of eight years; if a gun was used it might provide an "enhancement" of another two. Because a robber faced with such sentencing will demand a time-consuming trial by jury, there is likely to be a plea bargain by which the actual sentence is perhaps only four years for the robbery and another year for using a gun. With time off for good behavior, the robber is paroled in twenty-four months. A condition of parole is that he waive his rights against search for the duration of the parole, which will be only a few years. But parole boards could instead condition parole for those convicted of violent gun felonies on a *lifetime* waiver of their rights against search. Such felons would be deterred from having guns, knowing they are forever subject to police search at any time or place for any reason or none.

(A reviewer of this chapter doubts the constitutionality of this waiver scheme. But I think courts would uphold it, reasoning that the felon is only being given a choice: if he does not want to waive his rights he can just do his full sentence without parole. Three and one-third years—his term less "good time"—is surely not cruel and unusual punishment for gun robbery.)[70]

My last policy change would additionally incarcerate tens of thousands of violent gun criminals with only minor expenditure of scarce prosecutorial resources (though it would require extension of federal prison resources). Over the past twenty years many criminals have had state convictions for robbery, rape, or burglary with an enhancement for using a gun. Using these state convictions it is easily possible to add federal prison time to their state sentences by a systematic campaign to reconvict them under the federal law against felons having guns. Federal prosecutors in such a campaign will not need to plea-bargain with these felons. Of course, the felons will demand jury trials, but the issues to be tried will be extremely simple and straightforward, not requiring the calling of even one witness. All that the prosecutors need to present to prove their cases are two documents: (1) the defendant's record of conviction of some kind of felony and (2) the defendant's subsequent conviction of a felony involving the use of a gun. After being convicted on this simple evidence, tens of thousands of violent gun criminals will serve out their state sentences and then, instead of being released, go to federal prisons to serve out their additional federal sentences. By the time they finally emerge from prison, many or most will be in their mid-thirties or older. At that age most violent criminals realize crime is not a viable option.

Conclusion

A half-century of criminological research establishes that

- access to guns does not move ordinary people to commit violence;
- disarming them promotes violence by eliminating the most effective—for most people the only effective—means of self-defense;
- laws against gun possession by violent or mentally disturbed people are useful if for no other reason than that they allow incarceration of violators who are caught;

- such laws, rigorously enforced, might substantially reduce gun crime, but that requires financial investments the political system seems unwilling to make.

The premier authority in the field has emphasized the primacy of basic socioeconomic and cultural factors and the uselessness—indeed coun-terproductiveness—of focusing simplistically on the mere availability of some particular weaponry.

Fixating on guns seems to be, for many people, a fetish which allows them to ignore the more intransigent causes of American violence, including its dying cities, inequality, deteriorating family structure, and the all-pervasive economic and social consequences of a history of slavery and racism. And just as gun control serves this purpose for liberals, equally useless "get tough" proposals, like longer prison terms, mandatory sentencing, and more use of the death penalty serve the purpose for conservatives. All parties to the crime debate would do well to give more concentrated attention to more difficult, but far more relevant, issues like how to generate more good-paying jobs for the underclass which is at the heart of the violence problem.[71]

APPENDIX: TABLES

TABLE 1.   Intentional Deaths: U.S. vs. Continental Europe Rates[a]

	Suicide	Murder	Combined Rates
Russia	41.2*	30.6+	71.8
Estonia	40.1*	22.2+	62.3
Latvia	40.7*	18.2+	58.9
Lithuania	45.6*	11.7+	57.3
Belarus	27.9*	10.4+	38.3
Hungary	32.9*	3.5	36.4
Ukraine	22.5*	11.3+	33.8
Slovenia	28.4*	2.4	30.4
Finland	27.2*	2.9	30.1
Denmark	22.3*	4.9	27.2
Croatia	22.8*	3.3	26.1
Austria	22.2*	1.0	23.2
Bulgaria	17.3*	5.1	22.4
France	20.8*	1.1	21.9
Switzerland	21.4*	1.1[b]	24.1
Belgium	18.7*	1.7	20.4
United States	11.6	7.8	19.4
Poland	14.2*	2.8	17.0
Germany	15.8*	1.1	16.9
Romania	12.3*	4.1	16.4
Sweden	15.3*	1.0	16.3
Norway	12.3*	0.8	13.1
Holland	9.8	1.2	11.0
Italy	8.2	1.7	9.9
Portugal	8.2	1.7	9.9
Spain	8.1	0.9	9.0
Greece	3.3	1.3	4.6

Note: In order of highest combined rate; nations having rates higher than the United States are indicated by asterisk (suicide rate) or + sign (murder rate). These data should be considered in light of tables 2 and 3 and the explanatory note that precedes table 3.

[a]Based in general on *U.N. Demographic Yearbook* (1998) as reported in David C. Stolinsky, "America: The Most Violent Nation?" *Medical Sentinel* 5, no. 6 (2000): 199–201. It should be understood that, though the 1998 *Yearbook* gives figures for as late as 1996, the figures are not necessarily for that year. The *Yearbook* contains the latest figure each nation has provided the U.N., which may be from 1996, 1995, or 1994.

[b]The Swiss homicide figure Stolinsky reports is an error because it combines attempts with actual murders. I have computed the Swiss murder rate by averaging the 1994 and 1995 Swiss National Police figures for actual murders in those years. These are given in R. A. I. Munday and J. A. Stevenson, *Guns and Violence: The Debate before Lord Cullen* (Essex, England: Piedmont, 1996), 268.

TABLE 2.   European Gun/Handgun Violent Deaths[a]

	Suicide with Gun	Murder with Handgun	% Households with Guns	% Households with Handguns
Belgium	18.7	1.7	16.6	6.8
France	20.8	1.1	22.6	5.5
W. Germany	15.8	1.1	8.9	6.7[b]
Holland	9.8	1.2	1.9	1.2
Italy	8.2	1.7	16.0	5.5
Norway	12.3	0.8	32	3.8
Sweden	15.3	1.3	15.1	1.5
Switzerland	20.8	1.1[c]	27.2	12.2

Note: The data in table 2 should be considered in light of tables 1 and 3 and the explanatory note that precedes table 3.

[a]As set out in table 1, note a, these data are from the *U.N. Demographic Yearbook* reported by Stolinsky. The data on household gun ownership are from the British Home Office as printed in R. A. I. Munday and J. A. Stevenson, *Guns and Violence: The Debate before Lord Cullen* (Essex, England: Piedmont, 1996), 30, 275.

[b]Note that the data here are for West Germany and were obtained when that nation still existed as an independent entity. See table 3 for later (but differently derived) data for the current nation of Germany.

[c]Again, the Swiss homicide figure Stolinsky reports is an error because it combines attempts with actual murders. See note b for table 1.

Explanatory Note to Table 3: It bears emphasis that the following data come from a special UN report whose data are not fully comparable to those in tables 1 and 2 because they cover different years and derive from substantially differing sources. This special report is based on data obtained from the governments of the nations set out in table 3, especially data on gun permits or other official indicia of gun ownership in those nations. The data on suicide and murder in those nations also come from their governments, as do the similar data in tables 1 and 2, but for later years, and also include data on the number of firearm homicides and firearm suicides, which are not available from the UN source used in tables 1 and 2.

TABLE 3.　European Firearms: Violent Deaths[a]

	Suicide	With Gun	Murder	With Gun	Number of Guns per 100,000 Population
Austria			2.14	0.53	41.02[b]
Belarus	27.26		9.86		16.5
Czech Republic	9.88	1.01	2.80	0.92	27.58
Estonia	39.99	3.63	22.11	6.2	28.56
Finland	27.28	5.78	3.25	0.87	411.20
Germany	15.80	1.23	1.81	0.21	122.56
Greece	3.54	1.30	1.33	0.55	77.00
Hungary	33.34	0.88	4.07	0.47	15.54
Moldova			17.06	0.63	6.61
Poland	14.23	0.16	2.61	0.27	5.30
Romania			4.32	0.12	2.97
Slovakia	13.24	0.58	2.38	0.36	31.91
Spain	5.92		1.58	0.19	64.69
Sweden	15.65	1.95	1.35	0.31	246.65

[a]The data in this table derive from a survey (much more exhaustive than those referenced in tables 1 and 2) of legal firearms ownership in numerous nations that was carried out by researchers provided by the government of Canada under the auspices of the United Nations Economic and Social Council, Commission on Crime Prevention and Criminal Justice in 1997. The entire survey was published as a report to the secretary- general on April 25, 1997, as E/CN.15/1997/4. That report is analyzed in some detail in an unpublished paper ("A Cross Sectional Study of the Relationship between Levels of Gun Ownership and Violent Deaths") written by the leading English student of firearms regulation, retired chief superintendent of English police Colin Greenwood of the Firearms Research and Advisory Service. We are indebted to Chief Superintendent Greenwood for the opportunity to review his paper.

[b]The firearms ownership figure for Austria may be an undercount because an Austrian license is not limited to a single firearm but rather allows the licensee to possess multiple guns.

CHAPTER 3

The American Gun Industry:
Designing & Marketing
Increasingly Lethal Weapons

TOM DIAZ

At the turn of the nineteenth century the American gun industry—driven by the needs of the fledgling nation's military, fueled by government funding, and inspired by the inventive spirit of a few key minds—developed a system of mass production and uniformly interchangeable parts known as the "armory practice." Refined over several decades by the gun makers, the armory practice became broadly known as "the American system of manufacture" as it was spread by mechanical artisans to the manufacture of such commodities as sewing machines, clocks, farm machinery, bicycles, and automobiles. The American system in turn led to mass production and mass consumption.[1] Thus, the American gun industry is quite literally the father of the system of mass production of consumer goods that lies at the heart of American industry, indeed, of much of the world's industry.

Like the other industries it helped spawn, the gun industry learned that mass production of consumer goods carried within it a bitter seed. Production often exceeded natural demand. Techniques of mass marketing thus became the necessary handmaiden of mass production. The profession of "consumption engineer" arose in industry. The new profession's task was to "manufacture customers," principally through advertising.[2] One familiar example of such mass marketing is the automotive industry, the techniques of which were highly refined in the early twentieth century and resulted in the demand-generating artifice of the annual model change. That industry came to epitomize the relentlessly competitive "search for novelty" that characterizes mass marketing. The process consists of two stages: first innovative design and then exploitation of the new design, often through aggressive advertising.[3]

The mass-marketing techniques of the gun industry are less familiar to the general public than those of the automotive industry, but at bottom they are similar. Driven by the same imperatives as the automotive industry, the gun industry has diligently pursued design innovation and has aggressively exploited new designs to manufacture customers. Understanding these techniques is essential background for evaluating the contemporary debate about the industry's responsibility for gun violence. Lately, this debate has increasingly focused on assertions that specific gun designs developed in the race for innovation, and marketing techniques developed to exploit them, contribute to high rates of gun violence and resulting death and injury. This chapter offers an overview of the gun industry's contemporary mass marketing and an analysis of its impact on gun violence.

A Sketch of the Modern Gun Industry in America

The structure of the gun industry is relatively simple. Domestic and foreign manufacturers make the firearms. In a few cases, such as Glock handguns, the firearms parts are manufactured abroad, then imported and assembled at plants in the United States. Domestically manufactured or assembled firearms are distributed by the manufacturers, either through wholesalers (known in the industry as distributors) or directly to retail gun dealers. The pattern is not uniform—some manufacturers sell only through distributors, while others prefer to sell directly to retail dealers. Because retail dealers are typically thinly capitalized and in no position to bargain, the choice of distribution channels is the manufacturer's. It is made on the basis of whichever arrangement the manufacturer decides is to its financial, competitive, or contractual advantage.[4] Foreign-made guns, including stocks of military surplus that are not barred by U.S. law for civilian ownership, are brought into the country through importers and then enter the same channels of commerce.

Domestic firearms manufacturers, importers, dealers, and ammunition manufacturers are required to obtain Federal Firearms Licenses.[5] Firearms manufacturers and importers may deal in firearms at their licensed premises without obtaining a separate firearms dealers license.[6]

There is no separate federal license for wholesalers (distributors), as there is, for example, in the case of alcoholic beverages.[7] Distributors and retail dealers get the same federal firearms dealers license but function at different points in the stream of commerce. This licensing regimen affects the central purpose of the Gun Control Act of 1968—the core federal gun law—of supporting state control of firearms by basically forbidding interstate commerce in guns except through federally licensed dealers. However, Federal Firearms Licenses are issued on a virtually pro forma basis—anyone who is at least twenty-one years of age, has a clean record, has business premises, and agrees to follow all applicable laws can get a license good for three years upon paying a fee and submitting a set of fingerprints with an application form.[8]

New and imported firearms thus always transit in legal commerce through at least one federally licensed seller though the point of the first retail sale. (Some aspects of the illegal trade in firearms are discussed in a later section.) The federal Brady Act requires a background check as a prerequisite to any retail sale through a federally licensed dealer. However, once a gun has been sold at retail it may be resold in the secondary market—that is, not through a federally licensed dealer—using any one of a variety of channels, none of which require the federal Brady Act background check and most of which are unregulated by most of the states. Vehicles for these secondary market transfers include classified advertising in newspapers and newsletters, Internet exchanges, and informal sales between individuals at flea markets or gun shows. About 40 percent of all gun transfers are made through this secondary market, according to a 1994 national survey.[9]

The federal government does not regulate commerce in ammunition beyond the ammunition manufacturer's license (excepting only such minor constraints as the prohibition against civilian sale of armor-piercing handgun ammunition). Ammunition is therefore freely bought and sold in an opaque market, free of background checks, record keeping, and restrictions on interstate shipment to and from unlicensed individuals. This is a remarkable anomaly for two reasons. The first, in the words of a former industry executive, is that "ammunition manufacturers are the silent power in the gun industry."[10] A gun is a one-time sale for a firearm manufacturer, but ammunition manufacturers sell their product throughout the lifetime of the gun. Moreover, if ammunition manufacturers are unenthusiastic about a proposed firearm design involving a new ammunition configuration (e.g., caliber or case dimensions) and won't make ammunition for it on a commercial basis, the product will wither. The second is the curious result that, although felons are deterred from buying firearms by the system of background checks, they can have ammunition delivered to their doors with no questions asked once they obtain a gun through illegal channels.

One way to look at the business of guns is through the ubiquity of its products. Guns have been a central part of American life from its beginnings,[11] but no one knows exactly how many there are in America, their breakdown by type and caliber, or who owns them. The federal government estimates that 215 million firearms were in civilian hands in the United States in 1999.[12] This estimate was derived simply by adding the net of roughly known domestic manufacturing, export, and import data for the period 1995 through 1999 to the estimate of gun ownership produced by a 1994 sample survey sponsored by the Police Foundation. Given the limitations of the data sources—the industry is closely held and secretive, and the government collects a minimum of mostly tax-related data—this government estimate is as good as the available data allow.[13]

Given that the population of the United States in April 2000 was 281.4 million,[14] one might conclude that—at a ratio of seventy-six firearms per one hundred people—virtually every adult in America owns a gun. (Using later and slightly different figures in a 2003 report, the independent international Small Arms Survey arrived at the higher ratio of between eighty-three and ninety-six guns per one hundred people in the United States.)[15] Such a uniform distribution of firearms would have powerful political and policy implications.

However, the proportion of households that own firearms is declining, and gun ownership is increasingly concentrated in a minority of hands. Only about one-quarter of adults in the United States own a gun, and about one in six owns a handgun.[16] A national survey of gun ownership in 1994 found that "10 million individuals owned 105 million guns, while the remaining 87 million guns were dispersed among 34 million other owners."[17] In sum, fewer and fewer people own more and more guns. This has important and chronic implications for the gun industry. It has forced a premium on design and marketing innovation to stimulate people who already own guns to buy more and to attract new buyers to overcome a continual market contraction.

Even so, as the Small Arms Survey concluded in its report, "[b]y any measure, the United States is the most armed country in the world. It far surpasses second-highest Yemen, home to roughly 33 to 50 firearms per 100 people, or third-highest Finland with 39 per 100."[18] It is no wonder that an informed industry observer described the United States as "the last great market" for guns.[19]

Although the firearms industry is generally in long-term decline, it still enjoys peak years and is quite robust enough to generously slake the last great market's thirst. In 1999—the latest year for which domestic manufacture, export, and import data are all available—a net of 4,683,620 new firearms were made available for sale on the U.S. civilian market. Of these, 1,702,016 were rifles, 1,425,653 shotguns, and 1,555,951 handguns. Foreign imports accounted for 892,000 of those firearms. Two cautions are in order. One, these figures represent only new firearms entering the distribution channels of the civilian market, not actual retail sales, which might be more or less than the numbers given here, depending on the relation of sales to inventory. Information on retail sales of firearms is not collected on a national basis. Two, the figures do not include sales of used firearms, which is estimated to total about another 2 million a year, mostly in the secondary market.[20]

Another dimension of the gun industry is its economics. According to the 1997 report of the quinquennial Economic Census, 191 companies (representing 198 manufacturing establishments) manufactured small arms in the United States, producing total shipments worth $1.25 billion.[21] Although the number of manufacturing establishments increased from 184 reported in the 1992 Economic Census, the value of shipments declined almost 10 percent from $1.38 billion over the same period, a symptom of the industry's long-term ill health.[22] Another 108 small arms ammunition manufacturing companies (representing 113 manufacturing establishments) produced shipments worth $938.8 million in 1997.[23] The number of small arms ammunition manufacturing establishments grew from 102 in 1992, but the value of their shipments declined by slightly more than 8 percent from $1.02 billion in 1992.[24]

An interesting anomaly is the much larger number of persons licensed to manufacture firearms and ammunition in 1997 compared to the number of companies reporting actual production in the census. In that year there were 1,414 active firearms manufacturer licenses (as opposed to 198 manufacturing establishments reported in the census) and 2,451 ammunition manufacturing licenses (as opposed to 113 reported ammunition manufacturing establishments).[25] There is probably nothing sinister in this disparity. Some are possibly licenses issued to hopeful inventors or to very small operations. However, a chronic feature of the federal licensing system is the practice of acquiring licenses for personal convenience rather than for trade.

The total of 191 firearms manufacturing companies reported in the 1997 census is misleading if it is not kept in mind that the industry is in fact highly concentrated. It is a sort of inverted pyramid in terms of production, with a few big manufacturers at the top and a string of smaller companies scrabbling for the rest of the market, down to individual gunsmiths making only a few firearms each year in the equivalent of a garage workshop. In 2000, for example, three companies produced 53 percent of the rifles made in the United States, three companies produced 86 percent of the shotguns, two companies produced 76 percent of the revolvers, and four companies produced 55 percent of the pistols.[26]

Foreign imports represent a substantial addition to this domestic production. Contrary to popular belief, the United States has been uniformly a net importer of civilian firearms. From 1990 to 1999, net imports averaged about one million guns a year, of which about half were handguns.[27]

A perspective on the gun industry's size can be gained by comparing the $2.2 billion combined value of firearms and ammunition shipments reported in the 1997 Economic Census to the $28.3 billion reported by cigarette manufacturers and the $27.7 billion reported by distillers, wineries, and brewers.

There was a total of 81,325 dealer and pawnshop licensees in 1999, the last year for which comprehensive data is available. These licensees represent the main outlets for retail sales. However, according to the federal government, in 1998 a full 31 percent of these licensees had not sold a single gun during the previous year, a figure down from 46 percent in 1992. This large proportion of licensees who are not actively selling guns (sometimes called "kitchen table" dealers) is a consequence of the underlying value of the federal license—it enables the holder to purchase guns from out of state at wholesale prices, not only for himself but for friends and others.

Kitchen table dealers present a troubling potential for diversion of firearms into criminal channels. This has inspired a measure of reform.

In 1993 there were 284,117 federally licensed dealers in the United States. Passage of the 1993 Brady Act and the 1994 crime bill, both of which tightened licensing requirements, combined with administrative reforms pressed by the Clinton administration, dramatically reduced the number of licensees through such simple regulatory efforts as requiring licensees to specify a place of business and to notify local law enforcement authorities that they are in the gun business. Apparently, many informal dealers (and some storefront dealers) who were operating in violation of local zoning or licensing laws chose not to renew their federal licenses. In addition, federal and local authorities paid joint calls on license holders in Boston, New York, and other cities to ensure that they were complying with all applicable laws.[28]

There were 755 licensed importers in 1999.[29] There is no government data on the number of wholesalers (distributors), as they are simply licensed as dealers, but 132 firearms distributors were listed in a comprehensive directory published in 2002 by *Shooting Industry*, the premier industry journal.[30]

To sum up, the modern American gun industry is no titan compared to tobacco and alcohol, the other "sin industries." It is highly concentrated, ambiguously structured, faced with declining markets and foreign competition, and regulated at the federal level only through a system of licenses that are fairly easy to get.

A Brief History

The modern gun industry is a far cry from the preindustrial gun trade that existed from the colonial era to the turn of the nineteenth century. Guns throughout that period were either imported from abroad or made by hand by gunsmiths, who passed their skills down within the family or through apprentices in a typical craft system.[31] Design innovation was not an imperative and was achieved at a leisurely pace.

This all changed at the turn of the nineteenth century, when an organized firearms industry was first established at the instance and with the crucial support of the federal government. The events of the first several decades of that era established basic patterns and rhythms that have defined the industry to the present. These include a recurring cycle of boom and bust, industry reliance on design innovation to carve out new markets, the introduction of designs developed for military use into civilian markets, and aggressive marketing to promote sales.

The rebellious colonists founded the first government armory in 1777 at Springfield, Massachusetts, on land that had been used as a training field for militias since the 1600s. The Springfield Armory was a safe place to store and repair arms, out of reach of British sailing ships and the troops they brought with them. But no guns were actually made there until 1795.[32] Prior to that date, arms for the U.S. military were either imported from abroad or bought from suppliers, who delivered them to a handful of storage depots. But scandals associated with that system,[33] and later the looming potential of war with France, determined the new government to create its own independent source of weapons by first establishing in 1794 two manufacturing arsenals—one at Springfield and another at Harpers Ferry, Virginia—and later awarding arms contracts to private manufacturers.[34]

Concurrent with the new government's pursuit of an independent arms supply was a new doctrine's rise to favor in the Army's Ordnance Department, the overseer of contracts with the nascent arms industry. Originally articulated by a French military rationalist, General Jean-Baptiste de Gribeauval, the doctrine called for uniformly manufactured weapons with interchangeable parts. *Le système Gribeauval* was aimed at a major drawback of eighteenth-century warfare. Guns were basically handmade, parts were not interchangeable, and repairs were difficult and could not be made on the battlefield. An army that could issue standard firearms, as interchangeable as its conscripts, and repair them in the field would have the advantage in the new era of massed combat. Such a system was more easily envisioned than achieved, however. But it became a priority of the U.S. Ordnance Department, which ordered its arsenals to figure out how to speed up production and to make uniform firearms with interchangeable parts. In pursuit of the same ends, the Ordnance Department also awarded key contracts to private suppliers.[35]

Eli Whitney, the inventor of the cotton gin, was awarded one of those contracts and was for a time erroneously credited as the inventor of mass-produced firearms with interchangeable parts, in large part because of a rigged "demonstration" in Washington before President John Adams and other dignitaries.[36] Whitney was, in fact, a prescient promoter of the idea, but not an achiever. After several decades of development at the government armories, success was finally attained between 1820 and 1824 by John Hall, a subcontractor to the Harpers Ferry Armory.[37] The more efficient Springfield Armory arsenal then took the lead in developing the new system of "armory practice" and was a central source of widespread diffusion of the manufacturing process to other industries, such as clockmakers and sewing machine manufacturers.[38]

The Springfield Armory thus had a national influence that transcended its own production record. It established a new industrial base in the Connecticut Valley—which became known as "Gun Valley"—and attracted hundreds of skilled craftsmen. Many of these craftsmen became the core of the nation's new gun industry, and through them the system of armory practice quickly spread to the next new breed of gun makers—the makers of patent arms. As government contracts with private arms makers faded in the 1840s until the Civil War, these entrepreneurs "capitalized on forty years of government-sponsored development in manufacturing technology,"[39] combined the newly emerging mass-production methods with clever innovations in firearm design, and turned to mass-marketing techniques to generate sales in the civilian market.

Samuel Colt is the premier example of the Gun Valley patent arms maker. Colt invented the first practical revolving cylinder handgun design and won U.S. Patent No. 138 for it in 1836. The "revolver" made it possible for an individual to carry on his person a handgun that could fire multiple shots without reloading, arguably the greatest advance in civilian killing power in history. Although the idea of a handgun with a revolving cylinder was not new, Colt was the first to come up with a design that worked well.[40]

After initial promise, however, Colt's original company failed and began bankruptcy proceedings in 1842. Fate intervened in the form of a U.S. Army captain named Samuel H. Walker, who had been impressed with Colt firearms while fighting Indians in Florida and Texas. Walker's interest led to a contract for Colt from the U.S. Ordnance Department, and Colt found himself back in business, making a newly designed revolver called the Colt Walker.[41] Another gun, the Colt 1873 Single Action Army revolver, was named the Peacemaker and became popularly known as "the gun that won the West."[42]

In addition to design innovation and government largesse, Colt's success depended on his seizing another innovation in combination with the revolver—mass marketing. According to the company, "Sam Colt was later recognized as one of the earliest manufacturers to fully realize the potential of an effective marketing program that included sales promotion, publicity, product sampling, advertising, and public relations."[43]

Horace Smith and Daniel B. Wesson formed a partnership in 1852 to manufacture a handgun that fired a fully self-contained cartridge. This significant advance in firearms design made reloading much quicker than the cumbersome process of separately loading the bullet, powder, and percussion cap that the Colt revolver required.[44] Smith & Wesson is today the leading revolver maker in America, producing 41 percent of domestic manufacture in 2000. Other patent arms makers with similar histories became well known as "old-line" firearms manufacturers. They included trademarks such as Winchester, Remington, Marlin, High Standard, and Ithaca.

The Civil War gave the gun industry its next big boost. Conscripts who would never otherwise have had occasion to possess a firearm were introduced to guns. The Union army allowed its soldiers to take their guns home with them upon demobilization. Vast numbers of people thus became used to firearms and willing to buy them in the civilian market. For the next hundred years, the industry's fortunes waxed and waned. Civilian marketing emphasized self-defense, hunting, and marksmanship.

The modern firearms industry as it exists today began to stir as the nation emerged from World War II. New manufacturing enterprises were founded, many in states like California and Florida, far from Gun Valley but offering less costly production. Foreign gun manufacturers also discovered the vast American market and devised strategies to penetrate it. These included quietly buying out a number of well-known old-line American companies while keeping up the facade of their historic names, such that today many American gun buyers aren't even aware of the foreign ownership of these companies.

Some of the newer domestic enterprises went after the old-line companies head-on with innovative strategies aimed at producing traditional products in more competitive ways. The premier example of a successful such modern gun manufacturer is Sturm, Ruger & Company, Inc. Founded by William B. Ruger and Alex Sturm in 1949 to produce a .22 caliber semiautomatic target pistol, the company built its early business on manufacturing "western style revolvers"—handguns imitating the classic design of the nineteenth-century Colt Peacemaker.[45] Sturm, Ruger & Company has since branched out into modern designs and long guns. It has grown to become one of America's most prolific producers of all types of firearms for the civilian market.

The gun industry operated free of government restraint throughout most of this period. The first federal firearms law was the War Revenue Act of 1919, which placed a tax on the manufacture of firearms and ammunition to help pay costs of World War I. The National Firearms Act of 1934 and the Federal Firearms Act of 1938 together made up the federal government's first attempt at regulating the industry, largely through a taxation system that required manufacturers, importers, and dealers to register with the Treasury Department, to pay a tax, and to obtain a license. The system was largely ineffective as anything other than a revenue-raising measure, however. The few limitations it imposed on actual commerce in firearms were easily evaded and poorly enforced.

The assassination of President John F. Kennedy in 1963, the murders of Robert Kennedy and the Reverend Martin Luther King Jr. in 1968, rising rates of violent crime, and an explosion of handguns impelled Congress to pass the first truly comprehensive federal firearms law, the Gun Control Act of 1968, which somewhat tightened federal licensing requirements. The 1968 law encouraged another change in the American gun market. For the first time, the nation restricted the import of so-called Saturday Night Specials—small, easily concealable handguns poorly made of lower-quality materials—by imposing certain size, design, and performance standards on imported foreign guns. The law did not, however, subject domestic manufacturers to any such standards. This different treatment had two long-term results: domestic companies sprang up to fill the Saturday Night Special gap and foreign manufacturers created domestic manufacturing subsidiaries to evade import restrictions and to get back into the lucrative American market.

Southern California became the center of the domestic manufacture of cheap handguns. The rise and deleterious nationwide impact of these companies, collectively known as the "Ring of Fire" companies, was thoroughly and definitively documented in a landmark study by Southern California trauma surgeon Dr. Garen Wintemute.[46] Wintemute concluded that, although the Ring of Fire guns were marketed primarily for self-defense, their shoddy construction made them unreliable and unsuitable for personal protection. Yet, he found, the cheap Ring of Fire guns were disproportionately used in crime—3.4 times more likely to be involved in a crime than handguns from other major manufacturers.[47]

More generally, however, the spawning of the Ring of Fire companies marked the blossoming of the seeds Samuel Colt planted and the beginning of a consistent trend in the modern postwar gun industry: the mass marketing of lethality and "fire power."

Selling Lethality

All firearms are capable of killing, and indeed virtually all firearms are designed to do so. But not all firearms are capable of killing with equal efficiency. Specific design features affect lethality. Differences in ammunition capacity, caliber (bullet size), and concealability among firearms translate into greater or lesser likelihood that a firearm will be present in an encounter and, if it is, a greater capability to deliver lethal force in terms of the number of wounds and their seriousness. In short, design affects lethality.

The mix of firearm products sold in the U.S. civilian market has changed significantly over the last thirty years. Unlike many other consumer industries that grow along with population growth, the firearms industry in the United States has faced saturated, declining markets for at least the last twenty-five to thirty years.[48] The gun industry has used design change to stimulate its markets, and those changes have consistently been in the direction of greater lethality. This innovation was described in 1993 by Andrew W. Molchan, publisher and editor of *American Firearms Industry:* "Without new models that have major technical changes, you eventually exhaust your market. . . . This innovation has driven the handgun market."[49]

This deliberate enhancement of lethality contributes directly to the criminal use of firearms and to death and injury resulting from firearms use. On the other hand, the industry has not been equally innovative in designing or as eager to incorporate safety devices such as automatic load indicators, child-proof triggers, and magazine disconnects. The industry's defenders argue that enhancing the lethality of firearms simply improves a tool whose purpose has always been deadly force. Responsibility for misuse of that force lies with the user, not with the industry, they maintain.

The Rise of Handguns

The most striking change in the U.S. civilian firearms market since the end of World War II has been the rise to dominance of the handgun. Long guns (rifles and shotguns) dominated the civilian market throughout the first half of the twentieth century. From 1899 through 1945, handguns constituted 24 percent of firearms available in that market. In 1946 handguns constituted 11 percent of domestic manufacture. Because the United States was then a net exporter of civilian firearms, handguns accounted for only 8 percent of firearms available for sale.[50] Beginning in the mid-1960s this changed. Handguns rose fairly rapidly to dominate the civilian market and, with the exception of a brief resurgence of long guns in the mid-1970s, have continued to do so without interruption since 1979. Handgun sales per adult are now roughly twice the level of forty years ago, consistently averaging about 40 percent of the overall market.[51]

Conversion to Semiautomatic Pistols from Revolvers

Another striking trend has been the emergence of semiautomatic pistols over revolvers in the U.S. civilian market. Many more rounds (eight to seventeen) can be fired from a semiautomatic pistol, with less effort, than from a revolver (five to six), and the empty pistol can be reloaded more quickly than the empty revolver. This is especially true of the more modern high-capacity pistol magazines, designed to hold as many as twenty rounds. As pistol production increased, revolver production plummeted in the early 1980s. In 1987, for the first time, domestic pistol production surpassed revolver production, and it now leads the handgun market by a wide margin.

Two forces have driven this market. The first was the emergence of companies at the low end of the market specializing in small, cheaply made, easily concealable pistols in lower calibers. The second was the emergence, initially at the higher end of the market, of new pistols in higher calibers combined with high-capacity magazines. *Guns & Ammo,* the largest circulation gun enthusiast magazine, placed the market change among the "Top 10" gun trends of the 1980s.

> No class of handgun ever received the torrent of attention and developmental effort as did the modern, high-capacity, double-action 9mm pistol—the so-called wondernine. In 1979, there were only a few models available in the American market-place and they weren't particularly popular. . . . Then somebody opened the floodgates, because in short order we had a couple dozen new and interesting pistols in this category.[52]

Ultimately, the two ends of the market moved closer together. The cheaper gun makers increased the caliber of their guns, and many high-quality makers, aided by new developments in materials such as the emergence of plastics and stronger alloys, produced smaller and less expensive pistols.

Growth in Caliber and Diminution in Size

Another trend within the handgun market has been an increase in the manufacture of pistols in the upper range of commercial handgun calibers. Just as handgun caliber has been increasing, handgun size has been dimin-ishing. New materials have made it possible to design smaller handguns in higher calibers that would have been impossible to make, or dangerous to the user if made, in earlier generations of handguns.[53] At the same time, the success of a drive by the National Rifle Association (NRA) to change state laws to permit the concealed carry of firearms created a new market for small handguns.[54] The combination of technology and law change resulted in the widespread marketing of subcompact handguns (also known as "pocket rockets," mini-guns, and palm guns). The confluence of trends was summarized in 1997 by Bob Rogers, editor of *Shooting Sports Retailer,* a gun business magazine: "Firepower is increasing. So is the killing potential as guns shrink in size and concealibility [*sic*]."[55]

Emergence of Military-Style Weapons

A final phenomenon has been the appearance of two classes of mili-tary-style firearms: semiautomatic assault guns and sniper rifles. Histor-ically, surplus military firearms have often found their way onto the civilian market. Many of these have been suitable for such sporting uses as hunting. Semiautomatic assault weapons, however, are distinguished by their high ammunition capacity and by design features that facilitate rapid "spray" firing. Most semiautomatic assault weapons are slightly modified versions of guns designed for military use where it is desired to deliver a high rate of fire over a less than precise killing zone, a procedure often called "hosing down" an area.[56]

Generic design features that make them ideal for rapidly laying down a wide field of fire include (1) high capacity magazines (capable of holding from twenty to more than one hundred rounds of ammunition) and (2) devices that make it easier to simply point (as opposed to carefully aim) the gun while rapidly pulling the trigger. These pointing devices include pistol grips—or magazines that function like pistol grips—on the fore end of the gun and barrel shrouds, which are ventilated tubes that surround the otherwise too-hot-to-hold barrel, providing an area that is cool enough to be directly grasped by the shooter even after scores of rounds have been fired. Taken together, these features make it possible for the shooter of the civilian assault gun to "hose down" a relatively wide area with a lethal spray of bullets and to do it quickly. The NRA tested one such gun, the Calico M-100 Rifle, in 1987 and reported that "the full 100 rounds were sent downrange in 14 seconds by one flicker-fingered tester."[57]

A more recent phenomenon has been the marketing of military sniper rifles. These are not merely off-the-rack hunting rifles with telescopic sights but "purpose-designed" military weapons fielded by armies in conflicts around the world. These include such pieces as the Barrett M82A1 .50 caliber sniper rifle, used by U.S. forces during the 1991 Gulf War to destroy Iraqi light-armored vehicles, missiles, and artillery pieces at very long range.[58]

The Consequences of Deliberately Increased Lethality

These changes in the mix of firearms available in the civilian market have increased the lethality of armed encounters in the United States by enhancing three specific design factors identified as contributing to the likelihood of death or serious injury by firearm—availability (largely a function of concealability and thus portability), capacity, and caliber.

The greater ammunition capacity of firearms affects the outcome of armed encounters by increasing the likelihood that a shot will take effect. Although most handgun shootings occur at close range, most bullets fired, even by trained law enforcement officers, miss their targets.[59] For example, FBI agents are reported to have fired at least seventy rounds at two assailants in a fierce 1986 firefight in Miami, but only eighteen rounds hit the criminals.[60] Therefore, the more rounds a gun can fire quickly, the more likely it is that a given shooting will result in multiple wounds.

There are at least two ways to demonstrate the effect of increased capacity and caliber. One is to compare the demonstrable medical consequences of one's being shot more times by bigger bullets. The other is to examine the data of actual shooting incidents and look for changes linked to the introduction of the types of firearms posited to be more lethal.

The pathology of multiple wounds from large bullets is well established and tracks common sense. The dynamics of wound ballistics involve a complex of variables. But all other things being equal, larger bullets cause greater wound damage—"Of the bullets which attain desired penetration depth, those of larger diameter are the most effective, crushing more tissue," wrote the authors of a comparative study of police ammunition.[61] It should be noted that, although much of the writing about law enforcement and wound ballistics is addressed to the issue of "stopping power," that is, the ability to produce more or less immediate incapacitation, the issues of incapacitation and lethality are effectively equivalent in the case of handguns. That is, "[g]enerally, with handguns, to produce incapacitation, we've got to produce death."[62] The merits of such increased "stopping power" for self-defensive purposes has indeed driven the industry's enthusiasm for designs incorporating bigger and more bullets.

It is unfortunate that for a variety of reasons—including significantly fierce political opposition from organized pro-gun groups—uniform national data on firearm injury is not available. There is simply no resource from which one can obtain such useful data as types of handguns, caliber, and number of rounds taking effect in shootings. Nevertheless, a national survey of anecdotal medical evidence and a more intensive study of shootings in Philadelphia establish not only that more wounds increase the likelihood of death or serious injury in a given incident but that changes in firearm design have indeed driven an increase in the number of wounds in shooting incidents.[63]

Similarly with respect to the introduction of military-style weapons, law enforcement officials have noted anecdotally for some time that criminals are taking up "heavier arms in the form of assault rifles" and that "the rifle types most often used to kill officers encompass the most common assault rifle calibers in the world."[64] A recent study of FBI data by the Violence Policy Center found that at least 41 of the 211 law enforcement officers slain in the line of duty between January 1, 1998, and December 31, 2001—one in five—were killed with assault weapons.[65] This phenomenon is the consequence of the deliberate creation by the firearm industry of a civilian market for a class of weapons that simply did not exist before the mid-1980s.

Other Problem Areas

Defenders of the firearms industry often describe it as being heavily regulated, with no need for the discipline of the civil litigation to which other consumer product industries are subject. In fact, regulation of the industry at the federal level is largely a matter of pro forma licensing paperwork. There is no oversight of product design. This uniquely indulgent regulatory situation results from the structure of federal law, which exempts firearms and ammunition from the Consumer Product Safety Act and depends almost entirely on a system of licensing. Some responsibility also lies on the federal agency to which enforcement of that law is delegated—the Bureau of Alcohol, Tobacco, Firearms and Explosives (BATFE)—which has historically been far too lightly staffed to aggressively oversee its limited licensing mandate.

State regulation of firearms dealers varies wildly. Arizona has no statewide gun dealer licensing provisions and forbids local jurisdictions from regulating the sale, possession, or use of firearms. New Jersey, on the other hand, strictly controls who may have a state gun dealer's license. In any event, a minority of states impose their own gun licensing requirements, and most of these suffer from two basic flaws that make them easy to evade: either they do not adequately define what constitutes dealing in firearms (and thus the necessity to obtain a dealer's license), or they are limited to certain types of guns, such as handguns.[66]

Weakness in Federal Oversight of Licensed Dealers

The federal regulatory system enacted in the Gun Control Act of 1968 is primarily intended to restrict the interstate sale of firearms to gun dealers and thereby to prevent individuals without licenses from running over state lines to buy guns. Federally licensed dealers—including so-called kitchen table dealers—may have firearms shipped to them across state lines (e.g., from wholesalers, manufacturers, or other licensed dealers). They may buy and sell both new and used guns to and from other licensed dealers regardless of the latter's location, and they may buy and sell to or from residents of the state in which they are located. A licensed dealer also may sell long guns to a nonresident, so long as the sale is legal under the laws both of the dealer's state and of the nonresident's state. However, handguns may be sold across state lines only from one licensed dealer to another. In other words, a resident of Alabama may not legally buy a handgun in Georgia unless she has a Federal Firearms License.

In theory, the BATFE monitors the conduct of licensed dealers through a program of on-site inspection. However, BATFE has never had the staff to inspect more than a small percentage of retail licensees in any given year. In 1969, the first year of operations under the 1968 Gun Control Act, the agency inspected 54.7 percent of the new licensees created under the act. Thereafter, the agency's inspection activity declined dramatically, to an all-time low of 1.1 percent in 1983. In 1990, it conducted 8,471 compliance inspections, representing 3.1 percent of licensees. The number rose during the agency's aggressive scrutiny of retail dealers in the mid-1990s to a peak of 22,300 compliance inspections in 1993, or 7.9 percent of licensees, but fell back to 5,043, or 4.8 percent of licensees, in 1998.[67] At a 5 percent rate of inspection visits, it would take the agency twenty years to get around to inspecting each licensee once. In the real world, BATFE's resources are spread thin and most of its attention in the area of firearms goes to enforcing federal criminal laws relating to guns, not dealer compliance. The result is that the nation's fast-food outlets probably get more regular government attention from health, fire, and weights and measures personnel than the average firearms dealer gets from BATFE.

The problem of thin oversight is compounded by the historically weak action BATFE has taken against dealers who violate regulations—in the years 1975–99, BATFE revoked a total of only 373 dealers licenses.[68] The combination of cursory oversight and weak enforcement was exemplified in the case of a Tacoma, Washington, gun dealer whose store was allegedly the source of the Bushmaster assault rifle used by two snipers who terrorized Washington, D.C., in the fall of 2002.[69] The rifle was traced back to the store, but there were no records of its sale, and the dealer had not reported the gun stolen, as federal regulations required him to do.[70] In spite of the fact that at least four previous inspections since 1995 had uncovered numerous record-keeping violations and as many as 160 missing firearms that the store could not account for, no action was taken to revoke the dealer's license until after the Beltway shootings.[71]

Rogue Dealers and Straw Purchases

Given the power of the Federal Firearms License and BATFE's weak oversight of licensees, it is no wonder that, according to the testimony of a former industry official, "[t]he diversion of firearms to the illegal black market occurs principally at the distributor/dealer level."[72] Leakage from legitimate channels of commerce to illegal gun trafficking occurs at the retail or distributor level through several mechanisms, including theft, so-called straw purchases—frequently by organized gun traffickers—and corrupt gun dealers who knowingly use their licenses to directly or indirectly supply criminals with firearms.[73]

Expedient, legal access to firearms makes the corrupt dealer a "leveraged" force in criminal trafficking—an unlicensed dealer acting in concert with a corrupt licensee, for example, can obtain and divert to illicit channels many more weapons than he could if he were acting alone.[74] A BATFE study of gun trafficking reported that, although licensed dealers were involved in the smallest proportion of gun trafficking investigations, they were associated with the largest total of illegally diverted firearms.[75]

Straw purchasers are individuals who buy firearms on behalf of other persons, such as convicted felons, who are legally barred from possessing firearms. Small-scale straw purchasers and criminal straw-purchasing rings made up nearly half of the investigations in the BATFE study.[76]

The second largest source of illegally diverted firearms in the BATFE study was gun shows, fairs at which private citizens and licensed dealers alike sell firearms and related paraphernalia. According to BATFE, 4,442 such events were advertised in calendar year 1998.[77] Most gun transfers between private individuals are controlled only by state and local law. In most states, this means no control at all, since most states do not regulate private transactions. In theory, a private person could make so many "private" gun sales that he or she would be "engaged in the business" of selling guns under federal law and would thus be required to secure a federal firearms dealers license. Yet, federal law so generously defines the right of individuals to sell guns out of their own "collections" that in practice many such unlicensed hobbyists who sell at gun shows are indistinguishable from licensed firearms dealers. Brady Act background checks are not required for private transactions at gun shows, and most states also do not require background checks for such transfers. This has led to calls for additional legislation to "close the gun show loophole" by extending the Brady Act background check to sales at such shows.

Another problem area is the illicit traffic in firearms from states and localities with relatively lax gun laws or enforcement to states and localities with stricter laws.

Conclusion

Although often romanticized, fiercely defended on ideological grounds, and immune from common regulatory oversight, the modern American gun industry is at bottom simply a business, an industry that mass-produces a consumer product—firearms. I have attempted to demonstrate in this chapter that, faced with similar pressures resulting from production capacity exceeding natural demand, the modern gun industry mass markets firearms similar to the way the automotive industry mass markets new cars. I also have shown that the innovation the gun industry has relied on to generate demand in its markets has resulted in an overall increase in the lethality of its products. This results from specific design features the industry has incorporated into its products. These features, and the techniques that the industry uses to promote them, bear a demonstrably direct relationship to increased death and serious injury from firearms.

CHAPTER 4

A Cultural Critique of Gun Litigation

DAN M. KAHAN, DONALD BRAMAN,

& JOHN GASTIL

Like nearly all contentious political issues in our society, gun control has made its way to court. Is the new wave of lawsuits against the firearms industry a positive development? We don't think so. But our opposition to America's gun litigation isn't based on conventional grounds. We don't have an opinion on whether the plaintiffs' claims are well grounded in tort law. We aren't sure whether the remedies the plaintiffs seek would promote or impede public safety. We don't care whether the lawsuits are antidemocratic, disrespectful of federalism, or inconsistent with the Second Amendment. And we are passionately unmoved by the question of whether courts are as fit as legislatures or administrative agencies to craft efficient regulatory standards.

We oppose gun litigation because we think it's culturally obtuse. In courts of law, the gun debate is reduced to a set of contested factual claims about the consequences of firearms design and marketing. But in the court of public opinion, the gun debate inevitably broadens into a dispute over conflicting worldviews and the social status of those who adhere to them. Because Americans care just as much about what guns and the regulation of them say—about what we value and who we identify with, about what sort of society we live in, about whose stock is up and whose is down in the market for social prestige—any mode of decision making that focuses only on what guns do is bound to miss the point.

It turns out that this deficiency isn't unique to gun litigation. On the contrary, it's characteristic of mainstream gun control discourse wherever it takes place. Academics, criminal justice bureaucrats, and even elected representatives focus obsessively on consequences—"more guns, more crime" or "more guns, less crime"?—and stand mute on the broader cultural significance of gun control. And as the persistence and persistent acrimony of the gun debate in America attest, this "just the facts, please" approach hasn't gotten us very far.

It won't get us any further in the gun litigation, where consequentialist discourse will misfire for the same reasons it has in the political domain. One problem with emphasizing consequences to the exclusion of culture is logical. If citizens care, and care intensely, about the social meanings that guns express, then even indisputable empirical proof of the public safety consequences of a particular gun law won't give citizens sufficient reason to favor or oppose it. No matter what the outcome of the gun litigation, then, the political dispute over guns and gun control can be expected to continue—as the spate of recent statutory immunity provisions illustrates.

Another and even more potent objection to obsessive gun consequentialism is psychological. By virtue of a host of cognitive and social mechanisms, what individuals believe about the effects of gun control can't be disentangled from how they feel about them. For this reason, the factual debate inevitably reproduces the cultural—not just in result but in tone as well, since those on both sides inevitably conclude that those who disagree with them on the facts are motivated to do so by bad faith. Thus, however fact focused the gun litigation might look, its results will conform to the cultural priors of those who decide them.

The only way to resolve the American gun debate is to make its cultural underpinnings explicit. Policy analysts, elected officials, advocacy groups, and ordinary citizens must focus their attention on constructing procedures and framing policies that dispel the common anxiety that the outcome of the gun debate will necessarily elevate one understanding of what America stands for and denigrate all the others. The emergence of this form of constructive cultural deliberation is singularly unlikely to arise from gun litigation.

We will develop these claims in three steps. In section I, we will examine the cultural underpinnings of the American gun debate. To this end, we will analyze the debate within a framework derived from the cultural theory of risk perception, which furnishes a powerful explanation of the

mechanisms by which culture shapes factual beliefs about guns and con-
strains the power of consequentialist arguments to quiet political conflict
over them. In section II, we present a critique of the gun litigation, which
lacks the power to resolve the American gun debate precisely because it
misapprehends the psychological and social dynamics that figure in the
cultural theory of risk perception. We conclude with a call for expressive
deliberation, a mode of policy-making that we believe holds the key to
fashioning gun laws that appeal to Americans of all cultural persuasions.

I.   The Cultural Theory of Gun-Risk Perceptions

The "Great American Gun Debate"[1] isn't really one debate but two. The
first, conducted primarily in social science journals and in legislative
chambers, is empirical. Gun control supporters argue that pervasive gun
ownership makes society more dangerous by facilitating violent crimes
and accidental shootings. Opponents respond that it's gun control that
undermines safety by making it more difficult for potential crime victims
to ward off violent predation. The currency of this debate is factual data
in the form of opposing econometric regression analyses, contingent valuation studies, public health risk-factor analyses, and the like.

The second gun debate is cultural. Carried out (often heatedly) in letters to the editor and in town square rallies, gun politics consists in a
struggle to define what America stands for and who has standing in
America. Control opponents tend to be rural, southern or western,
Protestant, male, and white. For them guns symbolize a cluster of positive values, from honor to respect for legitimate authority to individual
self-sufficiency. Control proponents, in contrast, are disproportionately
urban, eastern, Catholic or Jewish, female, and African American. To
them, guns bear a host of negative connotations, from the perpetuation
of illicit social hierarchies to the elevation of force over reason to collective indifference to the well-being of strangers. The latter support gun
control as a way to repudiate these values and to affirm society's commitment to equality and solidarity; the former oppose it—with immense
energy and passion—precisely because they see it as intended to denigrate their cultural identities.[2]

The obvious question is how these two gun debates relate to each other. What matters more to ordinary citizens—consequences or values? Does it even make sense to suppose that the two are genuinely independent of one another?

The attention that mainstream policymakers and commentators afford to the consequences of gun control reflects their assumption that the empirical debate is autonomous and at least potentially decisive. Eventually, they reason, social scientists will reach consensus on whether "shall issue" laws, mandatory waiting periods, lock-box provisions, and the like make society more safe or less. When they do, moreover, we should expect the gun debate to come to a rapid and harmonious end. For as divided as they are on the nature of the good society and the place of guns within it, at least both agree that protecting innocent persons from harm is of paramount importance.

We, in contrast, think that the empirical side of the debate is derivative and hence impotent. Culture not only matters to citizens in the gun debate, but it determines how they evaluate and even what they believe about the consequences of gun control. Accordingly, it's futile to try to resolve the gun debate by bracketing culture and focusing on facts. This is the lesson we draw from the cultural theory of risk perception, the application of which to the American gun debate we will now examine.

Risk and Culture

Public evaluations of risk bear a notoriously uneven correspondence to the objectively measured dangers associated with various activities. Thus many individuals appear relatively tolerant of risk in their recreational activities but averse to it in their financial and workplace decisions.[3] They also tend to identify as extremely grave, and thus worthy of intensive regulation, many types of risks—from nuclear accidents to industrial pollution of waterways—that environmental experts view as relatively low, while essentially disregarding other risks—for example, accidental drownings in swimming pools—that experts rate much more highly.[4] Finally, risk perception has been shown to vary dramatically across different groups: ordinary citizens disagree not only with the experts but also with one another about how seriously to take various forms of environmental and industrial risk, not to mention risks relating to foreign aggression or economic collapse.[5]

Experts have traditionally advocated basing risk regulation on narrowly consequentialist measures of environmental and industrial hazards. Techniques such as cost-benefit analysis and comparative risk assessment rank hazards according to a uniform expected-utility metric. The policies they generate are defended as superior to any based directly on public risk perceptions, the unruly character of which is attributed to the public's lack of information about the hazards posed by various technologies and to cognitive limitations that distort laypersons' processing of such information.[6]

The inadequacy of this approach to risk regulation, however, is well known and, by this point, largely accepted even by many expert regulators.[7] The gap between various objective measures of risk and public perceptions of the same is not entirely (or even largely) a consequence of imperfect information or cognitive defects but rather a reflection of the diverse social meanings that ordinary citizens attach to risk. Individuals (a host of disciplines have taught us) don't have generic attitudes toward risky activities; rather, they evaluate them according to context-specific norms that determine what risk taking connotes about their values and attitudes.[8] Nowadays smoking, at least for some, conveys an irresponsible disregard for the future and a contemptible weakness of will, whereas mountain climbing (which is in fact much more hazardous) conveys for many a laudable attainment of physical discipline and courage.[9] It would be morally obtuse to expect individuals to evaluate the desirability of these activities solely according to their respective health risks without taking into account the value that they attach to their distinctive social meanings.

The same holds true for public risk regulation. Many citizens tend to view nuclear waste disposal and global warming with alarm not just because they pose risks of a particular magnitude but because running these risks (however small) conveys a host of undesirable meanings—of collective hubris, of generational selfishness, of disrespect for the sacredness of nature.[10] It would thus be morally obtuse for regulators to attempt to evaluate these risks relative to those associated with, say, recreational swimming (which regulators tend to view as much more serious)[11] without taking account of what citizens think the acceptance of the former says about their society's values and attitudes.[12]

Of course, what societal attitudes the law should express is often a matter of dispute. And that's exactly why risk regulation so often becomes the site of intense political conflict.

The best account of such conflict is supplied by the cultural theory of risk.[13] This theory relates variance in risk perception to individuals' allegiance to competing clusters of values, which construct alternative visions—egalitarian, individualist, and hierarchist ones, for example—of how political life should be organized. The selection of certain risks for attention and the disregard of others reflect and reinforce these worldviews. Thus, by virtue of their commitment to fair distribution of resources, egalitarians are predictably sensitive to environmental and industrial risks, the minimization of which reinforces their demand for the regulation of commercial activities productive of disparities in wealth and status. In contrast, individualists, precisely because they are dedicated to the autonomy of markets and other private orderings, tend to see environmental risks as low—as do hierarchists, in line with their confidence in the competence of authorities to solve society's problems. Hierarchists and individualists have their own distinctive anxieties—of the dangers of social deviance, the risks of foreign invasion, or the fragility of economic institutions—which egalitarians predictably dismiss.[14] Empirical testing suggests that cultural orientations so characterized more powerfully predict individual attitudes toward risk than myriad other influences, including education, personality type, and political orientation.

The cultural theory not only explains why risk regulation so often generates political disputes but also why consequentialist modes of decision making are powerless to solve them. No amount of expected utility analysis can tell us whose vision of the good society—that of the egalitarian, the hierarchist, or the individualist—to prefer. When commitments to ways of life figure explicitly into appraisals of societal dangers—"better dead than red!"—culture-effacing modes of risk assessment and decision making will simply miss the normative point.

To the extent that individuals treat social meanings as explicitly trumping consequentialist measures of danger, risk perceptions can be said to be morally derivative of cultural orientations. But perceptions of risk are likely to be cognitively derivative of culture orientations as well. By virtue of a collection of overlapping psychological and social mechanisms, individuals are likely to be relying on (and propagating) their worldviews even when they think that consequences are all that matter.

One mechanism that tends toward this result is cognitive dissonance avoidance.[15] It's comforting to believe that what's noble is also benign and what's base is dangerous rather than vice versa.[16] It's not comforting—indeed, it's psychically disabling—to entertain beliefs about what's harmless and what's harmful that pit one against commitments and affiliations essential to one's sense of self.[17]

Another mechanism is the contributions that affect makes to risk perception. Emotion is one of the basic faculties by which we discern risk; our judgments of how dangerous activities are track the visceral reactions that those activities trigger. Whether those reactions are positive or negative is determined largely by cultural influences.[18]

Finally and most important, cultural orientations condition individuals' beliefs about risk through culturally partisan forms of trust. When faced with conflicting claims and data, individuals usually aren't in a position to determine for themselves how large particular risks—for example, leukemia from contaminated groundwater, domestic attacks by terrorists, transmission of AIDS from casual contact with infected gay men—really are. Instead, they must rely on those whom they trust to tell them which risk claims are serious and which are specious. The people they trust, naturally enough, tend to be the ones who share their worldviews.[19]

The tendency of individuals to adopt views shared by others of their cultural orientation is self-reinforcing. If as a result of cognitive dissonance, affect, trust, or even simple accident the distribution of opposing beliefs about a risk starts out even slightly skewed across cultural groups, the propensity of individuals to defer to those who share their cultural allegiances will cause those beliefs to feed on themselves within groups, ultimately producing a highly polarized state of public opinion.[20]

Because for all these reasons individuals inevitably conform their appraisals of risk to their worldviews, only modes of analysis that explicitly address culture can meaningfully guide risk decision making. "Instead of being distracted by dubious calculations," to determine what sorts of dangers we are willing to face we must openly address the question of what "kind of society . . . we prefer to live in."[21]

Gun Risks and Culture

The consequentialist version of the gun debate is naturally framed as one between two competing risk claims: that insufficient gun control will expose too many innocent persons to deliberate or accidental shootings and that excessive gun control will render too many law-abiding citizens vulnerable to violent predation. Insofar as the worldviews featured in the cultural theory explain who fears what sorts of societal risks in general, it stands to reason that they would explain who takes which of these gun risks more seriously as well.

Various forms of public opinion data along with ethnographic, historical, and journalist accounts of the gun debate all support this hypothesis. Celebrated for their contributions to securing American independence and taming the American frontier, guns (at least for some) resonate as symbols of freedom and self-reliance, associations that make opposition to gun control cohere with an individualist orientation. Guns are also pieces of equipment integral to traditional male roles—father, hunter, protector—and badges of authority for institutions like the military and the police. These social functions imbue guns with connotations of honor, courage, obedience to authority, and patriotism, virtues distinctive of a hierarchic outlook.[22]

Aversion to guns and support for control, in contrast, cohere naturally with more egalitarian and communitarian (or anti-individualistic) worldviews. Precisely because they help to construct traditionally male roles and virtues, guns are often equated with a hypermasculine or "macho" personal style that many individuals, male as well as female, resent.[23] This egalitarian aversion is reinforced by the association of guns with the assassination of Martin Luther King Jr. and resistance to civil rights generally in the modern era[24] and with social and legal controls that made the possession of guns "an important symbol of white male status"[25] in earlier times. And while control opponents see guns as celebrating individual self-sufficiency, control supporters see them as denigrating solidarity: "Every handgun owned in America is an implicit declaration of war on one's neighbor. When the chips are down, its owner says, he will not trust any other arbiter but force personally wielded."[26]

We've confirmed the fit between the cultural theory of risk and gun control attitudes with independent research.[27] Using data from the General Social Survey (GSS) and the National Election Survey (NES)—the premier social science surveys of American public opinion—we constructed scales for measuring individual worldviews along two dimensions corresponding to hierarchy and egalitarianism, on the one hand, and individualism and solidarism, on the other. We then constructed regression models for each data set to test the influence of these cultural orientations on individuals' attitudes toward gun control. The relationship between cultural orientations and gun control attitudes was statistically significant and consistent with our prediction in both studies: that is, the more hierarchical and individualistic individuals were in their orientations, the more they opposed control; and the more egalitarian and solidaristic they were, the more they supported it.

Even more impressive, the cultural orientation measures, when combined, had a bigger impact on gun control attitudes than did any other individual characteristic. Indeed, in the GSS regression, cultural orientations subsumed many of the strongest demographic predictors of gun control attitudes altogether: after controlling for cultural orientations, there was no longer any difference in the attitudes of whites and blacks, southerners and northerners, or urbanites and country dwellers within the GSS model. The results in the NES model were similarly striking.

As it does for other risk-regulation conflicts, the cultural theory implies that consequentialist modes of analysis are bound to be politically inert in the gun debate. To begin, individuals' beliefs about the significance of competing gun risks, like their beliefs about other societal hazards, will be cognitively derivative of their cultural orientations. To avoid cognitive dissonance, egalitarians and communitarians will more readily take note of and credit evidence that insufficient gun control diminishes public safety; hierarchists and individualists will do the same for evidence that excessive gun control makes society less safe. Following the lead of socially constructed emotions, egalitarians and communitarians will instinctively recoil from guns in fear (as well as disgust), while feelings of security and confident self-sufficiency will impel hierarchists and individualists to reach out for them. And looking to those they trust to tell them whom to believe—the analysts and policymakers who say "more guns, less crime" or the ones who say "more guns, more crime"—individuals gravitate toward and become ever more firmly entrenched in the opinions dominant within their respective cultural group.[28]

Culture theory tells us that individuals' beliefs about gun risks will be morally derivative of their cultural orientations as well. Their preferred visions of the good society will figure explicitly in their evaluations of the competing risks that the gun debate comprises. When confronted with social science evidence purporting to show that shall-issue laws reduce crime, control supporters can be expected to spurn mass private weapons possession anyway as denigrating solidarity: better "a world with slightly higher crime levels . . . than one in which we routinely wave guns at each other."[29] No matter what the evidence shows, control proponents likewise will bridle at the idea that collective interests in security justify restricting the right of law-abiding citizens to own guns, which they see as a fundamental individual right.[30] Because of the influence that cultural orientations have in shaping perceptions of consequences, it's unlikely that many individuals would ever accept social science data that purports to contradict their priors on gun risks, but even those who can imagine being persuaded by such evidence would likely refuse to change their position on gun control as a result of it.[31]

These dynamics help to explain the persistent ineffectiveness of empirical data in the American gun debate. Using econometrics, contingent valuation surveys, public health risk-factor analyses, and the like, criminologists generate study after study on the consequences of various forms of gun control. But in the face of them, public opinion remains stubbornly immobile. Members of the public are either choosing to credit only the studies that confirm their priors or simply ignoring the empirics debate altogether. At least politically speaking, the lesson of the recent outpouring of high-quality empirical studies is neither "more guns, less crime" nor "more guns, more crime" but rather "more statistics, less persuasion."

The contribution of cultural orientations to the perception of gun risks also explains the remarkable stridency of the consequentialist debate. Commentators debating the "facts" engage in no less recrimination and name calling than do activists who explicitly see gun control as part of a "culture war."[32] This equivalence isn't surprising because, as culture theory makes clear, the fact and culture debates aren't genuinely independent. We know what to believe because our cultural orientations tell us what institutions and persons (for example, the Vatican or the National Academy of Sciences; Rush Limbaugh or the editors of the *New York Times*) we should trust. Those who disagree with us on the facts are thus implicitly (but unmistakably) conveying that they reject the authority of those persons and institutions and by extension the cultural allegiances that underwrite our deference to them. We inevitably conclude as a result that those who contest our version of the facts are not just stupid but evil.

The hope that consequentialist discourse can turn down the heat of cultural conflict turns is an idle one. Because cultural orientations determine what individuals believe and how they evaluate competing gun risks, policymakers and analysts, in this risk-regulation setting as in others, must suspend (at least temporarily) their fixation on consequences and openly address the question of what sort of values the law should express.

II.   The Cultural Obtuseness of Gun Litigation

Gun litigation won't accomplish this necessary refocusing of attention. Like the consequentialist modes of analysis that dominate the legislative arena, the tort theories that courts employ are concerned only with the empirical question of how to promote public safety. The cultural theory of risk suggests that juries will answer this question in the manner most congenial to their worldviews—a conclusion bolstered by existing empirical research on jury decision making generally. And because the litigation process does nothing to ameliorate the conflicting stance that competing worldviews take toward guns, the gun litigation will generate outcomes as divisive as those generated by any other lawmaking process that ignores culture.

The Trial Process: Facts In, Culture Out

Ordinary citizens are likely to find the empirical side of the academic and political gun control debate exceedingly difficult to penetrate. The competing claims made of shall-issue laws—that they undermine public safety by facilitating deliberate and accidental shootings and that they promote safety by enabling self-defense and deterring predation—might be straightforward enough, but the empirical methods used to test them are very complex. Most citizens have no clue how to interpret the basic components of an econometric regression analysis—standardized betas, t-statistics, R^2s, and the like. Nor are they in a position to evaluate the sorts of defects—missing variable bias, model misspecification, lack of robustness, endogeneity, and so forth—that critics make of their opponents' studies.[33]

The same is true in the legal arena. In the new negligent design cases, for example, the standard of "reasonable alternative design" appears straightforward at first: if a manufacturer knowingly fails to manufacture a safer device at comparable cost, then it may be negligent.[34] Force manufacturers and retailers to internalize the costs of less than optimally safe firearms, litigants argue, and the market will work its natural wonder. But alongside evidence that safety features save lives is evidence that these same features frustrate defensive gun use.[35] This not only has specific effects for those who can't access their firearms when they want to but also raises the issue of general deterrence effects: if fewer people will be able to use their legally purchased and owned weapons for self-defense, crime becomes less costly for criminals, potentially increasing crimes against persons.[36] Whose weighted tobit and weighted least-squared models and whose chi-squareds and log likelihoods will juries find more convincing?

The empirical debates that figure in public nuisance litigation are, if anything, even more difficult for ordinary citizens to understand. Liability in these cases is supposed to give manufacturers an incentive to prevent retailers from supplying guns to criminals. The costs associated with policing retailers in this way, however, will also make guns more expensive for individuals who desire to purchase firearms for lawful self-defense. To sort out the impact of these competing effects on public safety, jurors will have to grapple not only with the basic data relating to whether more guns mean more crime or less but also a host of additional issues relating to the impact of liability on the marketing of firearms.

One is the substitutability of used guns for new gun sales. At least some portion of the retail business with criminals that liability would prevent will simply be replaced by used gun sales, which typically are made by private individuals who face even fewer restrictions on whom they can do business with than do licensed dealers.[37] Would such a shift defeat the effect of liability or at least prevent it from diminishing gun sales to criminals enough to justify the impact that manufacturer liability would have in reducing the acquisition of guns for lawful self-defense?

The answer depends, in part, on the relative "elasticity of demand" for guns across criminals and law-abiding individuals. Perhaps law-abiding individuals, because they tend to buy relatively few guns and attach supreme value to them as instruments of self-defense, won't be discouraged from buying firearms by the increase in prices associated with manufacturer liability.[38] In that case, liability should have a greater impact in discouraging purchases by criminals than in discouraging purchases by law-abiding citizens. Or, in contrast, perhaps because personal self-defense competes with a host of other personal needs—such as food, shelter, clothing, transportation, and entertainment—individual citizens' demands for guns will be more sensitive to increases in price than will demands of criminals, who use guns as tools of the trade, and other persons especially intent on engaging in violence.[39] In that case, liability-induced price increases will disproportionately affect sales to law-abiding citizens.

This problem is likely to be bigger or smaller depending on how one measures the "positive externalities" associated with private gun possession. Tort law is supposed to promote efficiency by making individuals internalize "negative externalities"—the costs that their risk-taking behavior imposes on others.[40] But this model assumes that those who are engaging in the behavior are fully internalizing all the benefits of it; if they aren't—if their actions are also gratuitously conferring benefits on others—then making individuals internalize the full cost of their behavior will actually discourage them from engaging in as much of it as a (wealth-maximizing) society would desire.[41] At least in theory, the acquisition of guns by those who intend to use them for self-defense creates a positive externality of this sort, since the widespread possession of firearms makes criminals, who usually can't tell who is armed and who isn't, wary of attacking anyone. How much of a damages "break" should tort law give firearms manufactures to cover the positive externalities associated with private possession of guns?[42]

Jurors in gun suits will be bombarded with conflicting expert evidence on these and other issues. Since they are incapable of performing an independent investigation of the quality of the parties' competing claims and supporting empirical data, how will they resolve the "factual" disputes on which the gun suits turn? Cultural theory suggests they'll resolve empirical disputes here in the same way that individuals do in other risk decision-making contexts—namely, by conforming their factual beliefs to their cultural orientations.

This hypothesis is corroborated by a wealth of social science research on how individuals in general, and jurors in particular, evaluate ambiguous and conflicting evidence in legal disputes. One such body is the "story model" of juror decision making.[43] Devised by psychologists

Reid Hastie and Nancy Pennington, the story model furnishes the best comprehensive account of how jurors decide between competing factual claims and evidence.[44] Based on experimental studies, Hastie and Pennington show that jurors decide cases by fitting the evidence presented by the parties into one or more "verdict stories" and then selecting the one that appears most coherent to them.[45]

The verdict stories that jurors rely on come from culture, including shared experiences and socially constructed understandings of the natural and social world.[46] Naturally, then, cultural values exert a profound effect on jury verdicts, determining which types of evidence and which evidentiary inferences jurors find plausible or implausible. Indeed, as a result of their reliance on culturally constructed templates, jurors are unlikely to even *recall* evidence that is inconsistent with their preferred verdict story.[47] And, of course, to the extent that jurors in a culturally diverse society are likely to enter the jury room with diverse and even antagonistic cultural prototypes, they will sometimes disagree about what the evidence signifies for exactly that reason.[48]

Jurors will disagree about what the evidence in gun litigation signifies precisely because the cultures at war in the gun debate furnish competing stories or scripts about the relationship between guns and violence. Hearing accounts of school shootings, for example, those on both sides of the gun debate predictably assimilate the event to a preexisting account of how the world works: one side reacts with outrage because the assailants had access to a gun in the first place,[49] and the other side does so because students and teachers were not allowed to arm themselves on school grounds.[50] No one, significantly, changes their mind about gun control.[51] Conflicting evidence in gun litigation, the storytelling model predicts, will likewise not change jurors' opinions but rather will be conformed to the gun violence scripts they are already culturally programmed to accept.

Related bodies of jury research bolster this conclusion. The evidence underlying the "total justice" theory, for example, suggests that jurors in tort cases "strive to work their emotions and their judgments into a satisfying totality" even when this directly contradicts jury instructions about how to evaluate evidence.[52] This dynamic, too, suggests that jurors will conform their understanding of the evidence to their cultural values, which naturally determine *how* jurors morally and emotionally conceive of what "total justice" is in relation to firearms.

Similarly, studies of "commonsense justice" suggest that jurors apply (as they are encouraged to do so by jury instructions) their everyday reasoning ability to the issue before them.[53] But based on "adages, images, and rules of thumb," common sense, too, is deeply cultural in nature.[54] Jurors' commonsense understandings of the evidence in gun cases will thus reproduce their cultural scripts on guns—and reproduce as well the cultural cleavages of the larger gun debate the rules of inference and attribution vary dramatically as well.

These influences will be reinforced, most likely, by a process known as coherence-based reasoning.[55] If after assessing a conflicting body of evidence a decision maker finds one conclusion even slightly more persuasive than another—say, because that conclusion coheres more with culturally shaped prior beliefs—she will then reevaluate the body of evidence in a biased fashion, revising upward her perception of the persuasiveness of evidence that supports the favored conclusion and downgrading the persuasiveness of evidence that refutes it. After reevaluating the evidence in this way, the favored conclusion will appear all the more correct, inducing the decision maker to revise her assessment of the supporting and conflicting evidence all the more dogmatically, and so forth and so on—until she terminates the process without the slightest doubt as to either the correct outcome or the quality of the evidence that supports it.

As in most tort cases, issues of causation loom large in gun litigation. In resolving these issues, culture will loom just as large by virtue of a dynamic referred to by social psychologists as the "culpable causation" principle.[56] Culpable causation can be described as the tendency to attribute greater causal import to acts and greater responsibility to those who perform them when the acts are more morally blameworthy—even though the morality of the act is, strictly speaking, causally irrelevant. Thus, a driver involved in an accident will be perceived as more causally responsible for the accident if he was speeding on his way home to hide some drugs than if he was speeding on his way home to hide an anniversary present.

Studies of culpable causation tell us that jurors' moral sensibilities will strongly influence their understanding of how events are causally linked. Extensive empirical research and everyday experience tell us that these moral sensibilities vary and—especially with issues like mass torts against gun manufacturers—vary dramatically. The cultural theory of risk unites these two insights and articulates how this variation is, in large part, related to competing conceptions of the good society.

Studies of human cognition not only support the premise that culture will guide jury decision making in cases where the acts in question carry strong moral connotations, but they also tell us that, where the evidence is technically difficult, jurors will rely on these kinds of informal intuitions all the more. Because human reasoning is "domain specific,"[57] when individuals are presented with evidence outside or at the periphery of their normal experience, they are forced to rely less on strict forms of logical inference and more on their own informal heuristics.[58] As a result, experimental studies have shown, the more complex and controverted the causal evidence becomes, the more jurors turn to their own normatively inflected understandings of who to trust and what to believe.[59]

In the gun litigation cases, jurors will be asked to assess all manner of actions that can be seen in just such a normative light. To determine whether and how corporations should manufacture and market guns, juries will have to resolve complex factual issues about how liability might affect those practices and how any changes in these practices will influence the behavior of different groups of citizens. All the evidence that exists on jury decision making suggests that jurors will inevitably resolve these difficult issues by drawing on their assessment of whether the commercial marketing of guns and the private ownership of them comports or conflicts with their vision of an ideal society—an evaluation grounded in deeply held and widely contested cultural norms.

These conclusions are admittedly extrapolations from existing research, but they are already borne out to at least an extent by the small number of verdicts that gun suits have generated. In *Hamilton v. Accu-Tek*,[60] both sides relied heavily on expert witnesses to present voluminous, and radically conflicting, statistical analyses of the contribution that the defendant gun manufacturers' marketing practices were making to violent crime. "The jurors ignored almost all of it."[61] Almost immediately after deliberations commenced in the case, two jurors (one a statistician employed by Publishers Clearinghouse Sweepstakes and the other an accountant) "dismissed [the expert] testimony, telling their fellow jurors that numbers can be twisted to make almost any point."[62] Thereafter, according to one of the jurors, they "didn't really discuss the statistics for either side."[63] Instead, for six days, the jurors traded competing stories and impassioned speeches about crime and who is responsible for it; and because these were matters on which the jurors them-selves were apparently bitterly divided, the deliberations produced, unsurprisingly, a process of recriminatory give-and-take that was just as excruciating and conflictual as the American gun debate itself.[64]

Litigation and Cultural Polarization

The contribution that cultural orientations make to gun risk perceptions not only furnishes reason to doubt that litigation will generate the right answer, empirically speaking, to the public safety question. It also makes it impossible to believe that litigation will resolve the American gun debate. The lesson of the cultural theory of risk is that culture is prior to facts—not only in the risk perceptions of individuals but in the political decision making of communities that want to resolve societal risk dis-putes. Gun litigation won't work because it doesn't do anything to extri-cate the gun issue from the conflict between competing cultural styles in American life.

   Why might anyone suppose that gun suits could help dispel the cul-tural tensions that pervade the gun debate? The answer lies in the seem-ingly deliberative nature, and deliberation-forcing potential, of litiga-tion. The conventional picture of jury decision making, for example, sees it as a process of discursive give-and-take in which individuals of differing points of view reach consensus through considered, and con-siderate, exchange. Isn't it possible, then, that jury deliberations might enable individuals of hierarchic and individualistic persuasions and those of egalitarian and communitarian ones to find the common ground that has eluded them in the rough and tumble of electoral politics? And even if it doesn't, shouldn't we expect the outcomes of gun suits to make polit-ical deliberation more productive? Right now, the advantage that con-trol opponents enjoy in the electoral process by virtue of being small, well organized, and intensely interested makes it possible for them to block significant legislative interventions into the gun debate. But significant damages awards in gun suits—which are likely to be filed in the jurisdictions least supportive of guns—would give the control pro-ponents the leverage, and control opponents the incentive, needed to break up the culture-conflict log jam. Sadly, however, these conjectures turn out to be completely unrealistic.

The hope that jury deliberations might produce cultural respect and accommodation is at odds with a wealth of experimental data. These show that when groups deliberate on a disputed issue of fact or value their members tend to become more extreme in their positions, not more moderate.

This "group polarization" effect rests on a set of interrelated mechanisms. One is informational: if the members of the deliberating group are already leaning in one direction (or if the members with the strongest views are the ones most motivated to speak), arguments in favor of that position will predominate in discussion, thereby reinforcing the impression that that position is correct. Another mechanism is reputational: to gain the approval of others in the group, members who even weakly support what appears to be the dominant view will express unequivocal support for it, while those who disagree will tend to mute their opposition in order to avoid censure. The effect of reputational concerns on individuals' decisions to speak will in turn reinforce the skewed distribution of arguments, making it even more likely that members of the group will be persuaded that the dominant position is correct—indeed, indisputably so. Although group polarization has been shown to influence deliberations in a variety of contexts, some of the most compelling experimental demonstrations have in fact involved jury decision making.

Indeed, jury deliberations in gun litigation would seem especially vulnerable to this dynamic. Experiments suggest that group polarization is most intense when the issues in dispute are associated with competing social allegiances. In that case, the effect of both the informational and reputational mechanisms is magnified: the former by the credit that individuals naturally give to the views of those they trust and the latter by the desire that individuals naturally have to maintain good standing in their own social groups and to avoid the distinctive reproach afforded those who side with the groups' detractors. These pressures will predictably come into play in jury deliberations over guns precisely because beliefs about and attitudes toward guns are so conspicuously associated with competing cultural styles.

Accordingly, jury deliberations, far from dissipating the cultural conflict that fuels the gun debate, are much more likely to magnify it. Juries consisting of individuals who are already at least mildly predisposed in one direction will gravitate toward an unequivocal stance in that direction—in strong opposition to the stance taken by juries whose members consist of individuals who start out inclined, even mildly, in the other direction. And to the extent that particular juries start out with members of genuinely varying positions, deliberations are likely to propel them toward entrenched disagreement as individual jurors scramble to align themselves with their cultural peers and dissociate themselves from their cultural adversaries. Cultural polarization, within and across juries, will be the order of the day.

Although limited in number, verdicts in gun lawsuits bear out this surmise. After quickly concluding that expert "statistics" were irrelevant, the jury in *Hamilton* found itself unable to reach consensus on almost anything else. Beginning their deliberations deadlocked, the jurors remained so over the course of several excruciating days of emotionally assaultive deliberations.[65] "There was a lot of arguing, yelling and finger-pointing," one juror explained, as jurors (drawing on personal experience and anecdote) variously assaulted the gun industry as responsible for mass carnage, denied the extent of violent urban crime, and angrily disagreed about whether a finding of liability would open a floodgate of frivolous litigation. "Several jurors complained that the tension caused them physical pain," and one became violently ill and vomited during the course of the jury's discussions. After four days, the jurors sent the judge a note: "We are all very upset. We are starting to fight. We cannot reach a decision. We are emotionally drained and some of us feel physically ill!! Please, please give us more direction!!" The judge, Jack Weinstein, did just that, sternly advising the jurors: "Everybody has invested, including yourselves, too much in this case to allow you to throw up your hands prematurely." Two days later the jurors emerged with what was widely viewed as a nearly incomprehensible compromise verdict (one ultimately vacated as contrary to state law on appeal).[66] Another "advisory" jury in *NAACP v. AcuSport* likewise experienced a level of disagreement that prevented it from reaching a unanimous verdict.[67]

The hope that litigation outcomes might stimulate cultural dialogue in the legislative process is also idle. Multimillion-dollar verdicts in gun suits do surely invite response, but not of a culturally productive or accommodating kind. As we have emphasized, in the politics of risk regulation, factual dispute is simply cultural dispute by other means. What we believe depends on whom we trust, which in turn depends on what we care about. Thus, when others stubbornly resist our view of the facts, we naturally see them as attacking our worldviews and feel impelled to resist in cultural self-defense. That's why the gun control legislation (and, in the case of shall-issue laws, gun decontrol legislation) generates such impassioned conflict even when it is debated in purely empirical terms. There's no reason to think that verdicts against gun manufacturers, even when premised on a public safety rationale, will be seen as any less culturally threatening to those who attach positive social meanings to guns. Indeed, the rapid move to enact manufacturer immunity confirms that those individuals will aggressively respond with legislation that, no matter how seemingly instrumental in purpose, is ultimately motivated by (and opposed because of) its symbolic vindication of their values.[68]

Litigation, whether over guns or other culturally sensitive issues, systematically enhances cultural conflict in politics. This is in part an artifact of the way in which issues are framed in lawsuits, in which the winner inevitably takes all and the loser is saddled with a demoralizing loss of face.[69] But it is also a product of the preemptive-strike quality of litigation. By resorting to litigation, a party to a culturally charged politically charged dispute seeks to free itself of the constraints of a democratic process that might have forced it to listen and accommodate those who disagree and signals an intention to dictate its vision regardless of its appeal to members of the public. A move this brash and this alarming predictably energizes the other side—and ushers in a heightened state of cultural agitation in the political arena.[70] Cultural retaliation, not cultural logrolling, is what the new gun suits are likely to trigger.

III.   Conclusion

The litigation turn in the gun debate embodies the same two mistakes that pervade American gun politics generally. One is a basic misunderstanding of what the gun controversy is all about. Like most gun control legislation, gun lawsuits assume that what's at issue is what sorts of regulations will best promote public safety. What this view overlooks, however, is social meaning. Guns are at the center of an expressive struggle between the adherents of competing visions of the good society—one egalitarian and communal, the other hierarchic and individualistic. What gun laws *say* about the status of the groups who adhere to these visions matters at least as much to ordinary citizens as what gun laws will *do* to reduce or increase crime.

The second mistake concerns the process best calculated to resolve the American gun conflict. Consistent with the dominant approach to gun control policy-making, gun litigation assumes that the gun question can be settled by empirical methods. The attention that lawmakers, and now lawyers, pay to measuring the costs and benefits of gun regulation derives in part from the view that the gun debate is only about public safety. But the prominence of empirical methods also reflects a strategic or prudential concern on the part of many who understand full well the cultural underpinnings of the gun controversy. Precisely to *avoid* committing the law to picking sides in the struggle between the egalitarian and solidaristic proponents of control, on the one hand, and the hierarchic and individualistic opponents of it, on the other, some policymakers prefer the seemingly neutral idiom of econometrics.

But whatever motivates it, the preferred position of empirical methods is incapable of bringing the gun debate to a close. No matter how compelling, statistical proofs of the efficacy of gun control don't give citizens who care passionately about the meanings of guns a reason to change their minds. Indeed, precisely because they care so much about the values that guns express, individuals are unlikely to find compelling any statistics that purport to justify a gun policy contrary to the position they already prefer.

It's also idle to hope that empirical methods will reduce the intensity of cultural partisanship in the gun debate. The idea that it might do so reflects a naive understanding of the dynamics of expressive politics. Moderate citizens might find the apparent neutrality of costs and benefits appealing, but immoderate ones—those intent not just on avoiding cultural domination but on conquering their cultural adversaries—obviously won't. Seizing on the gun debate as an opportunity to deride their cultural adversaries and stigmatize them as deviants, they will prefer an unabashedly scornful expressive idiom. Control partisans thus ridicule their adversaries as "hicksville cowboy[s]," members of the "big belt buckle crowd"[71] whose love of guns stems from their "macho Freudian hang ups,"[72] while NRA president Charlton Heston declares "cultural war" against "blue blooded elitists" who threaten an "America . . . where you [can] . . . be white without feeling guilty, [and] own a gun without shame."[73]

But as obnoxious as these cultural extremists might seem, their messages cannot be easily ignored. Their language, however intolerant, resonates much more deeply with the social meanings of guns and gun control than do the statistics and the equations, the graphs and the figures, of the mainstream empirical debate. By assuming a posture of deliberate obtuseness in order to avoid giving offense, moderate commentators, politicians, and citizens cede the rhetorical stage to the expressive zealots. And as long as the zealots are the only ones with anything pertinent to say, the gun debate will remain divisive and unproductive.

The only way to resolve the gun debate is to correct the two mistakes that have deformed it over the course of the last half-century. *Moderate* citizens must openly attend not just to the consequences that gun control laws promote but to the cultural values they express. And they must do so through a deliberative process that makes it possible for individuals of diverse cultural orientations to see their identities affirmed rather than denigrated by the law.

Resolving culturally grounded political conflict isn't easy, but it *is* possible. Armed with a pertinent but pluralistic expressive idiom, those who favor compromise and accommodation will finally stand a fighting chance to defeat those who insist that everyone see only their vision of America.

PART II

Perspectives on Gun Litigation

CHAPTER 5

Private Lawyers, Public Lawsuits:
Plaintiffs' Attorneys in
Municipal Gun Litigation

HOWARD M. ERICHSON

One of the most telling details about modern mass tort litigation is this: the leading group of lawyers representing municipalities in their gun lawsuits was not a law firm but rather an ad hoc coalition of plaintiffs' lawyers who forged an alliance a decade ago for the sole purpose of suing the tobacco industry.

The group that represented New Orleans in the first municipal gun lawsuit, and subsequently filed suits on behalf of Atlanta, Cleveland, Cincinnati, Newark, and Wilmington, goes by the name Castano Safe Gun Litigation Group. "Castano" is not the name of one of the group's lawyers, nor is it the name of a handgun victim. Peter Castano was a smoker who died of lung cancer in 1993 at the age of forty-seven. His friend Wendell Gauthier, a prominent mass tort lawyer, vowed to pursue the cigarette makers with a force never before seen on the plaintiffs' side. Gauthier gathered over sixty of the nation's top plaintiffs' firms into a coalition to pursue a nationwide class action on behalf of Peter Castano's widow and some sixty million other nicotine-addicted persons or their families. The Castano Group, as the coalition came to be known, amassed a huge war chest and a wealth of legal talent and nearly succeeded in its efforts to obtain a nationwide class action or to negotiate a nationwide settlement. In 1996, a federal court of appeals decertified the nationwide class action, and the Castano Group turned its efforts to statewide tobacco class actions in a number of state courts. As the tobacco work faded, Gauthier became interested in pursuing another industry—guns. He persuaded about half of the coalition to join him in the new venture. Thus began the Castano Safe Gun Litigation Group, operating out of the same office space the group had established in downtown New Orleans as the headquarters for its tobacco operations. The fact that an ad hoc alliance of plaintiffs' lawyers formed for a particular class action should have continuing vitality for a subsequent mass tort speaks volumes about the business of mass tort practice and the role of plaintiffs' lawyers in generating and sustaining new mass tort litigation.

It ought to seem odd, perhaps, to focus on the role of private plaintiffs' lawyers in the gun litigation. The gun suits are, after all, public policy litigation at heart; the key plaintiffs in the recent wave of litigation were not individuals or class representatives but government entities seeking regulatory reform through injunctive relief and the threat of damages. When municipalities file suits casting blame on the firearms industry for the scourge of handgun violence on city streets, one reasonably might think that it is a story about the government's use of lawsuits for achieving policy goals, a story of social change litigation pursued by political actors. One would not necessarily think that it is a story of entrepreneurial initiatives by contingent fee trial lawyers. But the course of mass tort litigation in the past decade leaves no doubt about the importance of considering the role of private plaintiffs' lawyers and monetary incentives.

Without contingent fee plaintiffs' lawyers, the recent wave of gun litigation might not have materialized. It was private lawyers who drove the discussions that led to the filing of the first public entity lawsuit in New Orleans. It was, in part, private lawyers who encouraged other municipalities to join the fray. And it was private lawyers who poured their own resources into the litigation, laying millions of dollars on the line in a risky investment. Examining the role of plaintiffs' lawyers in the gun suits not only offers a richer story than simply one of political actors pursuing policy aims but also highlights the investment mentality that increasingly brings public policy debates to the courtroom.

We must be careful, however, not to exaggerate the centrality of trial lawyers' involvement in the gun litigation or to assume too neat a distinction between the strategic positions of contingent fee lawyers and political actors. Too many have mistakenly assumed that the gun litigation can be explained almost entirely as a sequel to the tobacco litigation, where mass tort lawyers played an indispensable role and where some of them earned fees of unprecedented proportions. While the gun litigation resonates with echoes of the tobacco litigation, each mass tort ultimately must be understood on its own terms.

A look at the role of plaintiffs' lawyers in the gun litigation suggests a more complex story than the now familiar refrain that trial lawyers, driven by greed, have co-opted legislative and regulatory power in order to soak money from one industry after another. The gun litigation is a story of mixed motives—moral, political, and financial—by diverse actors on the plaintiffs' side. Like tobacco, it involved several sets of players whose interests converged in the pursuit of an injurious industry. Like tobacco, it involved public entities that turned to elite mass tort plaintiffs' lawyers to supply the resources and litigation experience to pursue difficult tort litigation. And like tobacco, it involved mass tort lawyers who, frustrated in their attempts to use class actions to magnify the claims against their target, turned to government lawsuits as an alternative means to aggregate the litigation. But the gun litigation presented a unique set of alliances and rifts, in which gun control advocates faced fundamental disagreements among themselves concerning trial strategy, mayors with different political ambitions pursued different litigation paths, and the private mass tort lawyers found themselves embraced by some municipal plaintiffs and eschewed by others.

Activists, Politicians, and Trial Lawyers

The cast of characters in any public policy mass tort litigation includes three loosely defined groups of players on the plaintiffs' side: the activists, the politicians, and the trial lawyers. It is not difficult to place most of the leading players into one or another of the three categories, based in part on the extent to which their work is driven by policy, politics, or money. In the firearms litigation, the activists included Dennis Henigan of the Brady Center's Legal Action Project, Joshua Horwitz of the Educational Fund to Stop Gun Violence, and Professor David Kairys of Temple Law School. The politicians included Mayors Edward Rendell of Philadelphia, Marc Morial of New Orleans, and Richard Daley of Chicago, as well as New York State Attorney General Eliot Spitzer and Secretary of Housing and Urban Development Andrew Cuomo. The trial lawyers included Wendell Gauthier, Daniel Abel,

John Coale, Stanley Chesley, and Elizabeth Cabraser, all of whom participated actively in the tobacco litigation and other mass torts prior to their involvement in the gun cases.

While the activists, politicians, and trial lawyers approached the litigation with somewhat different sets of motivations and a different agenda, their motives overlapped in important ways. Indeed, one of the best ways to understand what makes public policy mass tort litigation viable is to examine the extent to which the interests of the three groups converge. At the same time, each mass tort displays different coalitions and divisions, which often cut across the more obvious groupings. In the handgun cases, different motivations and incentives drove participants on the plaintiffs' side to adopt different legal theories and settlement postures.

It was not until 1998 that the elite mass tort plaintiffs' bar turned its attention to guns and that courtrooms became a focal point for the gun control debate. Prior to that, individual plaintiffs had sued the firearms industry without success, although the *Hamilton v. Accu-Tek* case,[1] filed in 1995 in federal court in Brooklyn, drew widespread attention and had some initial success. Interestingly, the lawyer for the *Hamilton* plaintiffs had mass tort experience in the DES and breast implant litigation.[2] But it was the municipal lawsuits that drew the interest of the heavy hitters of the mass tort plaintiffs' bar and that brought the handgun litigation to national prominence. The municipal gun litigation can teach us about the role of private lawyers in public lawsuits and about the ways in which plaintiffs' lawyers of different stripes see their interests converge and diverge in public policy mass tort litigation. This chapter will look at the story of the key plaintiffs' lawyers in the public gun suits, particularly in the critical early stages of the litigation, and will then turn to an analysis of several aspects of that story.

Public Nuisance Advocates: The Philadelphia and Chicago Stories

The story of municipal gun litigation begins in earnest in 1996, when David Kairys advanced his strategy for suing the handgun industry on a public nuisance theory. Kairys, a law professor and civil rights lawyer, became immersed in the problem of handgun violence as a member of a Philadelphia task force on youth violence. Interested in reducing the availability of cheap handguns on Philadelphia streets, Kairys turned his attention to litigation options and focused on a strategy of municipal lawsuits against manufacturers, based on the legal theory that irresponsible marketing of handguns constituted a public nuisance.[3]

In late 1996, Kairys urged Philadelphia mayor Edward Rendell to consider pursuing a public nuisance suit against firearms makers. Rendell hired Kairys, at an hourly rate of $150, to draft a complaint. To learn more about suing the firearms industry, Kairys reached out to others who had been active in gun control work. He contacted Stephen Teret and Jon Vernick at the Johns Hopkins Center for Gun Policy and Research; Joshua Horwitz, a lawyer and gun control advocate who later represented the NAACP in its lawsuit against the gun industry; and attorney Elisa Barnes, who represented the plaintiffs in the *Hamilton* case. Kairys made contact with the Brady Center's Legal Action Project but avoided involving that organization as cocounsel in the lawsuit due to the mayor's concern that the gun control group's involvement would exacerbate the political tensions surrounding any lawsuit against the firearms industry.[4]

By the summer of 1997, Kairys was prepared to file the complaint, but the plans fell apart. Ten days before the lawsuit was to be filed, news of the lawsuit leaked to the press. Under public scrutiny and political pressure, Rendell balked at filing the complaint, and over the ensuing months Kairys came to realize that Rendell was unlikely to go forward with the nuisance claim against the gun manufacturers.[5] Some have speculated that Rendell, with gubernatorial aspirations, could not afford to alienate the large number of Pennsylvanians with pro-gun sentiments outside of Philadelphia.[6]

Frustrated with the mayor's failure to pursue the gun lawsuit, Kairys withdrew from representing Philadelphia in January 1998 and pursued the idea elsewhere. He sent copies of a paper he had written to over one hundred municipal lawyers across the country, offering his plan for lawsuits against the gun makers.[7] Mayor Rendell, rather than filing the suit, pursued talks with the gun industry about reforming industry practices. Rendell spoke at the U.S. Conference of Mayors in June 1998, praising efforts to bring the gun manufacturers to the negotiating table.[8] Kairys had failed in his initial attempt to generate a Philadelphia lawsuit, but his public nuisance strategy would take hold elsewhere.

In Chicago, the public nuisance strategy developed along a different path. Chicago had some of the most restrictive gun control ordinances in the country and a staunch gun control advocate in Mayor Richard Daley, but the city suffered from severe gang violence as guns continued to flood into the city.[9] In 1997, Mayor Daley asked the city's deputy corporation counsel, Lawrence Rosenthal, whether he could fashion a legal theory to hold the gun industry liable.[10] Rosenthal initially considered the problem in terms of product liability law and expected to respond to the mayor that product defect claims were unlikely to succeed.[11] But to learn more, Rosenthal met with officers from the Chicago Police Department gun unit. From the gun unit officers, and by looking at trace data on guns that had been used in crimes, he learned that Chicago gang members obtained their guns from a relatively small number of dealers outside the city limits.[12] Based on this information, he began thinking less about product liability and more about public nuisance.[13] As Rosenthal pursued the public nuisance idea, David Kairys learned that Rosenthal was making inquiries about the theory and contacted him. Rosenthal and Kairys began working together to turn the theory into a litigation reality.[14]

A former federal prosecutor, Rosenthal approached the problem with a law enforcement mentality. In August 1998, Chicago launched an elaborate three-month police undercover operation to gather evidence for the planned public nuisance suit. "Operation Gunsmoke" revealed that firearms dealers in Chicago's suburbs knowingly supplied guns to purchasers for criminal uses and for illegal possession in Chicago.[15] Information from the undercover operation would become a centerpiece of the city's complaint.[16] By November 1998, Daley and Rosenthal would be ready to go forward with Chicago's lawsuit, and the city lawyers enlisted the help of two Chicago law firms that agreed to work on the case pro bono.[17]

Product Liability Lawyers: The New Orleans Story

While the Philadelphia public interest lawyer-professor and the Chicago city lawyers pursued their ideas for reforming the gun industry through public nuisance litigation, a very different group of players began planning their own strategy for litigating against the gun industry. Wendell

Gauthier, the architect of the nationwide tobacco class action, was looking for a new target.

To understand Gauthier's entry into the gun litigation, we first must turn to his role in suing the tobacco companies and particularly his leadership of the Castano Group. By the time Peter Castano died of lung cancer, Gauthier already had developed a reputation as a highly successful trial lawyer with a style that combined expensive suits and down-home mannerisms, a mischievous sense of humor, and, above all, an ability to sign up clients wherever disaster struck. He had represented large numbers of plaintiffs in litigation arising out of the Continental Grain explosion, the MGM Grand Hotel fire, the Union Carbide chemical leak in Bhopal, the San Juan DuPont Plaza Hotel fire, the 1982 Pan Am air crash, and silicone gel breast implants.[18] With the wealth that he had accumulated from mass tort fees, Gauthier's small firm in Metairie, Louisiana, just outside New Orleans, had the resources to litigate at a top level, and Gauthier had earned a place among the nation's elite plaintiffs' lawyers.

But there was no plaintiffs' firm in the country with sufficient resources to litigate against the tobacco industry on a level playing field. For forty years, from 1954 to 1994, hundreds of plaintiffs had filed lawsuits against tobacco companies, with zero victories or settlements.[19] The tobacco defendants' strategy during this period involved, among other things, encouraging plaintiffs to drop their claims by making litigation intolerably expensive, and the strategy often succeeded.

Gauthier sought to level the field by creating an all-star team of plaintiffs' lawyers and amassing a sufficient war chest to allow the group to pursue the litigation without significant budgetary restraint. Each firm contributed at least one hundred thousand dollars toward litigation expenses. The group grew to include over sixty firms and many of the biggest names in the plaintiffs' bar: Peter Angelos, Melvin Belli, Elizabeth Cabraser, Stanley Chesley, John Coale, Russ Herman, Ron Motley, Dianne Nast, John O'Quinn, and many others.[20] The group filed a class action in federal court in Louisiana against the cigarette manufacturers on behalf of Peter Castano's widow and a class of some sixty million others. The group won certification of the *Castano v. American Tobacco Co.* nationwide class action in the district court, only to watch it get decertified by the federal court of appeals during a wave of appellate rejections of mass tort class actions.[21] The Castano Group proceeded to file statewide tobacco class actions around the country, which have not, on the whole, encountered much success.[22] The group played a peripheral role in the multibillion-dollar settlements between the tobacco companies and the state attorneys general in 1997 and 1998, although a number of the individual lawyers who had participated in the Castano effort went on to represent the states in their lawsuits. For the most part, the Castano leadership had wagered that the breakthrough tobacco litigation would be a class action and watched from the sidelines as the state recoupment lawsuits brought the cigarette makers to the bargaining table and brought massive fees to the states' contingent fee lawyers.

By the spring of 1998, as the Castano tobacco prospects diminished, Gauthier set his sights on guns. To Gauthier, tobacco and handguns both were dangerous products, causing widespread harm that imposed costs not only on individuals but also on society as a whole and manufactured by industries that were politically difficult to regulate. He saw handguns as unreasonably dangerous and the gun industry's conduct as negligent. Suing corporations for harm caused by dangerous products and negligent conduct was precisely what he knew how to do best.

Gauthier recognized that gun litigation would require a strong coalition of plaintiffs' attorneys. Rather than create a group from scratch, he and his partner, Daniel Abel, sought to draw the Castano Group's attention to guns. In May 1998, Gauthier pitched the idea to Stanley Chesley, a veteran mass torts lawyer and Castano Group member. According to Abel, Gauthier overcame Chesley's initial skepticism with the argument that gun lawsuits "fit the Castano philosophy of the plaintiffs' bar as a de facto fourth branch of government, achieving by litigation what had failed legislatively."[23] Gauthier also early on persuaded core Castano member John Coale, whom Gauthier had first met competing for clients in Bhopal, to join the effort.[24] Ultimately, thirty-seven firms—about half of the Castano Group lawyers—agreed to participate in the gun litigation. The participating firms in the Castano Safe Gun Litigation Group each contributed fifty thousand dollars in lawyer time and cash, with only twenty-five hundred dollars up front.[25] This represented a significantly smaller investment than the money and time each firm put into the Castano tobacco effort.

The Castano lawyers knew mass tort litigation as well as anyone, but they needed someone on board who knew gun litigation. For that expertise, they turned to Dennis Henigan of the Legal Action Project, the litigation branch of the Brady Center to Prevent Handgun Violence.[26] Henigan had left a partnership at the law firm of Foley & Lardner in 1989 to pursue public interest litigation through the Legal Action Project,[27] which offers pro bono representation to victims in suits against the gun industry. As a lawyer who had been pursuing lawsuits against gun manufacturers for years, Henigan arguably knew more about gun litigation and the gun industry than anyone else on the plaintiffs' side. Municipal lawsuits offered an opportunity for Henigan to put his knowledge of gun litigation to work with perhaps a greater chance of success than individual suits, which had proved difficult to win. Unlike those involved in the Philadelphia case, which avoided overt involvement by Henigan due to political concerns over the appearance of a gun control group in the case, the Castano Group welcomed Henigan's assistance.

Gauthier's gun litigation team took shape without a client. Soon, however, his hometown would give him the opportunity to fire the first shot in the municipal gun litigation. The October 1998 murder of New Orleans gospel legend Raymond Myles—shot with his own handgun—set the political stage for action against handgun makers. Mayor Marc Morial, who had known Myles since childhood, felt that the death could have been prevented by "smart gun" technology that would allow guns to be fired only by their owners. As a state senator, Morial unsuccessfully had sought to introduce anti-gun legislation. Now, as mayor, he considered litigation as an alternative means to achieve the same end. Morial was aware that a number of other municipalities were contemplating lawsuits against the gun industry; he saw this as an appealing option in a state where gun control legislation would be impossible to pass. Ten days after the Myles murder, Morial met with Gauthier to discuss the possibility of a lawsuit.[28] New Orleans retained the Castano Group to represent the city on a contingent fee basis: the attorneys would get 20 percent of the recovery if the case settled and 30 percent if it went to trial verdict. When asked later why he turned to top private plaintiffs' lawyers to handle the city's lawsuit, Mayor Morial responded, "You want lawyers who can take on giants."[29]

On October 31, 1998, Gauthier filed suit on behalf of the City of New Orleans against fifteen gun manufacturers. Abel and Henigan drafted the New Orleans complaint in terms of product liability, alleging that the manufacturers had failed to incorporate sufficient safety devices in their weapons, thereby making them unreasonably dangerous.[30] Gauthier signed the complaint with perhaps the oddest signature line in the annals of mass tort litigation: Wendell H. Gauthier, "Personally and for All Participating Castano Tobacco Attorneys."

Less than two weeks after the New Orleans complaint, Chicago filed its own lawsuit against the gun industry.[31] The two suits' temporal proximity makes it tempting to view them as a coordinated one-two punch by the plaintiffs. But, in fact, the contrast between the New Orleans and Chicago suits—in terms of the lawyering on the plaintiffs' side—could hardly be sharper. New Orleans turned to nationally prominent mass tort lawyers working on a contingent fee basis. Those lawyers conceived the lawsuit in familiar mass tort terms—as a claim about a defective product based on inadequate safety features. Chicago, by contrast, eschewed the private plaintiffs' bar. Deputy corporation counsel Lawrence Rosenthal emphasized that Chicago avoided using contingent fee lawyers to ensure that the lawsuit would be driven by public policy issues.[32] Instead, Chicago relied on its own city lawyers, aided by the investigatory work of the police department and with input from Professor Kairys. After it had developed its theory of the case and was ready to go forward, Chicago brought in two law firms on a pro bono basis. In contrast to the product liability theory pursued by the mass tort lawyers in New Orleans, Chicago's city lawyers favored a public nuisance theory. Whereas the New Orleans complaint looks like a mass tort case, the Chicago complaint resonates with the language of law enforcement.

After New Orleans and Chicago, other municipalities joined the fray. In January 1999, Bridgeport and Miami filed suit. Bridgeport, represented by a Connecticut law firm with assistance from the Legal Action Project, asserted both product defect and public nuisance claims, as well as a deceptive advertising claim.[33] Miami, also assisted by the Legal Action Project, focused on product defect claims, like the New Orleans complaint.[34] In the succeeding months, the Castano lawyers filed suits for Atlanta, Cleveland, Cincinnati, Newark, and Wilmington.[35] The benefits of the nationwide alliance were evident as the Castano Group sought to interest various cities in their services. In Cleveland, local Castano member John Climaco called the mayor to discuss the possibility of a firearms suit.[36] Prominent Cincinnati mass tort lawyer Stanley Chesley, also of the Castano Group, persuaded his city's Justice Committee to go forward with the lawsuit.[37]

As the municipal suits multiplied, more mass tort plaintiffs' lawyers jumped in. When San Francisco and Los Angeles filed their lawsuits in May 1999, they were represented by the nation's two leading class action law firms, Milberg, Weiss, Bershad, Hayes & Lerach and Lieff, Cabraser, Heimann & Bernstein. Elizabeth Cabraser, of the latter firm, had been an executive committee member of the Castano Group for the tobacco nationwide class action and had argued that group's motion for class certification. Subsequent tobacco work by Cabraser and her firm had created a rift between her and the other Castano members, however. When Cabraser's firm entered the gun litigation on behalf of thirteen California municipalities and counties, it did so independently rather than with the Castano Safe Gun Litigation Group. The Lieff Cabraser firm also served as co-counsel in gun suits brought by Boston and Camden, and when Philadelphia finally filed its lawsuit in April 2000—after Edward Rendell had left the mayor's office—Lieff Cabraser was on the complaint along with Philadelphia plaintiffs' firm Kohn, Swift & Graf. The firm of Cohen, Milstein, Hausfeld & Toll, which specializes in plaintiff class actions, served as co-counsel in the Camden, Los Angeles, and Philadelphia cases.

Within two years after Wendell Gauthier broached the gun idea with his Castano colleagues, many of the nation's leading mass tort plaintiffs' lawyers had entered the municipal gun litigation. Because of the gun litigation's strong public policy element, those private contingent fee lawyers found themselves working alongside other lawyers whose orientation was not that of trial lawyers but rather of activists or politicians. In most of the cases, Dennis Henigan and his public interest law colleagues at the Legal Action Project served as co-counsel with the private lawyers. Professor David Kairys worked on a number of the suits as well.

On the political side, the mayors and their city lawyers naturally were central figures in the municipal lawsuits, especially in Chicago, where the city handled its own litigation, did not retain contingent fee lawyers, and brought in pro bono counsel only after the city had already prepared its suit. But the gun litigation involved political figures beyond the municipalities. New York became the first state to sue the gun industry when state attorney general Eliot Spitzer saw the litigation as an opportunity to impose a code of conduct on the industry.[38] At the federal level, President Clinton and Secretary of Housing and Urban Development Andrew Cuomo considered a possible federal lawsuit against the gun industry;³⁹ Cuomo was instrumental in a March 2000 settlement with Smith & Wesson.⁴⁰

While a number of the lawsuits were dismissed by judges, the more interesting fact for our examination of the role of plaintiffs' lawyers is that two of the lawsuits were voluntarily dismissed by the plaintiffs. Boston dropped its suit in March 2002, and Cincinnati abandoned its suit in May 2003. In Boston, the court had rejected defendants' motion to dismiss, but its other legal rulings had rendered the plaintiffs' case difficult to prove. The city, represented by the Lieff Cabraser firm and other private mass tort lawyers, dropped the suit as litigation costs mounted and the chance of recovery became slimmer.⁴¹ Cincinnati's voluntary dismissal was surprising, coming less than a year after the Ohio Supreme Court's ruling in the plaintiffs' favor, a ruling that the Legal Action Project had acclaimed as the "greatest victory yet against the gun industry." Stanley Chesley, the city's Castano Group lawyer, recommended that the city drop the case, telling the city council that success was unlikely. Chesley's firm reportedly had spent $425,551 in billable hours and $136,296 in expenses; he waived his right to collect the $100,000 that the city council had set aside for expenses.⁴² The Legal Action Project, Chesley's co-counsel in the case, expressed disappointment about the decision to drop the case.⁴³

The picture that emerges from the story of the municipal gun litigation is one in which activists, politicians, and trial lawyers all played essential roles and in which the tensions between and within these groups played out differently in different cities, as the municipalities decided whether to file lawsuits, which claims to assert, and whether to persist in the face of mounting expenses and long odds. The story sheds light on public lawsuits as aggregation mechanisms and as investment opportunities. It also sheds light on the different mind-sets of trial lawyers, activists, and politicians with regard to public policy mass tort litigation. But perhaps more significant, it demonstrates the importance of understanding each mass tort on its own terms.

Public Litigation as an Aggregation Mechanism

What makes public policy mass torts an appealing opportunity for private plaintiffs' lawyers? The private lawyers involved in the gun litigation—like those involved in the state tobacco lawsuits and lead paint lawsuits—were largely either personal injury trial lawyers or class action specialists who handled securities and antitrust class actions as well as mass torts. These were not, by most people's definition, public interest lawyers. They were drawn, however, to suits by public entities seeking to hold industries accountable for widespread harm.

For successful mass tort plaintiffs' lawyers, the business model generally relies upon representing large numbers of injured persons with similar claims. In litigation involving widespread harm, defendants view the litigation in terms of the risk of massive liability and invest in their defense accordingly. To present a viable challenge to such high-stakes defense, plaintiffs' lawyers must invest heavily in discovery, experts, trial preparation, and other resource-intensive litigation work. Individual client representation ordinarily cannot justify the resources required to litigate such cases. By aggregating the claims of many injured plaintiffs, firms take advantage of economies of scale to reduce the per-plaintiff cost of pursuing claims. By presenting stakes on the plaintiffs' side in line with those seen by the defendants, aggregation encourages plaintiffs' firms to invest in the litigation.

The standard approach to aggregating claims is through procedural joinder mechanisms, most notably class actions. Even without a class action or other formal judicial aggregation, mass tort claims increasingly are informally aggregated by mass collective representation—the representation of many similarly situated individual plaintiffs by a firm. By representing large numbers of plaintiffs, either through class action or mass collective representation, a law firm can achieve scale economies, higher stakes, and enhanced bargaining leverage.

Lawyers pursuing gun litigation, however, found themselves unable to use either class actions or mass collective representation. Those who sought class certification in gun cases failed on the grounds that common questions do not predominate over individual issues in the claims of various gun victims or on the grounds that a class action would not be a superior method for resolving the dispute.[44] The gun litigation did not lend itself to mass collective representation, either. Unlike plaintiffs in pharmaceutical product liability cases and certain other mass torts, victims of handgun violence and accidents are not so numerous as to enable any law firm to sign up hundreds or thousands of individual clients, nor are they so similar as to permit an assembly-line litigation process for a large inventory of claims.

Plaintiffs' lawyers who find themselves unable to aggregate litigation by obtaining class certification, or by representing a mass of individual clients, devise other means to the same ends. Government entity clients present a perfect opportunity for plaintiffs' lawyers to achieve the effect of aggregation without the need for class action or any other judicial joinder and without the need for signing up numerous clients.

When a government entity sues an injurious industry to recoup money spent by the government to address a problem of widespread harm, the lawsuit has the effect of combining damages related to a large number of injured persons. This creates the economies of scale and increased stakes that plaintiffs' lawyers need in order to invest sufficient resources in the litigation. The state lawsuits against the tobacco industry created extremely high stakes because the states sought to recover for medical and other costs paid for millions of smokers. Likewise, the municipal firearms lawsuits sought to recover for municipal expenditures involving masses of gun victims.

In this sense, lawsuits by government entities function as a kind of representative litigation. The class action device permits the most explicit form of representative litigation, in which class representatives sue on behalf of themselves and on behalf of a class of all others similarly situated. In government lawsuits, the government in essence sues as a representative of its citizens. While the nature of the litigative representation differs significantly in the two types of cases, both magnify the stakes sufficiently to attract top plaintiffs' lawyers and to permit them to invest heavily in the litigation.

Government lawsuits hold an additional appeal for plaintiffs' lawyers. Not only do public entity lawsuits accomplish an indirect form of aggregation, but they also help plaintiffs' lawyers circumvent defenses that have proved successful against individual plaintiffs in both tobacco and gun cases. In tobacco cases, juries often blame the smoker and have proved unwilling in most cases to reward smokers for self-imposed harm. The strength of the state lawsuits came, in part, from the fact that the plaintiffs were not the smokers themselves. It is much more difficult to blame the state for the lung cancer of many of its citizens. In gun lawsuits brought by individual victims, the defense may blame victims and gun owners for carelessness in cases involving accidental shootings, and in cases involving intentional shootings, a key defense is that the gun maker should not be liable for another's criminal wrongdoing. As David Kairys realized early on, "when you focus attention on particular shootings, there's always that person pulling the trigger who is more immediately to blame for the bloodshed."[45] As a matter of causation, plaintiffs in individual gun cases have difficulty proving that different industry conduct would have prevented a particular victim's shooting. Municipal gun lawsuits, by treating the harm on an aggregate level in terms of the cost to the municipality, remove attention from any individual shooting and thus diminish the power of defense arguments that focus on blameworthy victims, owners, or shooters. Thus, the public entity plaintiff in tobacco litigation is less vulnerable to the defendants' "blame the smoker" argument for contributory negligence, comparative fault, or assumption of risk, while the public entity plaintiff in gun litigation is less vulnerable to the defendants' "blame the shooter" argument for superseding cause or for challenging actual causation. In sum, for the plaintiffs' lawyers, pursuing aggregate damages through government lawsuits not only provides a more viable business model than individual lawsuits for cases of widespread harm but also reduces substantive vulnerabilities.

Public Litigation as an Investment Opportunity

The previous discussion concerning the appeal of public lawsuits to private lawyers presumes a certain mind-set on the part of the plaintiffs' lawyers, in which the lawyers evaluate litigation opportunities in terms of their cost and the likely return on investment. The idea of entrepreneurial lawyering, well established in the academic literature, is one often embraced by those who support the use of money damages lawsuits to accomplish policy objectives, citing the role of plaintiffs' lawyers as "private attorneys general." In the context of the gun litigation, however, the idea of fee-driven lawyers often appears as part of a critique of the lawyers and the lawsuits.

Walter Olson, in his book *The Rule of Lawyers*, complains that "[t]he plaintiffs' bar searches out deep-pocketed institutions to sue for all varieties of human misery and woe" and that the onslaught of municipal gun litigation was simply another step in what he views as the dangerous trend of regulating through litigation. He disapprovingly notes that "it was the outside trial lawyers and not the city mayors who had provided the impetus for the suits by pitching the idea at presentations to city officials behind closed doors."[46] In Olson's view, contingent fee trial lawyers drove the litigation and operated as simple profit maximizers: "From the trial lawyers' point of view . . . it was at best a waste of effort to campaign against rinky-dink dealers and near-assetless individual buyers when much deeper pockets could be found among gun manufacturers."[47] Similarly, Michael Krauss writes of the "unholy alliance between government and the plaintiff's bar" and asserts that both the state tobacco suits and the municipal gun suits "were concocted by a handful of private attorneys who entered into contingency fee contracts with public officials."[48] Olson and Krauss overstate the centrality of contingent fee lawyers in the municipal gun litigation and exaggerate the extent to which the litigation was driven solely by money. But the importance of entrepreneurial incentives in the gun litigation, as in other mass torts, cannot be gainsaid.

Whether one views entrepreneurial lawyering as a social good or as a betrayal of professional ideals, one can point to aspects of the municipal gun litigation that tend to show the importance of entrepreneurial incentives. A number of the lawsuits, including the first filed, were handled by private lawyers with contingent fee arrangements. Most of the private lawyers were experienced mass tort plaintiffs' lawyers who were able to put significant resources into the litigation because of fees they had amassed from prior mass torts, especially asbestos and tobacco. It is entirely appropriate, as a general matter, to understand the litigation expenditures of mass tort plaintiffs' firms as reinvestment of earnings. Law firms in the mass tort arena see new and emerging litigation in part as investment opportunities and choose where to invest based on the perceived strength of the investment. Involvement in an emerging mass tort offers a law firm an opportunity, in effect, to diversify the firm's investment portfolio. For the Castano lawyers, whose tobacco class actions had largely fizzled, the gun litigation presented a chance to invest in something that might be more promising.

To say that the trial attorneys view public policy mass tort litigation as an investment opportunity is not to say that contingent fee lawyers are indispensable to such litigation. Chicago's lawsuit went forward without contingent fee lawyers. Deputy Corporation Counsel Lawrence Rosenthal handled the case with other city lawyers and with the help of Chicago law enforcement officials. Although the Chicago complaint was filed shortly after the Castano Group's New Orleans suit, it would be unfair to describe the Chicago lawsuit as a follow-up to New Orleans or in any way dependent upon the earlier suit. The Chicago lawsuit developed along a separate track, including an undercover investigation that began several months before the New Orleans suit was filed.

In addition to work by city lawyers, the municipal plaintiffs in the gun litigation found substantial assistance available free of charge. Chicago's experience demonstrates the willingness of private law firms to provide pro bono work on cases with a strong public policy element. Dennis Henigan and the Legal Action Project, as part of the donor-supported Brady Center, worked as co-counsel or advisors in most of the cases, offering their legal services free of charge. The Legal Action Project's involvement, moreover, was not the only example of donor-supported gun litigation. In 1998, the Center on Crime, Communities & Culture, endowed by financier George Soros, donated three hundred thousand dollars to assist the plaintiffs in *Hamilton v. Accu-Tek*.[49]

Even if we focus solely on the Castano Group and other contingent fee lawyers, it is difficult to explain the gun litigation purely in entrepreneurial terms, and it would be an exaggeration to say that the lawyers were motivated solely by money. After seeing the unprecedented fees lawyers received from the state tobacco settlements, plaintiffs' lawyers may well have hoped to find another pot of gold. The plaintiffs' bar quickly realized, however, that there was no pot of gold to be found in the gun litigation. It is not simply that the claims were long shots. As of 1994, tobacco claims appeared equally unlikely to succeed. Speculative investments can be appealing if the potential return is high enough, which was the draw for the tobacco lawsuits. But the gun manufacturers lacked the deep pockets of the tobacco companies. The earnings of the gun industry, while over one billion dollars per year, was a tiny percent of the earnings of the tobacco companies.[50] Moreover, even before filing the New Orleans lawsuit, Wendell Gauthier had determined that the gun makers did not carry liability insurance.[51] In terms of sheer investment appeal, the gun suits paled in comparison to tobacco and a host of other mass torts.

If it is hard to justify the gun lawsuits purely as a rational investment in the anticipated recovery, then what explains the involvement of so many leading mass tort lawyers? One possibility is that they simply made a bad investment, but many of the difficulties with the gun lawsuits were clear from the start. A stronger possibility is that the investment in gun litigation can be explained as long as the potential investment return is understood in broader terms than the fees generated by gun settlements or verdicts. If a gun case puts a lawyer's name in the newspaper, then the investment offers a payoff in reputational value and long-term client development, even if the case generates zero fees. The more prominent the public policy mass tort, the easier it is to explain its attractiveness to private lawyers even if the litigation looks relatively weak as an investment.

Investment, of course, need not be the only explanation for lawyer involvement in particular litigation. Indeed, the tone of the gun litigation suggests that some of the trial lawyers were committed to the litigation because they believed in the cause. While a certain amount of speechifying may be dismissed as mere rhetoric, there are hints that commitment to the anti-gun cause ran deeper. Gauthier continued to devote himself to both the gun litigation and the tobacco litigation even as he fought the cancer that claimed his life in late 2001. "I was already in the fight against tobacco and was in the early planning stages for the gun litigation," Gauthier explained in an interview reported in a book coauthored by one of his partners. "I was leading these two legal armadas, which is one reason I kept my bout with cancer a guarded secret. Few outside of my family and close associates knew. Radiation and chemotherapy would have attracted attention to the disease and would, therefore, have hindered the two big causes that meant the most to me. In any case, the odds were on my side."[52] The same book goes on to state that "Gauthier never counted on making a dime from the gun suits. In fact, the courtroom battle promised to cost the Castano Litigation Group millions of dollars in expenses. . . . The New Orleans attorney viewed the fight for gun control as the crowning achievement of his career; he knew he was in pursuit of something far more important than money."[53] This account of Gauthier's motives may be no more credible than the opposing accounts that describe the private lawyers in gun litigation as interested solely in money; the truth likely lies somewhere in between. Finally, no doubt part of the attractiveness of the gun litigation for trial lawyers was the sheer sport of it. A seemingly invulnerable industry makes an appealing conquest. As reported by Matt Labash, in his revealing account of the Castano gun lawyers, "[t]hose who know Gauthier best say litigation for him is not just about the settlements—or even the beloved children—it's about the contest."[54]

An appraisal of plaintiffs' lawyers' motives in public policy mass tort litigation must account for these other motives—reputation, genuine policy concerns, and the thrill of conquest—in addition to financial incentives. Self-promotion blends with self-identity as lawyers vie for the right to say, "I was there for that battle." Even so, an investment mind-set explains much of the conduct of the private lawyers in the municipal gun litigation. It explains their willingness to invest in the gun litigation but at a significantly lower level than in the tobacco litigation, given the lower expected return. It arguably explains their focus on a product liability theory, which lends itself to money damages. And it explains the willingness of contingent fee lawyers to drop the Boston and Cincinnati suits as their expenses escalated, despite favorable judicial rulings in both of those cities' cases.

Public Lawsuits, Private Lawyers, and Multiple Mind-sets

The story of the municipal gun litigation shows that the motivations of the three major groups of players on the plaintiffs' side—activists, politicians, and trial lawyers—are more complex than simply policy, politics, or money. As a starting point, it is reasonable to assume that financial considerations drive contingent fee lawyers more strongly than they drive the activists and politicians. The very notion of private attorneys general relies on the salience of entrepreneurial incentives for plaintiffs' lawyers. The conduct of private lawyers in the gun litigation bears out that contingent fee lawyers' decisions are driven, in part, by an investment mentality. Investment-based litigation decisions do not always correspond to the decisions that government officials would make as a matter of policy or politics. Indeed, this difference in mind-set forms the basis for some of the legitimate concerns that have been raised concerning the use of contingent fee agreements by public entity clients.

The difference between trial lawyers and others in pursuing public policy mass torts extends to the theories they tend to emphasize and the way they approach litigation. Private lawyers naturally bring a mass tort/product liability orientation, whereas public lawyers are more likely to bring a law enforcement orientation. The Castano Group's complaints in New Orleans and other cities relied largely on traditional product liability theories and focused upon handguns as defective products based on missing safety features. Other than damages, the approach mirrored what might have been asserted in an individual tort lawsuit or in a class action brought by handgun victims. Chicago's complaint, by contrast, relied on a public nuisance theory and focused largely on the handgun industry's methods of distribution. Moreover, whereas the Castano Group relied on usual mass tort discovery methods to gather evidence, Chicago's city lawyers gathered much of their evidence through a three-month police undercover investigation prior to filing the complaint. Many of the most interesting tensions in the gun litigation, however, occur not between the private lawyers and public lawyers but within groups.

Among politicians, the gun litigation played out very differently at the city and state levels. Big city mayors, on the whole, found the gun lawsuits appealing. Marc Morial of New Orleans and Richard Daley of Chicago, the first two mayors to file suits against the firearms industry, both were long-standing proponents of gun control. They and their constituents bore much of the cost of handgun violence and saw litigation as a way to address the problem. At the state level, gun owners and the NRA held greater sway. The citizens of rural Louisiana, Illinois, and Pennsylvania possessed very different attitudes about gun control than did the citizens of New Orleans, Chicago, and Philadelphia. A number of the cities, after filing their lawsuits, found themselves facing new state legislation immunizing gun makers from liability. Georgia's legislature enacted a protective statute only five days after Atlanta filed its complaint. And Philadelphia, where Professor Kairys first proposed his public nuisance idea, did not even file its lawsuit until the mayor's office was no longer occupied by a gubernatorial aspirant. In New York, by contrast, Attorney General Eliot Spitzer took an active role in the gun litigation, both as amicus curiae in private litigation and as the driving force behind the state's own lawsuit against the gun industry.

Among activists and law enforcers, despite sharing a common agenda on gun control, important differences emerged as to how to approach the municipal gun litigation. David Kairys and Lawrence Rosenthal both preferred a public nuisance theory that focused on distribution methods that allowed illegal guns to flood into cities, while Dennis Henigan enthusiastically embraced the Castano Group and its product defect approach. The difference is no minor tactical disagreement; it goes to the heart of the litigation. Later complaints tended to include both theories, but the decisions on how to frame the early lawsuits reveal much about the mind-sets of the decision makers. For Kairys and Rosenthal, the core problem was inner-city violence, especially handgun shootings involving drugs or gangs. The absence of trigger locks or smart gun technology had little bearing on these problems. Thus, they turned to a theory that addressed the very presence of guns in the city.

Henigan, however, was concerned not only about intentional shootings by owners but also about accidental shootings and unauthorized users. The Legal Action Project therefore threw its weight behind lawsuits that emphasized the absence of gun safety features, as well as lawsuits that also incorporated public nuisance theories. While both inner-city violence and accidental or unauthorized shootings present serious problems worthy of attention by public interest lawyers in a gun control nonprofit organization, it is plausible that, for the Brady Center's donor base, gang and drug shootings are not the most immediate concern. To many supporters of the gun control organization, the most pressing fears may concern the harm that could occur if children find an unlocked gun in a neighbor's house or if a Columbine copycat takes his father's gun to school. For constituents with these concerns, litigation that presses for trigger locks to prevent accidental shootings and for smart gun technology to prevent unauthorized use by nonowners surely resonates. For the law professor David Kairys or for the Chicago city lawyers, with no suburban donor base to satisfy, the public nuisance theory made more sense.

One can see why the product defect approach came naturally to the Castano Group and other trial lawyers, given their experience and success litigating such claims in other mass torts. One can see, as well, why it held some appeal for the Legal Action Project, given the likely concerns of some of its constituents. But what about Mayor Morial of New Orleans, who filed the first municipal gun lawsuit, which relied on the product defect theory? One might have expected the mayor to view the matter much as did Mayor Daley in Chicago. It may have been an odd factual twist that sealed the use of the product defect theory in New Orleans. Gospel singer Raymond Myles, whose murder was the catalyst for that city's gun lawsuit, was killed with his own Lorcin pistol. The murder, according to the plaintiffs, could have been prevented had the gun included the safety features they urged. Thus, Wendell Gauthier, Dennis Henigan, and Marc Morial—coming from the very different perspectives of trial lawyer, activist, and politician—saw their interests converge around the prospect of a municipal gun lawsuit for product liability.

The story of private plaintiffs' lawyers in the public gun litigation appears at first glance to suggest several themes concerning public policy mass torts. One theme might be the convergence of activists, politicians, and trial lawyers and the different mind-sets they bring to litigation. Another theme might be the use of public entity lawsuits as an aggregation mechanism by mass tort lawyers unable to obtain class certification. Yet another theme concerns entrepreneurial incentives and the investment mind-set of mass tort lawyers. Closer examination of the gun litigation, however, reveals that several of these possible themes are too simplistic to be applied usefully across a spectrum of mass torts. True, contingent fee lawyers drive most mass tort litigation and public policy mass torts bring together three major categories of players on the plaintiffs' side, but in the gun litigation, the noteworthy fault lines appeared within these groups as often as they appeared between them. The split between politicians at the city and state level and the split between public nuisance advocates and product liability lawyers proved more significant than the differences between activists, politicians, and trial lawyers.

Investment-minded contingent fee lawyers drive much mass tort litigation, but the gun litigation is harder than most to explain in purely entrepreneurial terms, given the difficulty of the claims and the relative lack of deep-pocketed defendants. Moreover, the heightened political and moral context of the gun litigation affects the motivations of some of the trial lawyers, even as it renders those private lawyers somewhat less essential to the cause by attracting activists, politicians, and their donors and supporters.

These fault lines, particular to firearms litigation, highlight the importance of understanding each mass tort on its own terms, even as we appreciate the broader themes and patterns. The choice of emphasizing public nuisance or product defect in a public entity recoupment lawsuit may come up in other cases, but it played out in the firearms litigation in a way that was particular to guns. Those primarily concerned about gang and drug shootings focused on gun distribution channels and thus emphasized a public nuisance theory, whereas those who cared most about accidental shootings and unauthorized users focused on trigger locks and smart guns and thus emphasized a product liability theory.

Similarly, political fault lines appear in other mass torts, but differently. In the tobacco litigation, the most salient political differences do not pit cities against states but rather involve tobacco-growing states, where the industry has the most clout, and states such as California, which has a lower tolerance for smoking. On the lobbying front, the tobacco industry has long held substantial power, unlike the gun manufacturers. But whereas cigarette smokers lack organization and do not constitute a particularly powerful interest group, gun users—represented by the NRA—possess undeniable power and wield it unabashedly.

The link between the tobacco and firearms litigation, so palpably embodied in the Castano tobacco group's renewed life as a gun litigation group, suggests that public policy mass torts display certain common features and develop along similar lines. It also suggests that private contingent fee lawyers play an important if controversial role. Scratching the surface of the gun litigation, however, we see not merely contingent fee lawyers but multiple groups of players whose interests converge and diverge in ways that are particular to the gun litigation.

CHAPTER 6

The NRA, the Brady Campaign, & the Politics of Gun Litigation

TIMOTHY D. LYTTON

The military strategist Karl von Clausewitz asserted that war is a continuation of politics by other means.[1] The same might be said of gun litigation. For many big city mayors and gun control advocates, filing lawsuits against the firearms industry represents a way to pursue gun control policies that they have failed to achieve through the political process. Efforts to pass laws mandating safer gun designs and imposing marketing restrictions have for many decades been thwarted by the National Rifle Associate (NRA) and its legislative allies. The mayors and gun control advocates blame their failure to achieve stricter gun laws on NRA corruption of the legislative process. So they have turned to the courts, asking judges to impose gun controls that they believe would otherwise be passed by an uncorrupted legislative process.

In response to these lawsuits, the gun industry, with help from the NRA, has turned to state legislatures and Congress for protection. Together, they have introduced bills seeking statutory immunity from suit in forty-six state legislatures and Congress, and industry immunity laws have been passed in thirty-two states, including Texas, Florida, Pennsylvania, Virginia, Georgia, Michigan, and Ohio. Supporters of these immunity bills have argued that plaintiffs are misusing the tort system, seeking through litigation gun control regulations that they have been unable to achieve legislatively, and filing municipal suits en masse in order to create overwhelming defense costs that will force the industry to settle, regardless of the legal merits of the claims against it.

Proponents of the lawsuits respond that the gun lobby's success in obtaining statutory immunity merely confirms its undue legislative influence, which explains the need for filing lawsuits in the first place. Furthermore, proponents of the suits point out that the industry's statutory immunity undermines the integrity of the tort system, determining liability on the basis of political muscle rather than judicial procedure. Thus, while the gun industry and its supporters accuse plaintiffs of misusing the court system in order to subvert legislative democracy, plaintiffs and their allies accuse the gun lobby of corrupting the legislative process and undermining judicial independence.

Both sides in the controversy over gun litigation have sought to gain an advantage by using one branch of government in order to compensate for lack of influence within another. The debate is no longer merely about the merits of gun control but also about whether to hold the debate in the statehouse or the courthouse. In this chapter, I critically examine the arguments of both sides. On the one hand, I question gun control advocates' justification of gun litigation as a response to legislative failure. There is reason to be skeptical of the claim that NRA influence has corrupted the legislative process and that this justifies recourse to the courts as a way to circumvent the legislative process altogether. On the other hand, I challenge defendants' use of immunity legislation to stifle litigation. Broad grants of statutory immunity undermine the integrity of the judicial process by resolving lawsuits on the basis of political power rather than legal principle, and they impair the capacity of courts to play a supportive role in refining and enforcing the legislature's own regulatory policies.

Both sides have taken extreme positions: insisting that either all of the litigation is justified or none of it is. If the first casualty of war is truth, then the first casualty of gun litigation has been moderation. In this chapter, I outline an intermediate position between these two extremes. In criticizing the use of gun litigation to circumvent the legislative process, I do not mean to reject all lawsuits against the gun industry, nor do I mean to deny that suits setting forth viable common law claims may have implications for the legislative process and that these implications play a legitimate role in the legislative process. Correlatively, in arguing against broad grants of legislative immunity for the industry, I nevertheless recognize the appropriateness of more focused legislative responses to litigation, where legislatures disagree with the policy implications of particular judicial decisions.

The polarization that characterizes the current politics of gun litigation rests on competing views about the proper division of labor between courts and legislatures. Whereas proponents of the suits see litigation as a ready substitute for the legislative process, opponents deny that courts have any significant role to play in policy-making. My more moderate position rests upon an alternative model of how courts and legislatures can and do work together in a complementary manner to fashion coherent and effective public policy. Within this model, legislatures, as the most democratic branch of government, relying on the expertise and experience of administrative agencies, take the lead in making policy choices and crafting solutions to social problems. Courts, through the adjudication of common law claims, play a secondary role that complements the efforts of legislatures and agencies to make and enforce public policy. In this chapter, I introduce this model of complementarity between legislatures and courts, which I refine further in chapter 10. My aim is to advance the politics of gun litigation beyond its current highly polarized state in which, in addition to their substantive disagreements, the two sides cannot even agree where to meet.

Gun Litigation as a Means of Circumventing the Legislative Process

For some plaintiffs and their attorneys, filing lawsuits against the gun industry represents a way to pursue gun control without having to face the obstacles of legislative politics. As the plaintiffs' attorney in one case explained, "We are taking the gun dealers to court because the political process failed us."[2] The plaintiffs' attorney in another high-profile suit put it somewhat more crassly: "You don't need a legislative majority to file a lawsuit."[3]

Gun control advocates often blame their failure to pass stricter gun laws on NRA corruption of the legislative process. They point out that the NRA mobilizes grass roots opposition to gun control using extremist rhetoric, engages in intensive lobbying at all levels of government, and uses campaign contributions to reelect its allies and punish its enemies. NRA success, they argue, is a textbook example of a special interest group capturing the legislative process, and the remedy is to file lawsuits asking courts to impose gun controls that would otherwise be passed by a truly representative legislature.[4] It is unclear, however, whether mobilizing opposition, intensive lobbying, and campaign contributions are symptoms of capture or instead signs of a healthy participatory democracy. Either way, gun control proponents should be less confident in their accusations of foul play since they engage in exactly the same activities. Furthermore, and perhaps even more to the point, even if capture is a useful way to characterize NRA legislative success, it is unclear whether litigation is an appropriate substitute for the legislative process. As we shall see, this strategic use of gun litigation as a response to NRA dominance of the legislative process threatens to undermine the integrity of the tort system and to weaken the possibilities for cooperation between legislatures and courts in making gun violence policy.

Does the NRA Exert Undue Influence?

By all accounts, the NRA is a formidable lobbying force. It has a long and successful record of opposing firearms restrictions. Proposals in the 1930s to impose sales restrictions and gun registration in response to high levels of gang violence met with strong resistance mounted by the NRA and were significantly scaled back in the National Firearms Act of 1934 and the Federal Firearms Act of 1938. Efforts to revise and strengthen these same regulations in the 1960s following the assassinations of President Kennedy, Martin Luther King Jr., and Robert Kennedy, culminating in the Gun Control Act of 1968, were similarly contested by the NRA. At the height of its powers in the 1970s and 1980s, the NRA repeatedly blocked attempts to expand gun control, notably exempting firearms from regulation by the Consumer Product Safety Commission established in 1972 and even repealing earlier sales restrictions and record-keeping requirements in the Firearms Owners' Protection Act of 1986. At the state level, the NRA enjoyed similar success, defeating a California handgun ban referendum in 1982 and convincing state legislatures to pass laws preempting local gun control ordinances throughout the 1980s. While NRA dominance of the legislative arena began to decline in the 1990s due to internal disputes within the organization and the rise of an effective pro-control lobby, it remains a powerful force at the federal, state, and local levels.[5]

Today, the NRA continues to exert considerable influence on the legislative process. In 2000, *Fortune* magazine ranked the NRA first on its list of the twenty-five most powerful lobby groups, ahead of the American Association of Retired Persons (AARP), the Association of Trial Lawyers of America (ATLA), and the AFL-CIO.[6] The NRA, one of the nation's largest membership organizations, boasts a current membership of 4.3 million members, received over $55 million in contributions in 2002, and spent $16.8 million in the 2000 election.[7] By contrast, its counterpart, the Brady Campaign to Prevent Gun Violence (formerly Handgun Control, Inc.), reports a current membership of 500,000, received $6.3 million in 2002, and spent $1.7 million in the 2000 election.[8]

The NRA is notorious for its success in using direct mailings to mobilize impassioned grass roots opposition to legislative gun control proposals. Legislators regularly report an overwhelming number of letters, telegrams, e-mails, and phone calls from NRA members demanding that they support the NRA position on particular bills. Aside from the sheer volume of these messages, some threaten violent retaliation against those who cross the NRA.[9] NRA members can be counted on to show up at town meetings and to call in on radio talk shows nationwide to attack politicians who support gun control. As one Senate staffer described it, what most influences politicians is not "the contributions they get from the NRA. They care about the piles of mail, these nasty calls, and people picketing their state offices."[10]

In addition to mobilizing grass roots activism, the NRA exerts influence within the legislative process. NRA allies in Congress chair key committees and successfully block hearings or votes on gun control bills.[11] During Ronald Reagan's presidency, NRA lobbyists worked with administration officials to draft legislation designed to head off more restrictive proposals.[12]

In electoral politics, the NRA has earned a reputation for hardball campaigning against those who oppose it. It even backed the socialist candidate Bernie Sanders against incumbent Republican Pete Smith in the 1990 Vermont race for the U.S. Congress after Smith announced his support for the 1989 assault weapons ban. The NRA and its local affiliates campaigned heavily against Smith. They attacked his credibility for having changed his views on gun control, printing bumper stickers that read "Peter Smith: The Big Lie." Gun shop flyers compared Smith to Hitler, his campaign yard signs were blasted with buckshot, and irate gun owners threatened his life and his family.[13]

NRA defenders characterize its lobbying activities as "democracy in action." To be sure, the organization's ability to mobilize widespread and intense grass roots opposition to gun control suggests that it represents a significant constituency. It is nevertheless true that the NRA's single-minded extremism and intimidating style have allowed it consistently to thwart moderate gun control measures favored not only by a majority of Americans but even by a majority of gun owners.[14] It is for this reason that gun control proponents have turned to the courts. As New Orleans mayor Marc Morial explained in justifying the city's suit against the gun industry, "With the legislature in the National Rifle Association's pocket, isn't this the only way we can go after them?"[15]

Two questionable assertions underlie the use of lawsuits to overcome the NRA's success in defeating stricter gun control laws. The first is that NRA lobbying power corrupts the legislative process. The second is that tort litigation is an appropriate response.

There are a number of reasons to doubt that NRA lobbying power corrupts the legislative process. For one thing, proponents of gun control engage in substantially the same lobbying tactics as the NRA. The Brady Campaign is no stranger to direct mailings, letter-writing campaigns, manipulation of legislative committee proceedings, access to the administration, and electoral politics. The Brady Campaign uses direct mailings to mobilize support for gun policies, and the Brady Campaign helped to organize the Million Mom March on Washington, D.C., on May 14, 2000. Throughout the 1970s, as chairman of the Senate Judiciary Committee, longtime gun control proponent Senator Edward Kennedy used his power to block consideration of bills to scale back firearms restrictions. In the 1980s, as a minority member of the committee, he blocked consideration of such bills by reading out loud the text of state gun statutes until committee members would leave the room out of boredom and the meeting would have to be adjourned for lack of a quorum. Democratic congressman Peter Rodino of New Jersey played a similar role as chairman of the House Judiciary Committee.[16] In the Clinton administration, the Brady Campaign found a willing partner in successfully passing the 1993 Brady Act mandating background checks for gun purchases. And like the NRA, the Brady Campaign contributes to the reelection of its allies and campaigns against its enemies.

Gun control proponents have attempted to distinguish NRA and Brady Campaign lobbying efforts. Whereas the NRA is a special interest group, the argument goes, the Brady Campaign is a public interest group. The NRA's larger and more active membership base, however, suggests that, if anything, the NRA is a more representative group than the Brady Campaign. This brings us to a second reason to doubt that NRA lobbying power corrupts the legislative process. Interest groups, even ones that represent minority views, make a valuable contribution to the legislative process.[17] There is a long-standing ambivalence in American politics toward the role of interest groups—what Founding Father James Madison called "factions"—in our democracy. On the one hand, we denounce "special" interest groups as antidemocratic in their use of money and influence to defeat popular legislation or to pass laws granting special favors. On the other hand, we praise "public" interest groups for representing not only their members but also large silent majorities or voiceless minorities. Popular distinctions between the two are largely rhetorical, expressing approval or disapproval of a particular group's aims rather than any real difference in the way that it operates or the role that it plays in policy-making. Whether the American Civil Liberties Union, the Moral Majority, the Sierra Club, the National Abortion Rights League, the NRA, or the Brady Campaign are special or public interest groups depends upon whom one asks. The fact is that all of these organizations, judging by membership, represent small minorities within the overall population. The Sierra Club, the largest of these groups aside from the NRA, claims only seven hundred thousand members. And, yet, interest groups such as these play a vital democratic role in a polity as large and as complex as ours. Joining and being active in an interest group is an effective, perhaps even the most effective, way for most individuals to participate in the political process. Interest groups provide a forum for the exchange of ideas among members, and their lobbying activities give voice to members' views in the legislative process. In addition, interest groups generate public information about all kinds of issues—from the political process to the environment—that is essential for an informed citizenry.

A third reason to doubt that NRA lobbying power corrupts the legislative process is that such assertions often rest on a romantic vision of the legislative process. NRA success in defeating popular legislation by means of parliamentary maneuvers such as watering down bills in committee, blocking consideration of them, and offering "killer" amendments is not evidence of corruption but rather is a normal feature of the legislative process. Legislation is, by design, hard to pass. Every bill, in order to become a law, must overcome a number of institutional hurdles: legislative procedures such as committee review, scheduling, filibusters, and floor debate, as well as constitutional requirements of approval by two legislative bodies and the executive. Popular legislation is regularly blocked, despite majority support, by a small group of committee members, a powerful majority leader, a minority faction of senators, or an executive veto.[18] Founding Father Alexander Hamilton viewed these procedural hurdles as a virtue, characterizing them as "security against the [enactment] of improper laws" and suggesting that "[t]he injury that may possibly be done by defeating a few good laws will be amply compensated by the advantage of preventing a few bad ones." His compatriot James Madison supported such procedures as not merely a safeguard but also as promoting legislative deliberation and refinement of bills. These hurdles, or "vetogates," as scholars have called them, block the vast majority of proposed legislation.[19] Of the 8,948 bills proposed in the 107th Congress (2001–2), only 377 were signed into law.[20] In New York State during the 2001 legislative session, 14,972 were proposed but a mere 188 passed and were signed by the governor.[21] Thus, killing legislation is as much a part of the normal legislative process as is passing it. In working to block legislation on behalf of their members, lobby groups do not corrupt but rather facilitate the normal legislative process.

While interest group activity is good for the legislative process in the ways I have mentioned, there is always a risk of abuse. Laws prohibiting bribery and extortion are designed to deter and punish the worst abuses. Death threats and other hardball tactics by the NRA or its affiliates are best dealt with by criminal prosecution of the perpetrators. Alternatively, or in addition, these abuses could be addressed by filing tort suits aimed at deterring the abusive conduct. But tort suits designed to thwart the NRA's lobbying goals, as opposed to its tactics, are not an appropriate response, as they interfere with the legitimate and beneficial lobbying role that the NRA, like all lobbies, plays in the legislative process.

Interest groups can also exert influence in ways that, while legal, are nevertheless troubling. They can use wealth or personal connections to influence the political process, and many decry the influence of economic and social elites within the political sphere.[22] Federal and state laws mandate the disclosure of lobbying activities in order to discourage those that might most offend public sentiment without imposing potentially unconstitutional constraints on lobbying. Using economic and social power to influence the legislative process, while common among many industry lobbies, is a charge that is difficult to level at the NRA, whose money comes in small contributions from a membership base made up largely of working- and middle-class gun owners who hardly constitute a social elite.[23]

The NRA's many members are perhaps the most impassioned of any interest group, and its reputation for swinging elections is, if somewhat inflated, well deserved. Its allies include many powerful legislators at both the state and federal levels, as well as many governors and, depending upon who is sitting in the White House, cabinet members and the president himself. While this formidable power does account for its persistent legislative successes, it does not, however, make a particularly strong case for denouncing this influence as undue or illegitimate.

Arguments against Using Litigation to Circumvent the Legislative Process

Even if charges of NRA corruption of the legislative process were true, tort litigation would not be an appropriate substitute. When parties attempt to fight legislative battles in courtrooms, they are prone to infuse the judicial process with the very same political forces to which they objected in the legislative process. While in the judicial context these political forces may play out to a different party's advantage, they ultimately politicize the courts in ways that are self-defeating and bad for the courts as an institution.

Some proponents of lawsuits against the gun industry have been open about their intention to use litigation as a means to circumvent the legislative process. As Wendell Gauthier, the lead plaintiff's attorney in the City of New Orleans's suit against the gun industry, put it, "The mayor tried to crack down on the [gun] dealers when he was a state senator, and the gun lobby crushed his efforts each time. He couldn't even get a bill out of committee. If lawyers hadn't launched *Brown v. Board of Education,* you would never have had school integration because it was so unpopular with lawmakers."[24] Gauthier went so far as to characterize the plaintiffs' bar "as a *de facto* fourth branch of government . . . [that achieves] regulation through litigation where legislation [has] failed."[25]

There are a number of problems with this justification for lawsuits against the gun industry. First, the failure to get a bill out of committee—by far the most common fate of legislative proposals—is not evidence of a problem with the legislative process that requires a remedy, much less one designed to circumvent the legislative process altogether. Second, the analogy with *Brown* is inapt. Whereas in *Brown* plaintiffs called upon courts to overturn school segregation laws as *unconstitutional,* in lawsuits against the gun industry attorneys like Gauthier are calling upon courts to contradict legislative determinations about gun control merely because they consider them *unwise.* Within our constitutional tradition, courts are empowered to strike down laws that exceed the limits of legitimate legislative power, but they cannot invalidate legislative determinations just because the court disagrees with them. While proponents of gun litigation may be eager to wear the mantle of civil rights, legally they are engaged in a very different exercise. And, finally, that gun controls achieved through litigation are the product of an unelected group of private lawyers acting as a "*de facto* fourth branch of government" in defiance of legislative policy choices is hardly something to boast about.

Treating the courts as merely a second front in legislative battles with the NRA threatens to politicize the judiciary even more than it already is. Of course, only a naive and romantic view of the courts would consider them apolitical. Most state court judges are elected, and appointment of the remaining state and federal judges is highly political. However, when there is bipartisan agreement that the primary function of courts should be to decide disputes in accordance with established legal principles, and that judges should exercise discretion only within the constraints of those principles and in line with legislative trends, then judges will be elected and selected largely for their commitment to restraint and not merely for their personal political views. As agreement over whether courts do or should conform to this model of judicial restraint breaks down, elections and appointment battles will become more partisan. We are then likely to see an increase in the lobbying activities that characterize the legislative process.

Proponents of lawsuits against the gun industry are betting that they will have more success with judicial than with legislative politics. In the short term, they may be right. The lobbying power of plaintiffs' attorneys in affecting judicial elections and appointments is likely greater than that of the NRA.[26] In the long run, however, there is no reason to think that the NRA would be incapable of shifting resources from legislative to judicial politics. Moreover, regardless of which side might win this particular battle to influence the judiciary, increased political pressure on the judicial process would encourage judges to abandon restraint whenever politically desirable. Failure to take seriously limits on the policy-making role of courts threatens to erode public confidence in their impartiality, which rests on a widely shared belief that they resolve disputes based on established legal principles rather than on judges' political views and that when judges' political views do enter into their decisions, they do so in a restrained way.

Gun Litigation as a Means of Influencing the Legislative Process

Some proponents of lawsuits against the gun industry view them as a way not to circumvent legislative debate but to change the terms of it. Indeed, one scholarly article recently characterized this as the primary function of the litigation: "Although the gun lawsuits are unlikely to have any near-term effect on storage, carrying, or gun misuse, litigation may have some indirect effect in each of these areas by strengthening the hand of gun control advocates in the legislative process."[27] There are two distinct ways in which this might occur. First, the prospect of bankrupting liability, or even just defense costs, might make accepting greater regulation in exchange for relief from the suits a more attractive legislative option for the industry and the gun lobby. Second, the language of the legal claims themselves—defective design, negligent marketing, and nuisance—might spill over into public and legislative discourse and reframe the problem of gun violence and options for addressing it. Tort litigation often has these implications for the legislative process—affecting the balance of power and the terms of debate—two of the many ways in which the resolution of private disputes inevitably impacts public affairs. Yet if this becomes the primary goal of suits against gun makers—using tort litigation as merely another lobbying tactic—it may undermine public confidence in the courts and provoke legislative backlash, resulting in significant damage to the tort system as an institution.

Litigation as a Bargaining Tool

In discussing the use of litigation as a bargaining tool within the legislative process, it is important to distinguish between the threat of imposing defense costs and the threat of liability. Threatening to impose defense costs on a legislative adversary involves a misappropriation of public resources. It is a misuse of the court system to employ the rules of pleading, discovery, and trial, which are enforced by the state and paid for by the public, as a lobbying tool. The purpose of these rules, and the justification for their costly imposition on parties to litigation, is to generate the information necessary to resolve private claims. They are not designed to help parties increase their bargaining power, and when they have been used in this way, such tactics have prompted reform.[28]

By contrast, using the threat of liability as a way to pressure a legislative opponent involves no such misappropriation of public resources. Liability, in contrast to defense costs, is a debt owed to the plaintiffs; it is a private resource that, unlike publicly funded procedural mechanisms, plaintiffs are entitled to use as a bargaining chip: to cash it in or trade it for something more desirable. Liability exposure—the risk of liability—is also a private resource, which can be valued at its potential payout discounted by the probability of winning a lawsuit.[29] Using liability or liability exposure as lobbying resources is no more objectionable than using other private resources such as money or the threat of demonstrations.

Of course, in practice, threats to sue often rely for their effectiveness not only on liability exposure but also on the specter of high defense costs. Nevertheless, it is important to distinguish between legitimate bargaining tactics such as threatening to sue under a theory that has a reasonable chance of surviving dismissal, as well as some chance of winning, and misuse of the legal process for private advantage, as when plaintiffs file multiple suits simultaneously merely in order to intensify defense costs. The two sides in gun litigation regularly fail to make this distinction: plaintiffs have at times shamelessly touted their ability to impose crushing defense costs on the industry, while the industry has too often whined about having to defend against "junk lawsuits," which not only survive discovery but also, in a few cases, result in verdicts favorable to plaintiffs.

Reframing the Terms of Debate

Aside from using defense costs and liability exposure to pressure the industry, gun control advocates see litigation as a way to reframe the policy debate over gun control both in legislatures and among the public at large. By changing the terms of debate, gun control advocates hope to gain a rhetorical advantage in the legislative and public arenas.[30] The way that issues get framed—the language used to describe a problem and the particular causal factors identified as the source of the problem—makes some policy alternatives more attractive than others.[31] From the very beginning, controversy over gun control has been fueled by persistent disagreement over how to characterize the problem of gun violence. On the one hand, gun control proponents assert that gun violence is a product of widespread and largely unregulated private gun ownership. Reducing gun violence, according to this view, requires clamping down on gun proliferation by restricting gun purchases. On the other hand, gun control opponents insist that gun violence is a crime problem, not a gun ownership problem. The proper response to gun violence, according to this view, is to punish criminals who misuse guns, not to deprive potential victims of an effective means of self-defense by restricting everyone's ability to purchase a gun. In support of this approach, gun control opponents frequently cite the Second Amendment, which they interpret as granting individuals a constitutional right to own and carry a firearm.

Lawsuits against gun manufacturers have focused attention on allegations of industry misconduct, and, in doing so, they have deemphasized the role of criminal assailants and discussion of gun ownership rights. When framed as a problem of industry misconduct, the obvious solution to gun violence is victim compensation at industry expense and industry regulation. The enemy is no longer individual gun owners but far less sympathetic corporate defendants.

Furthermore, lawsuits brought by individual victims have allowed gun control proponents to appropriate the rhetoric of rights, which has traditionally been the exclusive property of gun control opponents. Until recently, the gun control controversy was fueled by a tension between two fundamental American values—public safety and individual rights—that pitted proponents of protecting the public from gun violence against defenders of an individual's right to own firearms. Gun control proponents cited social science data suggesting that widespread and largely unregulated private gun ownership causes high rates of gun violence, while gun control opponents denounced gun controls, no matter how effective in reducing violence, as violations of a constitutional right. Lawsuits have allowed gun control proponents to develop their own rhetoric of rights, arguing that gun litigation, regardless of its regulatory implications, is primarily an effort to vindicate the rights of plaintiffs to be compensated for injuries caused by industry wrongdoers. The constitutional right to bear arms must now be weighed against the right to have one's day in court.

At the same time, lawsuits brought by government entities attempt to characterize the problem of gun violence not as a contest of rights but as a public health problem. By analyzing the incidence and impact of gun violence on different demographic groups—employing the same tools used to analyze disease—public health scholars have advocated strategies to prevent gun violence before it occurs. Not surprising, these strategies include modification of gun designs and restrictions on gun sales. The appeal of such strategies has been enhanced by an emphasis on preventing youth violence in particular. The rhetorical power of appeals to child protection—whether in campaigns against sexual assault, drug use, or tobacco control—has not gone unnoticed by gun control proponents within the public health community. Government entity lawsuits, which rely on crime statistics rather than individual victims and seek design modification and marketing restrictions, portray gun violence incidents in the aggregate and provide official endorsement of the public health approach to gun control as a question of how best to eliminate a disease rather than how to weigh competing rights. (In response, gun control opponents have shot back with social science data of their own, suggesting that well-armed communities enjoy lower rates of gun violence, known as the "more guns, less crime" argument. Thus, they too have sought to level the rhetorical playing field by deploying both individual rights and public safety arguments to support their position.)

Many factors influence issue framing, including media coverage, legislative lobbying, and litigation. In this respect, gun control is no exception. As long as lawsuits against the industry are based on plausible theories of liability aimed, in good faith, at winning rather than merely generating press coverage, then it is hard to see on what grounds one might object to their effect on the framing of legislative debates over gun control. If, however, plaintiffs pursue reframing as not merely a by-product of gun litigation but the primary aim, then they can rightly be accused of misusing the litigation process for a private advantage unrelated to the resolution of claims before the court.

Statutory Immunity as a Response to Gun Litigation

In response to the wave of lawsuits against the gun industry, the NRA launched a nationwide lobbying campaign in state legislatures and Congress to secure statutory immunity for the industry. So far, thirty-two states have passed such legislation. These laws vary widely in scope. Some of them merely prohibit municipalities from suing the industry. Others grant the industry blanket immunity from suit, with narrow exceptions for guns that malfunction (for example, guns that backfire) and breach of contract (for example, failure to deliver guns that have been paid for). In 2003 and early 2004, Congress considered a bill that would have granted the industry this type of blanket immunity nationwide. The bill, which enjoyed overwhelming support in both the House and the Senate, was scuttled at the last minute by its Senate sponsors who opposed amendments to the bill extending a ban on assault weapons and requiring background checks for gun sales at gun shows.

Gun litigation opponents justify statutory immunity as an appropriate response to lawsuits that seek to circumvent the legislative process. By granting such sweeping immunity, even against legitimate claims, legislatures have substituted their own judgment for that of courts and have rejected plaintiffs' claims without a hearing. Thus, while gun litigation opponents accuse plaintiffs of seeking to circumvent the legislative process, they are no less guilty themselves of attempting to circumvent the judicial process. And, unlike plaintiffs, they have been largely successful.

The Case against Immunity Laws

Sweeping statutory immunity for the gun industry is a bad idea for a number of reasons. First, it damages the doctrinal integrity of tort law. The primary purpose of tort law is to provide a system of predictable and stable rules for resolving private conflicts. While, in practice, the system contains inconsistencies, judges do attempt to employ similar considerations in deciding different cases so as to promote coherence within the system as a whole. There is even considerable uniformity among different states, despite the fact that tort law is state law and states are free to develop their own doctrines. Sweeping statutory immunity for the gun industry carves out an exception exclusively for one industry on the basis of political power rather than any concern for the doctrinal integrity of tort law. This, no less than filing suits in order to circumvent the legislative process, is a politicization of the tort system.

Second, sweeping statutory immunity for the gun industry usurps judicial power. It is the job of courts, not legislatures, at least in the first instance, to judge whether particular legal claims fall within established liability doctrines. Judges know and understand the limits of tort doctrine better than legislatures, and their judgments are based on deliberation rather than interest group politics. Of course, politics does affect judicial decision making. Unlike the legislative process, however, a number of structural features of judicial process mitigate this influence, such as the issuing of written opinions, appellate review, and a sense of judicial role. And, in any case, courts have dismissed the majority of claims against the gun industry at the outset, which undermines the need for statutory immunity in the first place. Within our constitutional scheme, legislative adjudication, no less than judicial legislation, erodes the separation of powers.

Third, sweeping statutory immunity for the gun industry weakens the capacity of tort litigation to complement legislative policy-making and effective administrative regulation. Lawsuits against the gun industry complement legislative and agency policy-making in a number of ways. The discovery process in some lawsuits has already uncovered hidden information about the industry, which has been less than forthcoming about its experiences with safer design alternatives and its knowledge about the risks of different marketing practices. Findings of liability can fill gaps in the system of laws and agency rules that regulate the industry. And liability can supplement scarce enforcement resources by providing an additional incentive for the industry to comply with existing regulations. By eliminating the complementary regulatory role of the tort system, sweeping statutory immunity is detrimental to a legislature's own policy-making effectiveness.

Narrower immunity laws focused merely on prohibiting municipal suits are, however, less open to these objections. Most of these laws reserve to the state the right to sue the industry. They impose a uniform governmental approach to suing the industry by depriving local governments of the right to sue, while allowing the state itself to sue should it choose to do so. Laws such as these that define the rights of local government do not carve out politically motivated exceptions to core tort doctrines; they fall squarely within the traditional province of state legislatures, and they preserve a complementary role for the tort system insofar as they leave individual suits unaffected.

A number of municipalities have mounted court challenges to immunity laws. The cities of New Orleans, Atlanta, and Detroit have argued that immunity laws passed after they filed suit, attempting retroactively to preempt their claims, are unconstitutional. The Louisiana Supreme Court rejected the New Orleans challenge, holding that, as a municipal corporation created by the state, the City had no federal constitutional rights that it could assert "in opposition to the will of its creator" and that, under the state constitution, the immunity law was a valid exercise of the state's police power.[32] Georgia and Michigan appellate courts rejected challenges by Atlanta and Detroit on similar grounds.[33] Immunity bills so far appear to be an effective tactic in extinguishing both pending and future municipal claims against the gun industry.

Federal Immunity

The Protection of Lawful Commerce in Arms Act, considered by Congress in 2003 and early 2004, is the most sweeping statutory immunity measure yet, both in its broad protection from liability and in its federal scope. The bill, which ultimately failed, enjoyed overwhelming support. It had 250 cosponsors in the House of Representatives and 55 in the Senate. While it passed by a margin of 285–140 in the House, it was ultimately defeated in the Senate after the NRA and its Senate sponsors withdrew their support in opposition to amendments extending a ban on assault weapons and requiring background checks on gun sales at gun shows. Given the strong support for gun industry immunity in Congress, the issue is likely to come up again.

Federal gun industry immunity is especially vulnerable to the objections raised previously to state immunity laws. There can be little doubt that the Protection of Lawful Commerce in Arms Act was more a product of interest group politics than of careful deliberation about reforming tort doctrine. Democratic opponents of the bill in the House of Representatives denounced its sponsors for cutting off Judiciary Committee discussion of the bill after a mere three hours and maneuvering to limit debate and amendments during floor consideration of the bill. Furthermore, the bill's insensitivity to the separation of powers is manifest in its "findings," which begin with a declaration that "[c]itizens have a right, protected by the Second Amendment to the United States Constitution, to keep and bear arms" and goes on to state that imposing liability on the industry would "constitute a deprivation of the rights, privileges, and immunities guaranteed to a citizen of the United States under the Fourteenth Amendment to the United States Constitution."[34] Thus, the act, motivated by a desire to preempt judicial overreaching, itself begins by purporting to interpret the Second and Fourteenth Amendments to the Constitution—a power traditionally reserved to the courts. Moreover, the act also passes judgment on the legal theories at issue in lawsuits against the industry, asserting that "[t]he liability actions commenced or contemplated by the Federal Government, States, municipalities, and private interest groups are based on theories without foundation in hundreds of years of the common law and jurisprudence of the United States and do not represent a bona fide expansion of the common law."[35] From a separation of powers perspective, it is one thing for a legislature to overturn common law rules by statute; it is another thing altogether for it to declare what the common law is.

Notable also is the extent to which this immunity legislation is itself a vehicle for framing the terms of debate over both gun control and tort reform. One hears in congressional debate a contest for ownership over resonant terms such as *rights, junk,* and *nuisance:* the "right to keep and bear arms" versus the "right to have one's day in court"; groundless "junk lawsuits" versus unsafe "junk guns"; and "nuisance suits" versus "liability for nuisance."[36] In an ironic twist, Republicans, normally champions of regulatory federalism, have appropriated the traditionally Democratic insistence on the need for a national standard, while Democrats, for their part, have offered impassioned pleas on behalf of the states to make their own determinations about gun industry immunity. While the highly rhetorical and somewhat unprincipled character of the debate is a normal feature of legislative politics, this legislation, if ultimately successful, will be notable for the damage that it is likely to inflict on the integrity of the tort system, the separation of powers, and the capacity of courts to play a supportive role in regulating the gun industry.

Focused Legislative Responses to Particular Judicial Decisions

Immunity laws are not the only legislative responses to gun litigation. In 1988, the Maryland legislature passed a law overturning the doctrine of strict liability for the manufacture, distribution, and sale of Saturday Night Specials established by *Kelley v. R.G. Industries* and creating in its place a board of experts to identify and restrict the sale of handguns with a high risk of criminal misuse.[37] In 2002, the California legislature repealed a provision of the Civil Code granting immunity to the gun industry against product liability claims in response to the California Supreme Court's rejection of *Merrill v. Navegar*, which relied on the provision.[38] In both of these instances, the legislature effectively overturned a particular judicial rule because it objected to the policy implications of the rule.

In criticizing sweeping immunity laws, I do not mean to suggest that legislatures should refrain from overturning common law doctrines when the legislature disagrees with the policy implications of those doctrines. I do mean to suggest, however, that the legislature should do so in a restrained way, one that respects the preeminence of courts in shaping tort doctrine and preserves the regulatory benefits of tort litigation. Legislative responses in Maryland and California exemplify this approach. Unlike sweeping immunity laws, these more focused responses promote the integrity of tort doctrine, respect the separation of powers, and preserve a regulatory role for the courts.

Maryland's Rejection of Judicial Doctrine Established
by Kelley v. R.G. Industries

The Maryland legislature's response to *Kelley v. R.G. Industries* exemplifies a restrained approach to legislative review of judicial policy choices. In deciding *Kelley*, the Supreme Court of Maryland recognized that it was creating a novel theory of recovery—one, however, that it believed fit within the structure of existing doctrine. And in promulgating this novel theory, the court sought to do so in accordance with "the public policy of the State set forth by the General Assembly of Maryland."[39] After a lengthy analysis of legislative policy, the court concluded that "the policy implications of the gun control laws enacted by both the United States Congress and the Maryland General Assembly reflect a governmental view that there is a handgun species, i.e., the so-called Saturday Night Special, which is considered to have little or no legitimate purpose in today's society" and which therefore merited distinct treatment from that accorded to other firearms or consumer products. In creating a new common law rule, the court took the unusual step of making it prospective, applying it only to the *Kelley* case and to sales of Saturday Night Specials occurring after the date of the opinion.

The Maryland legislature disagreed with the court's new rule and three years later passed legislation replacing it with an administrative scheme designed to achieve substantially the same results. The Maryland law repudiated the *Kelley* doctrine, stating that "[a] person or entity may not be held strictly liable for damages of any kind resulting from injuries to another person sustained as a result of the criminal use of any firearm by a third person."[40] At the same time, the law established a nine-member Handgun Roster Board charged with creating a list of handguns that could legally be sold in the state. The board comprises representatives from law enforcement, the gun industry, the NRA, gun control organizations, and the general public. Approval for sale is based on a number of criteria designed to exclude cheap, easily concealed guns. In theory, the legislature's purpose in creating the board was to ban the sale of Saturday Night Specials within the state. In practice, the board has excluded relatively few handguns—only thirty-four compared to the over fifteen hundred approved as of 2002—due to insufficient firearms expertise, lack of information, vagueness of exclusion standards, and gun-lobby influence in appointments.[41]

The Maryland legislature's focused response to *Kelley* has three notable virtues. First, overturning the novel doctrine established by the case introduced no inconsistency into tort doctrine. Strict liability for the manufacture, distribution, and sale of Saturday Night Specials was itself an exception to tort law's approach to firearms in particular and consumer products in general, which are not subject to strict liability absent a defect. If anything, eliminating the *Kelley* rule made tort doctrine more consistent. Second, the Maryland legislature's rejection of *Kelley* respected the separation of powers, focusing on the particular rule at stake without delegitimating the court's authority to declare the common law. Absent from the statute are "findings," such as those in the federal Protection of Lawful Commerce in Arms Act, concerning the constitutionality of the litigation or what the common law is. Third, the legislature's response did not interfere with the court's capacity to complement the regulatory process. Instead of attempting to remove the court altogether from deciding gun litigation, the legislature merely overturned a judicial policy choice with which it disagreed, thereby providing guidance to the court in future cases. Given the legislature's establishment of the Handgun Roster Board, it could be said that the legislature in fact agreed with the court's policy aims of eliminating the sale of Saturday Night Specials and did not so much overturn *Kelley* as replace it with an administrative mechanism that it believed would be more effective.

California's Repeal of Gun Industry Protections in Response to Merrill v. Navegar

The California legislature's response to *Merrill v. Navegar* offers a second example of a more restrained approach. In *Merrill*, the California Supreme Court rejected plaintiffs' negligent marketing claim that the manufacturer of a semiautomatic pistol designed for close combat-style assaults should have limited promotion and sale of the gun to military and law enforcement, the only consumers who might have legitimate use for such a weapon. Citing Section 1714.4 of the California Civil Code, the court explained that "the Legislature has declared as a matter of public policy that a gun manufacturer may not be held liable '[i]n a products liability action . . . on the basis that the benefits of [its] product do not outweigh the risk of injury posed by [the product's] potential to cause serious injury, damage, or death when discharged.'"[42] The court held that the plaintiffs' negligent marketing claim was essentially a "products liability action" barred by the statute since the claim relied on assertions about the particular design of the gun and its potential to cause serious injury.

In response to the *Merrill* decision, the California legislature repealed Section 1714.4. The legal effect of this action was to remove the statutory obstacle to gun manufacturer liability and leave the courts free to decide gun industry liability based on common law or, depending on the case, based on Civil Code tort provisions as interpreted by the courts.[43] This response has the same three virtues as the Maryland legislature's response to the *Kelley* decision. First, the California legislature acted in a way that enhanced, rather than detracted from, the consistency of California tort doctrine. Section 1714.4 was a special exemption for the firearms industry from the product liability principles applicable to all other consumer products. In repealing it, the legislature removed an inconsistency that it itself had created back in 1983. Second, the legislature respected the separation of powers, leaving clarification of how the common law and the Civil Code applied to gun litigation up to the courts. Third, the legislature's repeal not only preserved but encouraged the courts to revisit the issue and to play a complementary role in gun industry regulation. The *Merrill* decision and the subsequent repeal of 1714.4 illustrate a high degree of cooperation, mutual respect, and complementarity between the California Supreme Court and the legislature on the issue of gun violence policy: the court showed great deference in its interpretation of the legislature's policy preferences, and the legislature responded by indicating a contrary preference and leaving the court to work out the doctrinal implications.

Exercising Mutual Restraint:
The Complementary Roles of Legislatures and Courts

The analysis throughout much of this chapter relies on a model of policy-making and regulation in which legislatures and courts play distinct and complementary roles. According to this model, legislatures should take the lead in shaping public policy. The perception of democratic legitimacy makes them better suited than courts to broker political compromises between competing interest groups. Furthermore, they have the power to establish, fund, and supervise agencies capable of gathering information and developing special expertise in a particular regulatory area. At the same time, legislatures should leave room for courts to play a secondary role, one that, in the end, can strengthen the effectiveness of their own policy choices. In responding to court decisions with which they disagree, legislatures should exercise restraint, overturning the particular doctrinal choices with which they disagree without eliminating altogether future court involvement in an area of public policy. Legislatures should also exercise restraint in replacing common law rules with statutory substitutes, especially when this introduces inconsistencies into tort doctrine. When Congress has occasionally granted a particular industry immunity from tort liability—as in the case of the coal industry, vaccine makers, or the airline industry following the September 11, 2001, terrorist attacks—it has provided an alternative compensation system for victims.[44] Similarly, when passing legislation that preempts state tort law, Congress has relied heavily on particular agencies equipped to regulate the relevant industry. Such limitations on the role of the tort system should be justified by the public interest, not by political influence.

As for the role of courts within this model, the primary duty of common law courts is to provide a stable and predictable system of rules for resolving private disputes. Insofar as it is highly deliberative and insulated from political pressures, the judicial process is well suited to this task. When ambiguities arise in the application of existing rules, judges must exercise discretion and should be guided in part by the public policy implications of different options for deciding a case. In making policy choices within the context of resolving doctrinal ambiguities, the idea of complementarity suggests that courts should show deference to legislative policy preferences where discernable. By playing a complementary role, courts can enhance legislative policy-making by uncovering hidden information, filling gaps in the regulatory regime, and supplementing scarce enforcement resources. In chapter 10, I develop this complementary model further.

Conclusion

In this chapter, I have criticized the efforts of gun control advocates to use litigation as a means of circumventing the legislative process. These efforts threaten to politicize the judiciary, and they are likely, in the end, to be self-defeating as the gun lobby focuses its superior political power on judicial elections. I have also criticized the gun lobby's largely successful attempts to secure statutory immunity for the gun industry as a way to stifle litigation. Such sweeping immunity damages the doctrinal integrity of tort law, undermines the separation of powers, and impairs the capacity of tort litigation to support legislative regulatory efforts. Tort litigation should not be used merely as a means of promoting an unsuccessful legislative agenda, and immunity legislation is no substitute for individual adjudication of private claims.

While I have denounced blatantly political suits, I do not mean to deny that private litigation can play a legitimate role in public policy debates. The threat of liability is a legitimate bargaining tool in the legislative process, and the reframing of issues among the general public and within legislative debates is a normal by-product of high-profile litigation. Furthermore, in arguing against broad immunity legislation, I do not mean to deny that focused legislative responses to judicial decisions are a healthy part of the interplay between legislatures and courts, one that reasserts, when necessary, the primacy of legislatures in the policy-making process.

Throughout, my analysis has been based on a model of policy-making in which legislatures and courts work together in a complementary fashion to shape and to carry out coherent and effective regulatory choices. The viability of this model depends upon the ability of legislatures and courts to exercise mutual restraint. In the case of gun litigation, this means that courts should dismiss purely political suits and legislatures should leave courts to adjudicate legitimate ones.

CHAPTER 7

Gun Litigation in the Mass Tort Context

RICHARD A. NAGAREDA

Lawsuits by individuals and municipalities against the gun industry exemplify a new form of mass tort litigation, what one commentator aptly dubs "social policy tort" litigation.[1] Plaintiffs in gun litigation seek conventional civil damages for tortious misconduct in the past. But a complementary goal—arguably, the predominant goal of the lawsuits by municipalities—is to precipitate prospective changes in the marketing practices of the gun industry as a whole. This prospective dimension of gun litigation by municipalities has led critics accurately to see it as an attempt to bring into being, through settlement of litigation, the kind of regulatory regime that gun control advocates have failed to secure from legislatures or public regulatory agencies.[2]

   I initially explain how the social policy dimension of contemporary gun litigation distinguishes it from most previous instances of mass tort litigation. This is not to suggest that those litigating against the gun industry somehow are a monolithic force, united in all respects about objectives and strategy. As Howard Erichson cautions in chapter 5 of this volume, gun litigation is as notable for the variations in its origins and objectives as it is for its common features. My initial point is simply that there is a substantial social policy dimension to gun litigation—arguably, a dimension in some tension with the conventional tort goal of compensation for individual plaintiffs—and that one may frame that dimension within the backdrop of mass tort litigation generally. I then advance two claims about gun litigation as a species of social policy tort litigation.

My first claim is that one can fit the emergence of social policy tort lit-igation within two longer-term trends: developments in tort theory and a roughly contemporaneous transformation in the political landscape for regulatory programs in the public sector. Theorists of tort law today tend to conceptualize tort litigation largely as a convenient occasion for regulatory policy-making through the vehicle of the common law. At the same time, critics of public regulatory programs have called into doubt their efficacy and, indeed, their very legitimacy. The confluence of these two developments has meant that tort law is seen as an arm of reg-ulatory law but that political support for expansion of the regulatory state is tenuous. It should come as no surprise that, in such a world, ambitious regulatory programs should come to the fore through the avenue of tort litigation. There is more than a hint of irony here. The implication of this initial claim is that gun litigation today is the unex-pected and unintended outgrowth of two developments that many free-market conservatives would applaud: the instrumental conception of tort law associated with the law-and-economics perspective and the Reagan revolution in regulatory policy.

My second claim is that gun litigation seeks to implement its regula-tory program in a manner strikingly unmindful of the lessons learned about conventional regulation in the public sphere. Recent decades have witnessed a reorientation of regulatory policy-making, one implemented through measures embraced by such divergent political regimes as the Reagan and Clinton administrations. This reorientation has two compo-nents of significance here: (1) systematic comparison of proposed regu-latory interventions based upon their relative cost-effectiveness, broadly defined; and (2) greater emphasis on political accountability in the mak-ing of regulatory policy decisions. By contrast, gun litigation by many municipalities seeks to frame the questions surrounding industry mar-keting practices on a stand-alone basis, as matters to be addressed irre-spective of other interventions to protect public safety and through arrangements for the financing of litigation that often are removed from the conventional budgetary process.

Two specific subpoints stand out here. First, the challenge to industry marketing practices in gun litigation seems, at first glance, to comprise a new kind of allegation in the mass tort world. On closer examination, however, this challenge actually replicates—indeed, accentuates—the difficulties associated with both tort litigation and regulation with respect to products alleged to cause latent disease. This too should come as no surprise, given the efforts of some gun litigation advocates to recast the social consequences of gun availability as an issue of public health.[3] I expose here the conceptual relationship between the negligent marketing claim at the heart of gun litigation and more conventional allegations of latent disease associated with the kinds of pharmaceutical products characteristically the focus of mass tort lawsuits.

Second, the growing disconnection between social policy tort litigation and public regulation is more than a matter of theoretical interest. The rise of social policy tort litigation presents free-market conservatives today with the ironic consequences of their own successes. But social policy tort litigation in the future could proceed along lines that would be deeply ironic for liberals. A world in which social policy tort litigation emerges as a vehicle through which to recoup the costs to the public fisc of private behavior that the government has not regulated directly—perhaps cannot regulate directly—would be a world quite amenable to a social conservative agenda. The only question would be how to gain control of the political offices with the authority to arrange for litigation in the name of the government. Gun litigation, if anything, demonstrates that social policy tort suits may proceed on a local, rather than a state or a national, basis. And, as no less than James Madison famously recognized in *The Federalist,* narrow factions of all sorts are more apt to achieve political dominance on a local, rather than a national, level.

Gun Litigation as a New Form of Mass Tort

Recent decades have witnessed a transformation in the nature and objectives of mass tort litigation. Before turning to that transformation, however, one must bear in mind the features of mass torts in more conventional forms. I use the term *mass torts* to describe tortious misconduct alleged to affect large numbers of geographically dispersed persons and to give rise to latent disease.[4] Mass torts thus differ from mass accidents—such as an airplane crash or a hotel fire—which might cause injury to large numbers of people but generally do not involve latent disease. Mass torts also differ from toxic torts—such as might arise from the release of toxic chemicals from an industrial facility—which involve allegations of latent disease but only on the part of persons within a relatively circumscribed geographic area.

Each feature that defines a mass tort—numerosity, geographic dispersion, and latency—presents a host of challenges for the conventional tort system. The sheer number of claims makes unwieldy, at best, the processing of individual tort lawsuits by a litigation system that remains geared around discrete, idiosyncratic wrongs. Geographic dispersion accentuates the problem by spreading cases across multiple judicial systems, thereby making difficult the coordination of pending litigation. And the phenomenon of latent disease pushes at conventional principles of causation and injury to such an extent that some commentators call for new principles of tort liability predicated upon the imposition of risk itself.[5]

For all the practical and conceptual challenges that they pose, however, mass torts are quite conventional in one significant respect: mass tort suits seek damages based upon allegations of tortious misconduct in the past. To be sure, the sheer scale of such damage liability can raise difficulties of its own—hence, the tendency of mass torts to lead defendant manufacturers to opt for corporate reorganization under the Bankruptcy Code. But the point remains that the focus of mass tort litigation is overwhelmingly retrospective in temporal orientation. Mass torts characteristically carry the possibility of effecting prospective change only remotely and at a high level of generality by enhancing the deterrence of risk taking by corporate America as a whole. In conventional mass tort litigation, the defendant manufacturer typically has ceased to market broadly—often to market at all—the underlying product in question. This account describes the vast majority of examples commonly used to illustrate the mass tort phenomenon. Such illustrations include litigation over asbestos, the defoliant Agent Orange, the Dalkon Shield contraceptive device, silicone gel breast implants, and the diet drug combination fen-phen.

Three features characterize the emergence in recent years of social policy torts as a genre of mass tort litigation. First, litigation proceeds not simply on multiple fronts in geographic terms but also in the name of both private persons and the government itself. For the government, the predicate for litigation consists of a public benefit program, whether state-funded health care benefits in the case of tobacco litigation[6] or locally funded police and other public services in the case of gun litigation. The crux of the government's argument for liability consists of the claim that the defendant industry's tortious misdeeds have resulted in some increment of additional outlays from the public fisc. The government, as plaintiff, often seeks not only damages to recoup those additional outlays in the past but also injunctive relief against the underlying marketing practices of the defendant industry, so as to alleviate the need for similar outlays in the future.

The financial engine for social policy tort litigation by the government is also noteworthy in many instances. Such litigation frequently takes place not through the use of budgetary resources for law enforcement but, instead, through the retention of law firms within the plaintiffs' bar on a contingency fee basis.[7] In tobacco litigation, for instance, the law firms retained by state governments generally consisted of those spearheading litigation by individual smokers or classes thereof.[8] One must take care, however, not to paint with too broad of a brush. Some municipal lawsuits against the gun industry are financed in the ordinary fashion, through the allocation of budgetary resources to that end.[9] The important point about litigation finance, nevertheless, is that many of the government suits aspire to what one might describe as a budgetary freebie: recovery of funds for the public fisc, but not through the financing of litigation from the public fisc.

Second, from the standpoint of defendants, the practical effect of social policy tort litigation on multiple fronts is to give rise to its own *in terrorem* effect, such as may lead corporate executives to contemplate seriously the prospect of a comprehensive settlement agreement. This is not to say that the multifront aspect of social policy tort litigation is the result of conscious, coordinated decision making by plaintiffs' lawyers and governments. Again, the plaintiffs' side of social policy tort litigation is not monolithic. The absence of coordination on the plaintiffs' side notwithstanding, the multifront nature of social policy tort litigation has the effect—intended or not—of placing the defendant industry in the position of having to prevail in all, or virtually all, fora in order to avoid the imposition of injunctive relief that, as a practical matter, might well entail the restructuring of industry marketing practices as a whole.

To observe that the multifront nature of social policy tort litigation has its own *in terrorem* effect, moreover, is not to say that the defendants ultimately will succumb. Many, though not all, suits by municipalities against the gun industry have met with dismissal on legal grounds.[10]

And, thus far, only one firm in the gun industry—Smith & Wesson—has gone the settlement route, a strategic choice that has made the company the subject of considerable scorn from other gun makers.[11] A substantial facet of social policy tort litigation nonetheless remains its *potential* to effectuate, through comprehensive settlement, a regulatory program by means that do not necessarily require an extended series of clear-cut victories in court.

Third, social policy tort litigation both accentuates and transforms the preexisting tendency of mass torts toward a convergence of tort and criminal concepts.[12] Conventional mass torts often involve substantial factual questions about the existence of a causal link between the alleged tortious misconduct of the defendants and the particular maladies suffered by the plaintiffs. At the same time, mass torts frequently involve substantial evidence of fault on the defendants' part—perhaps a lax attitude toward product safety or, even worse, a conscious corporate program to mislead consumers with regard to product risk. But fault does not, in itself, make for causation. Defendant manufacturers simply may have had the sheer good luck—the "outrageous fortune," one might say—not to have caused injury to anyone. To take perhaps the most famous illustration from the annals of mass torts: notwithstanding a less than exemplary regard for product safety on the part of manufacturers, silicone gel breast implants still do not cause autoimmune disease as a scientific matter.[13]

Existing commentary marks the tendency of mass tort litigation along the foregoing lines toward "commingling" by civil juries—a willingness, often spurred by plaintiffs' counsel, to overlook substantial factual questions of causation in the presence of formidable evidence of blameworthy conduct on the defendants' part.[14] One tendency in conventional mass torts, in short, is to impose civil liability as a way to punish defendants for their misdeeds, with little regard to whether they actually caused the harm suffered by plaintiffs. This is not to say that such a tendency is necessarily unjust in the overall scheme of the law. The criminal law punishes on this basis with regularity, through its recognition of attempted crimes in addition to completed ones. I simply suggest that this approach is uncharacteristic of tort law.

Social policy torts introduce a new twist to this familiar pattern. For all the factual questions that frequently surround conventional mass torts, their legal underpinnings typically are secure. The usual allegation is that the defendants failed to warn consumers about some risk associated with their product. To be sure, the facts may not bear out this assertion in a given instance; but the underlying notion of liability for failure to warn remains well established in tort doctrine. Not so with regard to many theories of liability invoked in gun litigation. As existing commentary observes, even individual tort suits predicated on negligent marketing by gun manufacturers raise formidable questions of legal duty where the harm to the plaintiff comes, most immediately, as a result of criminal misconduct.[15] Challenges to industry marketing practices at the behest of the government raise substantial legal questions of their own. As currently conceived, the "free public services" doctrine deems unrecoverable public expenditures made in the performance of government functions.[16]

Social policy tort litigation raises a prospect of commingling of a new sort: not simply the prospect that civil juries will overlook factual barriers to liability when confronted with substantial evidence of defendants' blameworthiness but, additionally, that some courts in some jurisdictions might come to regard the problem of gun availability in modern America as so pressing and of such societal consequence as to warrant the surmounting of doctrinal barriers to liability. Thus far, the constraints of existing tort doctrine have largely held firm in gun litigation. But, once again, the multifront dimension of social policy tort litigation comes into play. It is not enough for the defendant industry, over time, to win in many, or even most, fora if the prospect of losses in some effectively would make for the implementation of marketing changes along the lines demanded by litigation proponents.

Intellectual and Political Context

Its implications for mass tort litigation aside, the emergence of social policy tort litigation in recent decades highlights the unexpected confluence of two larger developments in the late twentieth century, the implications of which have become apparent only in recent years. The first development is intellectual in nature, though it is by no means one confined to academia in its repercussions. The second development is political in character and defines the landscape for public regulatory initiatives to the present day.

An intellectual history of tort theory in the United States is well beyond the parameters of this chapter.[17] A bird's-eye view nonetheless suffices to frame—with some risk of generalization, I admit—the rise of social policy tort litigation as a distinctive species of mass tort. Put simply, the dominant theoretical account of tort law today sees tort litigation as a convenient occasion for regulatory policy-making by common law judges—as an invitation for the crafting of tort doctrine to achieve, among other regulatory goals, the optimal deterrence of risk taking by product manufacturers. As one commentator tellingly observes, tort law today tends to be conceived as a gigantic enabling act, one that delegates to common law judges—and, by implication, to their counselors in the academy—the authority to enact a wide range of regulatory policies on the basis of their judgment as to how best to promote social welfare.[18]

This regulatory perspective has a lengthy intellectual pedigree, tracing its origins at least to Oliver Wendell Holmes's famous account in *The Common Law* of tort law as a vehicle for social regulation.[19] Holmes's writings mark the early stirrings of Legal Realism, a movement whose proponents, by the mid-twentieth century, would tout explicitly tort law as a form of "public law in disguise" for the achievement of regulatory ends.[20] In his landmark 1941 *Handbook on the Law of Torts*, William Prosser would include an early section overtly describing tort law as an exercise in "Social Engineering."[21]

Later scholars—most prominently, Richard Posner and Guido Calabresi—would endeavor to lend precision to the regulatory force of tort law by bringing to bear on its doctrines the concepts and rigor of economic analysis. Common law judges, for example, could target the regulatory force of liability principles in order to place the costs of accidents on the "least cost avoider."[22] One commentator captures the central thrust of these developments, observing that, by the 1960s, "[a]mbitious judges and scholars viewed tort rules not as a direct reflection of the mores of the citizenry, but as a means of implementing social policy decisions arrived at through the application of philosophical, scientific, and technical knowledge to social problems."[23]

All of this is not to suggest that the regulatory account of tort law stands unchallenged. The major theoretical rift in tort law for some time has pitted the instrumentalist heirs of Holmes, Posner, and Calabresi against a competing camp of scholars who see tort law not in terms of the regulatory ends that it might advance but as a vehicle for the achievement of corrective justice as between the plaintiff and the defendant.[24] One may find in commentary on gun litigation ripples from this larger theoretical debate. In a telling recent exchange, law-and-economics scholar Barry Adler defends gun litigation—indeed, strict liability for the gun industry—as a vehicle through which to internalize the social costs of gun availability and to spread those costs through the mechanism of gun prices.[25] Corrective justice theorists Jules Coleman and Arthur Ripstein, by contrast, insist that tort law must understand gun litigation not as "a matter of fixing prices" but as "a matter of doing justice," by which they mean the making of judgments about "responsibility and wrongdoing."[26]

My enterprise here is not to settle the theoretical debate but simply to fit the emergence of social policy tort litigation within the larger intellectual context of tort theory. This is not to suggest that conventional tort litigation somehow lacks a social policy agenda. The demise of the privity limitation in products liability, for example, could not have occurred unless someone had sued and demanded such a change in doctrine. The distinctive feature of social policy tort litigation is not that it has a regulatory agenda but rather that it has the potential to implement that agenda not necessarily through definitive judicial rulings but through the dynamics of tort litigation itself—through settlements that would implement prospective changes in defendants' practices in the face of doctrinal uncertainty. No less of a tort-as-regulation proponent than Gary Schwartz remarked with regard to the multibillion-dollar state attorneys general settlement with the tobacco industry: "Never has so much money changed hands on account of lawsuits in which the legal theories have been so uncertain."[27] By conceptualizing torts as occasions for *judicial* policy-making, regulatory accounts unwittingly have opened the possibility of policy change not so much through the decisions of enlightened judges schooled in economic or other regulatory analysis but, instead, through the dynamics of litigation itself.

Social policy tort litigation not only exhibits a kinship with regulatory theories of tort law. One also must understand the phenomenon in light of other developments in the political realm. Here, too, I compress a complex story to highlight key points. The election of Ronald Reagan in 1980 marked a transformation of the political landscape for ambitious new programs of government regulation. Famously declaring that "[g]overnment is not the solution to our problem; government is the problem,"[28] President Reagan embarked on an extensive program of deregulation. Indeed, as I shall discuss momentarily, significant facets of the Reagan administration's approach to regulatory policy have had enduring effects that transcend partisan lines. No less than President Clinton would declare two decades later that "[t]he era of big Government is over."[29]

Whether the Reagan revolution in regulatory policy transformed public perception of government or largely capitalized on preexisting political trends will remain a subject of debate among historians for the foreseeable future. A variety of contemporaneous developments undoubtedly contributed to a dwindling of the 1960s zeitgeist that new public regulatory programs should occupy the forefront of efforts to address social problems. The Reagan revolution was much in keeping with the undermining of public regard for government generally in the aftermath of the Watergate scandal and the Vietnam War. In addition, attention to the costs of the regulatory state for both industry and the government itself is consonant with the slow economic growth prevalent in the 1970s and the deepening public distaste for taxes during the same period.

The ascendance of regulatory theories of tort law and the emergence of a political landscape inhospitable to demands for government regulation have made for a potent combination, one that has created a hospitable intellectual and political environment for the development of social policy tort litigation. This observation should give pause to free-market conservatives who attack gun litigation as an effort to expand marketing restrictions on firearms through means other than ordinary political channels. Gun litigation, properly understood, is the unanticipated consequence of developments that free-market conservatives largely applaud—indeed, have taken a prominent role in implementing. This is not to suggest that law-and-economics scholarship is uniformly hostile to government regulation or, even more fancifully, that all who practice it somehow harbor a deregulatory agenda. To the contrary, an increasingly important branch of law-and-economics scholarship—behavioral law and economics—aspires to build a richer and more precise case for government regulatory interventions.[30] Nor do I mean to imply that the innovations in government operations deployed to implement the Reagan revolution were not used later by the Clinton administration to support a dramatically different vision of the regulatory state. My point is simply that those who tend, on the whole, to applaud the rise of law and economics as an account of tort law and to laud the Reagan revolution in regulatory policy need to confront starkly the unanticipated consequences of their own successes. By simultaneously accentuating the regulatory dimension of tort law and downplaying the efficacy of the regulatory state, free-market conservatives have unwittingly created a climate ripe for the use of social policy tort litigation to sidestep the political arena.

Gun Litigation as Risk Regulation

Apart from its ironic intellectual and political roots, gun litigation undertakes its regulatory enterprise in a manner oblivious, for the most part, to the major lessons learned over the past two decades about prospective risk regulation. These lessons are twofold, and, most important, they transcend partisan political lines.

First, regulatory policy post-1980 has emphasized both precision and comparison in the evaluation of regulatory programs. The intellectual starting point for this development consists of the now famous chart developed in the early 1980s by the Office of Management and Budget (OMB) to compare across agencies the cost-effectiveness of various regulatory measures intended to advance public health and safety. The OMB chart later formed the centerpiece for a book in which Stephen Breyer calls for the prioritization of regulatory interventions based upon their capacity to deliver the greatest health and safety benefits for the least compliance costs.[31] Subsequent academic commentary has called into question the methodology of the OMB chart specifically.[32] The larger lesson nonetheless remains: Sensible regulatory policy in a world of limited social resources calls for precision in the identification of the costs and benefits associated with regulatory interventions and for prioritization of interventions according to their anticipated cost-effectiveness, broadly defined.

In the Reagan administration, the principal vehicle for the reorientation of regulatory policy along the foregoing lines consisted of Executive Order 12,291.[33] The Reagan Order demanded cost-benefit analysis of proposed regulatory interventions and provided for centralized oversight of the regulatory process by OMB to implement the policy agenda of the president. The most striking feature of the Reagan Order is not so much its content as the durability of its basic framework across partisan lines.[34] President Clinton entered office with a markedly different view of government regulation. But his counterpart Executive Order 12,866[35] largely retained the framework for regulatory policy analysis set forth in the Reagan Order. If anything, President Clinton went a step further, issuing directives to administrative agencies with regard to particular regulatory policies, sometimes at preregulatory stages of the agency decision-making process.[36] President George W. Bush likewise has embraced a process for regulatory review centered upon cost-benefit analysis across administrative agencies, as reflected in his Executive Order 13,258.[37]

Gun litigation unquestionably addresses a substantial risk to public safety—that posed by gun violence. But gun litigation—like all social policy tort litigation—proceeds on a distinctly noncomparative basis, framing the response of the law simply in terms of changes in gun marketing practices. This is not to say that gun litigation advocates ignore the costs and benefits of their preferred policy course or even that they agree on the microlevel details of the changes in industry marketing practices that would be most desirable. It is only to say that the inquiry is not comparative in the sense embraced in the realm of public regulation. As a matter of regulatory policy, the question is not simply whether the benefits of additional limitations on gun marketing outweigh their costs—a question that tort litigation, particularly on a regulatory conception, might explore. The question also is whether such an approach gives the law the biggest bang for the buck compared to other ways to address the safety risks posed by gun violence, some of which might not center on changes in manufacturers' conduct at all.

Second, regulatory policy post-1980 has come to appreciate the inherently political character of its enterprise and the consequent centrality of political accountability in the making of regulatory decisions. The Reagan, Clinton, and Bush Orders all reflect this view, calling for coordination of regulatory initiatives across administrative agencies not only for reasons of cost-effectiveness but also to ensure that agencies implement the overall policy agenda of the president. That agenda differed, of course, from Reagan to Clinton to Bush. The point, however, is precisely that. Absent the setting in stone of particular regulatory policies by Congress, the question of whether regulatory policy at a given time should be marginally more or less receptive to government intervention is quintessentially a political question and, as such, one suited for resolution by the institutional actor, aside from Congress itself, accountable to the populace as a whole.

Gun litigation, by contrast, uses tort liability as a vehicle for regulation in a manner that, in substantial part, sidesteps the ordinary political process. Insofar as elected officials in municipal governments have authorized gun litigation, many have tended to do so through the use of contingency fee arrangements that do not require budgetary authorization and, hence, are not subject to budgetary limitation at the behest of the legislature. Where ordinary political channels have raised their head in this area, they have done so through legislation at the state level to disempower municipalities from bringing or maintaining suits against gun makers.[38]

My overarching point here is not to come definitively to rest on the question of whether additional regulation of gun marketing stands as desirable policy from the vantage point of post-Reagan regulatory policy analysis. My claim, instead, is simply that a vision of social policy tort litigation as a vehicle for risk regulation makes for a growing disconnection between tort law and regulatory policy. That would not be so incongruous if tort law itself were seen as achieving something different from regulation—say, corrective justice between the parties. But it is a distinctly curious thing in a world in which tort law is conceptualized primarily as public regulatory law "in disguise."

Here, many advocates of gun litigation seek to walk a very thin tightrope. Their legal allegations fit within the prevailing theoretical account of tort law as a privatized vehicle for risk regulation. That account holds the promise of enabling them to obtain the kind of regulatory program that they have been unable to secure from the political system—one captured, some might say, by the gun industry and its supporters. Yet advocates of gun litigation tend not to subject their chosen vehicle of risk regulation to the kind of comparative, politically informed inquiry now regarded, on a bipartisan basis, as the hallmark of sound regulatory decision making. They want the regulatory force of tort law, but only if they can control how and where that force is targeted. As I now explain, social policy tort litigation against the gun industry tends to skirt even the parameters that the civil justice system has managed to fashion for the handling of conventional mass tort litigation.

Gun Violence as Latent Disease

Like mass tort litigation, the regulatory system too must confront the prospect of products suspected to cause latent disease. Cost-benefit analysis in the regulatory sphere depends upon precision in risk assessment, an ability to estimate the marginal benefit to public health associated with regulatory interventions. As a consequence, epidemiology—a field of scientific research concerned with the incidence and causes of disease in human populations—has come to the forefront of regulatory decision making. This is not to say that any branch of science can eliminate the need for regulators to make difficult value judgments in the face of uncertainty. The point nonetheless remains that mere speculation about the benefits of proposed regulatory interventions—speculation unsupported by the intellectual norms of science—is unlikely to carry weight in the policy debate. Science, in short, can serve to delineate the terrain within which political judgment takes place.

Attentiveness to the intellectual norms of science is not a notion confined to the regulatory sphere. The signal development in mass tort litigation practice in recent decades has been the exercise by trial courts of enhanced supervision over the admission of expert scientific testimony. In its 1993 decision in *Daubert v. Merrell Dow Pharmaceuticals, Inc.*, the Supreme Court posited a "gatekeeping" role for trial judges with respect to expert scientific testimony.[39] Appropriately enough, *Daubert* itself involved a conventional tort suit brought late in the sequence of mass tort litigation over the morning sickness drug Bendectin—in particular, after the development of a "vast" epidemiological literature documenting that children of mothers who consumed Bendectin during pregnancy suffered no increased incidence of birth defects as compared to children not so exposed.[40] The *Daubert* Court directed trial judges to differentiate expert testimony grounded in "scientific knowledge" from faux expertise backed only by "subjective belief or unsupported speculation."[41]

Elaborating on the foregoing distinction in subsequent decisions, the Court has recognized the need for scientists to draw inferences from underlying data but nevertheless has underscored the role of the trial court to determine whether, in a given instance, there is "simply too great an analytical gap between the data and the opinion proffered."[42] Along similar lines, the Court has underscored the trial court's responsibility "to make certain that the expert . . . employs in the courtroom the same level of intellectual rigor that characterizes the practice of an expert in the relevant field."[43] *Daubert* and its progeny have spawned whole treatises[44] and a vast array of scholarly articles. The important point for present purposes is that, after *Daubert*, speculation ungrounded in the intellectual norms of science is likely to have as little impact in mass tort litigation as in a regulatory process with an emphasis on cost-benefit analysis.

The most striking feature of the negligent marketing claim at the heart of gun litigation is that it replicates the analytical challenges associated with difficult causation issues in conventional mass tort litigation but without the "intellectual rigor" of an established branch of expertise. The negligent marketing claim arises in both individual lawsuits by victims of gun violence and litigation by municipalities under the rubric of tort liability for the creation of a public nuisance.[45] The claim has many dimensions that speak to, among other things, the adequacy of defendant manufacturers' monitoring of gun retail sales practices and manufacturers' tolerance of what one might describe as interjurisdictional arbitrage, whereby guns initially sold in jurisdictions with less stringent regulatory controls come to be transferred on the secondary market to jurisdictions with greater regulation. Details aside, the essential thrust of the negligent marketing claim is that the practices of manufacturers make guns readily available to persons inclined to use them in the commission of violent crime—a phenomenon that, in turn, results in some increment of additional expenditure by local governments. The negligent marketing claim in gun litigation is part of a larger genre of "enabling torts,"[46] situations in which the tortious misconduct of the defendant facilitates the commission of an intentional tort by a third party: here, the gun-wielding criminal offender.

Though not cast in scientific terms, the negligent marketing claim bears more than a passing resemblance to the sorts of epidemiological questions common in both conventional mass tort lawsuits and public regulation. Epidemiologists use the concept of "relative risk" to describe the relationship between a given substance and human disease.[47] As the term suggests, relative risk expresses the incidence of disease in the population exposed to the substance in question as compared to the incidence in an unexposed population similar in all other relevant respects. Thus, relative risk greater than 1.0 indicates that the incidence of disease in the exposed population is greater than that in the unexposed population—a finding that reflects an association between the substance and the disease, though not necessarily a causal relationship. Epidemiological research might seek to estimate relative risk in a variety of ways,[48] but the crux of the methodology remains to *compare* exposed and unexposed persons who are otherwise similar.

The comparative nature of epidemiological research is central to its power, both as a tool for scientific inquiry and as evidence of causation in tort litigation. The existence of a strong association between, say, silicone gel breast implants and autoimmune disease does not demonstrate the existence of a causal relationship between the two. One needs to know more about what toxicologists describe as the background or baseline risk of disease—in the present example, the prevalence of autoimmune disease among persons without the disputed implants. The concept of baseline risk relates closely to the counterfactual nature of the causation inquiry in tort litigation. The question of "but-for" causation in tort law asks whether the plaintiff would have suffered the same disease, even in a world without the misconduct that she attributes to the defendant[49]—or, to rephrase the question, whether the association between the product and her case of disease is simply coincidental.

As Aaron Twerski and Anthony Sebok note with respect to gun litigation, "it is the responsibility of the plaintiff to identify the differential between the baseline risk produced by non-negligent marketing and the ultimate risk produced by the defendants' negligence."[50] Translated into epidemiological terms, the central question surrounding the negligent marketing claim concerns the *magnitude* of the relative risk. As an intuitive matter, there is more than a little plausibility to the idea that, but for the challenged marketing practices of gun manufacturers, the incidence of gun-related violent crime might be lower. Evidence produced by the plaintiffs in recent unsuccessful litigation by the NAACP against the gun industry on a theory of public nuisance identifies a "significant relationship" between deficiencies in gun retailer care and the eventual use of the guns sold in criminal activities.[51] The calculus of additional outlays from the public fisc nevertheless is not a matter for intuitive guesswork based upon evidence of such an association—evidence that, in itself, advances no systematic comparison of the world with and without negligent gun marketing. To determine the additional increment of outlays from the public fisc attributable to negligent gun marketing, the hard question is whether and, if so, how much relative risk exceeds 1.0. And the magnitude of that excess itself affects the confidence with which one can infer a causal relationship, as distinct from a mere association.

For individual tort litigants advancing a negligent marketing claim, an additional question would be whether the particular plaintiff's injury—say, her shooting at the hands of a criminal offender—would have occurred even absent the negligent marketing of the defendant manufacturers. That question, however, is no different conceptually from that of specific causation in conventional mass tort litigation. Even if one is confident that a given product is capable of causing disease in humans generally, an individual mass tort plaintiff still must demonstrate that the product more likely than not caused her particular case of disease.[52] The attraction to municipalities of the negligent marketing claim as a basis for the recouping of budgetary expenditures is that it enables them to ground liability simply upon a showing of general causation—or, more specifically, to avoid the need to identify which gun-related injuries to which citizens come within the additional increment associated with the negligent marketing practices of the defendant manufacturers. This observation is in keeping with Howard Erichson's account in chapter 5 of this volume of how municipal lawsuits operate, in practice, as a form of litigation aggregation.

The nature of the negligent marketing claim is such as to make it exceedingly difficult to identify the magnitude of the relative risk through anything approaching a scientific method. As noted earlier, the way that epidemiologists estimate relative risk for products suspected to cause latent disease is by differentiating exposed from unexposed persons. In conventional mass tort litigation—say, over a pharmaceutical product—this kind of differentiation is straightforward. Some people consumed the product, whereas others did not. This observation is not to belie the methodological challenges inherent in the design of a sound epidemiological study—chiefly, the identification of human populations comparable in all relevant respects, except for the exposure at issue. But it is at least possible as a practical matter to deploy such a methodology.

The nature of the negligent marketing claim in gun litigation confounds any methodology that differentiates between exposed and unexposed persons. Here, exposure itself is a generalized phenomenon. Whereas only some persons in the populace come to be exposed to a pharmaceutical product and, as such, can be distinguished from unexposed persons in epidemiological research, everyone in the United States has been "exposed" to the disputed marketing practices of the gun industry. What is needed in gun litigation is the social science equivalent of epidemiology. But the nature of the causal chain at the core of the negligent marketing claim is such as to confound the prospects for such a methodology. The result is to cast the causation inquiry with regard to the negligent marketing claim in largely impressionistic terms at odds with those on which conventional mass tort litigation and the regulatory process have come to address conceptually similar issues.

Alabama and Beyond

The regulatory account of tort law gives defenders of gun litigation an avenue of response to criticism that they have cast the civil justice system adrift from recent learning in both regulatory policy and mass tort litigation practice. If tort law is to be judged principally by the regulatory outcomes that it facilitates, then one might defend gun litigation from an instrumental standpoint as at least better than the other approaches realistically on the regulatory horizon. Better to do something about gun violence through social issue tort litigation, so the argument goes, than to continue to leave the matter in the hands of a suspect political process inclined to inaction, at best. Better to rely on impressionism to a degree, some might say, than to await the development of an epidemiology of gun violence.

There is a certain appeal to this line of thinking, if all one cares about is reform of gun regulation in America. Social policy tort litigation undoubtedly has enhanced the public profile of gun industry marketing practices and, in so doing, has jump-started debate over the appropriate regulation of gun marketing. And the social meaning of gun availability itself is a matter surely worthy of public deliberation, as Dan Kahan, Donald Braman, and John Gastil observe in chapter 4 of this volume.

My concluding observation nonetheless is more in keeping with the classic song "Who's Next?" composed by humorist Tom Lehrer at the height of the cold war and the civil rights movement in the South.[53] Lehrer begins with the observation that "[f]irst we [the United States] got The Bomb, and that was good, 'cause we love peace and motherhood." He then lists the other nuclear powers at the time. For instance,

"France got The Bomb, but don't you grieve, 'cause they're on our side, I believe." Lehrer's list then extends fancifully to such nations as Luxembourg and Monaco, fading out with the lyrics: "We'll try to stay serene and calm when Alabama gets The Bomb. Who's next? Who's next?"

A regime of social policy tort liability unmoored to parallel considerations of risk analysis in the regulatory or mass tort litigation sphere is a dangerous animal. Serenity and calm may well prevail, while social policy tort liability, like The Bomb, stands to be wielded only by those who "love peace and motherhood"—or, more precisely, who wish to reduce the incidence of smoking, to lessen gun violence, and to combat the health effects of fast-food consumption. But social policy tort litigation is not by nature a creature beholden to any particular regulatory agenda. The marketing practices of various industries—manufacturers of violent video games overtly marketed to teenagers; producers of rap music touting violence against women and law enforcement officers; and purveyors of sexually explicit, nonobscene entertainment—might well be thought unamenable to direct regulation through conventional channels but nonetheless to precipitate, however remotely, some increment of additional outlay from the public fisc. For that matter, the concept of adverse "secondary effects," including crime, is already a dimension of the First Amendment debate over direct regulation of nude dancing.[54] Alabama may not get The Bomb, but municipalities there, or elsewhere, might welcome social policy tort litigation, just on a different account of enlightened social regulation.

Seen in the foregoing light, the emerging debate over social policy tort litigation bears more than a passing resemblance to that over the wisdom of another modern-day legal innovation that presses at the bounds of conventional structural limitations in the service of other instrumental goals: the independent counsel statute. This resemblance actually is no surprise. A conception of tort law as simply an occasion for regulatory policy-making has difficulty accounting for the institutional role of the plaintiff. Whereas corrective justice theories readily explain the plaintiff's presence in a tort lawsuit as the specific person mistreated by the defendant, regulatory theories can explain the involvement of the plaintiff only as a private attorney general. The plaintiff is simply as convenient a person as any to initiate suit and, in so doing, to create the occasion for regulatory policy-making by the court. Though not literally a private actor, the independent counsel—as the title suggests—operates nominally within the scheme of government but nonetheless outside ordinary prosecutorial channels.

Challenged as a violation of the constitutional separation of powers, the independent counsel statute survived review by the Supreme Court.[55] At the time, only a lone dissenter among the justices penned a dire warning of the potential for abuse of the independent counsel position—of its tendency toward a process of " 'picking the man and then searching the law books, or putting investigators to work, to pin some offense on him.' "[56] Less than a decade later, one might say metaphorically that Alabama got The Bomb. And the attitude of the legal academy toward the office of the independent counsel has undergone a transformation. One waits, with watchful eyes, to see whether the same sequence will prevail in the world of social policy tort litigation.

CHAPTER 8

Comparing Tobacco & Gun Litigation

STEPHEN D. SUGARMAN

Cigarettes and guns are enormous problems. Cigarettes kill more than four hundred thousand Americans each year, perhaps 10 percent of whom are victims of secondhand smoke and approximately one thousand of whom are victims of cigarette-started fires.[1] Firearms these days kill nearly thirty thousand Americans annually, including about eleven thousand homicide victims, more than sixteen thousand suicide victims, and about one thousand victims of the accidental discharge of firearms.[2]

This chapter first compares tobacco control and gun control from the public health perspective. It then examines possible aims of litigation against tobacco and gun companies, linking those aims to the public health goals earlier described. The results of tobacco litigation are then discussed, followed by an exploration of the implications for gun litigation.

The chapter concludes that, based upon the experience with tobacco, gun litigation should not be viewed as a central policy strategy for making public health gains with respect to firearms, especially given the highly uncertain prospects for the claims that cities have brought against the gun industry. Nonetheless, individual tort litigation might play a modest role in the broader public health initiative on guns.

Comparing Tobacco Control and Gun Control Goals and Strategies

Why Not Prohibition?

Many Americans wish that no one smoked cigarettes and that only law enforcement officials had access to handguns (and that ownership of other firearms was sharply restricted and regulated). Some favor strict legal bans on smoking and on gun owning. In June 2003, U.S. Surgeon General Richard Carmona said he favored abolishing all tobacco products, and over the years gun control advocates have urged the government to make it generally illegal to *possess* handguns.

Yet, such aspirations are unrealistic given current social norms. Tobacco and gun prohibition would make criminals out of millions of Americans who are addicted to cigarettes and/or who would hold onto their weapons regardless of the law. While smoking prevalence has shrunk about 50 percent since 1964, when the surgeon general issued his famous report on the health risks of smoking, today about 22 percent of American adults (more than 40 million people) regularly smoke cigarettes. Americans currently own more than 200 million guns, including more than 70 million handguns; indeed, between one-third and one-half of U.S. households reportedly contain a working gun. Moreover, experience with alcohol and marijuana prohibition shows that criminalizing tobacco and gun possession, if at all seriously enforced, would likely bring with it huge costs in the form of law enforcement and prison operations, the abuse of civil liberties, and an increase in organized crime.

Even apart from enforcement issues, individual liberty claims make gun and tobacco prohibition problematic. Although most adult smokers began as teens and say they are addicted, many enjoy cigarettes by choice. Given public support of personal autonomy and privacy, it would be highly troubling to criminalize smoking at home. As for guns, first there is the libertarian value that underlies the popular understanding of the Second Amendment. Second, there is the long-standing belief in the right of self-defense with guns that would be difficult to dislodge in a nation as violent as ours—a belief reenforced by some scholars who claim that violence is reduced when ordinary citizens are allowed to own guns because the fear of being shot deters some "bad guys" from committing crimes. Beyond these policy considerations are practical political considerations arising from the power of the tobacco industry and the NRA.

This is not to say that a prohibition policy for cigarettes and/or guns is totally unimaginable forever. After all, a few American locales have made handgun possession a crime (with minor exceptions), and in the era of alcohol prohibition, some states also criminalized tobacco possession and use—albeit with widespread violation of these laws.

Nonetheless, more realistic tobacco and gun control advocates do not focus on prohibition. Whether limited policy changes are actually seen by gun control advocates as second-best steps en route to gun prohibition is contested and has made compromise on gun control policy very difficult. By contrast, although tobacco control advocates are sometimes called "health Nazis," it appears that few wish tobacco use to be criminalized in the way marijuana and cocaine use have been.

Putting legal prohibition aside, tobacco and gun control efforts may be grouped under three headings: (1) changing social norms, (2) user harm reduction, and (3) protecting third parties.

Changing Social Norms

With respect to changing social norms around tobacco, the underlying assumption is that many people smoke because of the influence of others. The core idea, then, is to encourage people to be nonsmokers by making smoking seem deviant, not something one routinely encounters fellow citizens doing like eating, driving, or even drinking alcoholic beverages. Restrictions on tobacco advertising and secondhand smoke regulation (as well as the current campaign to curtail smoking by actors in motion pictures) are policies aimed at changing social norms by providing people with a daily environment in which they no longer widely observe people (or visual representations of people) enjoying cigarettes.

Put more strongly, the goal is to convince the public either that those who smoke must have been duped by an evil tobacco industry or else that they are fools. When efforts to demonize the tobacco companies through publicly funded antismoking ads are added to the policy package, the broader message intended is that smoking is decidedly not "cool."

A parallel with respect to guns is to convince ordinary folks that keeping a firearm for self-defense reasons is unwise or inappropriate. The underlying assumption here is that, if Americans who have guns were voluntarily to get rid of them, homicide, suicide, and accidental death rates would decline for the reason that guns obtained for self-protection are sometimes used irresponsibly, impulsively, or carelessly (perhaps by a different household member).

Changing this social norm is problematic for a number of reasons, however. Whereas getting one hundred people to quit (or not to start) smoking generally translates into perhaps fifteen or twenty years of extra life for perhaps fifty people, the consequences of one hundred ordinary citizens giving up their guns are much less certain. For one thing, to the extent that the fear that ordinary citizens are armed now dissuades criminals from attacking them, widespread voluntary disarmament could actually stimulate more assaults. Moreover, even if accidental and impulsive violence could be reduced by getting ordinary Americans voluntarily to give up guns, it is not clear what policy strategy can be employed in furtherance of that goal (although laws recently adopted in many states that permit people to carry weapons away from home would seem a step in the wrong direction).

Some gun control advocates depict the choice to possess a weapon for self-defense not only as foolish (i.e., you might accidentally shoot yourself or a family member or provoke an intruder to shoot you) but, worse, as depraved (i.e., what kind of society is this in which we individually resort to frontier justice instead of relying on collective security?). Hunting and other "sporting" uses of guns are also disparaged by some as inappropriately callous and macho. Yet, it is not clear whether these attitudes toward guns are being embraced by Americans who aren't already anti-gun and don't own them anyway. After all, for many responsible Americans, having guns in the family is a long-standing cultural pattern.

Of course, were our society to become dramatically less violent—were robberies and worse personal crimes to decline to low levels—then people who now obtain guns for self-defense purposes might be considerably less inclined to do so. Indeed, put more broadly, were there less poverty, less alcoholism, and less drug abuse; were Americans less depressed; and were effective mental health facilities more accessible, then one would expect fewer homicides and suicides generally, including fewer caused by firearms. But that is a different reality from ours.

One way to entice people to abandon gun possession is to impose a high tax on the purchase of guns. It has been estimated that the discounted present value of the harm to third parties caused by handguns is something like $850 per gun. Although this is not a precise scientific estimate, if a sum like that were added to the price of owning a weapon, this would probably have a substantial impact on gun ownership. People who currently can buy a pistol for $100 are likely to have second thoughts if they faced a cost of $1,000. Maybe a burglar alarm would seem a better investment; maybe the worried householder would make do with a club. "Sporting" users of guns might go in for other sports. In short, as with cigarettes, there is good reason to believe that a gun purchase is price sensitive. But, so far, nothing like that sort of tax on guns has been seriously considered, let alone adopted.

One explanation for why cigarette taxes are increasingly popular and yet governments have not imposed high taxes on gun purchases is that policymakers and voters see guns differently from cigarettes. Society seems quite content to increase the financial burden on everyone who smokes. But many gun owners are viewed as legitimately entitled to their weapons, and to price them out of the market (or even to heavily burden them financially) seems inappropriate to many. This sentiment is similar to that concerning alcohol, which tends to be relatively lightly taxed and which is responsibly used by most drinkers.

Besides, given the vast arsenal of existing guns, even if a high tax on the purchase of new guns influenced the market price of used guns, it is hard to imagine that anyone really keen on obtaining firearms would be discouraged from doing so—especially given estimates that at least five hundred thousand guns are stolen each year. (High taxes on new guns might also have the undesirable effect of encouraging owners of older less safe guns not to replace them with newer safer ones.)

The discussion of social norm change with respect to guns has focused on convincing ordinary citizens to disarm. A different idea is to change the social norms around the use of guns by "criminals" by making both threats with firearms and the firing of guns at victims culturally taboo. Unfortunately, it is not clear how our society might go about achieving this change without compulsion. Hence, more coercive policies aimed specifically at keeping guns out of the hands of "bad guys" are considered in a later section.

User Harm Reduction

"Harm reduction" has been embraced by the public health community with respect to illegal drugs, which views clean needle exchanges and less disabling heroin substitutes as good examples. But tobacco control advocates have been leery of harm reduction and have tended to follow the mantra of conservatives in the war on drugs—"just say no." Tobacco control advocates have been cool to the notion that there might be safer cigarettes or even that smokers should be encouraged to cut down on how much they smoke, fearing that these approaches would draw from people who otherwise would quit entirely, thereby causing more harm than good.

Moreover, the tobacco control community is highly suspicious of the tobacco companies. Such advocates believe that tobacco companies have insidiously conned smokers into thinking that filtered cigarettes and so-called low tar or light cigarettes are safer, when those advocates are convinced that such products are at least as dangerous as traditional products. Because of this experience, the public health community is generally hostile to the recent development by tobacco companies of products such as additive-free cigarettes and sharply reduced nicotine cigarettes.

Nevertheless, some tobacco control advocates have pointed out that the public health would be considerably improved if, for example, masses of smokers were to switch to chewing tobacco (even though there would be a rise in oral cancers). Moreover, the tobacco control movement seems content with products such as the nicotine patch or nicotine gum used in transition from being a smoker to a nonsmoker. Still, there are fears. What if more youths start using chewing tobacco as a gateway to cigarette smoking? What if people use alternative nicotine products in addition to smoking (e.g., drinking "nicotine water" while on a long flight)? What if such products make some people less fearful about taking up cigarette smoking in the first place? In short, many tobacco control leaders remain skeptical about whether there are genuine tobacco analogies to such efforts as the clean needle exchange.

By contrast, harm reduction appears promising to many gun control advocates. They imagine that guns could be made that young children with limited strength could not fire, that gun triggers could be locked and unusable by anyone without the key, that indicators could make clear when a gun is loaded, and that improved unloading and cleaning technology could reduce the risk of an unintended firing. Alterations like these might especially reduce accidental deaths (and injuries) from guns. In short, safer weapons are seen as decidedly feasible, whereas safer cigarettes are still generally viewed as a fantasy.

Yet, while even saving a modest number of lives is a good idea, one should not be overly optimistic about the potential gains from safer guns, given that rather few guns are now accidentally fired by children who would be prevented from doing so by triggers that are harder to pull and given that gun owners motivated by fear of attack might well choose to leave their guns unlocked despite the availability of locks. Moreover, many accidental gun shootings today result from irresponsible behavior by those with guns in their hands that technology is not likely to overcome.

Protecting Third Parties

Now that secondhand smoke is believed by scientists and the public to cause thousands of deaths from cardiovascular and lung diseases every year, restrictions on where people can smoke are primarily promoted to legislators on the ground that they protect involuntary third-party victims. (As noted earlier, these controls also importantly serve to make smoking appear to be an uncommon and deviant behavior. Furthermore, researchers have found that zoning out smoking at work and other locations helps smokers to quit or former smokers not to relapse.)

Homicides caused by guns (as well as the wounding of third parties with firearms) are obviously of enormous public concern. And it seems clear that, even though data show that many more people die from secondhand smoke than are murdered, Americans view the risks to third parties from guns as a more important social problem than third-party risks from tobacco. Perhaps this is because the gun risk seems so arbitrary or random to most people or because guns are often used to kill young people in gruesome ways as compared with the slower deaths of generally older people from tobacco.

Rather than disarming the entire population, however, for the past several decades the central gun control strategy with respect to third-party harms has been to try to prevent "bad guys" from obtaining firearms or, as a less effective substitute, to keep them from obtaining especially dangerous weapons. The thinking is that, if "irresponsible" users do not have guns, the homicide rate would decline sharply (acknowledging that "bad guys" could resort to other weapons even if they did not have guns).

One problem with this strategy, of course, is trying to predict in advance who might use a gun to kill or wound, so as to know who should not be allowed to have one. Because making accurate predictions is so difficult, policymakers have had no choice but to employ under- and overinclusive substitute measures instead. For example, it is currently illegal to purchase a gun if you are a convicted felon, an illegal alien, mentally ill (by certain criteria), or a minor. Of course, many who kill with guns are not in these categories and not everyone in these categories is likely to do so. But finer tuning is difficult. Where the baseline rule allows people to own guns, it is politically hard to add categories to this list except those describing people whose past conduct is viewed as sufficiently stigmatizing to justify this "penalty."

To be sure, even an underinclusive policy might yield substantial social benefits. But a second serious problem is actually keeping guns from those who, according to official policy, should not have them. Certain licensed retailers often fail to comply with the law requiring a background check before making a sale—out of carelessness, indifference, or worse. Some headway can be achieved here by improved technology and the investment of more law enforcement resources. However, in addition, there is the vast secondary market for guns. People who are not supposed to possess guns can readily obtain them at flea markets, at gun shows, from want ads, from underworld sources whose identity spreads via word of mouth, from friends making "straw" purchases from legitimate dealers, from family arsenals, as well as by theft. Gun show regulation and straw purchase regulation, currently hot topics, are probably steps in the right direction, but they are likely to have only a modest impact.

This gun access problem is similar to the problem of controlling youth access to cigarettes. Teens are not supposed to be able to purchase tobacco products from licensed retailers, but, in practice, most find it easy to obtain cigarettes anyway.

New gun technology might change this. For example, if guns could be connected to users by some sort of fingerprint identity (which has been proposed and which some companies are working on), then such "smart guns" could be fired only by the registered owner (unless an overriding technology were developed). This should undercut the secondary market for such new guns. Even so, it could be many years before the vast supply of existing guns would break, be lost, or be confiscated in the normal course of police business. In an era of fingerprint-connected weapons, perhaps some headway might be made on the problem of the existing stock of less safe guns, if government both bought back and increased penalties for possession of older guns—although existing gun buy-back programs and existing laws that make it a crime for convicted felons to possess guns seem to have had little effect.

Looking from Gun Control to Tobacco Control with Envy

Although some new national gun control measures have been adopted in recent years, these federal laws (including, most importantly, the Brady Bill, enacted in the early 1990s) appear to have had relatively little impact on reducing gun violence. To be sure, violent crime (including handgun crime) is significantly down nearly everywhere in the country as compared with, say, a decade ago. But in most places it does not seem credible to view gun control measures as a major cause. In some places, such as New York City, strong gun control laws and determined policing efforts to enforce those laws may be making a difference.[3] Yet few other locations appear to be copying New York's approach.

Moreover, whereas the "gun problem" was previously viewed by many as essentially an urban matter involving minorities and gangs, the spate of suburban school shootings of whites by whites has caused many now to view the gun problem as much more of a national concern.

When gun control advocates look to tobacco control, they might conclude that the grass there is considerably greener. Tobacco control legislation appears to be much more widespread, and in several places across the nation considerable headway has been achieved in enacting much of the tobacco control community's agenda. In California, for example, there are very tough controls on secondhand smoke; cigarette taxes have been boosted to a high level by U.S. standards; there is a reasonably funded antitobacco control campaign that, among other things, pays for hard-hitting antitobacco ads; many local legislative bodies have adopted controls on the marketing and promotion of tobacco products; new efforts are continually made to restrict youth access to tobacco; and many public pension plans have rid their portfolios of tobacco stocks. Moreover, cigarette smoking levels in California continue to drop and are now well below 20 percent of the adult population (quite a low rate by U.S. and worldwide standards, albeit still far higher than tobacco control leaders would like).

Beyond legislative comparisons, a further point of comparison between the movements concerns the place of litigation. Now that we have witnessed a blizzard of tobacco litigation, some of which is perceived to have been quite successful, many have wondered whether that success can be carried over to gun control.

Litigation as Part of the Tobacco and Gun Control Strategy

Before turning to details, it is important to emphasize where the analysis will wind up. First, despite widespread sentiment to the contrary, there is reason to doubt that tobacco litigation has achieved, or will achieve, a great deal by way of tobacco control. Second, it is not at all clear that legal strategies that have succeeded, or might succeed, against tobacco companies would succeed against gun companies. Third, on the other hand, in certain modest respects there may be greater prospects for successful gun litigation than for tobacco litigation.

Most of the litigation against tobacco companies has been tort (or personal injury) litigation, although some important cases, most significantly those brought by states and the federal government, have been based on other areas of the law.[4] Individual victims (or a victim and a spouse) have brought most of the cigarette lawsuits, although a few celebrated cigarette cases have been class actions. The same general pattern applies to the lower volume of gun litigation.

This section explores, in a general way, potential goals of tobacco and gun litigation and links them to the public health objectives discussed previously. The next sections examine actual and likely litigation achievements.

Put Product Manufacturers out of Business

One possible goal of litigation against cigarette and gun manufacturers is to put them out of business. It is not altogether clear how the goal of financially crushing the industry fits with the public health themes discussed earlier. At its most powerful, litigation that has destroyed an industry might be a backdoor way of achieving prohibition that is politically implausible through regular legislative processes.

But even if existing companies were financially destroyed, would new companies step in to replace those driven out? Or would they too face threats of legal liability that would dissuade them from entering this line of business? The answers may depend on the legal theory behind the litigation. If based on past misconduct in which future entrants need not engage, the answers could be very different than if the theory behind the litigation would make any future manufacturer equally financially at risk.

Furthermore, even if existing "legitimate" manufacturers are driven out of business and there are no "legitimate" new entrants, the issue of product supply remains. For cigarettes, this is primarily a matter of the potential for smuggling cigarettes into the United States and the possibility of homegrown (or perhaps simply home-rolled) cigarettes. This parallels the problem of illegal sources of drugs like marijuana today, as well as illegal sources of alcohol during prohibition. The same concerns apply to guns, but for guns there is the additional matter of the huge existing inventory of handguns in the United States.

A different issue is whether what might appear to be financially crippling litigation would actually put the existing product makers out of business. Existing firms, faced with crushing legal judgments, might seek the protection of bankruptcy courts. Resolving those claims via the bankruptcy process, firms could emerge from bankruptcy (perhaps with different owners) and continue making the same product (guns or cigarettes) in the future.

With respect to tobacco companies, although some tobacco control advocates would like to destroy the American cigarette industry, most observers of tobacco litigation have viewed lawsuits as unlikely to achieve that result. At most, there has been half-serious talk about putting the major companies into bankruptcy without stopping their production of cigarettes (although a few tobacco control activists dream of the possibility that the U.S. government would take over the industry and manufacture unbranded cigarettes that doctors could provide to addicted smokers—a kind of methadone analogy).

In any event, whatever aspirations some tobacco control activists might have, even in the $250 billion Master Settlement Agreement

(MSA) with the state attorneys general (discussed in more detail later), arrangements were carefully made for the industry to pay huge sums to the states over time and in ways that minimized the chances that these financial obligations would put the companies out of business. And none of the rest of the cigarette litigation (as detailed later) has so far seriously threatened to destroy the industry.

By contrast, because the gun industry is much smaller overall than the tobacco industry, and because the major gun makers are not financial giants like Philip Morris, R. J. Reynolds, and British-American Tobacco, there is a greater chance that successful industrywide gun litigation could destroy the *existing* manufacturers. Indeed, the financial burdens of defending lawsuits, regardless of their outcomes, could eventually overwhelm the gun companies. But, given ease of entry into the handgun business by companies with very limited capitalization, even if existing gun makers are driven out of business, they might readily be replaced by waves of newcomers who, in turn, would earn a quick profit and then disappear.

Fully Internalize the Injury and Illness Costs of the Product into Its Price

A different vision of litigation against some product makers (including cigarette and gun makers) is that lawsuits could force them to fully internalize all the injury and illness costs of those products into the price of their products. This litigation goal seems most consistent with the public health aim of changing social norms around smoking and owning guns.

For tobacco, it has been estimated that, with full cost internalization, smokers might be forced to pay, say, twenty dollars or more for a pack of twenty cigarettes. Buying cigarettes at this price would confront buyers with the full costs of the risks *they* run—such as shorter lives, lower earnings, and extra and earlier health-care costs—as well as the full costs their smoking imposes on others via secondhand smoke. Of course, smokers (and their families) today already bear a substantial share of those costs. But they bear them in the future when they become ill and die. By contrast, a mechanism that fully internalizes those costs at the time of purchase would make vivid to the buyer the enormity of those costs and would probably sharply reduce consumption.

In a parallel way, fully internalizing the costs of guns in the price of guns could possibly increase the price of typical handguns from between one hundred dollars and four hundred dollars to, say, upward of two thousand dollars. This price hike could substantially reduce the acquisition of guns.

But finding a valid legal ground that would achieve full cost internalization via litigation is quite another matter. For cigarettes, the funding of the MSA was loosely based on the idea that the cost to states of having to pay for health care for indigent smokers should be internalized into the cost of smoking. This is clearly only a tiny share of the total costs of smoking. And while the MSA, as noted earlier, is scheduled to yield payments in the range of $250 billion over the next two decades, on a per-pack basis this is thought to amount to something like thirty-five cents. Yet, as already noted, a full cost internalization approach would involve an increased cost of many dollars a pack. No serious tobacco litigation strategy so far attempted envisions such an outcome.

Gun litigation brought by cities and others (discussed later) that has been modeled on tobacco litigation is also not aimed at full cost internalization—although it is worth noting that, as a general matter, it seems that a larger share of the costs of guns is borne by third parties and public services (as contrasted with gun users themselves from suicides and accidental self-shooting) than is the case for cigarettes.

At least so far as tort law is concerned, the main problem with the full cost internalization aspiration is that there is no existing legal theory readily applicable to cigarettes or guns that would achieve this outcome. Although tort law does recognize what is called "strict liability," this does not mean absolute liability for all the costs associated with the use of the product. Were that so, then automakers, power tool makers, and alcoholic beverage makers, to take but three important examples, could be held liable and forced to internalize the costs of all injuries and deaths associated with their products. That simply does not occur.

The reason for this result as a legal matter is that product makers are only meant to be forced by tort law to internalize the costs of "defective" products they put into the market. This means paying for harms arising from defective automobiles, for example, but not for harms connected to autos in general.

The basic way that products are determined to be defective (or not) is by carrying out a risk-benefit analysis. In principle, the risk-benefit analysis could be done by asking whether the product is so dangerous that, in the jury's view, it should not have been marketed at all. But, in practice, courts generally require that the "defect" be measured by comparing the design of a product with a safer alternative design that the plaintiff proposes.[5]

It is true that the Restatement (Third) Torts for Products Liability no longer contains a provision found in the Restatement (Second) Torts that made clear that ordinary cigarettes were not defective products.[6] Moreover, the Restatement (Third) Torts opens the door a crack for the possibility of condemning certain socially unacceptable products as "defective" without claimants' having to prove a safer alternative design.[7] Yet, the narrow invitation to courts to consider embracing strict liability for unacceptably dangerous products without substitutes has so far come to nothing.

A second legal strategy might try to have the selling of cigarettes and guns deemed "abnormally dangerous activities" to which strict liability in tort attaches.[8] Under this branch of the law, for example, companies are permitted to set off dynamite when it is reasonable to do so, but if the dynamite injures anyone, those doing the blasting are liable for the harm done regardless of whether they acted with due care. Although some writers have suggested that this branch of strict liability in tort should apply to cigarettes and guns, courts have been unreceptive to this theory. If nothing else, note that it is those who engage in dynamite blasting, not sellers of dynamite, who are strictly liable.

It is imaginable under the common law of torts that courts could adopt a new category of strict liability that is not based on the existing "abnormally dangerous activity" or "defective product" rationales, and were they to do so, it is easy to envision both cigarettes and handguns at the top of the list of likely candidates for inclusion. Indeed, judges in Maryland did just that some years ago for at least a certain class of handguns.[9] Yet, this decision has not been followed in other states, and in Maryland the court's ruling was overturned by state legislation.[10]

Therefore, for the present, it seems wiser to focus on whether litigation against tobacco and guns might achieve other goals.

Promote Safer Products and Safer Practices

To many, the most important goal of tort litigation is the deterrence of unreasonably dangerous acts, and in the product setting this means stimulating product manufacturers to make safer products. The basic economic idea behind this goal is that, faced with the risk of legal liability if their product is proved unduly unsafe, firms will, in advance, take precautions to make it safer. Second, some argue that once a manufacturer is shown through litigation to be producing an unacceptably unsafe product, that company and others in its industry will get the message and begin to produce a safer product. Finally, some argue that litigation can pry secret safety information from defendants that not only shows that they all along knew about dangers that could have been reduced but also paves the way toward safer products in the future.

There is no reason to believe that, because of the threat of litigation, cigarettes smoked today are safer than they would otherwise be. Indeed, plausibly safer cigarettes may not have been introduced by the leading companies for fear that this would make them vulnerable to lawsuits by those who smoked the older more dangerous versions. On the other hand, some tobacco control activists believe that, if tobacco companies were held liable for the consequences of their current products, they would soon have something safer on the market.

Although the connection with litigation is not entirely clear, it is notable that some tobacco companies have recently been experimentally marketing new products that might possibly be safer than traditional cigarettes. However, so far there has been little market acceptance of these quasi-cigarette products, and, as noted earlier, public health activists are generally leery of them.

By contrast, with respect to guns, as noted earlier, there is hope in some circles for the development of much safer guns, and some genuine progress seems under way on this front. Although the threat of legal liability might be driving these technological advances, that is not self-evidently so. After all, guns that would actually provide greater safety to users would probably be readily purchased by many people who are determined to buy a gun, at least so long as the safety feature did not add too greatly to the gun's cost or usability.

In any event, when it comes to promoting safer products, one can at least see the connection between the public heath aims and the aspirations of litigation. Indeed, depending upon what sort of safety improvements were achieved, this safety-promoting goal of litigation could further both the aim of reducing user harm and the aim of providing better protection for third parties.

Beyond changing the products themselves, another related goal of litigation is to prompt what could be termed the "safer" marketing of products. Both the tobacco control and gun control movements strongly object to the marketing practices of the industries they attack. If nothing else, these objections demonstrate that fear of tort liability has not prevented these product makers from marketing in the way they do. Nonetheless, industry opponents have hoped that they can alter marketing practices for the future through litigation efforts that charge tobacco companies with false and misleading advertising and charge gun companies with improperly marketing high-power weapons and improperly distributing guns in ways they know will put them into the hands of criminals.

It is also important to appreciate that, while tort law is meant to promote safety by the threat of and imposition of money damages, litigation brought by the government against the tobacco and gun industries is based on a different approach. Although the governmental lawsuits also seek money damages, those cases typically seek injunctive relief as well. Moreover, it is clear that government plaintiffs from the start have been seeking settlements with both industries that, apart from any financial payments, would include promises of behavioral changes by the defendants. It is this "regulation by litigation" approach that has especially infuriated those who believe that the plaintiffs' lawyers in these cases are making an end run around the political process. Yet, to the extent that the defendants (or their downstream distributors) are violating laws properly enforceable by public officials, this objection seems to miss the point that injunctive relief and settlements based on promised behavioral changes are regularly obtained by district attorneys, state attorneys general, and the like.

Provide Financial Compensation to Victims

A traditional tort law role is to compensate victims of wrongdoing by providing them with money. To be sure, one-third or more of the money collected in a successful lawsuit usually goes to the claimant's lawyer and the other costs of litigation, and another hunk typically reimburses health insurers who have paid for the victim's medical expenses. Nonetheless, successful tort claimants can wind up with money that replaces the uninsured income they lost, pays for uninsured health-related expenses, and provides a not inconsiderable lump sum as a solace for the pain and suffering they have had to, and continue to, endure.

Furthermore, some tobacco litigation has sought to secure other compensation. In one series of cases, smokers who are not yet ill have sought compensation for ongoing medical monitoring that they would undergo in hopes that it would provide early warning of adverse health consequences of smoking. In an altogether different vein, in a recent wave of litigation smokers have sought reimbursement for the money they have paid for cigarettes on the theory that they were duped into thinking that light cigarettes were safer than regular cigarettes and that, absent such fraud, they would not have bought cigarettes at all. Neither of these sorts of claims has an evident application to gun litigation.

Beyond the medical monitoring remedy, it is not clear that the compensation goal per se is well connected with public health aims (apart from any product price increases it may in the end bring with it, a topic discussed next). This is because the compensation goal is generally backward looking, whereas the public health focus is forward looking.

Internalize Some Costs to the Product

Although it was noted previously that tort and other litigation theories currently available to claimants are unlikely to force the full internalization of the costs of products like cigarettes and guns into the price of those products, somewhat more promising theories exist that, if successful, might internalize some of those costs. From the public health perspective, any strategy that increases the cost of providing such products, and hence forces sellers to raise their prices, is potentially a social gain. This litigation goal seems most connected to the public health theme of changing social norms.

For cigarettes, if higher prices only forced people to switch to lower-priced generic brands, this by itself would not yield a public health gain since those products are as dangerous as premium brands. But the evidence is clear that higher cigarette prices actually reduce consumption and, most important, reduce the smoking prevalence rate. The only awkward aspect of higher cigarette prices is that addicted smokers will have to devote even more of their money to their addiction, and they are increasingly from the ranks of the working class and the poor.

As for guns, as noted earlier, higher prices should also mean fewer sales—although it is contested whether this alone would yield a net reduction in violence. Also, some buyers may respond to higher prices by purchasing what today are cheaper guns. This may be better than nothing if cheaper guns in general are less accurate and therefore a bit less lethal.

Punish Manufacturers for Misconduct

If companies (or whole industries) badly misbehave, then government prosecutors can pursue them, seeking fines and other financial penalties and possibly even individual penalties (as severe as prison sentences) against those inside the firm who were responsible. This government litigation could be of a civil or criminal nature (or both).

Private litigation can also be deployed for arguably similar purposes, especially when claimants seek punitive damages as a remedy. Punitive, or exemplary, damages are meant as a punishment for outrageous conduct, and the threat of such damages is meant to deter such conduct in the first place. In the corporate setting, punitive damages are basically imposed on companies, not on individually culpable employees. Yet, it is possible that, if punitive damages are awarded, wrongdoers inside the enterprise may be fired or otherwise punished (provided they are still connected to the firm, which often is not the case). Moreover, punishing the firm itself can sometimes punish the misconduct of management by driving down the price of the firm's stock (and the value of stock options), which executives often depend on as part of their compensation. (Of course, this consequence also penalizes all investors in the enterprise, many of whom are not personally blameworthy.)

Many tobacco and gun control advocates are angry at the industries they are trying to control, and their rhetoric often sounds highly vindictive, as though they are seeking a kind of vengeance against what they view as evil actors. While this is perhaps understandable, and while punishing those industries and their leaders may also help fortify fellow activists, as well as attract new supporters, it is not clear that punishment *by itself* serves a public health objective. Perhaps it can best be seen as a warning to others who undermine the public health that a similar fate may await them. Or it may be instrumentally seen as part of the effort to delegitimize the target industry so as to weaken it politically—for reasons noted next.

Weaken the Industry in Legislative Battles by Creating and/or Maintaining a Public Image of the Industry as "Evil"

Litigation can be used as part of an attempt to tarnish (or keep tarnished) the reputation of a company or industry. This result might be achieved simply by announcing that a lawsuit has been filed and/or by publicizing documents obtained in discovery—that is, without actually winning a case. In short, litigation, and the media attention it receives, can be a vehicle for educating the public. Moreover, litigation (or even its prospect) may itself spur whistle-blowers to come forward with evidence disparaging defendants.

If, through litigation, an industry can be branded in the public's eye as an evil outlier, this may make it more vulnerable in legislative battles. Legislators may be less willing to take contributions from such an industry and more willing to vote for legislative changes designed to regulate such an industry. The tobacco industry appears quite concerned about this. Philip Morris, for example, engages in a variety of activities that seem aimed at (re)gaining the admiration of at least parts of the public.

This goal of using litigation to politically weaken the tobacco and gun industries is not connected to any particular public health goal. Rather, it may be seen as potentially facilitative of whatever is on the public health legislative agenda that could no longer be blocked by the political might of those industries.

Discourage Consumer Patronage by Exposing and Documenting Company Misconduct

Quite apart from weakening an industry on the legislative front, stigmatizing an industry via litigation could cause many of that industry's customers to withdraw their patronage. The underlying idea is that consumers may dislike buying from "bad guys," especially those they now believe have been trying to dupe them. This idea seems most aligned with the public health goal of changing social norms around smoking.

With respect to guns, although publicity around litigation may be effective in (re)arousing the ire of those who already favor gun control, it is less clear whether exposing even the most troubling marketing practices of some gun makers will turn off many would-be purchasers.

This completes the review of potential goals of litigation. The next sections describe the status of cigarette and gun litigation. One important overall point is that, in terms of actual final legal victories, both tobacco and gun control forces so far have rather little to show for their efforts.

Tobacco Litigation Overview

Smokers (and their spouses and heirs) have been suing the tobacco companies in tort cases for more than fifty years. Until recently, these cases have all failed. Claimants generally have lost because they could not prove that the smoker was actually harmed by smoking, because they could not convince the jury of tobacco company wrongdoing and/or because they could not prove that better disclosure of the risks of smoking by tobacco companies would have made any difference in the smoker's behavior.

Of late, the tide has turned somewhat at the trial level, as about a dozen juries have become convinced that the tobacco industry badly misbehaved and that had it not done so the victim would not have become ill.[11] In a first-ever victory, a Florida case (*Carter v. Brown & Williamson Tobacco Corp.*) was won at trial, and, after all appeals were exhausted, in March 2001 the victim was actually paid about one million dollars.[12] In mid-2003, something less than two hundred thousand dollars was paid to another Florida smoker who had won at trial.[13]

Beyond that, claimants have now won approximately ten other verdicts around the nation. Several of these victories include enormous sums (many millions of dollars) as punitive damages. But all these cases are still on appeal. Moreover, tobacco company defendants continue to win jury verdicts in a substantial share of individual smoker tort cases, so the future prospects for these cases remain cloudy.

The legal prospects for lawsuits claiming harm from secondhand smoke injuries are also uncertain. Although the tobacco companies have won most of these cases so far litigated, a flight attendant plaintiff has won an important trial victory, but that case too is on appeal.[14]

Class actions on behalf of ill (and deceased) smokers have not fared well. One enormous temporary exception was the Florida class action (*Engle v. R.J. Reynolds Tobacco Corp.*) in which a jury awarded nearly $150 *billion* in punitive damages against the tobacco companies, as well as substantial compensatory sums to three individual smoker victims.[15] However, in 2003 the intermediate Florida appeals court threw this case out entirely, concluding, among other things, that a class action never should have been allowed in the first place.[16] That case too is not yet fully resolved.

Class actions seeking medical monitoring remedies, noted earlier, have also fared poorly, and the two most promising cases, in West Virginia and Louisiana, have recently been lost by plaintiffs (although in Louisiana the jury awarded smoking cessation benefits to smokers, a result likely to be tied up in court for some time).[17]

Although, as explained earlier, the tobacco control movement has been skeptical about making cigarettes safer for smokers, potentially "fire-safe" cigarettes are another matter. If cigarettes self-extinguished more quickly and reliably, tossed lighted cigarettes might cause fewer fires. In 2003, however, Philip Morris agreed to a settlement in a case brought on behalf of a burned child—albeit in what is widely viewed as an extraordinarily pro-plaintiff local jurisdiction.[18]

Health-care providers and foreign governments have also sued tobacco companies, seeking reimbursement for expenditures they incurred in the treatment of those with smoking-related diseases. But these cases have essentially all been won by the defendants (with a couple of special exceptions not likely replicable elsewhere).[19]

During the Clinton administration, the Department of Justice brought a wide-ranging federal lawsuit against the tobacco industry that initially contained several causes of action. Trial of the potentially most damaging claim—that the defendants violated the federal racketeering act (RICO)—finally began in late 2004. Whether the government will prevail is quite uncertain, although, if it does, the financial consequences for the tobacco companies could be enormous.

As noted earlier, several class actions have recently been filed claiming that tobacco companies duped smokers into thinking that light, or low-tar, cigarettes are safer than traditional cigarettes when, it is claimed, they are just as dangerous (or perhaps more so), given how they are actually smoked. These cases seek financial reimbursement for the cigarettes that lawyers say victims would not have purchased had they known the truth. Although these cases have been dismissed in some states, they are moving ahead elsewhere, and in Illinois, a trial judge has awarded the class an astounding twelve billion dollars (including punitive damages).[20] This case, too, is on appeal.

As the story of tobacco litigation has so far been detailed in this section, the record ought to make one wonder just what gun control advocates might be seeing in tobacco litigation to make them want to pursue this same trail. But this retelling has so far ignored the MSA.

Starting in the 1990s a few state attorneys general, with critical help from the personal injury bar, sued tobacco companies, seeking huge financial recoveries. Soon they were joined by the attorneys general of most states (with the support of many of the same personal injury lawyers). The legal theories underlying these cases were varied and, in the end, largely untested.

Although many describe these cases as a new form of tort litigation, there is reason to reject this characterization. Governments who provide health care to indigent smokers do potentially have rights under established tort principles, but these are *subrogation* rights. And that means that the government must step into the legal shoes of the smokers whose care they funded, seeking reimbursement from defendants against whom the smokers themselves have valid legal claims. But it was absolutely clear from the outset that the state attorneys general were making legal claims that did not depend upon proving what individual smokers themselves would have to prove if their own claims were to succeed.

These state lawsuits prompted an effort by the tobacco industry to reach a so-called global settlement that, among other things, would have protected the industry against future class actions and future punitive damages claims and would have capped their potential annual financial obligations in individual lawsuits. The agreement was understood to require adopting a confirming and implementing federal statute. But that never happened. Simply put, the tobacco control side got much greedier once the global settlement was presented to Congress, and as their Democratic supporters sought more money from, more concessions from, and fewer concessions to the industry, the tobacco companies pulled out of the deal and had their Republican supporters kill it.

This left the tobacco companies in a somewhat difficult position, however. In the run-up to the global settlement, they opted to settle the most advanced cases (in Mississippi, Florida, and Texas) before trials could begin, and then they settled the Minnesota case during trial (when things were looking good for the "home team"). After the collapse of the global settlement, the MSA, agreed to by the other states (plus jurisdictions like the District of Columbia and Puerto Rico), provides about one-third less money than the global settlement would have, and, although it contains public health concessions, they are weaker than those the global settlement would have contained. Yet, the MSA does not contain the litigation protections that the global settlement would have provided the tobacco industry, although, of course, it did get rid of the highly threatening, if legally uncertain, state attorneys general lawsuits.

Many public health experts believe that the behavioral measures agreed to in the MSA (such as an end to billboard advertising and certain magazine advertising)—despite their aim of changing social norms around smoking—are too narrow in their reach and as a result have had, and will continue to have, little impact on smoking and health. The money provided by the MSA gives states as a group around ten billion dollars a year, which is a large sum, although many tobacco control activists bitterly complain that, in most states, none or next to none of the money is being used for tobacco control.

Hence, the primary impact of the MSA, apart from generating huge legal fees for the private lawyers involved, appears to be an increase in the price of cigarettes, estimated to be around thirty-five cents a pack, which reliably reduces the volume of cigarettes sold. Of course, this same result could be much more directly achieved by an excise tax increase. Furthermore, it is worth noting that some of the MSA provisions that are said to protect the public health also serve to protect the market shares of existing tobacco companies and to discourage new entrants.

Overall, the record of tobacco litigation is at best a mixed success from the public health perspective.[21] Safer products have not been achieved, although, arguably, somewhat less seductive marketing methods were agreed to in the MSA. Hardly any victims have been compensated. A very modest share of the costs of smoking has been internalized into the price of the product. The industry has not yet been financially punished by the litigation.

Although the reputation of the tobacco companies surely must be far worse now than it was, say, ten years ago, it is unclear how much of that reputation decline should be attributed to litigation of the past decade. Litigation has unearthed documents that are embarrassing to the tobacco industry, but disgruntled insiders revealed similar information apart from the litigation.[22] Moreover, the industry has been under attack in the media for reasons unrelated to litigation.

In any event, while this worse reputation may have made the industry politically weaker, federal regulation of tobacco products remains extremely modest, suggesting that the national tobacco control movement has been unable to capitalize on the altered political balance. State and local tobacco control efforts have grown. However, the most important measures put in place—higher taxes and tougher secondhand smoke controls—may well be the result of an increasing majority of nonsmokers ganging up on the much smaller and increasingly marginalized number of smokers.

To be sure, smoking levels are way down since 1964, although a large share of the decline occurred well before the recent wave of litigation. States like California have achieved significantly reduced smoking rates even in recent years, but apart from the MSA-based price increase, again it is by no means clear that tobacco litigation has played a major role in this outcome.

Lessons for Gun Litigation

Seeing governments obtain a lot of money and at least some policy reform measures via the MSA, it is easy to understand why lawyers, and especially personal injury lawyers who earned vast sums in the tobacco cases, would think about a parallel litigation campaign against handgun makers.[23]

From the viewpoint of gun control advocates, the main attraction of the MSA approach is the possibility of achieving injunctive relief or a favorable settlement with the gun industry—remedies that might get gun companies to adopt public health measures that are politically implausible through normal legislative channels.

In addition, gun lawsuits modeled on the state tobacco cases could be used as part of a publicity campaign to expose what gun control advocates view as extreme misconduct by some gun makers. Using litigation in this way, as described earlier, should be understood as part of a strategy for generating greater public support for gun control in general and as a way of weakening the pro-gun political lobby, regardless of the outcome of the litigation.

Finally, gun control advocates can imagine that funds obtained through successful government gun cases could be earmarked for further gun control activities, thereby avoiding the fate of the tobacco control community in the MSA.

So far, however, most state attorneys general and governors have not supported lawsuits against gun makers. Indeed, at the state legislative level, often with the support of the governor, many states have adopted statutes designed specifically to preclude such cases. Moreover, in early 2004 Congress came very close to adopting a sweeping national ban on many types of gun litigation, an issue that is not likely to disappear quickly from the congressional docket.

The upshot is that government cases (in states where they have not been legislatively precluded) have mostly been filed by cities with the support of the mayor. (Parallel to the third-party lawsuits filed in the tobacco area by health insurers, there has been some third-party effort in gun cases as well, as best illustrated by a now unsuccessful lawsuit filed in New York by the NAACP.) So far, these cases have not fared well.

As with the tobacco cases, it is not clear whether there is a valid legal theory underlying the cities' gun cases, although several inventive theories have been advanced. Speaking generally, most of the claims have been primarily based on public nuisance law and/or on a theory of negligent marketing. Both of these legal approaches imagine that tighter controls on the legitimate distribution of handguns will keep many "bad guys" from obtaining handguns. Some of the lawsuits also seek to make guns safer. Details of these cases are provided in other chapters in this book.

During the Clinton administration, the federal government, led by Department of Housing and Urban Development head Andrew Cuomo, joined with New York attorney general Eliot Spitzer to try to achieve a deal with the gun industry. But this effort failed. One major gun maker,

Smith & Wesson, eventually reached a deal with government officials, but other companies did not go along. Moreover, once isolated, Smith & Wesson wound up facing an enormous backlash from the NRA and gun owners and significantly withdrew from its commitments.

In sum, achieving gun control via government lawsuits turns on whether the remaining cases being pursued by cities will ever become a sufficient threat to the industry as to force major concessions. Several California cities recently obtained what appear to be minor concessions from gun distributors, but those cities' legal claims against gun makers have, so far, been dismissed. Moreover, a continuing worry is that restrictions forced on (or agreed to by) existing gun makers and distributors would prompt entry into the gun market by outlaw providers.

As noted previously, individual tort cases against tobacco companies, in important respects, are about advertising and promotional strategies. That some tobacco cases are beginning to succeed also provides some hope for gun control advocates who have been promoting the use of tort law in individual gun cases also to go after advertising and distribution practices.

Gun control plaintiffs seek to put a stop to marketing practices such as the flooding of gun shops in the suburbs with weapons that everyone knows will largely wind up in cities and to discredit ads that flaunt certain weapons as especially dangerous and suited for killing people. Legal hurdles confronting these cases include the problem of proving that an individual victim would not have been shot had the industry changed its conduct.

Perhaps legally more promisingly are defective product gun cases brought by individual plaintiffs. As already noted, cigarette cases have not generally been based on design defect theories. But gun cases have begun to be, and, based on the previous public health discussion, that is understandable. Moreover, convincing a jury that guns could be made safer, and that had a certain one been made so, then a particular victim would not have been injured or killed, presents a lawyer with the sort of product liability challenge that is litigated all the time with respect to auto injuries, tool injuries, and the like.

To be sure, defective gun cases are likely to prove most attractive only in special instances of accidental shootings, and, to be sure, many of the superficially best targets of this litigation may be insolvent or out-of-business gun makers. Nonetheless, a few victories that rest on the general idea that guns can be made less dangerous could pave the way for even more aggressive gun safety claims over time.

In conclusion, guns and cigarettes present public health problems that are both similar and different. Although public health strategies for dealing with these two problems fall into the same broad categories, the details are very different. Tobacco litigation is probably given credit for achieving more by way of public health than it actually has to date. One should not be optimistic that gun litigation will yield a dramatic decrease in homicide, suicide, or accident rates. Yet, gun litigation might have a useful complementary role to play as part of a mixed legislative, regulatory, and litigation approach to gun control.

PART III

*Gun Litigation as a Regulatory
Response to Gun Violence*

CHAPTER 9

Why Regulating Guns through Litigation Won't Work

PETER H. SCHUCK

The assault against the gun industry is a peculiarly American form of guerrilla warfare. The insurgents have fielded their commandants and foot soldiers, deploying them along diverse fronts. They[1] have eagerly and imaginatively recruited spies and turncoats to ferret out the enemy's documents and strategies. Both they and their industry adversaries have exploited modern tools of communication and persuasion—lobbying, publicity, expert studies, legislative hearings, propaganda, opinion leader vouching,[2] and disinformation—to mobilize support among politicians, the media, the uncommitted, and the uninformed. And both sides have wielded a variety of weapons ranging from the traditional to the most technologically advanced.

Legislative tactics having failed either to bring down the gun industry or to produce the more extensive controls that the reformers seek, they have made litigation their new weapon of choice. Although we are by now thoroughly inured to the spectacle of mass tort actions against companies that market controversial products of one kind or another, litigation against an entire industry remains relatively unusual. The main precursor, of course, is the tobacco litigation, which in its current phase seeks to move the focus from the traditional individual claimants to class actions and other forms of mass claims aggregation.[3] In view of the remarkable success of the tobacco plaintiffs (and especially of their handsomely compensated lawyers), it is hardly surprising that the gun control advocates regard the tobacco litigation as a template for their own efforts, while also introducing some new wrinkles of their own devising.

(Stephen Sugarman, in chapter 8 of this volume, analyzes the relevance of the tobacco model.)

Litigation, then, is the most remarkable site of gun control efforts today in the United States.[4] As of this writing (November 2004), the plaintiffs' lawyers in the gun litigation have invested a great deal of time and money on this campaign[5] with very little to show for it in terms of either new liability-promoting legal doctrine or jury awards sustained on appeal.[6] Indeed, this litigation may be producing the worst possible outcome from the reformers' perspective. Their lawyers, after all, are drilling dry holes at great cost, creating adverse legal precedents, and further energizing already militant pro-gun groups. State legislatures are adopting statutes that bar or limit such litigation, and Congress is actively considering legislation that would grant the industry nationwide immunity from liability. Such controls are a direct, categorical response to the plaintiffs' litigation campaign.[7] From a purely consequentialist point of view, this campaign must be considered an almost total failure.

I say *almost* because the gun litigation has produced certain outcomes cheered by the plaintiffs. It has forced at least one small gun manufacturer (Davis Industries) into bankruptcy;[8] induced another (Colt) to discontinue production of seven handgun models;[9] convinced a third (Smith & Wesson) to agree to alter its design, marketing, research, and distribution practices to reduce gun-related risks;[10] and obtained some concessions from some small gun dealers.[11] Whether these outcomes will in fact reduce gun-related risks or merely shift the demand to other brands and dealers[12] remains to be seen, but gun control advocates regard them as victories. In addition, the litigation has unearthed information from industry files that helps to discredit its public position,[13] and Judge Weinstein's decision in July 2003 dismissing the most prominent private tort case against the industry was written in a way that creates a roadmap for plaintiffs' lawyers in other cases.[14] Finally, as Philip Cook and Jens Ludwig argue, litigation may succeed in altering the political starting points and encouraging compromise solutions that would otherwise be more elusive.[15]

The analysis that follows constitutes an exercise in comparative institutional analysis. My purpose is to illuminate the relative advantages and disadvantages of undertaking gun control through common law litigation versus other forms of social policy-making and implementation. In doing so, I shall take as a premise—although this premise is in fact

highly contestable[16]—that gun control (in some form) is a desirable public policy and that the relevant question is not whether to undertake such
control (in some form) but whether to do so through litigation or instead
through some other public law technique that I shall call "risk regulation."[17] When my answer to this question depends either on which particular form of gun control the decision maker chooses or on how its
choice would be implemented, I shall note this conditionality. In short, I
mean to focus this analysis as much as possible on the institutional differences between judicial and nonjudicial regulation. To this end, I
finesse the substantive issues of gun control policy as much as my focus
on comparative institutional analysis—which prefers the management
of gun risks through legislative or administrative regulation rather than
adjudication—will permit. Being only human, however, I cannot resist
using the conclusion to state very briefly my own policy views, which
would place a priority on developing improved technologies to detect
illegal possessors and to identify illegal users rather than extending the
kinds of existing controls that have been demonstrably ineffective.

Needless to say, the gun control movement is reluctant to forswear litigation about gun risks in favor of legislative and administrative regulation. After all, they have already tried and failed in their political pursuit
of the latter. Nor is it necessarily true that regulation and litigation are
mutually exclusive. Indeed, as Timothy Lytton argues in chapter 10,
these two forms of social control may in some circumstances actually be
complementary. My analytical project, however, will be that of an
Olympian designer of an optimal regime for controlling gun-related
risks, one who compares the litigation option as it now exists to the regulatory option that would become viable were the gun control movement to achieve greater political success in the future. Finally, my discussion will refer to legislators and administrative officials collectively as
risk regulators unless I mean to distinguish between the two categories
for analytical purposes.

The Logic of Institutional Comparison

Institutional comparison is rooted historically in the legal process school
of jurisprudence strongly identified with the work of Henry Hart and
Albert Sacks at Harvard Law School in the 1950s.[18] The methodological

premises of the legal process approach are well established in a rich literature with linkages to work in political science, public administration, and economics. At the most foundational level, this approach is concerned with the structure and behavior of institutions. Political theorists have recently elaborated a deep conceptual understanding of the nature of institutions,[19] but such abstraction is unnecessary for my purposes. The institutions of chief interest here are the three standard structures of political governance and policy development—legislatures, courts, and administrative agencies—as well as the less formal institutions that surround them: the plaintiffs' and defense bars, the media, the gun industry, gun control groups, and the market.

The legal process approach holds that different institutions exhibit distinctive structural elements that shape the behavior of those individuals and groups that constitute them in patterned, recurrent, recognizable ways. Some of these elements—such as how the institution's leaders are appointed, how they must exercise their authority, and how the institution relates to other institutions—are constitutional in nature. Others are prescribed by external statute or internal regulation. Still others are informal, generated by the goals, incentives, and interactions of the officials and of outsiders with interests in the institution's decisions. These structural elements, taken together, fashion an institution's routines and tendencies—and, over time, its traditions, organizational values, self-conception, and sense of mission.

All of this institutional development is designed to legitimate its decisions and authority as it competes against other institutions for resources and influence in a political world where they are always being hotly contested. In this competition, each institution exhibits characteristic (because largely structural) strengths, weaknesses, and trade-offs. Simply stated, each institution is good at some things and poor at others—compared to other institutions. Such judgments about comparative institutional performance or competence, of course, are largely in the eye of the beholder; they depend on her particular values and empirical assessments. There simply is no Archimedean point outside the system of evaluation from which an observer can derive and render authoritative, uncontroversial judgments about how institutions perform.

These judgments about comparative institutional competence are inherently difficult. First, the notion of competence, properly understood, extends far beyond mere technical expertise. It also requires an assessment of an institution's capacities across a number of criteria: normative (its ability to instantiate the distinctive values for which it stands), political (its ability to generate and sustain the necessary public support), and instrumental (its ability to effectively and efficiently implement the decisions it makes). Second, such assessments are necessarily contingent; they vary according to the nature and history of the specific issue being addressed by each institution, the resources available to it, political factors outside its control, and many other variables. Accordingly, an assessment must be qualified and context sensitive, not categorical and timeless. Finally, institutional performance is inevitably suboptimal, which means that an institutional comparison is inevitably a comparison among what Neil Komesar calls "imperfect alternatives" (which is the title of his important analysis of how society should choose among different institutions to achieve its goals).[20] Thus, the fact that an institution is less than ideal for a particular policy task is not necessarily a reason to reject it and choose another; for all its limitations, it may still be better than the alternatives.

Although the particular assessments required by the institutional comparison approach are likely for these reasons to be controversial, the approach itself might seem self-evidently correct. After all, who can object to judging and comparing institutions according to their capacities to handle the kinds of questions that come before them? The answer, however, is somewhat more complicated—at least where important legal rights are concerned. Some commentators indeed object to basing the assignment of responsibility for determining and protecting legal rights on an institutional assessment that takes this rationalistic, instrumentalist, cost-benefit balancing form. In particular, those legal scholars and others who tend to prefer judicial fora to legislative and administrative ones resist this approach, celebrating the courts' traditional role in recognizing and enforcing individual rights, whether those rights be constitutional, statutory, or judicial in origin. They are often beguiled by the common law process, which purports to elaborate law from previously adopted principles rather than making a synoptic judgment at the threshold of decision about which of the various institutional possibilities for lawmaking is best suited to the task. Courts engaged in common law adjudication seldom ask institutional competence questions unless, as in many gun liability cases, the novelty of the plaintiffs' claims at common law is clear and the claims' broad policy implications make such questions impossible to finesse.[21] And even when the courts do ask institutional competence questions in gun cases, they seldom analyze them in a systematic or thorough fashion. In some cases, this juridico-centrism (as I have called it)[22] may be the outcome of a self-conscious institutional comparison by the court, but more often it represents either a kind of reflexive or ideological preference for judicial resolution or a prudential judgment that the particular right in question will fare better (or worse, as the case may be) in adjudication than in a political or bureaucratic forum.

The institutional competence literature is now large. Much of it has been a response to earlier waves of class action litigation designed to reform large public bureaucracies like school, prison, police, and mental health systems where the legal claims and especially the legal remedies being urged upon courts strain, and perhaps exceed, their institutional capacities.[23] Less of this literature has been concerned with the challenge of designing a process to manage social problem solving more generally.[24] The analysis that follows is written in this broader spirit.

The Criteria for Institutional Comparison

In order to conduct an institutional comparison, of course, one first needs to specify the criteria according to which the competing institutions are to be appraised. Although the relative weights assigned to each criterion in the overall judgment are bound to be controversial, the criteria themselves should elicit general agreement. I propose six of these criteria; obviously I could identify many more. Each of these six criteria pertains to the institutions' propensity to develop and implement sound gun control policies. Again, this is true almost without regard to the substance of those particular policies. In order for an institution to make and implement policy effectively, it must (1) generate the technocratic information needed for gun-related policy-making; (2) generate the political information needed to frame an acceptable policy; (3) mobilize the array of different policy instruments necessary to establish and implement the policy; (4) promote social learning (short feedback loops) and flexible adaptation to new conditions; (5) generate predictable rules; and (6) secure and sustain the policy's legitimacy.[25]

In the discussion that follows, I shall often speak of regulation in gen-

eral terms as a kind of useful shorthand. Even at this abstract level, however, it is important to emphasize that the properties and propensities of
various regulatory systems may differ significantly from one another.
We might broadly distinguish between two types of such systems. One
is a regime in which an agency supervises and specifies a multitude of
design, production, transportation, and other decisions by the industry
in minute, technical detail and on a continual, dynamic basis. Air pollution control is a familiar example. A quite different regime is one in
which the regulator imposes relatively few limitations on what the industry may or may not do. These standards tend to be fewer and more static, and their enforcement does not require the elaborate regulatory
machinery of an Environmental Protection Agency but relies on more
conventional agencies such as police departments and the Bureau of
Alcohol, Tobacco, Firearms and Explosives (BATFE). I imagine that
the regulation of gun-related risks will likely take this simpler form. It
already does so with regard to registration requirements, background
checks, bans on the sale and transport of specific weapons, and so forth,
and may do so in the future if regulation requires, say, ballistic markings
or certain new safety features. I do not mean to prejudge the specific
forms that gun regulation might take. My point, rather, is to refine the
discussion of gun regulation by contrasting it, even at this abstract level,
to the far more complex regimes found in other areas of risk regulation
policy.

Technocratic Information

Information is the lifeblood of intelligent lawmaking. A legal system's
ability to mobilize high-quality policy-relevant facts for the lawmakers
at a relatively low cost is perhaps the most important precondition for the
effectiveness of its policies—and ultimately for their legitimacy, as I discuss later. The term *facts* here encompasses empirical evidence concerning, among other things, the nature and magnitude of gun-related risks;
how well existing policies work; which public and private resources can
be brought to bear on which aspects of the problem; how alternative
policies might affect the world and through which causal pathways and
with what substitution effects;[26] the magnitude of the costs and benefits
created by these alternatives and the intergroup distribution of these

costs and benefits; and how markets will respond to particular policy changes. I call the information about such facts "technocratic," distinguishing it from the "political" information that is the subject of the next section.

For any complex policy problem, of course, the available information, technocratic or otherwise, is always incomplete, imperfect, subject to competing interpretations, and costly to obtain or improve. This is simply a fact of life for policymakers. The relevant question is this: Which institution or combination of institutions[27] is best equipped to minimize this informational deficit with respect to this particular policy problem?

We are in a better position to answer this question today after experiencing more than three decades of legislation, administrative regulation, and mass tort litigation directed at major public health risks—especially asbestos, tobacco, and gun-related violence.[28] During the 1960s and 1970s, federal and state legislation established regulatory agencies designed to mobilize technical expertise, to identify significant public health risks, and then to act to reduce them. These regulatory schemes, it was thought, could render private tort lawyers ancillary, if not superfluous, to the regulators engaged in risk management.

Alas, as has frequently been true in the history of the administrative state, this promise proved to be false, or at least vastly exaggerated. Environmental, occupational, and product risks are actually identified through complex processes in which many actors—endowed with different resources, responding to different incentives, and employing different methodologies—play a role. Often, these risks are first revealed by research scientists, public health and environmental organizations, specialized science and health journals, and other private groups. These risk monitors then communicate their research findings to those who are in a position to act upon this information—mass media, industry-specific newsletters, labor unions, policymakers, and services that publish and distribute this information to lawyers.

Sometimes, plaintiffs' lawyers are alerted to litigation-worthy health risks by an accumulation of workers' compensation awards, consumer complaints, public health agency reports, or media coverage. This information flow triggers what I have called a "lawyerization" of risk, in which plaintiffs' lawyers drive the policy-through-litigation process forward. Only seldom does formal regulatory action spawn mass tort litigation; in cases as diverse as asbestos, Dalkon Shield, DES, Agent Orange, auto safety, and tobacco, the regulatory agency took action, if at all, only years after the risk had been at least partially lawyerized.

Gun litigation is quite different. Whether and how to control gun violence have been prominent public policy issues for a very long time—since 1927 at the federal level and at various times at the state and local levels (1911 in New York)[29]—yet the tort lawyers did not get into the act in a serious way until the late 1990s.[30] They cannot claim responsibility for developing the policy-relevant information about the nature or magnitude of gun-related risks, which have long been well known.

It is true that the litigation process tends to produce a good deal of information from and for the parties. After all, discovery can be notoriously aggressive and intrusive, and the plaintiffs' lawyers have every incentive to demand as much existing information from the defendants as the discovery rules, the judge or discovery master, and their photocopying budgets will allow. But this access to existing files hardly translates into providing the decision maker, be she a judge or juror, with the kind of information that she would want if she were a rational risk regulator, and, in any event, few litigants possess the resources needed to adduce it. The adage "there is many a slip between cup and lip" has its tort litigation counterpart in the many screens that lawyers impose between discovery documents and presentation of evidence.

It is also true that the plaintiffs' lawyers have discovered documents bearing on the industry's allegedly negligent distribution and marketing practices.[31] Although these documents have not yet succeeded in establishing tort liability, they are surely useful to risk regulators seeking to identify available pressure points for reducing gun-related harms. Nevertheless, it is hard to believe that risk regulators engaged in this task would not have developed this kind of information through the conventional information-gathering techniques available to them. The publicity surrounding the litigation certainly raised the issue of gun-related harm to greater public prominence, but this is not the same as producing policy-relevant information that regulators would not otherwise have adduced. Then again, my belief on this point may only reflect the advantages of hindsight.

Indeed, it is quite plausible to suppose that litigation, or the prospect of it, may actually *discourage* the gun industry from undertaking new risk-related research. Manufacturers are the only group with a possible economic incentive to invest in such research, but at least two obstacles exist. The new risk information (unless protected as intellectual property) would be a public good, so no individual manufacturer would be able to recover the costs of producing it, while any research cost-sharing agreement among industry competitors would court potential antitrust liability. More to the present point, any new information that the research might yield—for example, ways to manufacture or market in risk-reducing ways—would likely be used by gun control groups to press for expanded civil liability or government regulation, at least insofar as the rules of evidence permit them to use this new information against the manufacturers.[32]

In contrast, risk regulators can encourage or even subsidize research on gun-related risks, as they have for many other public health problems like lead paint poisoning, pollution, teenage pregnancy, and a host of diseases. They can also direct which particular research issues should be investigated rather than rely on the probably vain hope that the tort system's liability signals will indirectly induce manufacturers to research the specific issues that, from regulators' more disinterested point of view, are likely to have the greatest public health payoff. In particular contexts, of course, risk regulators may fail to undertake the needed research for political, technical, or other reasons—and some would say that this has been the case with respect to the gun industry's marketing and distribution practices. To the extent that this is so, litigation-induced research may be all the more valuable—although the fact that it is driven by litigation or funded by the parties may adversely affect its quality and reliability as an instrument of policy.

Judges as policymakers are technocratically disadvantaged in several other ways relative to their risk regulator counterparts. They are trained as generalist lawyers (usually as litigators), not as policy specialists, and thus are unlikely to acquire, or to know how to exploit, the kinds of information that a competent policy analysis requires. As already noted, judges only receive the information that the litigants choose, for their own self-interested reasons, to provide. Moreover, these litigants represent only a fraction of the many social interests probably affected by the legal rule, and the selection biases that drive the decision to litigate mean that the relatively few tort cases that reach trial are likely to be unrepresentative of the set of all tort disputes, much less the social reality that a policy must address.[33] The tort case, then, is a most unpromising vehicle for generating public policy that will govern a relatively large number of often disparate situations.

But the system contrives to keep judges even more ignorant than this. The rules of evidence further limit—and, in the name of protecting other legal values, distort—the kinds of information that judges can receive or that they may take into account if proffered. Other legal rules render certain factual issues legally irrelevant to a tort claim and thus unlikely to be developed by the parties and introduced into evidence. A rational regulator of gun risks, for example, might want to know about the industry's revenues, costs, and profits in order to assess the feasibility of alternative policy interventions, yet this kind of economic information might be inadmissible in a tort case where the issue is whether and how the defendant harmed the plaintiff.[34] Similarly, the same risk regulator would regard information about liability insurance practices in the industry as highly relevant. Yet this information, which judges might or might not take into account in deciding whether a manufacturer owes a legal duty to a remote victim, would be inadmissible before a jury and, if hinted at by a lawyer, might even prompt a mistrial.

More generally, risk regulators are less interested in the adjudicative facts concerning a particular gun manufacturer and the people its products injured than about the legislative facts bearing on the much larger risk environment. Indeed, unlike a judge who is confined to assessing the risk presented by a particular case that happens to come before her and cannot easily choose not to decide, a rational risk regulator considers not only gun risks but all other risks that compete with it for regulatory resources. After reviewing the larger risk environment, the regulator may decide that it could better use those resources to regulate, say, smoking rather than guns or to regulate guns of one type rather than the type used in the case before the court. Although in reality regulators seldom use risk information as synoptically as this, in principle they should do so and in practice they sometimes do. Common law judges almost never do, and in principle they should not.

Again, the distinction between the production of adjudicative and legislative facts in different fora should not be overdrawn. The gun litigation, for example, has generated useful legislative-type facts about the feasibility of alternative designs and marketing practices, while risk regulators are often influenced by individual narratives that they believe, rightly or wrongly, exemplify more general problems. The important point here is about the general tendencies and distinct properties of different institutions.

Political Information

Policymakers need good *political* information at least as much as the technocratic information. This category encompasses information about, among other things, the various outcomes different groups of voters want; the intensity of those preferences within those groups; the stakes that different policy proposals would create for different groups and the political resources that they will invest in the policy process; the levels and modes of their participation; the support enjoyed by the groups' leaders; the media's likely take on the issue; the legislative, bureaucratic, and organizational alliances that policymakers can form or mobilize; the likely sources of opposition; the carrots and sticks they can deploy to elicit the necessary support; and a variety of local, often arcane knowledge about what motivates the key political actors, which concessions they would accept and on what terms, and how they will behave in particular situations.[35]

Merely to recite this (incomplete) list of political information, of course, is to suggest how elusive and intricate it will be for any policy proposal, and all the more so as its importance and complexity increase. Consider just one of these factors—the intensity of voters' preferences.[36] Policymakers need to know not what voters want in the abstract but how strongly they want it and what they are willing to sacrifice in order to obtain it. This vital political intelligence is hard to obtain. While a competitive marketplace can readily register the intensity of consumers' preferences, only a political bargaining process in which alternative outcomes are "priced" through exchanges among the participants can measure how intensely voters feel about policy outcomes. Interest groups provide an important index of voters' willingness to "pay" for their policy goals. Being a member of a group usually entails some cost; members' actions on behalf of the group such as letter writing, grass roots work, reading-group materials, and lobbying are even more costly to them. For this reason, voters' group memberships are a crude proxy for the intensity of their policy preferences, one whose accuracy will depend on the cost of membership, the ease of exit, and so forth. Skillful policy-makers learn to gauge these factors as they gain knowledge about the various groups that are actively concerned with particular policy issues, but it is harder for them to do so with respect to preferences around which groups cannot easily organize, either because the preferences are diffusely or weakly held or because the individuals who share them lack political resources.

Common law courts are walled off from this vital political information by institutional design, lack any expertise in interpreting it, and are precluded by both tradition and doctrine from integrating it into their decisions. To observe this is emphatically not to say that judges are political innocents. In fact, they often have political experience and by profession and inclination are interested in and aware of political developments. Nor is it to suggest that judges do not advert to what they imagine are the political consequences of their decisions or take those consequences into some account. They do both. The important point for my purposes is that they are singularly disabled from gathering and using this kind of information systematically or effectively—and anything less than this information is likely to lead them astray, from a political point of view.

The gun litigation may be an example of this political ineptitude, although for reasons about to be explained one cannot be certain. The first decision to hold a gun manufacturer strictly liable in tort for injuries inflicted by a third party, *Kelley v. R.G. Industries, Inc.*,[37] was quickly rejected by the Maryland legislature, which overturned the decision and adopted a statutory nonstrict liability alternative. Subsequent gun litigation has generated a political backlash against these claims in many other states and, most notably, in Congress. These political actions do not necessarily mean that courts upholding such claims were wrong as a matter of tort law. After all, courts are free to interpret tort law as they see fit and to let the political chips fall where they may, while legislatures are entitled to revise the courts' understandings of tort law through statute. This kind of pas de deux is by no means uncommon or necessarily unwelcome; the California legislature, for example, has rejected its courts' imposition of social host liability to victims of alcohol-related accidents.[38]

Nor do such political responses preclude the possibility that the judicial decision helps to produce some important policy changes. Indeed,

Timothy Lytton demonstrates in chapters 6 and 10 that this has occurred in the wake of some unsuccessful gun litigation. One suspects, however, that some courts have not fully grasped the extent of political opposition to the new doctrine. Institutionally speaking, political intelligence gathering is not part of their job. This limitation, far from being a cause for regret, is generally salutary for the legal system.

Policy Instruments

Effective policymaking is impossible unless the implementing officials can deploy the variety of policy instruments to create and shape the incentives necessary to secure compliance by the members of the public and other officials who are the policy's targets. A risk regulator's kit bag contains a large number of these instruments, enabling her to impose fines or taxes, subsidize, educate, reorganize, inform, hire, fire, insure, establish bureaucracies, build political coalitions, or coerce third parties—to name just a few of the tools available to her. In contrast, judges in tort cases possess few instruments for securing compliance, and they tend to be weak, inflexible, or both. With the exception of nuisance cases, where injunctive relief may be possible, all that judges can do is order A to pay B a prescribed sum of money for breaking a rule. The damage remedy that they can deploy is undeniably important in shaping some kinds of behavior—including the pricing decisions of insurers, as Tom Baker and Thomas Farrish explain in chapter 12—but it affects quite a narrow band on the broad spectrum of human motivation.

Another instrumental factor that severely limits courts' ability to implement their policy views is the institutional imperative to decide cases on ostensibly principled grounds rather than on the basis of legislative-type choices. For example, modern courts that decide to abandon the traditional rule of contributory negligence nearly always feel constrained to adopt the alternative approach of "pure" comparative fault. One reason may be that courts think they can derive a "pure" regime from general tort principles, whereas any of the "modified" approaches—which might make better policy and which legislatures usually choose—would require judges to select arbitrary percentage cutoffs as legislators routinely do but traditional, legitimacy-conscious judges shrink from doing. This judicial bias in favor of principled reasoning, of course, does not prevent courts from importing policy consid-erations into their decisions, as a vast number of contemporary tort law attests, and some of them produce rules that are necessarily arbitrary even when policy justified—for example, the multipart tests for bystander and economic loss recoveries. My point is simply that this con-cern to decide according to general principles of justice constitutes an important institutional constraint, largely actuated by legitimacy con-cerns, on their practical ability to engage in policy-making in an open, unapologetic, and systematic or thoroughgoing fashion.

Nor are general tort standards likely to be as effective as specific reg-ulations in targeting the particular behaviors that are most pertinent to sound gun control policy. In part, the relative ineffectiveness of these standards is because it is juries who apply them. Of course, juries apply general standards such as reasonableness, proximate cause, contributory fault, and knowledge of risk to conduct in the normal course, but as an institutional matter they do so in an opaque and conclusory fashion—through general verdicts and without explanation. Especially when applied in this delphic fashion, such standards lack the capacity of highly specific regulations to focus the attention of firms and officials on the behavioral variables that actually shape gun-related risks—variables such as record keeping, advertising, selection and monitoring of dealers, firearms education, weapons storage, threatened criminal violence, com-pliance with licensing, and technological innovation. I do not mean either to deny the superiority of standards in many contexts or to suggest that rules do not also entail endemic disadvantages. My point, rather, is that courts do not have the same range of choice between rules and stan-dards that other risk regulators possess.

The common law damage remedy, of course, is often perfectly ade-quate for the purpose of inducing defendants' straightforward compli-ance. Where gun litigation is concerned, however, recalcitrance is more predictable. First, many gun manufacturers—in sharp contrast to the cigarette producers—are relatively small, thinly capitalized businesses that may be rendered insolvent by a large tort judgment.[39] Second, the manufacturers suspect that the real motivation behind the gun litigation, as it was in the cigarette litigation, is less to reform their production or marketing practices than to end their nongovernmental business.[40] The plaintiffs' assumption, on this account, is that there is no such thing as a safe gun in a world where guns are routinely stolen and find their way, despite the risk of tort liability and criminal law enforcement, into the hands of violent criminals, vulnerable children, sociopaths, and civilians who misuse them. In such an environment, the gun industry concludes, it is literally fighting for its economic life and must resist compliance as strenuously and resourcefully as it can. This may be one reason why Smith & Wesson, after agreeing to a widely publicized settlement praised by the president of the United States, backpedaled and ended up altering its marketing practices only marginally.[41]

Third, the behavioral response of a gun defendant, even one that pays the tort judgment or alters its practices in order to minimize its liability, can take a number of different forms. For my purposes, the crucial point is that a court cannot control which of these choices the manufacturer makes, and some of its choices may simply shift the risk of gun-related harm around or even increase it.[42] Gun control scholar James Jacobs speculates, for example, that unscrupulous manufacturers might respond by selling only to wholesalers or only to wholesalers who promise to distribute guns responsibly, which might encourage shady dealers to cash in by becoming wholesalers for these manufacturers. Alternatively, they could divert their guns into the secondary market or simply go out of business, thereby leaving the manufacture of guns to the black market, as has occurred with certain illicit drugs.[43]

In contrast, a risk regulator can decide to regulate particular behaviors of gun firms with some confidence that the firms will either comply with the regulations or violate them in ways that the regulator can then identify, address, and perhaps punish. The regulator can encourage or mandate new behaviors that it thinks will best address the gun-related risk it wants to alter, or it can discourage or prohibit existing ones. Again, I am not suggesting that regulators always secure compliance while judges cannot—far from it—but rather that the former are institutionally more capable of getting their way. The list of regulatory failures is long indeed—and, as Timothy Lytton argues, BATFE's failures may be among them—but those failures are more often instances of regulators choosing the wrong policies in the first place than they are instances of choosing the right ones but being unable or unwilling (given their resources) to implement them.[44]

Finally, any institutional comparison of policy instruments must consider the crucial role of markets. The effectiveness of every public policy is significantly affected, if not determined, by how that policy interacts with the market forces that influence those on whose behavior the policy's success depends. Strong market forces, particularly when reinforced by powerful social norms, may simply overwhelm law, distorting or disabling it. If those forces are strong enough, they will spawn corruption, smuggling, or other illegal markets. On the other hand, well-designed policies can harness market dynamics to the law, thereby strongly advancing the law's goals.

These considerations are particularly relevant to gun control policy. There are now about 275 million firearms in the United States, distributed among 35–45 percent of all American households; those households possess between 2.5 and 4.5 weapons on average.[45] This bespeaks immense and rapidly growing firearms markets, legal and illegal—markets that are notoriously difficult for the government to limit. Indeed, Jacobs shows that regulatory control efforts have largely served to expand gun markets by driving them underground, where they defy even conventional law enforcement. My point here, then, is not that risk regulators possess policy instruments for effectively controlling gun markets; rather, it is that courts do not. As Jacobs's analysis suggests, their only tool, the damage remedy, could actually strengthen illicit markets.

Social Learning

Perhaps no resource is more essential to a society's policy wisdom than its capacity to learn and to adapt swiftly and creatively to changing conditions. This learning capacity in turn depends on the society's ability to generate, aggregate, process, disseminate, deploy, and (as necessary) correct the information it needs in order to discover what its collective purposes are and might be and then to pursue them effectively.

Courts lack any reliable way to obtain feedback on their policies' real-world effects, and, as noted earlier, they are poorly equipped institutionally to assess the policy implications of the new evidence. Judges depend for their information largely on the particular litigants and disputes that happen to come to their courtroom, and the later case is an appropriate vehicle for policy change only if it raises the same policy issues that the earlier case raised but manages to adduce better information for decision. Even if the precedent can simply be distinguished, disregarded, or overruled, a court that realizes belatedly that it erred earlier must ordinarily wait for a properly framed new case to come along that provides it with a vehicle for changing doctrinal course. In its recent *Lawrence v. Texas* decision,[46] for example, the U.S. Supreme Court announced that the rule it had adopted in *Bowers v. Hardwick* was wrong not only in 2003 but from *Bowers*'s inception. Nevertheless, it took the Court twenty years to find a case (and the necessary votes) that enabled it to correct its error. This situation, moreover, is not at all typical; as the Court emphasized in overruling *Bowers,* that decision had been relentlessly and severely criticized from its first day. In contrast, the court in the usual tort case is far less likely to learn about the nature and extent of its error.

A risk regulator, in contrast, has numerous opportunities to revisit its earlier decisions and revise them whenever it seems appropriate. Indeed, regulators have institutionalized formal techniques for doing so—oversight hearings, notice-and-comment rule making, reauthorizations, and the like—and access to the information and expertise needed to assess the case for change and the various reform options that are available.[47] And interest groups such as the National Rifle Association (NRA) and gun control advocates engender rapid social learning by giving regulators, the media, and the general public almost instant feedback about the costs of public policies to the groups that claim to bear them. Whether one regards their efforts as examples of valuable public education or of irresponsible distortion—the gun control debate has many examples of both—may depend largely on one's views about the merits of these controversies. It is also a question in any particular situation of whether the risk regulators were actually informed by this feedback, ignored it, or merely used it as a pretext for decisions reached on other grounds. What is certain is that such regulators are more likely than courts to receive such feedback from a wide variety of sources and in a forceful and timely fashion.

Predictability

An effective public policy must be predictable. That is, those who will interpret, enforce, or comply with the policy must be able to determine—in advance of its application, with a high degree of accuracy, and at low cost—what it means and (which is much the same thing) how it applies in a variety of factual circumstances. This in turn may require that its purposes be fairly transparent. Predictability is vital in any legal system, but particularly in a liberal one where citizens are expected to govern themselves with maximum freedom and a minimum of official intrusion. Predictability also advances certain other values such as the rule of law (by facilitating the treatment of like cases alike) and efficiency (by minimizing transaction and enforcement costs). The need for predictable rules on guns is particularly great because of their ubiquity in the United States. These rules, then, must be determinate and transparent enough to enable a vast number of ordinary citizens to know their gun-related legal rights and obligations.

Tort rules are much less determinate and transparent than regulations, other things being equal. In part, this reflects tort law characteristics that have already been discussed: the generality of its rules; their "black box" application by juries; the state-by-state variations; and the glacial and somewhat opaque process by which tort decisions accumulate, congeal into "rules," and become recognized as authoritative precedents. In addition, appellate decisions are contingent on the specific facts of those cases—or so the courts, eager to maintain their decisional leeway for the future, insist—yet common law legal reasoning means that we can never know which of the many facts were pivotal unless and until some court writes an opinion in some future case that tells us. A related feature of tort law, lack of codification, makes it harder for even lawyers to access and interpret its doctrines.

In short, a manufacturer, dealer, user, or victim of guns would find it much easier to find and comprehend what the regulatory law of guns prescribes—with regard, say, to licensing or background checks or concealment rules—than what tort law rules prescribe with respect, say, to distribution patterns, intervening criminal use, or gun technology. In such complex contexts, the standard of reasonableness is not a very useful guide to manufacturers that must predict what the courts (or, more precisely, juries) will require and make their long-term investments in technology and distribution networks accordingly. Tort law's uncertainties create costs for the industry and legitimate users—and, as Jacobs points out, opportunities for illicit gun market participants. To be sure, regulations may immunize practices that comply with the letter of the law but perhaps not with its spirit, while the indeterminacy of tort standards may sometimes induce compliance beyond what the law would have required. These problems, however, can be solved better through regulatory drafting that is more precisely tailored to the desired outcomes than through the uncertain compliance (too much or too little) that vague tort standards may induce.

Legitimacy

Legitimacy is a much-discussed but ill-defined criterion. It is easier to describe why it is necessary in a democratic polity than to explain where it comes from, how it is sustained or lost, and why some institutions enjoy more of it than others do in some situations while the reverse is true in other situations. What seems clear, however, is that legitimacy is not simply the sum of the other criteria of competence that I have discussed here. Criteria-based assessments certainly affect an institution's legitimacy, but it does not exhaust its meaning.

The public perception that law is legitimate constitutes a social resource of incalculable value. It nourishes respect for both polity and principle and hence for the claims of one's fellow citizens. It induces people to comply with law even when, as often occurs, narrow self-interest counsels disobedience. Indeed, it invites people to broaden their conception of what their interests are and perhaps to identify them with the interests of others. It reflects an often compelling vision of social justice. Law's legitimacy, however, is always fragile in a vibrant, liberal society. Political and economic actors attack laws that constrain them while supporting those that constrain their competitors. Law's moral claim to obedience rests ultimately on the public's perceptions of its procedural fairness, its substantive justice, and its practical efficacy. Because the lawmaking process invariably compromises these values, its legitimacy is always contestable. Law's legitimacy is most vulnerable when it seeks to transform a deeply embedded social practice like gun ownership that enjoys its own public legitimacy, for here the gap between the law's promise and its performance is likely to be widest. Indeed, this gap can become a chasm whose breadth contributes to the decline in public respect for law and government.

These general reflections on legitimacy, and particularly on the relation between the law's practical efficacy and its legitimacy, are highly pertinent to an institutional comparison of risk regulators and courts in addressing the problem of gun-related violence. There is something of a paradox here. In general, judges are more highly esteemed in the public mind than are politicians and bureaucrats, yet when it comes to solving this particular problem through tort law, judges are (so I argue) comparatively less competent and less legitimate as an institutional matter.

The paradox is resolved, I think, by the special policy-making demands that contemporary gun litigation places on the courts, demands that I have analyzed in this section.[48] The relatively high repute of courts is probably more a vestige of what courts traditionally did than a tribute to what some courts are now attempting to do. Even today, the usual task of a court (and jury) in a tort case is the relatively straightforward one of applying given standards, vague though they may be, to a given set of facts. In contrast, the tasks of risk regulators tend to be more intellectually challenging, involve more complex and fluid problems, demand more information, arouse more political controversy, require more skill at persuading and mobilizing constituencies, and are harder to implement. Unlike federal and many state judges, legislators must also face at the polls those who bear the costs of their policies as well as those who benefit from them. It should come as no surprise, then, that risk regulators have seemed to fail while courts remain popular and successful, for they are playing very different games by altogether different rules. When courts take on the kinds of comprehensive problem-solving, policy-making functions that risk regulators routinely exercise, their failure rate—and the level of public disappointment in them—is likely to rise as well. Courts may believe that inaction by the risk regulators has forced their hand, but this belief begs the essential question as to the reasons and justifications for inaction in the face of what are often daunting policy dilemmas, and it elides the question of the institutional role.

The problem of gun-related violence implicates both of these questions. The risk regulators' failure to solve the problem during the last four decades speaks volumes about its political and practical intractability. But if this failure speaks, what does it say? Gun litigation advocates offer some answers. This failure, they argue, says that risk regulators, particularly legislators, lack the imagination and, more important, the political will necessary to solve it. Exhibit A in their argument is the fact that the NRA is by many accounts the single most powerful lobbying group in the nation.[49] This argument, however, simply pushes the question back a step: why is the NRA so politically powerful? The most straightforward answer is that the NRA is powerful because its more than three million members and other gun owners constitute a bloc, according to polling data, of from twenty-three to twenty-seven million voters in all parts of the country, and these voters intensely oppose most forms of gun control.[50] In a democracy, politicians are supposed to respect these voters' preferences on gun issues and the legislative procedures that often have the effect, if not the purpose, of protecting the status quo from impulsive reforms—and they do. Needless to say, this does not mean that the NRA's positions are necessarily correct or that politicians who accept those positions do so for public-spirited reasons. It means, rather, that one cannot infer a failure of democratic process from the NRA's frequent political efficacy.

A second inference that litigation proponents draw from the politicians' failure to enact more stringent gun control is this: even if the politicians' opposition to gun control is legitimate, the courts are legitimate legal institutions too, and their institutional duty is to adjudicate the cases that come before them on the basis of settled legal principles (here, tort law) as applied to new, or at least newly compelling, social problems (here, gun-related violence). But this position also begs the more fundamental questions of whether it would be just for courts to stretch those principles to impose liability in these cases and whether doing so would squander the courts' legitimacy.

On the question of justice, almost every appellate court that has addressed the issue has concluded that existing legal principles cannot properly be stretched so far, and I am inclined to agree with them—even assuming that manufacturers have not controlled their distribution networks as well as they might. I would expect that the legislative reversals of such a stretch would be swift and sure,[51] and the courts' public reputation would suffer accordingly—and, in terms of practical results, for naught. Indeed, by circumventing the essential process of cultural accommodation, such judicial decisions could exacerbate social conflicts over guns rather than ease them.[52] Having said this, I hasten to add a caution that I offered some years ago about how the Supreme Court's legitimacy has fared when it entered political thickets.

> In a long line of cases, the Court has turned aside warnings of just this kind, and has instead proceeded to take on project after daunting project of broad political and social reform. At the time, even sympathetic observers often believed that these projects [long list

omitted] would strain judicial capacities to the breaking point. Yet more often than not, the Court seemed to sustain its projects without losing either perceived legitimacy or prestige. Indeed, the Court has returned from these engagements bearing the battle ribbons and the public esteem of a military hero. Its struggles with the politicians and the bureaucrats have only served to enlarge its reputation for moral purity, constitutional wisdom, and real-world effectiveness.[53]

It is hard to say how applicable this cautionary tale is to the courts in gun litigation. State courts do not enjoy the same iconic reverence as the U.S. Supreme Court, and they presumably have less accumulated prestige to draw down. Because most gun cases involve only common law principles, not constitutional ones, the courts' pronouncements lack the oracular, almost hieratic quality of constitutional rulings. Because their rulings in gun cases can be, and often are, overridden by the legislature, they may seem less authoritative and worthy of respect. My sense—and it is no more than that—is that members of the public who favor gun control will praise the courts for exhibiting courage and independence in contrast to what they see as the politicians' abject obeisance to the NRA, while pro-gun forces will denounce the courts for eroding what they view as a precious constitutional right. Beside professors and other (high-minded) pundits, few will devote much attention to issues of institutional legitimacy, competence, or separation of powers, issues that will strike them as academic.

Conclusion

Since my comparative institutional analysis leads to the conclusion that risk regulators are far better equipped than judges to address and manage the problem of gun-related violence, the obvious question remains: what should the regulators do about the problem? Although my writ in this chapter does not run to that question, I do have some views on it, with which I shall conclude.

First, I am convinced by Jacobs's recent and comprehensive review of existing and proposed laws to keep guns out of the hands of those who should not have them that such laws—call it a "Brady-plus" approach—are unlikely to succeed. There are many reasons for this pessimism: the existence of a vast secondary market that is probably impossible to regulate as a practical matter; a large and elusive black market; the powerful incentives and ample opportunities for criminals to obtain guns in the secondary and black markets; the approximately 275 million guns that are already in people's hands; the spur to new gun purchases that any reform proposal would create during the periods before enactment and before it becomes effective; the marginal (at best) effectiveness of the Brady Act itself and of other laws along the same lines; the massive noncompliance with existing controls on felons' access to guns; the large-scale exemptions that any control regime must contain; and so on.[54]

This pessimism does not mean throwing up one's hands in futility, but it does suggest a need for more modest expectations and greater realism about Brady-plus reforms. A more promising approach is technological in nature—making guns safer (although relatively few gun-related injuries are inflicted on or by careless, innocent users)[55] and more easily traceable to those who fire them. Further research on "smart" guns, ballistic fingerprinting, trigger locks, and other such fixes is clearly warranted. Whether and to what extent this research should be publicly subsidized is a separate question, but the possibility that the large and growing costs of gun litigation may on balance be diverting manufacturers' resources away from such research is a disturbing one.

An even more promising approach is the use of surveillance technology to enable the police to detect guns in public spaces and at safe distances while obviating the need for making dangerous, discriminatory, and intrusive "stop and frisks" of individuals without probable cause for suspicion. This would vastly increase the ability of police officers safely and effectively to disarm people who have no legal right to carry weapons. It is only a matter of time before such technology is available. If it is to be deployed, however, it must safeguard individual privacy rights under the Fourth Amendment. Whether and how this can be done is already the subject of some scholarly debate.[56] My guess (and it is only a guess) is that the vast majority of Americans will view the use of a reliable surveillance technology limited to concealed guns in public spaces and subject to strict legal controls against unwarranted profiling and intrusion as constituting a reasonable search, one whose crime- and violence-reduction benefits would more than justify the small invasion of privacy entailed. If so, and if the politicians adopt such a measure, the courts will probably uphold it. As an institutional matter, however, the courts are ill-equipped to promote or appraise such technological developments.

Compared with these kinds of direct, narrowly targeted, legally manageable, technology-based forms of risk regulation, tort litigation is a remarkably indirect, indiscriminate, crude, and unpromising remedy for the plague of gun-related violence. It has advanced valuable social ends by generating new policy-relevant information about gun-related violence and by capturing the industry's undivided attention. These are significant achievements, and perhaps—the question is an important one—we would not have gained them had the litigation not been prosecuted. At this point, however, it amounts to a costly and institutionally inappropriate distraction from the real political and policy tasks before us.

CHAPTER 10

The Complementary Role of Tort Litigation in Regulating the Gun Industry

TIMOTHY D. LYTTON

Tort claims against gun manufacturers call on judges to make policy choices about firearm design and marketing. There is much debate over whether judges should be in the business of making policy choices. On the one hand, traditionalists denounce judicial policy-making as violating the constitutional separation of powers, which reserves policy-making to legislatures and consigns courts to resolving individual disputes between parties.[1] Moreover, according to this view, courts lack the breadth of perspective necessary to make good public policy, a breadth that legislatures achieve through initiating investigations or holding hearings.[2] In addition, courts of general jurisdiction lack the technical and scientific expertise that administrative agencies lend to legislative policy-making.[3] On the other hand, progressives embrace judicial policy-making as part of a public law vision of the tort system. According to this view, courts should craft creative solutions to social problems when deadlocked or corrupt legislatures fail to act.[4] Furthermore, by using procedural techniques that allow for the consolidation of many claims into one legal proceeding, courts can resolve individual claims en masse, thereby avoiding the possible inconsistencies and inefficiencies of piecemeal adjudication on a case-by-case basis.[5]

In this chapter, I advocate an intermediate position. I argue that courts should play a secondary role in policy-making that complements the regulatory efforts of legislatures and administrative agencies. Against the traditionalist position, I assert that judges are wise in attending to the public policy implications of their rulings in individual cases. The nature of common law adjudication is to apply old legal principles to new problems. The proper application of these principles, however, is often unclear, and judges are required to resolve ambiguities on the basis of something other than clear precedent. It is here that policy analysis plays a legitimate role in judging. Against the progressive position, I argue that courts should confine their policy analysis to the resolution of doctrinal ambiguities. Courts should use policy analysis to gradually refine tort law's system of rules for resolving private disputes in ways that serve the public interest. Radical shifts in doctrine, even when supported by sound policy choices, undermine the legal stability that in our constitutional scheme courts are uniquely qualified to protect. Furthermore, I argue that in making policy choices, courts should, where possible, follow the lead of legislatures. To the extent that there are discernable trends in legislative consideration of a problem, it undermines the legitimacy of judicial decision making for judges to contradict them. The danger of unrestrained judicial policy-making is greatest in mass torts, where the aggregation of claims and industrywide liability exposure can easily transform the resolution of private disputes into the crafting of innovative solutions to social problems, without due regard for doctrinal integrity or legislative preferences.

A complementary policy-making role for courts is not a new idea, but it has found few, if any, proponents in the highly polarized controversy over gun litigation.[6] My analysis reveals that tort claims against gun manufacturers can complement legislative efforts to regulate the firearms industry and can thereby make a modest contribution to decreasing gun violence. It cautions, however, that the mass tort features of some of the more recent cases threaten to undermine the legitimacy of the whole enterprise.

My defense of a complementary policy-making role for courts in regulating the gun industry involves several steps. I begin by defending tort claims against gun manufacturers that offer opportunities for complementary policy-making by courts. Next, I caution against the use of mass tort strategies in gun litigation based on their tendency to view the tort system as an alternative, rather than a complement, to legislative policy-making. I then address common objections to the complementary model that I am advocating, and I conclude with some general remarks about the regulatory advantages of allowing the tort system to play a complementary role in making public policy.

Opportunities for Complementary Policy-Making

Some tort claims against firearms manufacturers present courts with an opportunity to play a complementary role in regulating the gun industry. Allowing these claims would not imply new rules or special exceptions that would undermine the doctrinal consistency of the tort system, and the policy choices involved—concerning firearms design and marketing—would support existing legislative mandates in these areas. Consider the following examples.

Halberstam v. Daniel: *Regulating Gun Kits*

Federal law requires that those regularly in the business of selling guns obtain a Federal Firearms License; conduct background checks on all buyers; restrict out-of-state purchases to other Federal Firearms Licensees (FFLs); and comply with federal, state, and local firearms laws. In addition, the law requires that all guns carry a serial number on the frame or receiver of the gun in order to assist law enforcement in tracing the sales and ownership history of the gun if used in a crime. One strategy for evading these regulations is to sell guns disassembled in the form of parts kits, since the regulations apply to firearms but not to firearm parts.[7] The case of *Halberstam v. Daniel* arose out of just such a scheme.[8] In that case, the plaintiffs were shot by a criminal assailant using a semiautomatic pistol that had been assembled from a mail-order parts kit manufactured and sold by the defendants. While the statutory definition of a firearm includes "any combination of parts from which a firearm . . . can be assembled," the defendants' gun kits included all the necessary parts except a frame.[9] The kits did, however, include sheet metal flats that, when folded, were designed to serve as frames. In this way, the defendants succeeded in circumventing federal licensing restrictions on gun sales.

The plaintiffs claimed that this marketing scheme was negligent insofar as the defendants failed to exercise reasonable care to prevent acquisition of their guns by individuals with a high risk of criminal misuse.[10] In support of their claim, the plaintiffs described the defendants' sales methods, including out-of-state sales to non-FFLs, taking orders by phone, postal delivery, reduced prices for bulk purchases, no requests for any information other than that relevant to payment and shipping, and failure to keep any sales records. Furthermore, the defendants avoided having to place serial numbers on their guns since the unmarked sheet metal flats did not constitute frames until folded. At trial, the defendants testified that they did not care who purchased their weapons.

The trial judge in *Halberstam* refused to dismiss the plaintiffs' claim, implying that the manufacturer owed a duty to exercise reasonable care in marketing its weapons and allowing, for the first time, a negligent marketing case to reach a jury. The jury, however, rejected the plaintiffs' claim, finding that, while the defendants' marketing practices were negligent, they were not a substantial factor in causing the plaintiffs' injuries. At trial, the defendants had produced an affidavit and a deposition by the criminal assailant in which he stated that he had purchased the gun from someone on the street and that he had never had any business dealings with the defendants.

While the plaintiffs' claim foundered on the issue of causation, given the particular facts of the gun purchase involved, *Halberstam* illustrates a type of case where imposing liability would be consistent with general tort principles and would complement legislative efforts to regulate the gun industry. As I discussed in the introduction to this volume, the primary obstacle to negligent marketing claims is the absence of a duty to exercise reasonable care in marketing firearms. The establishment of such a duty requires showing that gun violence injuries are a foreseeable risk of marketing guns and that gun manufacturers have a unique capacity to reduce this risk. The existing regulatory regime lends credibility to both of these assertions. This regime is based on the premise that gun violence is a known risk of selling guns and that this risk can be reduced by regulating gun sales through dealer licensing and background checks on purchasers. When manufacturers sell their guns at the retail level, as did the *Halberstam* defendants, they are engaged in conduct that, according to the regulatory regime, entails a foreseeable risk of harm. One might argue that, even when selling further up the distribution chain, the risk is no less foreseeable. Furthermore, the practice of manufacturing and marketing guns in the form of unregulated mail-order parts kits reveals that manufacturers have, in some circumstances, a unique capacity to manipulate this risk. If the regulations are premised on the idea that they reduce the risk of gun violence, then marketing guns in a way that evades the regulations would presumably increase it. These arguments weigh heavily in favor of imposing a duty of care on gun manufacturers, and, even if they are not sufficient by themselves, they at least show that such a duty is an option consistent with traditional doctrinal requirements of foreseeability and a unique capacity to reduce risk.

When doctrinal considerations alone cannot definitively settle a question, judges should consider the public policy implications of different options. In doing so, they should be deferential to policy choices already made by legislatures, since the legitimacy of judicial policy-making is weakened when it contradicts legislative policy choices. In cases like *Halberstam*, these considerations further favor the imposition of a duty of care on manufacturers. Selling guns in the form of unregulated mail-order parts kits, while legal, undermines the existing regulatory regime developed by Congress over the past sixty years. The fundamental purpose of this regime is to prevent firearms purchases by criminals and other disqualified persons. Dealer licensing and background checks on purchasers are the chosen means to achieve this aim. The absence of similar regulations governing the sale of gun parts reflects a legislative decision that regulating the acquisition of spare parts for existing firearms would do little to prevent criminals and other disqualified persons from illegally purchasing guns. This rationale for not extending licensing and background checks to gun parts hardly supports the legislative failure to include gun kits. The most likely explanation for the failure to regulate gun kits is that Congress simply did not anticipate this strategy for evading the regulations on gun sales.[11] The failure to impose licensing and background check restrictions on the sale of a gun merely because it is sold disassembled is a gap in the regulatory regime detrimental to its underlying purpose.

The existence of this gap in the regulatory regime, and the ability of tort liability to plug it, favors imposing a duty on gun manufacturers to exercise reasonable care in marketing firearms. The *Halberstam* verdict indicates that at least some juries are likely to find that reasonable care requires using the same precautions when marketing guns in the form of gun kits as when marketing them fully assembled. This form of tort liability would complement legislative regulations by deterring manufacturers from using marketing practices designed to evade them.

Smith v. Bryco Arms: *Mandating Safer Gun Designs*

Federal administrative agencies regulate the safety of a wide range of products. Agencies such as the Food and Drug Administration (FDA), the Environmental Protection Agency (EPA), the National Highway Transportation Safety Administration (NHTSA), the National Boating Safety Administration (NBSA), and the Consumer Products Safety Commission (CPSC) promulgate rules that mandate safety features in medical devices, pesticides, automobiles, boats, and many other products. No federal agency, however, has the power to regulate firearm designs. The Bureau of Alcohol, Tobacco, Firearms and Explosives (BATFE) is empowered to enforce only sales and ownership restrictions, and guns were explicitly excepted from the jurisdiction of the CPSC.

Another source of product safety regulation is the tort system. Potential liability exposure provides manufacturers with a powerful incentive to equip products with safety features that prevent injuries that could give rise to lawsuits. Lawsuits over the failure of manufacturers to equip light construction vehicles with anti-tipping devices or to equip food processors with cut-off switches have led to safety improvements in these and other products. The case of *Smith v. Bryco Arms* illustrates how gun litigation has the potential to similarly improve firearm designs.[12] In that case, the plaintiff was injured when he was shot with a gun by a friend who believed that the gun was unloaded because the magazine had been removed. The plaintiff sued the gun manufacturer for defective design insofar as the gun could have been equipped with a safety feature that would have prevented the gun from firing when the magazine was removed. An intermediate appellate court reversed the trial court's dismissal of the claim, holding that the plaintiff's theory that inclusion of a magazine safety was a feasible, cost-effective alternative design fell squarely within New Mexico product liability doctrine. "[W]e do not perceive," noted the court, "anything so unique about handguns that they cannot or should not be subject to normal tort law concepts, norms, and methods of analysis. . . . [T]he application of our tort law can be expected to . . . increase the safety of handgun use."[13]

To the extent that passing judgment on the reasonableness of gun designs involves policy choices, the appellate court in *Smith* considered those choices to be a well-established and legally uncontroversial aspect of adjudicating product liability cases. In answer to the trial court's assertion that product design regulation is a matter for legislatures, not courts, the appellate court explained: "The notion that courts cannot speak in the area of products liability without legislative guidance has been considered and rejected by the New Mexico Supreme Court . . . New Mexico courts have long held manufacturers and distributors responsible in strict liability or negligence for failing to include safety devices in their products."[14] This is equally true of other states as well.

It might be objected that while evaluating design choices is indeed a normal part of adjudicating product liability claims, in the case of guns, this sort of judicial policy-making contradicts a federal legislative mandate against regulating gun designs, implied by the exclusion of gun designs from regulation by the CPSC or the BATFE. Rather than playing a complementary role, courts like the *Smith* court are in competition with legislative policy choices. The problem with this objection is that it misconstrues the exclusion of gun designs from regulation by the CPSC and BATFE as a legislative mandate against regulation by the tort system. The Consumer Product Safety Act (CPSA), which established the CPSC, recognizes the independent regulatory role of the tort system. The CPSA does not pretend to provide a comprehensive regulatory scheme; it excludes not only firearms but other consumer products such as tobacco, motor vehicles, pesticides, aircraft, boats, drugs, medical devices, cosmetics, and food, the regulation of which are left to other federal agencies. Furthermore, Section 25(a) of the act explicitly states that "[c]ompliance with consumer product safety rules or other rules or orders under this Act shall not relieve any person from liability at common law or under State statutory law to another person."[15] Thus, the exclusion of firearms represents a decision not to establish CPSC regulation of gun designs, not a decision to forbid all regulation of guns by other agencies, state legislatures, or the tort system. This is equally true of the absence of BATFE regulatory authority over gun designs. The federal gun control acts that BATFE is charged with enforcing do not include any mandate concerning gun designs. It is a mistake to interpret congressional silence on this matter as precluding other sources of regulation. Congressional silence on the regulation of gun designs reflects merely the lack of a mandate to replace decentralized regulation by state and local legislatures and common law courts.[16] This type of regulation, as the *Smith* court pointed out, is a well-established function of the tort system.

City of Chicago v. Beretta: *Defending the Integrity of Local Gun Regulations*

In addition to federal laws, there are many firearms regulations promulgated by state and local governments. The most restrictive of these tend to be municipal ordinances in large cities with high crime rates. For example, the cities of Chicago and Washington, D.C., ban civilian gun possession altogether. Yet, despite such measures, cities like Chicago and Washington continue to suffer from high rates of gun violence. City officials blame the failure of these restrictive policies on the ready availability of firearms from suburban gun dealers who sell guns to city residents.

The City of Chicago's public nuisance suit against the gun industry illustrates how tort litigation can complement the regulatory efforts of local governments. As explained in the introduction, the City's claim alleged that gun manufacturers' unrestricted supply of guns to suburban gun dealers with a record of illegal sales or who have sold many guns eventually used in crimes constitutes a public nuisance—an "unreasonable interference with a public right." The Supreme Court of Illinois rejected Chicago's claim, holding that manufacturers and wholesale distributors owe no duty to the public at large to guard against the criminal misuse of guns.[17] Notwithstanding the dismissal of Chicago's suit, suing gun manufacturers, distributors, and dealers for public nuisance offers cities a way to eliminate a significant source of weapons that undermine their attempts to ban or otherwise restrict the sale or possession of firearms. Thus, tort liability enables cities to protect their legislative policy choices from threats by gun sellers and manufacturers who are outside of their legislative jurisdictions, but not beyond the reach of tort claims.

A problem with municipal claims like Chicago's is the question of remedy. Chicago's suit demanded the payment of money damages for the gun violence costs incurred by the city as a result of the nuisance. Calculating these damages requires isolating that portion of gun violence attributable specifically to oversupply, lack of dealer supervision, and illegal sales practices—a complex calculation to say the least. The suit also requested injunctive relief in the form of marketing restrictions designed to limit the flow of guns into the city from surrounding suburbs. Such restrictions could be viewed not merely as a strategy for protecting a city's own regulatory regime but as an attempt to thwart the regulatory decisions of suburban governments—to use tort litigation as a way to impose the city's will on its neighbors. While a city may have chosen to ban guns, suburban governments often choose to permit easy access to guns within their borders. To the extent that a municipal public nuisance suit would greatly restrict the availability of guns in surrounding suburbs, it might be characterized as an attempt to exercise regulatory power beyond the city limits, and they may run afoul of state home rule provisions. Only if a city can identify limited measures aimed specifically at abating the nuisance by reducing the risk of sales to city residents can the city make its claim look less like an attempt to impose its will on suburban governments and more like a garden-variety cross-border nuisance suit. Insofar as municipal suits have regulatory implications beyond state borders, they may raise concerns based on the U.S. Constitution's dormant Commerce Clause doctrine. Chapter 13 takes up this issue in greater detail.

Market Share Approaches to Causation: Generating Regulatory Information

It is often the case that guns used in crimes are never recovered, so many gun violence victims cannot identify the particular manufacturer that made the gun used against them. Some plaintiffs have suggested shifting the burden of proving causation. Under this approach, defendants would have to prove that they did not manufacture the gun in question in order to avoid liability. Failing such a showing, they would be held liable in proportion to their share of sales within the total gun market or within the market for the type of gun used to injure the plaintiff. The idea behind such "market share" theories is that, although defendants will not be held liable for the entire amount of damage that they caused to any particular plaintiff, they will over time be held liable to all plaintiffs for a fair share of the total damage that they caused. In *Hamilton v. Beretta*, discussed in the introduction, the plaintiffs could not identify the manufacturers of the weapons used to injure them. They argued that the defendant manufacturers should each be held liable in proportion to the percentage of guns that they sold, or, if either party could narrow it down to a class of guns (for example, .25 caliber handguns), the defendant manufacturers should each be held liable in proportion to the percentage of guns that they sold within that class.[18]

Shifting the burden of proving causation where no gun was recovered is another way in which the tort system can complement legislative regulation. Most federal and state gun regulation focuses on sales restrictions aimed at reducing the risk that guns will be sold to criminals and other disqualified persons. Shifting the burden of proving causation onto manufacturers would provide them an incentive to maintain and disclose sales records, since this information would be essential to exoneration. The information would also be useful in enforcing federal and state sales regulations and in better understanding the link, if any, between gun marketing and crime. In this way, gun litigation can generate information that is helpful to legislatures and administrative agencies in enforcing and further developing effective industry regulation. In addition, this information would be useful in courts' own consideration of the duty issue in negligent marketing cases.

Exceptional doctrines such as market share liability should be applied with caution. In some versions of the doctrine, defendants cannot avoid liability even if they do establish that they did not make the product that injured the plaintiff (the idea being that others who cannot prove this are nonetheless held liable to each plaintiff in proportion to their market share and that holding everyone partially liable in every case is fair in the aggregate).[19] Applied to gun litigation, this version of the doctrine would eliminate manufacturers' incentive to keep sales information and would thereby undercut justification for the doctrine based on the complementary role of tort law.

Problems with Mass Tort Strategies for Gun Litigation

Tort law is first and foremost a mechanism for resolving private disputes between parties. In this chapter, I have argued that, where the law leaves room for judicial discretion in resolving private disputes, judges should take into account the public policy implications of their decisions, and they should seek to complement the public policy choices of legislatures where possible. Some suits against gun manufacturers do not fit this vision of the tort system. These suits employ mass tort strategies that treat the tort system as an alternative, rather than a complement, to legislative policy-making.

Undifferentiated Damages and Regulatory Remedies

One mass tort strategy is to consolidate many individual injuries into one lawsuit. Recovery for these injuries may be sought against one defendant or, as is increasingly common, against all members of an industry. The aggregation of claims and defendants forces judges to balance many distinct interests in search of a global solution that may require crafting complex remedies and an administrative apparatus to execute it. The judicial resolution of mass tort claims has increasingly given rise to complaints that judges have exercised quasi-legislative powers beyond their traditional role.[20]

Some lawsuits against the gun industry aggregate individual gun violence injuries and seek complex regulatory remedies. For example, municipal suits aggregate thousands of individual injuries in calculating costs occasioned by gun violence. Since the cities, even according to their own claims, are entitled only to those gun violence–related costs caused by industry wrongdoing, granting them recovery requires separating out that portion of gun violence due to design flaws and unreasonable marketing practices. Plaintiffs have so far been unable to provide data isolating these costs, and even if they could, any conclusions would likely be highly speculative. Some suits seek complex regulatory injunctions in addition to or instead of monetary compensation. For example, the City of Chicago's suit demanded a court injunction that would force defendant manufacturers to "market personalized firearms that can only be used by the lawful purchaser," "participate in a court-ordered study of lawful demand for firearms and to cease sales in excess of lawful demand," "provide adequate training to . . . dealers," "systematically monitor . . . dealers," and "terminate shipments of firearms to dealers" who fail to adopt voluntary sales restrictions such as limiting purchasers to one gun per month and refusing sales to Chicago residents "unless the purchaser can prove that he has a legal place to maintain the firearm outside of the City of Chicago."[21] The design, administration, and enforcement of such a regulatory scheme would engage courts in a legislative enterprise well beyond their traditional powers, one that would draw much criticism and could erode respect for the courts.[22] Moreover, such a scheme would subvert the legislative refusal in many states to limit purchasers to one gun per month.

Regulatory Settlement

Another mass tort strategy is to use aggregation as a means of applying pressure in settlement negotiations aimed at securing regulatory outcomes beyond remedies that courts could or would provide. In pursuit of such regulatory settlements, some plaintiffs have litigated in ways designed less to clarify issues at the heart of their dispute than to intimidate their opponents. This degrades the litigation process, transforming a respected public institution into a private tool of extortion.

Within a year of the first municipal suit against the gun industry (filed by the City of New Orleans), twenty-seven other similar suits were filed by cities and counties across the country, and eventually the total rose to over thirty. One aim of suing simultaneously was to increase the industry's defense costs so as to pressure them into settlement. Philadelphia mayor Edward Rendell vowed that municipalities would file one hundred suits if the industry refused to adopt marketing restrictions, and Secretary of Housing and Urban Development (HUD) Andrew Cuomo threatened to unleash additional suits by local housing authorities nationwide if the industry refused to accept settlement terms proposed by city attorneys and state attorneys general.[23] The settlement terms included design specifications, marketing restrictions, and an industry oversight commission. One manufacturer—Smith & Wesson, the nation's largest gun maker—eventually did accept the settlement, only to face denunciations from other manufacturers, a boycott of its product by angry gun owners, sale of the company, and eventual withdrawal from the settlement.[24] Two California gun dealers and three national distributors recently settled claims against them brought simultaneously by twelve California county and municipal governments. The dealers and distributors agreed to refrain from selling weapons at gun shows and to implement background check and record-keeping systems beyond those mandated by law.[25] The coordination of municipal suits, which individually may not be without merit, uses the litigation process to make public policy privately, independent of judicial restraints and legislative oversight, without justification based in either the rule of law or the democratic process.[26]

The Regulatory Benefits of Tort Litigation

As the foregoing analysis illustrates, allowing the tort system to play a complementary policy-making role can enhance legislative efforts to regulate the marketing and design of firearms, defend the integrity of local gun control efforts, and promote the establishment and maintenance of information systems that are essential to effective oversight of the industry. Generalizing from the case of gun litigation, this section outlines the regulatory benefits of allowing the tort system to play a complementary role in making public policy.

Information

Effective regulation requires reliable information about risk and industry misconduct. Tort litigation can uncover such information.[27] Plaintiffs' lawyers are often more tenacious and civil discovery rules more invasive than legislative hearings or agency investigations. The gun industry has been less than forthcoming about many of its business practices. Do gun makers intend, as many lawsuits allege, to design their weapons in ways that appeal especially to the criminal market for guns? Do the industry's current distribution practices make it too easy for criminals to obtain guns? Lawsuits against the gun industry have produced testimony from former industry executives indicating that manufacturers know more about the relationship between their marketing strategies and criminal markets than they have been willing to admit.[28]

While regulatory information is a valuable by-product of tort litigation, the courts should beware of potential abuses. For one thing, the high litigation costs associated with discovery can be used to threaten or harass an industry even if the underlying legal claims are without merit. For another, interest groups may file groundless suits as a means of obtaining information. Dismissal of actions prior to discovery offers judges an effective tool to protect the industry against these kinds of abuse. A more detailed analysis of the role of tort law in uncovering useful regulatory information is the subject of the next chapter.

Gap Filling

In crafting rules designed to regulate conduct, a legislature cannot possibly anticipate all situations. So the rules inevitably fail to cover conduct that the legislature would have wanted to regulate if it had contemplated the conduct. Tort litigation offers an efficient and effective way to fill these legislative gaps in accordance with the policy goals of the legislature. In the case of gun control, we have seen that liability for the unrestricted selling of gun kits can deter manufacturers from exploiting gaps in sales restrictions that do not cover guns when sold disassembled. In seeking to fill gaps in legislation, however, courts should be careful not to mistake the limitations of a rule for gaps in the rule. That is, legislatures often limit the conduct that they wish to regulate, and the absence of regulation may indicate not an oversight but rather a desire not to regulate. So, for example, courts should be wary of imposing liability for the unrestricted sale of individual gun parts since the omission of gun parts from the legislation regulating gun sales indicates a legislative desire not to regulate gun parts. Distinguishing between gaps and exceptions in legislation is a difficult but customary task of courts for which there is a long tradition of statutory interpretation and for which courts are well equipped.

Enforcement

Legislative regulation is often ineffective due to poor enforcement. The threat of tort liability can provide individuals and corporations with a powerful incentive to comply with regulations where enforcement resources are limited. For example, each year BATFE is able to inspect only about 10 percent of the roughly one hundred thousand licensed gun dealers, and the agency is limited to one unannounced audit of a dealer in any given year.[29] Tort liability based on violation of federal sales regulations provides added incentive for dealers to comply with the law, even if they are unlikely to be inspected by BATFE. This benefit of tort liability requires that tort rules be clear and tailored to legislative mandates in order to provide effective notice to dealers and to refrain from deterring conduct that BATFE wishes to leave unregulated.

Federalism

One advantage of a decentralized approach to regulation is that it provides an opportunity to test different regulatory strategies in different jurisdictions. Decentralization also makes possible the use of different rules based on different local circumstances. The major disadvantages are lack of uniformity, predictability, and federal agency expertise.[30] Congress balances these competing regulatory approaches and often adopts a decentralized, or federalist, approach to regulation simply by not choosing to regulate. In doing so, Congress leaves regulation in many areas up to the states. State tort law is and has historically been an important part of state regulation. The regulation of gun designs through product liability in state courts is entirely consistent with Congress's desire to exempt them from centralized CPSC regulation and is, as the New Mexico appellate court said in *Smith*, a traditional role of state courts. Tort litigation in general and gun litigation in particular promote the benefits of a federalist approach to regulation.

Objections to a Complementary Policy-Making Role for the Tort System

At this point, I would like to address three objections to the complementary policy-making role for the tort system that I have been advocating. The first objection, from traditionalists, asserts that legislatures are perfectly able to plug their own gaps and to correct their own mistakes without the involvement of courts. Nothing prevents legislatures from investigating the results of their policy choices and revisiting them where necessary. The problem with this objection is that it assumes an idealized vision of the legislative process. The committee structure and deliberative nature of legislatures are designed to make it *hard* to pass legislation.

Of the thousands of bills proposed in large state legislatures or Congress each term, only a small fraction are passed into law. Legislative policy-making is cumbersome, slow, and highly inefficient. Such is the price of deliberative democracy. Furthermore, the outcome is often incomplete or internally inconsistent, reflecting not so much a clear policy choice as the numerous compromises necessary to pass legislation. Courts, by contrast, can more efficiently and more coherently plug gaps or correct contradictions so as to make legislative policies more effective. Agencies also perform this function of gap filling, subject to review by courts. Where courts err egregiously or overstep their legitimate complementary role, this will usually create enough controversy to attract legislative attention and action, as it did in the *Kelley* case, discussed in chapter 6.

A second objection, from progressives, questions why courts owe any deference at all to legislative policy choices, especially when those choices are dictated by special interest lobbies. For one thing, our constitutional tradition of judicial review empowers courts to sit in judgment of legislative policy choices. For another, as was just mentioned, if legislatures do not approve, they can always pass legislation more to their liking. The problem with this objection is that it fails to distinguish between judicial decisions based on constitutional concerns and those based on policy preferences. There is an important difference between a court's claiming that a legislative decision is illegitimate—that the legislature had no right to make such a decision in the first place—and claiming that a legislative decision is wrong—that, all things considered, the choice of policy is a poor one. The former is no law at all, while the latter, no matter how misguided, is valid law. While our constitutional tradition of judicial review does empower courts to contradict the policy choices of legislatures when they are illegitimate, it expects them to defer to legitimate legislative policy choices, even when wrong. Moreover, as hard as it is to make legislative policy, independent judicial policy-making would only make it harder. And while the legislature is free to replace judicial policy choices with its own, this is, as I have mentioned, a difficult process. It took the Maryland legislature three years to overturn the policy established by the *Kelley* case. Courts should refrain from regularly testing the limits of their policy-making powers, for the cumbersome corrective capacity of legislatures will work best if taxed only rarely.

A third objection, from those sympathetic to the general approach of the complementary model, questions the model's usefulness to judges in deciding cases. It is not enough that the model offers an attractive intermediate position between those who would deny judges any role in policy-making and those who would grant them unfettered discretion. In order to be useful in practice, the model must clarify specific constraints that define the complementary role in a way that provides guidance to judges when they are adjudicating cases. In other words, how does the concept of a complementary role help judges distinguish legitimate judicial policy-making from overreaching? How is a judge to determine, in a way that can be articulated and without the benefit of hindsight, whether the policy implications of a decision are consistent with a complementary role?

There is no simple response to this objection. Defining the judicial role and the proper limits of judicial discretion have been persistent difficulties throughout the history of jurisprudence, and I do not purport to have solved them. I can, however, further develop the concept of a complementary policy-making role in ways that may offer practical guidance in adjudicating claims.

The complementary policy-making role of courts, as I have developed it so far, is defined by two elements. First, the primary function of common law courts should be to provide a stable and predictable system of rules for resolving private disputes. Second, judges should engage in policy analysis only insofar as this is necessary to resolve doctrinal ambiguities and should make policy choices that support discernable legislative trends. This formulation, however, is too simple, for it fails to account for occasions where courts justifiably overturn established doctrines. For example, the products liability "revolution" of the last century was carried out by courts willing to overturn established precedents and to create new doctrines that drastically altered the regulation of consumer product safety. Landmark cases such as *MacPherson v. Buick Motor Co.*, overturning the privity requirement in negligence cases, or *Greenman v. Yuba Power Products*, establishing strict liability for defective products, now, ninety years later and forty years later respectively, stand for well-accepted, indeed foundational, doctrinal principles.[31] If a model of common law adjudication does not accommodate widely respected doctrinal transformations such as these, so much the worse for the model.

In order to accommodate cases such as *MacPherson* and *Greenman* that overturn established doctrines and set new directions for public policy, let me offer both a refinement of my model and a more subtle view of these two landmark cases. From this discussion will emerge a more specific delineation of the complementary judicial role that I am advocating. In order to maintain a stable and predictable system of rules for resolving private disputes, the rules must be, or at least be perceived as, fair by most people in most situations. A system of rules that is widely viewed as unjust is likely to become unstable and unpredictable. Judges and juries will be more likely to ignore them, litigants will be more prone to resist enforcement of them, and legislatures will be more apt to reform them. All of these reactions, which will intensify the more the rules are perceived as unfair, undermine the stability and predictability of private dispute resolution, the primary function of the tort system. The long-term maintenance of a system of stable and predictable rules for resolving private dispute may therefore on occasion require replacing rules perceived as unfair with rules perceived as fair. This explains how the complementary model could countenance the occasional reversal of established tort doctrines.

The unfairness of particular doctrines is not enough, however, to explain the decisions in *MacPherson* and *Greenman*. In *MacPherson*, Justice Cardozo not only viewed the privity rule as unfair because it failed to recognize the realities of manufacturer-consumer relations in the age of mass production and national distribution; he also considered the rule substantially compromised by prior decisions that carved out increasingly significant exceptions to it for "inherently dangerous products," a gradually expanding category that included poisons, guns, and scaffolding.[32] *MacPherson* did not so much signal a sudden revolution in tort doctrine as the culmination of a gradual shift away from privity. Moreover, in overturning the privity rule, Cardozo was concerned with updating the tort system as a whole by expanding the scope of negligence liability. He was not merely using the litigation as a means of addressing the particular social problem of auto accidents. These two observations are even more true of *Greenman*. Justice Traynor in the *Greenman* decision did not dramatically change the rule governing injuries caused by defective products from negligence to strict liability; rather, he merely recategorized an existing strict liability rule in contract—implied warranty—as a strict liability rule in tort. And, like Cardozo in *MacPherson*,

Traynor was concerned about the larger doctrinal system governing product-related injuries, not the specific social problem of power tool accidents. In both of these cases, judicial policy-making was characterized by gradual, incremental change rather than sharp, sudden departures from precedent and a concern for the integrity of the tort system as whole rather than a specific solution to a particular social problem. By contrast, cases like *O'Brien v. Muskin Corp.*, establishing liability for defective design even where the plaintiff can propose no safer alternative, known as "generic" or "product-category" liability, and *Kelley v. R.G. Industries*, establishing strict liability for the manufacture or sale of "Saturday Night Specials," lack these qualities.[33] The rule in *O'Brien*, subsequently overturned by the New Jersey legislature, marked a sudden departure from existing precedent. The rule in *Kelley*, overturned by the Maryland legislature, was more focused on proposing a solution to the particular problem of gun violence than on the systemic integrity of tort doctrine.

In the end, the judicial role is a sensibility rather than a set of determinate rules. It is more an aesthetic than a set of principles. In the complementary conception of this role, judicial policy-making is constrained by a concern for the doctrinal integrity of the tort system as a stable and predictable way to resolve private disputes. This means that judges generally restrain their policy analysis to resolving ambiguities in existing doctrine and their policy choices to options that support legislative trends where discernable. Even on the extraordinary occasions when judges overturn established doctrines in favor of fairer rules, they do so in an incremental manner guided by a concern for the systemic integrity of tort doctrine. Thus, when adjudicating gun cases, judges should generally dismiss those claims unsupported by existing doctrine and should resolve doctrinal ambiguities in ways that avoid contradicting legislative policy choices. Should parties on either side call on judges to overturn existing doctrine, judges should do so only if they are convinced that such a change would best serve the doctrinal integrity of the tort system as a whole.

Institutional Complementarity as a Regulatory Virtue

Complementarity between courts and legislatures is difficult to maintain. At times, courts ignore doctrinal restraints or make policy choices without regard for legislative preferences. The realities of the legislative process often make it difficult, if not impossible, to pass legislation overruling such decisions. It takes more than a mere legislative majority to get a bill through the many procedural hurdles of the legislative process. Similarly, legislatures occasionally take it upon themselves to influence pending litigation or to hand out immunity based on political considerations without respect for the role of courts or regard for the integrity of legal doctrine. In most instances, there is little that courts can do to correct such legislative overreaching. The litigation process is slow, and judicial action is limited to deciding the cases that happen to appear before the court. Thus, complementarity is less an enforceable rule than an institutional virtue to which courts and legislatures should aspire.

The complementary role of courts is based on the view that the primary duty of common law courts is to provide a stable and predictable system of rules for resolving private disputes. Insofar as it is highly deliberative and insulated from political pressures, the judicial process is well suited to this task. When ambiguities arise in the application of existing rules, judges must exercise discretion and should be guided in part by the public policy implications of different options for deciding a case. In making policy choices within the context of resolving doctrinal ambiguities, complementarity suggests that courts should show deference to legislative policy preferences where discernable. By playing a complementary role, courts can enhance legislative policy-making by uncovering information, filling gaps, enhancing enforcement, and, where desirable, being part of a decentralized, federalist approach to regulation.

For their part, legislatures too should play a complementary role in making public policy. Legislatures should take the lead in shaping public policy. The perception of democratic legitimacy makes them better suited than courts to broker political compromises between competing interest groups. Furthermore, they have the power to establish, fund, and supervise agencies capable of gathering and developing special expertise in a particular regulatory area. At the same time, legislatures should leave room for courts to play a secondary role, one that, in the end, can strengthen the effectiveness of their own policy choices. In responding to court decisions with which they disagree, legislatures should exercise restraint, overturning the particular judicial rule with which they disagree without eliminating altogether future court involvement in an area of public policy. Legislatures should also exercise restraint in replacing common law rules with statutory substitutes, especially when this introduces inconsistencies into tort doctrine. Such inconsistencies should be justified by the public interest, not political influence.

Again, when courts and legislatures transgress these norms, there is usually little if anything that the other can do about it. It is up to judges and legislators themselves to promote institutional integrity and to cultivate the benefits of complementarity between courts and legislatures. Doing so will strengthen both private law and public policy. While cultivating mutual respect and complementarity between courts and legislatures may not be enforceable, it is nevertheless essential to good government.

CHAPTER 11

Stubborn Information Problems &
the Regulatory Benefits of Gun Litigation

WENDY WAGNER

By all accounts, the gun litigation has been an utter failure. Plaintiffs claim no significant courtroom victories and appear pleasantly surprised when their case survives a motion to dismiss.[1] Even more damning, the litigation has provoked a violent backlash. Gun control opponents, most notably the National Rifle Association (NRA), lobbied for broad new legislative protections with impressive success.[2] At the same time, those gun executives who were even slightly receptive to a settlement of the municipalities' claims found themselves either out of business or out of a job due to the gun owners' hostile reaction to their concessions of industry responsibility.[3] Given this series of events, assessing the success of the gun litigation is not difficult.

The practical failure of the gun litigation does not necessarily mean that the larger project is misguided, however. Particularly since the weight of scholarly opinion seems to be turning against the litigation, this chapter adopts a deliberately sympathetic view, offering a best-case interpretation of the litigation and its results. From this vantage point and in spite of its real-world setbacks, the gun litigation can be defended as necessary to produce new information about product safety in a setting where the gun industry faces numerous, unchecked incentives to keep incriminating information regarding gun distribution and manufacture to themselves. When relevant information is asymmetrically held, both markets and the political process may be less capable than civil litigation of forcing the disclosure of relevant, internally held information. The political process offers affected parties only blunt mechanisms for accessing private information. By contrast, the courts provide litigants with direct access to industry files and personnel, which serves to enhance industry accountability in a way that might not be possible if industry oversight were left exclusively to the political process and agency enforcers.

This chapter argues that, to the extent that important information regarding gun distribution and manufacture is privately held, the gun litigation may be the best and perhaps the only way to access and publicize privately held information relevant to gun safety. Support for this argument follows in three sections. The first section argues that, contrary to recent criticism, the gun litigation is institutionally justified due to the courts' superior ability to divulge this "stubborn" (privately held) information relevant to social problem solving. In the second section, this more abstract justification for the gun litigation is compared against reality. The section concludes that, despite its theoretical promise, the gun litigation has failed to force the disclosure of much privately held information relevant to safer gun manufacture and distribution, largely for reasons specific to the litigation itself. The final section highlights the modest informational gains that the litigation has made with respect to gun safety and discusses potential additional gains in the future.

A Defense of Regulatory Litigation

Gun litigation is part of a larger family of "regulatory litigation" that seeks to counteract the unchecked powers of industry with respect to public health and safety. Much of this regulatory litigation, which is characterized by mass litigation that seeks a regulatory objective (that is, encouraging safer products through damage awards), has been criticized by prominent commentators. Their criticisms take two forms. First, critics question the fundamental legitimacy of regulatory litigation under prevailing principles of civil and, more specifically, tort law. Second, critics argue that as compared to other institutional alternatives, the courts are an inappropriate mechanism for bringing about social regulation. In this section, the gun litigation is justified by responding to these criticisms of the larger family of regulatory litigation to which it belongs.

The Principles of Tort Law

The first set of arguments against regulatory litigation, and the gun litigation in particular, asserts that the litigation stretches tort law beyond its doctrinal boundaries. More specifically, critics argue that this form of tort litigation "represents an illicit warping of common law principles" and violates the "corrective justice" principles of tort law.[4]

While these breaches sound devastating, in truth they are not, for the simple reason that theorists currently disagree on what the underlying principles of tort law are or even whether coherent principles exist at all, including the amorphous conception of "corrective justice."[5] Until some consensus is reached on these core principles, then, it is impossible to say that they have been violated. Moreover, since tort law has been in a dynamic state of expansion since the turn of the twentieth century, it is also difficult to make a case that there is some static doctrinal point beyond which tort law becomes illegitimately overreaching. As Prosser noted in his treatise on the subject, tort law is composed of a disorganized set of "miscellaneous civil wrongs"[6] that adjust swiftly to changes in times and social needs.[7] Without a viable standard for evaluating the legitimacy of the incremental expansions and retractions of tort liability, the courts, not legal commentators, serve as the final authority for determining the legitimacy of claims brought under the common law.

The Judicial versus the Political Process

Second, some commentators have argued that the gun litigation is not legitimate or justified because there is a more appropriate institution— the legislature—to address complex regulatory issues like gun control.[8] These commentators rightly point out that, for a number of reasons including its superior competency and representative capacity, the legislature is better situated, relative to the courts, to resolve complex social problems.

Yet these isolated attributes of the legislative process ignore ex ante issues of whether the political process is also capable of extracting the information needed for informed and reasoned debate, especially when the information is stubborn and resists disclosure or production. If political institutions are incapable of generating information needed for competent problem solving, then their superior capacities in resolving the problems once the information is produced are beside the point. Analysts must account for stubborn information problems or run the risk that their institutional comparisons will be incomplete.

This section outlines the importance of accounting for stubborn information problems in comparative institutional analysis. The discussion then turns to the superiority of the courts, as compared with the political process, to divulge and publicize this stubborn information.

STUBBORN INFORMATION PROBLEMS

Stubborn information arises when information is privately held and there are no incentives or subsidies to encourage its production or sharing. As a result, the information is closely guarded and deliberately withheld from other participants in the policy-making process. Stubborn information problems arise frequently in public health and safety regulation. Actors who create risks to health and the environment amass specialized private expertise about the ways their activities or products could cause harm, but sharing this information often threatens to lead to increased liability or regulation.[9] These actors are thus rewarded for concealing the potential adverse effects of their activities on public health and are able to maintain an advantaged position in the information-deficient debate. For example, gun manufacturers understand that investments in research on gun safety may reveal negligent past practices, which in turn could lead to increased liability and regulatory responsibilities as well as unpopularity in the marketplace. Under these circumstances gun manufacturers and dealers might be more willing to perpetuate ignorance rather than contribute to greater public knowledge regarding gun safety. In a related way, manufacturers and dealers might actively lobby against laws that require the production of new information if they believe the information will be incriminating. When these types of stubborn information problems prevail, the remaining participants in the political process are put at a severe disadvantage.[10] If there is little credible information on the benefits of greater regulation of the gun industry, for example, the attentive public may decline to participate, even though they might participate vigorously were they informed.[11] By contrast, those who do participate despite the lack of accurate information may be more likely to take a polarized, value-laden position. As a result, the absence of information on a social problem makes productive political discourse, and in some cases any discourse at all, difficult.

In the case of stubborn information problems, even "public interest" organizations may be unable or unlikely to encourage the generation of new, important information needed to address complex social problems. Sociologists observe that nonprofits are typically unable to motivate the public to participate in social issues when there is no "credible risk" or other documented problem.[12] To the extent that relevant information is expensive to obtain or in the superior control of private parties, interest groups in the political process will be stymied. In addition, since the new, additional information that is produced might not ultimately support the interest group's mission, crusades to generate more information are risky propositions. Credit claiming, a feature vital to the survival of individual public interest groups, is also difficult for projects that seek only to generate new information because other nonprofits can free-ride and attempt to claim partial credit for the revelation of the new information. Perhaps because of this constellation of obstacles, at least in the area of environmental and health regulation, nonprofit groups rarely dedicate resources to producing new information, even when there are gaping holes in knowledge of adverse effects of industrial activities on health or the environment.[13]

For social problems with especially stubborn information problems, then, the political process may encounter participatory paralysis. It is in these situations that regulatory litigation finds its niche. In contrast to the political process, which provides few mechanisms for individuals to generate needed information or to pry it from secretive private parties, the courts provide a far better institutional setting in which to generate socially useful information. Armed with the threat of contempt sanctions and the authority to conduct broad discovery, litigants availing themselves of the judicial system are able to gain access to private documents and company employees to learn the extent of a defendant's expert knowledge about the safety of its product, including whether the defendant compromised safety in order to increase sales. Even though it is fraught with compliance problems, the discovery process still provides litigants with far better access to private information than does the political process.[14] Also in contrast to the political process, where nonprofits can find it difficult to claim exclusive credit for informational discoveries, tangible benefits accrue to litigants who succeed in locating and disclosing new information in the course of litigation. Even though the information that emerges produces a public good, it also provides significant private financial benefits to the litigants if they are successful.

The fact that the judicial process excels relative to the political process at breaking through stubborn information problems is confirmed in practice. Stubborn information problems are the defining feature of the regulatory litigation over asbestos,[15] the Dalkon Shield,[16] DES,[17] lead,[18] ultra-absorbent tampons,[19] Bendectin,[20] breast implants,[21] and tobacco.[22] In each of these cases, the defendant manufacturer was insulated from regulatory accountability because it withheld or failed to produce, often under regulatory order, private information regarding the safety of its product. This critical private information was uncovered only after the litigation proceeded through discovery.

The litigation system also has built-in protections to ensure that cases brought to uncover this superior information are socially beneficial and will generally outweigh their costs to the judicial system and society at large. As a simple economic matter, plaintiffs' attorneys invest in cases that promise to divulge privately held information only when they believe that that information exists and will support their damages claims.[23] The legal requirement that plaintiffs state a claim upon which relief can be granted and the various penalties for bringing frivolous litigation, including ethical violations, provide additional checks on the unrestricted use of litigation to address stubborn information problems.[24]

HYBRID INSTITUTIONS

Comparative institutional critiques of regulatory litigation also suffer from limiting comparisons to single institutions that act in isolation from one another rather than considering how institutions can work together in a complementary fashion. For example, in settings where the political process is likely to falter because of stubborn information problems, the courts may emerge as the single best institution to overcome stubborn information at a preliminary stage, even though they may not be the best or only institution to resolve the larger social conundrum. Once litigants expose critical information that private parties conceal from the political process, the information can be used in the legislative process (or even the marketplace) to reach a more sophisticated outcome than the courts could manage with their own crude, incremental rulings or settlements.[25] The information can also be used to catalyze the political process by alerting the broader public to problems that were previously concealed. This heightened political awareness, in turn, can stimulate legislation and regulation that uses the new, critical information to arrive at a more refined and democratic response.

This hybrid model also reflects practice. Legislatures often, although not always,[26] respond to controversial judicial decrees with adjustments, codifications, or even revocations. The Maryland legislature's and the Massachusetts attorney general's reactions to the Maryland Supreme Court's imposition of strict liability on the manufacturer of the "Saturday Night Special" gun provide an apt illustration. The information produced from the litigation fueled the political process. Although the Maryland state legislature overturned the doctrine of strict liability imposed by the court, it created in its place a board of experts to identify and restrict the sale of handguns most vulnerable to criminal misuse.[27] The attorney general of Massachusetts similarly developed more vigorous state regulation of guns in response to the Maryland litigation.[28]

Gun Litigation: There's a Place for It

With a theoretical justification for regulatory litigation in place based on the superior ability of the courts to divulge stubborn information, it is still necessary to determine whether the current constellation of lawsuits comprising the gun litigation conforms to this theoretical niche for regulatory litigation. In this section it is argued that the gun litigation does address stubborn information problems and that, because much of this missing information is privately held, other forces such as interest groups and market pressures are unlikely to dislodge the needed information on their own. In such a system, the role of gun litigation as catalyst seems not only legitimate but necessary to jump-start discourse on an issue blocked by the absence of information that lies in significant part with the gun industry.[29]

Stubborn Information Problems in Gun Safety

Information on the potential safety gains from alternative, safer gun designs or distribution practices is seriously deficient. Both the Harvard Injury Control Research Center[30] and the National Academy of Sciences[31] have noted the alarmingly deficient information available to evaluate regulatory options for gun control. As a result, both institutions are actively engaged in collecting the available information and identifying short- and long-term research needs. Since this limited information suggests that improvements in gun design and distribution will prevent gun violence, there is reason to believe that still more research will be valuable.[32]

Stubborn information problems explain some of the gaps in knowledge regarding the safety of gun design and distribution since a considerable amount of the necessary information either appears to lie with manufacturers and dealers or is most cheaply and comprehensively produced by them. Simply from their position as internal experts on the subject of gun manufacture, gun manufacturers have considerable access to information about how guns can be designed more safely to prevent accidents and are best positioned to use this information in their own technological innovations. Illustrative evidence of ways that manufacturers enjoy superior information over gun safety is provided in table 1, which presents an excerpt from an internal, "highly confidential" memorandum by Colt discovered during the gun litigation.[33]

Gun manufacturers' superior expertise and informational advantages regarding safety improvements to gun design and distribution are corroborated by more general accounts of the gun industry. Tom Diaz's book, *Making a Killing*, dedicates much of its 250 pages to documenting the superior information and expertise that the gun industry enjoys regarding design and distribution decisions.[34] Other literature reinforces Diaz's general conclusion that a large amount of privately held information regarding safety devices and distribution is held exclusively by gun manufacturers and dealers.[35] Still, the extent of the manufacturers' superior information over gun safety remains illusive because manufacturers often classify safety-related information as trade-secret protected, a protection that exempts the information from public disclosure. Manufacturers also succeed in sealing some of the safety-related information uncovered in private litigation through the use of gag settlements.[36] (Further complicating access to information is the fact that all but one of the gun manufacturers is a privately held corporation.)[37] The gun industry's effort to insert a rider into an appropriations bill exempting the Bureau of Alcohol, Tobacco, Firearms and Explosives (BATFE) data on dealer transactions from the Freedom of Information Act (FOIA) provides still more evidence of the industry's eagerness to conceal embarrassing information on unsafe gun distribution practices from the public.[38] In fact, some evidence shows that the manufacturers not only conceal privately held information on possible innovations in gun design and distribution, but they might use this information in perverse ways to make guns less safe and more available to criminals to maximize their sales in an otherwise saturated gun market.[39]

Even when they do not have safety information in their immediate possession, evidence suggests that manufacturers and distributors are best situated to reduce the illegal flow of guns to criminals because of

TABLE 1.   Excerpt from Internal, "Highly Confidential" Memorandum for iColt and Colt

---

Colt management has not wanted to tip its hand in terms of how close Colt is to launching its first 'Smart Gun' product. Colt's official position is that a law enforcement model of the 'smart gun' could be introduced in two to three years and a consumer model could be introduced in two to three years after that. The reasons Colt management has not kept the public informed with its recent exceptional progress, which may result in a quicker time to market, includes the following:

1. One of the complaints lodged against the industry is that the industry is deliberately delaying the introduction of the 'Smart Gun.' As Colt is perfecting the design, management does not want the press, legislators, or plaintiff lawyers influencing the launch decision as Colt is testing and evaluating its first generation models.
2. Colt has had a limited budget to invest in 'Smart Gun' technology. Virtually the entire industry has publicly stated they are against the concept and believe it to be virtually impossible. One or two companies have the resources to start catching up if it is believed that viable 'Smart Gun' were about to be released.
3. Colt is working in Washington to help put $20 million to $40 million in the federal budget for research on 'smart gun' technology. Depending how the press reports the current state of the 'smart gun,' it could be perceived by Congress that further research dollars are not needed.

Source: Memorandum from Steven M. Silwa, CEO and president of Colt, to Zilkha Capital Parters et al., June 28, 1999, "iColt Offering Memorandum Draft," 27, http://www.gunlaw suits.org/pdf/docket/041803.pdf.

their superior access to this information. With the help of BATFE's data, for example, manufacturers can learn of and disenfranchise corrupt dealerships and develop internal tracking systems to improve dealership compliance.[40] Manufacturers can even "[t]race information [on guns used in crimes or other suspect circumstances] that identifies a retailer or distributor's name or FFL number[, information that] is not publicly available until the trace request is more than five years old."[41] In a lengthy opinion resolving the NAACP's nuisance suit against manufacturers and distributors in New York City, Judge Weinstein concluded that "the manufacturers and distributors . . . [are peculiarly situated], through the use of handgun traces and other sources of information, [to] substantially reduce the number of firearms leaking into the illegal secondary market and ultimately in to the hands of criminals in New York." The 136-page district court opinion lists a variety of ways that the manufacturers and distributors currently are in a superior position to discourage dealerships from allowing straw purchases and illegal sales.

Despite the meaningful role that gun manufacturers could play in reducing the supply of guns to the criminal market, the political process has largely exempted manufacturers from meaningful regulatory oversight. At the federal level, manufacturers of guns are exempt from virtually all consumer safety regulation.[42] While federal legislation has effectively banned the manufacture and civilian sale of some semiautomatic weapons and machine guns,[43] BATFE has no authority to regulate the design of the large, remaining set of rifles and handguns that are allowed on the market or to order their recall.[44] Manufacturers also have no legal responsibility to track or oversee the behavior of dealers or to report adverse information on their products.[45] If defects in a line of guns are discovered, litigation is the only recourse, with after-the-fact liability.[46]

Federal regulation of dealers is only slightly more vigorous. Dealers must obtain a license from BATFE in order to operate, and under the terms of the license, dealers' sales to certain individuals are proscribed and the dealers are required to keep records of all sales.[47] In order to ensure compliance with these requirements, BATFE has the authority to conduct on-site inspections at dealerships, but inspections governing compliance with record-keeping requirements are limited by law to no more than one unannounced inspection per dealer per year.[48] The only penalties available to BATFE to deter corrupt dealers are to either pursue a criminal prosecution or revoke a license.[49] BATFE's greatest regulatory handicap, however, is its lack of enforcement resources.[50] The agency is able to finance inspections of only a fraction of licensed dealers (roughly 10 percent as of 1993), and in these inspections BATFE routinely discovers a high rate of noncompliance (34 percent), suggesting that the dealers also consider BATFE enforcement to be lax.[51]

Yet without a meaningful regulatory presence, deficits in information regarding gun safety are perpetuated. Unlike manufacturers of other potentially dangerous products—including drugs, food additives, pesticides, toxic substances, polluting activities, motor vehicles, and consumer products—gun manufacturers are not required to provide any information regarding their product design or distribution or to report adverse information other than trace-relevant data to regulators or public officials under limited circumstances.[52] Even for grandfathered products, manufacturers of potentially dangerous products other than guns must disclose information on adverse effects, provide warnings, and respond to regulators' requests for information.[53] None of these requirements are imposed on gun manufacturers, despite the fact that firearms are second only to motor vehicles as the major cause of product-related deaths in the United States.[54] As one commentator noted, even the design of feebly regulated consumer products, such as toy guns and teddy bears, is regulated more vigorously than the design of concealed handguns and rifles.[55]

Of course, forcing the disclosure of industry information on gun safety is not a panacea, and, once produced, this information will obviously not resolve all debates on gun regulation. However, additional credible information about gun design and distribution options is likely to narrow the available, plausible positions of those for and against government-imposed regulation of guns. Indeed, even Kahan, Braman, and Gastil's cultural critique of the gun litigation in chapter 4 of this volume concedes the value of credible information when it is endorsed by trusted experts on both sides of the gun debate. Thus, while it is important to recognize that additional empirical information will not answer all questions, it is a mistake to underestimate the grounding effect that credible information can have on political debate and regulatory progress. This is especially true for regulatory litigation, where experience reveals the dramatic difference that new, credible information can make to health protection.

The Failure of the Dominant Interest Groups Operating in the Political
Process to Overcome Stubborn Information Problems regarding Gun Safety

Dominant interest groups on both sides of the gun control issue might
attempt to remedy the dearth of information on gun safety, but as discussed earlier, these groups are generally not rewarded for efforts that
have as their sole end the production of new information. Even more
troubling in some settings, these groups may be inclined to actually exacerbate, rather than reduce, information deficits. Without information,
interest group leaders are emboldened to advocate extreme positions that
are difficult to question. Advocating extreme positions, moreover, can
serve to encourage greater donations and financial support if organization leaders convey a sense of crisis. As a result, the positions of dominant interest groups may become more ideological, value laden, and
irreconcilable. One of the primary causes of the cultural conflicts that
Kahan, Braman, and Gastil discuss in chapter 4 may in fact be public
choice behavior by interest groups on both sides of the debate strategi-
cally keeping positions polarized in order to generate a steady flow of
revenues from members.

These concerns regarding the counterproductive behavior of interest
groups when policy-relevant information is scarce are not merely theoretical but in fact characterize at least some of the current debate about
gun regulation. The gun debate has been deadlocked for decades by
interest groups who take extreme positions supported by little credible
information. With limited information on the risks of the unregulated
manufacture and distribution of guns, gun control proponents for their
part resort to portraying the "credible risk" as the gun itself. Rather than
advocate more moderate gun regulation, some groups advocate a complete gun ban. In the view of these gun control advocates, safer gun
design is not even an appropriate gun control objective since it undercuts
the dominant goal of banning guns.[56] As one gun control advocate con-
ceded: "On the one hand, [safer guns] could help reduce fatal accidents,
unintentional injuries. . . . On the other hand, if you make the 'safe handgun' are you giving the industry a whole new marketing tool? . . . I'm not
really sure where I come down on it."[57] Even Brady Center lawyers who
openly embrace the need for safer guns have been portrayed by the gun
industry as too ideological. One gun manufacturer, Glock vice president

Paul Jannuzzo, maintained that the Brady lawyers, as opposed to the attorneys from the Justice Department or the firms, "'blasted what should have been a straight line to settlement'" between the gun manufacturers and some of the municipalities. Jannuzzo recounts that, after lengthy settlement discussions about the ways manufacturers could design guns to prevent accidental shootings, a Brady lawyer responded, "'but what about suicides?'"[58]

There is still more damning evidence that organizations opposing gun controls—such as the NRA and other smaller organizations[59]—regularly take positions on gun control that diverge from a majority of their membership.[60] A survey of 607 gun owners by Harvard researchers Weil and Hemenway revealed that most NRA members supported types of gun control, such as registration and waiting periods, that the NRA leaders actively lobbied against.[61] The authors conclude from the survey that "the leadership positions of the NRA do not represent the views of either the typical NRA member or nonmember gun owners with respect to important gun control policies."[62] There is also evidence that some of the NRA's specific positions—for example, its attack against Smith & Wesson for agreeing to settle the gun litigation—diverged from the preference of the majority of its members.[63]

The Harvard study leaves unresolved why persons might support organizations that do not represent their views. Weil and Hemenway offer some explanations, such as multiple benefits from membership and the advocacy of even more important policy positions, such as the right to bear arms, that could eclipse specific disagreements with NRA's positions on narrower issues relating to gun control.[64] Another possibility based on the survey results, and reinforced by studies of nonprofits in other settings, is that the members are not fully aware of the leadership's opposition to all forms of gun control.[65] For example, 90 percent of the NRA members in the study said they "agree[d] with the positions of the NRA," yet their preferences for gun control diverged to a significant extent from the NRA's on virtually every gun control issue.[66] Indeed, the NRA's greatest losses in member support appear to occur when more sophisticated members become aware of the NRA's specific lobbying positions. For example, both former president George H. W. Bush and the police associations separated from the NRA because of disagreements with its specific policy positions on gun regulation.[67] Several insiders have also exited the NRA after divulging in depositions that the strong, small, and very extreme group in charge of the organization "silences voices for reform within the industry."[68] In most circumstances, however, rank-and-file members may not have the time or resources to critically evaluate the NRA's positions, especially since the information they use to evaluate issues relating to gun regulation comes largely from the NRA and its affiliates, including the gun press.[69] Distorted or incomplete education of members, especially when that education helps keep members from leaving the organization, may be a recurring problem with nonprofit representation more generally in information-deficient arenas.[70]

Market Failure

At least in the sale of guns, the marketplace is also unlikely to overcome stubborn information problems. There are positive spillovers associated with safer gun design and distribution practices that may not be covered in market transactions. Gun purchasers, for example, might discount or even disregard the need to purchase guns with safety devices that guard against accidental shootings, especially if a gun is more expensive with a safety device than without.[71] In any case, even if some consumers prefer safer guns with respect to either design or distribution, manufacturers might not provide these options for other reasons, for example, the fear of tipping off regulators or political constituents who might attempt to codify technological advances into industrywide regulatory requirements.[72] In fact, market forces could actually reward manufacturers with more sales when they increase the power and concealability of their weapons and sell to corrupt dealers,[73] leading to what Diaz calls the spiral of lethality.[74]

Evaluating the Litigation: Missed Opportunities for Overcoming Stubborn Information Problems

As discussed in the previous two sections, the most compelling justification for regulatory litigation is its potential to overcome the information asymmetries that handicap the political process. Yet despite its theoretical appeal, as a practical matter the gun litigation has failed to divulge important, privately held information. Instead, it has provoked a powerful backlash. These disappointments are detailed in this section

Little New Information Has Been Discovered

Since judges have determined that many of the municipalities' claims fall outside the outer bounds of permissible tort law, much of the gun litigation has been dismissed before discovery can commence. Without the divulgence of industry information on gun safety, however, the litigation is able to make little headway in informing the options for gun control. But even the limited information that has been produced through discovery has not been transformative. Gun manufacturers' files are generally not filled with smoking gun memoranda and meeting notes that reveal a strategic effort to saturate the criminal gun market to increase profits. The evidence, at its most embarrassing, paints only a picture of corporate inattention to the harms that might flow from careless design and distribution practices.[75] Although this evidence is certainly unflattering, it does not begin to approach the secret industry memos uncovered in the tobacco litigation that revealed, for example, the industry's manipulation of the addictive properties of cigarettes.[76]

The litigation has also failed to create incentives for significant additional research on the relationship between the design and distribution of firearms and their contribution to gun injuries and deaths. Because of the quick dismissal of most cases, no new studies have been commissioned by plaintiffs or the gun industry, as has sometimes been the case in other mass litigation.[77]

Nevertheless, there has been some modest informational progress as a result of the litigation. Gun litigation, for example, does confirm that the industry enjoys a great deal of private information and expertise that it is not sharing or using in ways that optimize health and safety. For example, in deposition testimony and expert surveys of the gun industry, it has become clear that the manufacturers can equip their guns with integral locks at low costs, from two to ten dollars per gun.[78] The manufacturers' and dealers' settlement agreements (both the Smith & Wesson failed settlement[79] and the California settlement discussed later) and the

NAACP litigation also provide evidence that gun manufacturers can play an important role in safer gun design and distribution practices.

Because Stubborn Information Is Not Produced, the Political Process Has Generally Been Catalyzed in the Wrong Direction

Regulatory litigation that loses in the courts and fails to produce a significant body of information on the risks of unregulated guns is not likely to generate popular support. Without salient smoking gun evidence, the hoped-for David and Goliath image of beleaguered, crime-laden cities and victims taking on the greedy gun manufacturers that profit from crime is transformed into the opposite image. Plaintiffs' attorneys, sitting on obscenely large winnings from the tobacco litigation and portrayed as having an almost insatiable appetite for high-stakes litigation, look much more akin to Goliath than David. The quick bankruptcy of several of the smallest gun companies following the litigation,[80] coupled with a realization that even the biggest manufacturers are relatively small in relation to other tort defendants like tobacco,[81] complete the flipped image. At the same time that the litigation is failing to produce significant informational gains, the NRA is churning out negative publicity and inflaming its grass roots chapters against the litigation.[82] With the skilled organizational efforts of the NRA, a tidal wave of state legislation barring the municipal litigation was passed in thirty-two states and considered in all but four, and Congress is also debating immunity legislation at the federal level.[83] Public perceptions of the litigation have become so negative that the NRA was even successful in its efforts to urge gun consumers to boycott the one manufacturer, Smith & Wesson, willing to entertain settlement discussions.[84]

It remains to be seen whether a different chronology of events could lead to a different outcome. Experience reveals that when regulatory litigation does produce privately held industry information that documents important public harms in the face of regulatory failure—as it has in the asbestos, DES, lead, Dalkon Shield, and tobacco cases—the litigation is reluctantly acknowledged as legitimate, in spite of the fact that its approach to solving these problems is costly. By contrast, when regulatory litigation fails to produce information on the connection between the product and social harms, as in the breast implant and Bendectin litigation, the litigation is widely regarded as abusive and unjustified.[85]

The Final Chapter of the Gun Litigation:
Unexpected Advances in Gun Safety

From the standpoint of its proponents, the gun litigation is lacking the traditional markers for success. Yet scratching below this surface reveals several more subtle accomplishments of the litigation. Most important and in spite of its failure in the courts, the litigation may be causing internal changes in the industry with respect to safer design and distribution practices. Second, the litigation might be taking a more democratically responsive step toward gun control than has been accomplished in the political process. Third and finally, recent developments remind us that regulatory litigation is dynamic, making it wise to suspend a final evaluation of the gun litigation until it is finally over.

Encouraging Industry Accountability

Despite the strong backlash and rash of immunity laws, there is surprisingly positive evidence that, as a result of the litigation, the gun manufacturers have focused more attention on safer designs and the dealers have voluntarily instituted efforts to make distribution less susceptible to criminal trafficking.[86] For example, after the litigation was filed, Colt discontinued its most dangerous and inexpensive models.[87] The Brady Center reports that other manufacturers, "including Beretta, Heckler & Koch, Kimber, Remington, Sako, Smith & Wesson, Springfield Armory, and Steyr, . . . beg[a]n for the first time to sell guns with internal locks," with other manufacturers now advertising this feature in future guns.[88] According to the *Arizona Republic*, in 2000 the annual SHOT Show featured safety as the overriding theme in "display after display" for the first time in its history.[89] The National Association of Firearms Retailers now posts on its web site the BATFE's training video for ways that retailers can prevent straw purchasers.[90] Even product liability insurance has become costlier for the manufacturers of more dangerous guns in the wake of the gun litigation.[91] Although there is still no way to assess the significance of these changes, industry behavior has moved, on its own, in the direction that the gun control litigants had hoped.

Although it seems counterintuitive that manufacturers and dealers might change their behavior in response to the failed litigation, this increased attention to safety may simply be a rational reaction to economic realities. Prior to the litigation, manufacturers faced no probability of sanctions for careless distribution or design practices. After the litigation was filed, the manufacturers faced a probability of at least a lawsuit and the small probability of substantial sanctions. At least in rational choice terms, the change in accountability could lead manufacturers to make some investments in safety if they believed they could limit or stave off further lawsuits by doing so.[92] There may be other reinforcing reasons for this changed behavior, including the possibility that the industry itself was unaware of the gap between its practices and the public interest or that outside investors and insurers began to pressure the industry for changes given the risk of successful litigation. Most explanations, though, are tied to the fact that, even if the litigation failed to produce useful new information to the public or the political process, it caused the industry to engage in internal self-evaluation. Others have observed similar voluntary industry changes as a result of regulatory disclosure requirements, which can bring about improvements in industry practice through greater internal and external accountability.[93]

No matter how rational this industry behavior might seem in hindsight, the gun industry's response to the failed litigation is certainly a surprise ending to conventional thinking about deterrence. The gun litigation teaches us that the courts may have the power to bring about a swift and productive change in industry practice simply by virtue of having their jurisdiction invoked. If this industry reaction is not an anomaly (and economic modeling suggests the reaction is in fact rational), then as an institutional matter, some of the greatest gains in deterrence might be accomplished through the clear and present threat of litigation rather than judicial rulings or legislative deliberations.

Democratic Representatives: Interest Groups versus Litigants

One of the sharpest criticisms of the municipal gun litigation is that it involves "less public input and accountability than government regulation."[94] These critics argue that, by institutional design, neither the attorneys nor the judges are able to solicit or are likely to be much affected by public input. Yet, as a quirky empirical matter, it appears that the mission of the gun litigation—to increase regulatory oversight over gun manufacturers and dealers—is actually more in keeping with majority preferences concerning gun regulation than any of the current legislation and regulation. One set of surveys, published in the *New England Journal of Medicine* and set forth in table 2, found that a majority of the public, including a solid majority of gun owners, favor greater regulation of guns.[95] Gun owners who do not join the NRA are even more amenable to gun control than the majority of NRA members, with up to 20 percent increases in support on various issues.[96] Other studies corroborate this finding.[97]

Of course, the gun litigation's closer match to public preferences than existing legislation may simply be a convenient coincidence. But it also could suggest that the political process may diverge dramatically from public preferences on issues for which there is little information and, as a result, may enable nonprofit organizations to proceed with more extreme positions and become deadlocked in the information-deficient debates. In such cases, one might expect to see regulatory litigation come closer to majority preferences than existing regulation simply because the claims must be supported by some information and the merits of the claims undergo the scrutiny of the courts.

TABLE 2.   Support Among Respondents for the Regulation of Guns as Consumer Products

	Percentage Who Favored or Strongly Favored the Policy	
Policy Option	All Respondents ($N = 1,200$)	Respondents Who Owned Guns ($N = 338$)
Governmental regulation of gun design	68	64
Same standards for domestic guns as for foreign guns	94	93
Childproofing of all new handguns	88	80
Personalization of all new handguns	71	59
Magazine safety for all new pistols	82	75
Loaded-chamber indicator for all new handguns	73	60

Note: All results shown are from the 1997–98 survey.

Regulatory Litigation Never Dies, It Just Fades Away

Just as the gun litigation docket is drying up, it may—in its last dying gasps—be finally producing the kind of embarrassing information and resulting political activity that justifies its existence. In the California municipal gun litigation, unlike much of the other gun litigation nationwide, the manufacturers' cases were dismissed, but the court declined to dismiss the dealers from suit. Plaintiffs were thus given the opportunity to conduct discovery. Although incriminating information came from several sources during discovery, the most devastating was the deposition testimony of longtime NRA and gun executive Robert Riker in February 2003, who testified, among other things, that " 'until faced with a serious threat of civil liability for past conduct, leaders in the [gun] industry have consistently resisted taking constructive voluntary action to prevent firearms from ending up in the illegal gun market and have sought to silence others within the industry who have advocated reform.' "[98]

In textbook fashion, this incriminating evidence began to change the character of the litigation. In late August 2003, the dealers entered into a settlement to end the litigation and agreed to undertake a number of actions to prevent criminal trade in guns.[99] Presumably because this settlement worked to silence future whistle-blowers from having their testimonials recorded as deposition testimony, the NRA and other gun industries have, for the most part, refrained from denouncing the settlement.[100] The information also appeared to catalyze some modest legislative activity. Several weeks after the settlement was announced, the California legislature passed a law—this one addressed to manufacturers—requiring guns sold in California to be equipped with indicators that show whether there is a round of ammunition in the chamber or requiring that guns be impossible to fire if the ammunition magazine is not inserted in the gun.[101]

This turn of events, especially when compared with other regulatory litigation, serves as an important reminder of the dynamic nature of emergent information and its importance to the ultimate fate of regulatory litigation. Recall that other regulatory litigation that began with strong success, like breast implant and Bendectin litigation, ultimately failed as new information emerged showing that the harms were less than suspected.[102] By contrast, regulatory litigation such as the tobacco, lead, and asbestos suits that suffered losses in the early years, sometimes for decades, ultimately emerged as victorious as information surfaced to validate the claims. Thus, especially given this new turn of events, it is premature to reach any final conclusions about the merits of the gun litigation.

It should also be noted that, although the California developments are the first sign that the gun litigation has served to catalyze political action in favor of gun regulation, other examples of gun litigation leading to legislative action predate the municipal suits. Successful litigation against the Saturday Night Special in 1988 spurred legislative and regulatory oversight of gun manufacturers in Massachusetts and Maryland.[103] While it is certainly premature to extrapolate too broadly from the recent California experience, there is at least the possibility that California's activities could be the first of an ongoing series of sympathetic state legislative actions that, over time, could reach a "tipping point" that results in a torrent of new regulatory laws across the United States.

Conclusion

The gun litigation has produced a number of surprises. Just when it appeared that the immunity legislation advocated by the NRA provided the last, irrefutable evidence of the litigation's failure, damaging evidence produced in discovery may begin to slowly inform and catalyze political discourse on gun regulation. Given the history of other regulatory litigation, if privately held information begins to paint gun manufacturers and dealers as responsible for unnecessary social harms, the California settlement and legislation may not be the last chapter in the gun litigation but instead the first chapter in new and more vigorous legislative and perhaps voluntary efforts to make gun design and distribution safer. Much will depend on how the new and emerging information is portrayed and publicized in the months that follow.[104] If regulatory legislation or related developments do follow, however, the gun litigation's catalytic role will be difficult to ignore.

CHAPTER 12

Liability Insurance & the Regulation of Firearms

TOM BAKER & THOMAS O. FARRISH

Along with the recognition that we live in the age of the insurance state has come the recognition that private insurance institutions play governmental roles.[1] If the core "governmental" activities have become the traditional "insurance" activities of risk spreading and loss prevention, then insurance *is* governance and, accordingly, all insurance institutions are governmental. For that reason, any comprehensive account of regulation should at least consider the role of insurance institutions—all the more so when one of the forms of regulation under examination is tort law, because liability insurance has the capacity to translate tort law's incentives into prices and directives.

This chapter has three goals. First, the chapter presents a preliminary description and analysis of liability insurance as a form of regulation. Although we have not finished all of the work required to present a completely satisfactory picture of insurance as regulation, the progress that we have made has informed considerably our research on guns and insurance, and we offer the conceptual framework presented here in that spirit. Second, and most important for this volume, the chapter describes what the U.S. liability insurance industry does (and does not do) to regulate gun activity. In the process, we consider how liability insurance addresses several kinds of gun-related litigation: intentional and accidental shooting cases, traditional products liability lawsuits, and the recent mass tort litigation. Finally, the chapter reflects on the implications of this case study for understanding liability insurance as a form of regulation and for understanding tort law as a deterrence and loss-spreading institution.

Regulation by Liability Insurance

The paradigmatic form of regulation by insurance is facilitative. Insurance spreads the costs of loss, which facilitates activities that might cause loss. Absent insurance, people might be unwilling to proceed in the face of the risk of loss (or, in the case of profit-oriented activity, might demand a higher potential return before proceeding) and might well have to cease activity if and when the risk matured into an actual loss. An early seventeenth-century Act of Parliament described this role of insurance in the shipping trade as follows.

> [B]y meanes of whiche Policies of Assurance it comethe to passe, upon the losse or perishinge of any Shippe there followethe not the undoinge of any Man, but the losse lightethe rather easilie upon many, then heavily upon fewe, and rather upon them that adventure not then those that doe adventure, whereby all Merchantes, sp[ec]ialie the younger sorte, are allured to venture more willinglie and more freelie.[2]

While this description emphasizes the benefits of first-party insurance (insurance that we buy to protect our own property, life, or health), loss spreading is the main attraction of liability insurance as well. By spreading the costs of liability among insurance purchasers, liability insurance helps individuals avoid financial ruin when they cause harm to others.

The fact that the "costs of liability" are based on the "costs of injury to others" means that liability insurance also spreads the costs of injury. In other words, liability insurance is not only a shield for defendants, it is also the institution that makes it possible to think of tort law as a loss-spreading system. Of course, the fact that tort law can be understood as a loss-spreading system does not necessarily make it an effective one. Among other structural problems, the fact that people buy liability insurance for the purpose of protecting themselves from the claims of others (and not for the purpose of protecting those others) creates very significant complications for injury cost spreading, some of which will be illustrated in this case study.

Almost every other aspect of regulation by insurance follows from the facilitative, loss-spreading role of insurance. The power to refuse to take the risk gives an insurance company leverage over the party with the risk. And the decision to take the risk gives the insurance company incentive to manage that risk, both before and after it matures into loss. This leverage and incentive translate into the following broad categories of regulation by insurance: gatekeeping, loss prevention, engagement with public regulators, liability limitation, selective exclusion, management of loss costs, and research and education. The sections that follow briefly describe each using examples from a variety of insurance contexts.

Gatekeeping

Obtaining insurance is often a prerequisite to other activity. You can't register a car without auto insurance, take out a mortgage without homeowners' insurance, obtain a commercial loan without business owners' insurance, bid on a government contract without a surety bond, advertise on network television without media liability insurance, finance a movie without cast insurance, sign a commercial lease without commercial property and liability insurance, obtain practice privileges at most hospitals without medical malpractice insurance, and so on. All these legal or institutional requirements make insurance companies important *gatekeepers* in large sectors of the U.S. economy (and undoubtedly in other parts of the developed world as well).

Liability insurance requirements arise in two main contexts. First, governments sometimes mandate insurance as a way of making sure that people or businesses that engage in certain activities will be financially responsible (at least to some degree) for their liabilities. Automobile insurance is the most common example; other examples include medical malpractice insurance requirements in some states and environmental insurance requirements for hazardous waste handlers.[3] Second, commercial contracts often require that parties have insurance either to make sure that the parties will be able to cover losses to the counter-parties (e.g., landlords requiring tenants to purchase insurance) or to make sure that the parties will be able to cover the losses of people who would otherwise sue the counter-parties (e.g., hospitals requiring physicians to have malpractice insurance).

Going through the gate requires meeting the insurance companies' standards, as well as paying the necessary premiums. This gatekeeping role gives insurance companies the potential to serve as very significant regulators (while at the same time making access to "private" insurance an intensely "public" issue).[4]

Loss Prevention

Once an insurance institution assumes responsibility for the financial consequences of a given harm, it has an incentive to prevent that harm. Insurers prevent harm in four main ways, each of which is potentially applicable to liability insurance: by establishing underwriting procedures that make loss prevention activities a condition of obtaining insurance, by establishing pricing structures that give policyholders an incentive to undertake specific loss prevention activities, by adopting risk-based pricing more generally, and by engaging in loss prevention–oriented monitoring during the course of the insurance relationship.[5] Risk-based pricing is a means of internalizing the loss costs associated with a range of activities. Provided that the policyholder has control over the level or type of activities covered by the insurance, this cost internalization can promote decisions that balance the costs of harm and prevention.[6]

Engagement with Public Regulators

Insurance organizations regularly work with public agencies to further loss prevention and related risk management goals. Although much of this aspect of regulation by insurance could fit under the more general heading of "loss prevention," the involvement of the state makes it different enough from private contract requirements to deserve special attention. Insurance organizations attempt to influence the agencies that are responsible for housing codes, road and highway design, automobile safety regulations, environmental cleanup procedures, and many other activities that affect the frequency or magnitude of insured losses. From the perspective of insurance institutions, the involvement of the public agencies helps with enforcement of loss prevention norms. In addition, the public agency can become a potent source for the collection and transmission of loss-related information, which helps in pricing future policies.[7]

Elimination or Reduction of Liability

From a social perspective, the liability insurance "loss" is the harm that forms the basis for the underlying liability that is insured. From the economic perspective of the people who are liable, however, the loss is not the harm itself but rather the liability arising from that harm. From a potential defendant's perspective, "loss prevention" is really "liability prevention," and the elimination of liability is just as effective as the elimination of the harm and, at least potentially, much cheaper.

As this suggests, insurance organizations can prevent *insured* losses by reducing or limiting the liability that forms the basis for liability insurance claims. Although completely eliminating liability would hardly further the interests of liability insurers (eliminating liability eliminates the need for liability insurance), eliminating some potentially very costly liabilities could serve insurers' interests, at least in the short term, particularly when the insurance that might otherwise cover those liabilities has already been priced and sold. This may explain why insurers have been involved in a number of efforts over the years to "reform" tort law in a manner that reduces liabilities across the board (e.g., damages caps) or that addresses specific kinds of liabilities (e.g., asbestos and environmental liabilities). Whatever else one may think about it, elimination or reduction of liability regulates—or, better yet, deregulates—activities through the withdrawal of the incentives and institutional arrangements that follow from tort liability.

Selective Exclusion

Insurers also can reduce the number of insured claims by refusing to provide coverage for specific kinds of losses. In general, these "selective exclusions" arise out of three kinds of circumstances: moral hazard, known losses, and potential losses that insurers determine are too uncertain. The most common example of moral hazard exclusion is the exclusion of intentional harm. Known loss exclusions include exclusions for asbestos claims and other product-specific exclusions inserted into manufacturers' liability insurance policies once mass tort litigation involving that product has commenced (commonly referred to as "laser exclusions" because of their narrow focus). Exclusions for losses that are deemed too uncertain include exclusions for environmental claims in standard liability insurance policies. In practice, selective exclusion can amount to the elimination of the liabilities that are excluded, particularly when the potentially liable parties are individuals (because of the obstacles to collecting real money from real people)[8] but also if and when the liabilities overwhelm the assets of organizational defendants.[9]

Management of Loss Costs

Along with working to prevent loss (or liability), insurance companies also attempt to reduce the cost of harm that does occur. Loss cost management is a significant focus of almost any kind of insurance arrangement in which the insurer promises to indemnify the policyholder for a given type of loss (as opposed to an insurance arrangement in which the insurer promises to pay a fixed amount in the event of loss). While there is nothing a life insurer can do to manage its loss costs after a covered death has occurred, there is a great deal that a health insurer can do to manage medical costs, that a disability insurer can do to promote rehabilitation, and that a liability insurer can do to manage the defense of claims. Within the medical and legal profession, loss cost management is one of the most visible forms of regulation by insurance, as doctors (who are regulated by managed care practices) and tort defense lawyers (who are regulated by litigation management guidelines) can report. Nearly all of tort law is systematically affected by the loss cost management aspect of liability insurance, because it is tort loss cost management that turns almost all tort lawsuits into a contest with a "repeat player" on the defense side.[10]

Research and Education

Insurance was among the earliest information businesses. Indeed, from a certain perspective an insurance company is simply a tool for the collection, analysis, and use of information. The core analytical task of an insurance enterprise is identifying future losses, choosing which of those losses it is willing to insure, estimating their frequency and magnitude, preparing insurance contracts that reflect those choices, and then deciding how much to charge which classes of people in return for this protection. In addition, insurance companies need to learn how to motivate people to buy their insurance, and they ought to learn as much as possible about how to prevent loss. All of this produces knowledge, much of which can have consequences beyond the insurance enterprise. For example, over the years, insurance institutions have been a significant force in the development and dissemination of harm-reducing technologies and practices. While of course insurers use this research in their underwriting and pricing, consumers also use this information to make decisions about what kinds of products to buy. Examples of such research and education in the liability context include risk management seminars and advice provided to doctors, lawyers, and other professionals; the occupational safety and related research carried out under the auspices of (or in cooperation with) workers' compensation insurers; and at least some aspects of the extensive efforts by insurance-supported groups in the automobile safety arena (although much of this research can be understood as an effort to reduce first-party property insurance losses).

Gun Regulation by Insurance?

In exploring how the U.S. insurance industry approaches gun risks, we focused our efforts on liability insurance. Health and disability insurance primarily is sold through employment-based group policies that do not present an opportunity to engage in individual underwriting, and life insurance companies do not appear to consider gun-related risks in underwriting and pricing their products.[11] Moreover, the focus of this volume is on gun-related tort liability, which is the province of liability insurers. Although we did not set out to learn about property insurance for guns, we could not avoid learning something about that topic because liability insurance commonly is sold together with property insurance. We focused on insurance for gun manufacturers, wholesalers, and retailers, as well as organizations and consumers involved in the recreational use of guns. We did not investigate insurance for public or private law enforcement organizations.

Personal Lines Liability Insurers

Personal lines liability insurers have adopted as their only approach to gun-related injuries the strategy of *selective exclusion*. Individual coverage for nonoccupational liability risks is provided as part of standard residential package insurance policies (such as a homeowners' or renters' policy). These insurance policies universally include an exclusion for intentional harm, which eliminates coverage for the vast majority of gun-related injuries.[12] Allstate and some other insurers have adopted an even more restrictive version of the intentional harm exclusion that excludes coverage for harm resulting from criminal acts, regardless of whether the harm was intentional.[13] Allstate has applied this exclusion to accidental injuries involving firearms, and, on the whole, courts have upheld this approach.[14]

Typically, insurers with the largest market share in this market do not inquire whether applicants have guns, except in situations in which it appears likely that the applicant may have very valuable guns that require the purchase of additional insurance protection to guard against theft.[15] As a result, there is no effort to engage in gun-related prevention through underwriting or pricing, and gun risks do not play a role in personal lines insurance gatekeeping.

This hands-off approach to gun ownership makes sense because the intentional harm exclusion means that only a very small percentage of gun injuries are even potentially covered by liability insurance. In addition, we learned of a controversy involving State Farm that suggests that being perceived as hostile to gun owners may pose some reputational risk to an insurance company.[16] This controversy notwithstanding, we are inclined to discount any conspiracy explanations for personal lines insurers' decision to ignore gun-related liability risks. Were insurance companies to be persuaded that changes in gun designs (e.g., internal locks or personalized, "smart" guns) would pay off in significantly reduced liability insurance claims, they might well offer homeowners' insurance discounts based on gun design. After all, it's not "anti-gun" to offer a discount for a safer gun.[17] But, given the relatively low cost of the liability insurance portion of homeowners' insurance (as compared to the property insurance portion) and the relatively small number of accidental gun injuries,[18] we are inclined to doubt that insurers will ever offer such discounts.[19]

Commercial Liability Insurers

With regard to commercial gun risks, insurers employ a somewhat broader array of regulatory techniques. Selective exclusion is the main tool, but there is evidence of gatekeeping and prevention. In this section we will first describe the insurance environment for gun-related businesses and then characterize insurers' approaches in terms of our conceptual framework.

COMMERCIAL INSURERS AND GUN RISKS

Unlike personal lines insurers, commercial insurers do differentiate between those customers that present gun risks and those that do not. Although the treatment of a gun risk is left to the discretion of the individual insurer, and in some cases the individual underwriter, there are industrywide recommendations that channel that discretion.

When deciding whom to insure, and at what price, many insurers rely on statistical and actuarial data compiled by the Insurance Services Office (ISO). ISO collects loss data from insurers and other entities and organizes it according to the type, or "classification," of business that produced the loss. As a result, ISO's classifications effectively make up a set of de facto industry standards. If ISO classifies, say, lamp manufacturers differently from lamp shade manufacturers, the insurers who rely on ISO's statistics will classify and price them differently as well.

ISO's classification scheme shows that there are relatively few instances in which gun-risk businesses are classed differently from other, similar businesses. Retail sporting goods stores all carry the same general liability classification (18206) whether they sell firearms or not.[20] Pawnshops are also classed the same whether they deal in guns or not. Jewelry stores, liquor stores, and bars are classed the same whether or not they keep guns on premises for security purposes.

Gun-risk businesses that have their own classifications are primarily those that present significant products liability exposures. Firearms manufacturers, for example, are classed separately. Ammunition manufacturers are classed separately as well and indeed are further divided between those that manufacture smokeless powder and those that do not. Other gun risks that do not present significant products liability exposures but nevertheless have their own classifications include gunsmiths, shooting clubs, and shooting galleries.

Although industry standard setters do not set mandatory rules for the treatment of gun risks, they do recommend that insurers take such risks into account. The *A.M. Best Underwriting Guide*, for example, characterizes firearms risks as a "serious exposure" in which the "potential for injury is severe."[21] Best offers a number of recommendations to underwriters who are considering insuring such risks, depending on the type of business seeking coverage.

Sporting Goods Stores.   Although ISO does not class gun-selling sporting goods stores differently than gun-free ones, Best's *Underwriting Guide* advises the underwriter that the "hazard index" presented by a gun retailer is higher. Interestingly, the primary area in which Best sees heightened exposure is not in general liability but rather in property insurance coverage—commercial crime and fire in particular. On a scale of one to ten, Best characterizes the general liability hazard index of a sporting goods store at six whether it sells guns or not. But the underwriter is advised that the ordinary commercial crime hazard index of five becomes "higher with the sale of firearms and ammunition." Due to the heightened crime and fire exposures, Best recommends that the insurer consider several factors before agreeing to insure a gun retailer.

Given this focus on fire and crime, it is not surprising that most of Best's recommendations have to do with the prospective insured's gun and ammunition storage practices. Best recommends that the underwriter investigate whether guns are kept in locked display cases constructed of tempered glass. In addition, Best recommends that the underwriter determine whether firearms are stored unloaded and separately from ammunition. It recommends that the insurer investigate the type of ammunition stored on premises—black powder presents explosion hazards that small rifle cartridges do not—and it recommends that the insurer confirm that the insured follows all state and federal regulations in the storage of ammunition.

Best does not offer many specific recommendations concerning the general liability and products liability perils. It reminds the underwriter that the potential for injury is severe and that a retailer is likely to be named as a defendant in any products liability suit brought against a manufacturer.

Information on how carriers are implementing these recommendations is sparse. One carrier (The Hartford) will not insure a sporting goods store that sells handguns.[22] Another carrier (Safeco) will insure a sporting goods store if its gun sales are "incidental." Safeco regards gun sales as incidental if they are less than 15–20 percent of the store's total sales, and the underwriter accounts for the incidental gun risk by manually adjusting the premium upward.[23] The four largest U.S. writers of commercial insurance (AIG, CNA, Travelers, and Liberty Mutual)[24] declined requests for interviews.

Anecdotal evidence suggests that it is becoming increasingly difficult for a gun retailer to get general liability insurance, notwithstanding Best's relatively unthreatening portrayal of the exposure and the actions of individual carriers such as Safeco. John Badowski, managing director of the National Association of Firearms Retailers and director of retail partnership programs for the National Shooting Sports Foundation (NSSF), has noted an increase in the frequency with which firearms retailers are reporting refusal or nonrenewal of insurance.[25] Badowski's assessment is confirmed by Robert Chiarello, an Elizabeth, New Jersey, insurance broker who administers an insurance program endorsed by the National Association of Sporting Goods Wholesalers.[26]

Badowski indicates that the NSSF has attempted to increase gun retailers' attractiveness to insurers by conducting its own loss control activities. The NSSF has created a dealer education program entitled "Don't Lie for the Other Guy" that is intended to increase the dealer's ability to recognize and prevent straw purchases. NSSF, in consultation with a team of engineers, has created a gun display case highly resistant to "smash and grab" thefts. Badowski reports that these loss control efforts have yet to show success in reducing insurer reluctance to accept retail gun risks.[27] This may be because of the general "hardening" of the property casualty insurance market at the time of our interviews over the last three years,[28] as well as concern that retailers may be drawn into the mass tort gun litigation (though that latter concern is addressed in part through selective exclusion, as explained later).

Gunsmiths. ISO maintains a separate classification (95620) for gunsmiths. Gunsmiths are those businesses that are primarily engaged in the "repair and maintenance of firearms" and may also engage in "engraving, bluing, fitting a gun specifically to a customer, suggesting gun improvements to a manufacturer, and selling firearms and other shooting equipment on a retail basis." "In addition to conducting their own business, some insureds also will do warranty work for major manufacturers, much like an authorized service center."[29]

Although a gunsmith's entire business is gun related and a sporting goods retailer's business is only partially so, Best's general liability hazard index is lower for gunsmiths than for sporting goods stores. On a scale of one to ten, Best rates the general liability hazard index of a sporting goods retailer at six and that of a gunsmith at four.[30] This might suggest that Best sees other sporting goods (rollerblades, treadmills, etc.) as more productive of general liability losses than guns.[31] Best rates the products liability hazard index of both gunsmiths and sporting goods stores at six and the crime hazard index of both at five. Best sees a sporting goods retailer as a higher fire hazard than a gunsmith—the former is a six, the latter a five—but the fire exposure presented by a gunsmith is said to be "much higher with ammunition on the premises." Workers' compensation is the only line in which the hazard index is higher for a gunsmith (eight) than for a sporting goods retailer (four). This is due in part to the presence of firearms but also to the presence of cutting and drilling machinery.[32]

As with sporting goods stores, Best's *Underwriting Guide* recommends that the underwriter survey the applicant's gun and ammunition storage practices before agreeing to insure her. Best also recommends that the underwriter review any contracts the gunsmith may have signed with manufacturers for whom she does warranty work, with a view to determining whether the gunsmith has agreed to indemnify the manufacturer for any personal injuries arising from serviced guns. In addition, Best recommends that the underwriter review the professional qualifications of the applicant, since her skill in gunsmithing ought to be directly proportional to the rate at which her repairs will fail and produce products liability losses. The underwriter is also advised to determine whether the gunsmith designs any parts or assemblies for gun manufacturers, since such work would increase the likelihood that the gunsmith would be named in a products suit against the manufacturer.

Best also makes a number of recommendations specific to lines of insurance other than general liability. Since gunsmiths frequently need to test-fire guns to ensure that their repairs are satisfactory, Best recommends that workers' compensation underwriters determine whether the gunsmith's employees have received proper training in the firing of guns. Best also recommends that crime underwriters look closely at the crime rate in the insured's neighborhood and at the types of guns on which she works. Gunsmiths who work on valuable antiques will have more severe bailee losses.

Hunting Clubs, Rifle Clubs, and Shooting Ranges. We were unable to obtain access to Best's recommendations for these kinds of risks. We were able to locate other documents that provide a window into how insurers approach these risks, however. Carpenter Insurance Service of Annapolis, Maryland, administers a hunting club insurance program for the Northland Insurance Company, an arm of Travelers. We obtained a copy of Northland's application for hunting club liability insurance, and the underwriting questionnaire contained in that application tells us much about the risks that Northland perceives in such clubs. Applicants are asked whether they allow the use of horses on their premises; whether they own any vehicles or allow the use of members' vehicles on their premises; whether they hold a liquor license or allow members to participate in hunting or shooting activity while under the influence of alcohol; whether they use tree stands; and whether all members carry proper firearms permits.[33] Another insurance program for hunting clubs is available through the National Rifle Association (NRA). The NRA endorses a program administered by Lockton Risk of Kansas City. Lockton is willing to quote, if not issue, insurance for a hunting club on the strength of an exceptionally short questionnaire. Lockton's application asks the prospective insured to report the number of members it has; whether it uses tree stands; whether it is NRA affiliated, and what its locations are.[34]

Lockton Risk also offers an NRA-endorsed insurance plan for rifle clubs and shooting ranges. Here, the questionnaire is more extensive. Before Lockton will issue a quote, it requires the applicant to reveal the type of range to be insured (indoor, outdoor, rifle, archery, skeet/trap, etc.), the number of range lanes, and the design of the range. In addition,

Lockton requires a description of the range's safety practices, including whether it has posted range safety rules, on-site range safety officers, and required ear and eye protection. Lockton also asks the prospective insured about its environmental practices, including the range's ventilation and its disposal methods for spent lead shot.[35]

Gun Manufacturers and Distributors.   Little public information exists on the insurance environment for gun manufacturers and distributors. Gun manufacturers and distributors appear to be unable to obtain insurance from the standard commercial insurance market and, thus, can only obtain their insurance from a special, less heavily regulated type of insurance known as "surplus lines" insurance. Although it is difficult to generalize about such a flexible insurance instrument, surplus lines insurance tends to be more expensive and offered by organizations that are administratively leaner and, accordingly, less likely to engage in the more hands-on approaches to risk management (prevention, engagement with public regulators, research, and education). Some of the leading surplus line insurance companies are subsidiaries of well-known insurance groups (AIG, Zurich, Travelers, etc.) and, thus, would seem to have access to very significant administrative resources. Nevertheless, these subsidiaries tend to be run relatively autonomously.

Interviews with industry participants indicate that, even in the context of the ordinarily expensive surplus lines environment, gun manufacturers and distributors are experiencing a "hard market" for insurance. Robert Chiarello, the New Jersey insurance broker, indicates that a number of carriers have withdrawn from the gun manufacturer products liability market. To Chiarello's knowledge, there are "only about five players" remaining in the market. AIG writes products liability for manufacturers and distributors through its Lexington Insurance subsidiary. Admiral, Granite State, and New Hampshire Insurance have manufacturer and distributor programs as well.[36]

In addition to these providers, insurance is available through a captive insurance company founded by some of the larger gun manufacturers. The captive—Sporting Activities Insurance Limited, or SAIL—is a Bermuda corporation formed in 1986 with the assistance of Chiarello.[37] It insures or has insured Smith & Wesson and Navegar, among others.[38] Tom McDermott, a New York attorney who investigates fraudulently undercapitalized insurance companies, classifies SAIL as a "legitimate insurer" and not as an example of the "sleazy insurance" problem addressed later.[39]

Chiarello reports that gun insurers do not directly discriminate between "reputable" gun manufacturers such as Colt and "junk gun" manufacturers such as Bryco but that some of their underwriting guidelines indirectly produce the same practical result. The rating basis for a gun manufacturer—indeed, for manufacturers generally—is gross sales. But "carriers will look not only at the gross dollar amount of sales but also at how those sales are earned. A company that makes a million dollars selling a thousand units will present a different exposure than someone who makes the same million dollars selling one hundred units." So while the underwriter might not enter the process expecting to treat a Bryco differently from a Colt, the two manufacturers end up being treated differently because of the larger number of exposure units Bryco presents per each unit of sales. In addition, Chiarello reports that underwriters understand consumers of expensive guns to be better educated in the use of firearms and therefore less likely to injure themselves. Chiarello cites Anschutz, the German manufacturer of competition air rifles used in the Olympics, as a manufacturer with an enviable loss record. "Anyone who spends three thousand dollars on an air gun probably knows what he's doing."[40]

Chiarello provided us with documents that expand on his verbal description of the underwriting concerns of gun insurers. Chiarello has taken the underwriting concerns of the several market participants and synthesized them into a common insurance application. By asking his customers to answer every underwriting question asked by any of his markets, Chiarello saves his customers from having to fill out a separate application for each insurer that may express interest in the risk. An accidental by-product of this customer service measure is that the Chiarello application gives us a composite view of the underwriting concerns of the market as a whole.

Chiarello's application is actually two separate documents—one for general liability coverage generally and another for products liability specifically. Commercial liability insurance policies typically exclude products liability coverage from the "general liability" coverage and provide it under a separate "products liability" heading. Chiarello's general liability application asks the prospective insured about business history, gross sales and payroll, the nature of her operations, the type of building occupied, loss history, and trade group affiliations.[41] In addition, it asks distributors about the sources of their products—evidently the carriers Chiarello represents are more concerned with distributors of foreign guns than with distributors of domestic ones, presumably because they suspect that plaintiffs will not want to locate foreign manufacturers and will instead sue their distributors.

The products liability application asks many of the same questions. In addition, it asks deeper questions about the insured's business background, including whether the insured purchased any businesses and, if so, whether it assumed that business's liabilities. The application also asks the prospective insured to describe quality control and loss control activities and to break down sales according to the type of gun produced—rifles, shotguns, or handguns. Finally, the application asks about claims history at a greater level of detail.[42]

THE "SLEAZY INSURANCE" PROBLEM

A December 2002 article in the online journal *Slate* claimed that insurers abet the marketing of "junk guns" by helping irresponsible gun manufacturers put up a facade of financial responsibility.[43] According to the article, makers of junk guns teamed up with "sleazy" insurance companies to defraud firearms distributors and retailers into believing that they—the manufacturers—could face their products liability obligations. If not for the contributions of sleazy insurance companies to this scheme, distributors and retailers would not have marketed junk guns and the public would have been safer as a result.

The primary source for the article was Tom McDermott, the New York attorney referred to earlier, and the example presented in the article was an insurance company called Leeds and London. According to McDermott, Leeds and London was conceived by an insurance broker and a principal of the now defunct low-end gun manufacturer Lorcin Engineering. In addition to Lorcin, Leeds and London insured another low-end manufacturer by the name of Davis Industries; McDermott says that Davis "had to have known" that the insurance provided by Leeds and London was illegitimate because the premium was too low.[44] Evidently Leeds and London branched out, offering to cover hard-to-insure operators of carnival rides. A Maryland carnival operator discovered problems with Leeds when a state inspector refused to accept its certificate of insurance, and the company collapsed soon after.[45]

McDermott believes that Leeds-issued certificates of insurance persuaded distributors and retailers to market products that they otherwise would not have marketed. He attributes the existence of the scheme to a near-collapse of state monitoring of insurer solvency in the surplus lines arena[46] and reports that gun distributors and retailers will have to monitor the quality of the insurance carried by the manufacturers they represent, because "no one else is."[47]

Robert Chiarello, the New Jersey insurance broker, disagrees with McDermott's characterization of the reach of what he calls the "rogue insurer problem" but agrees that distributors and retailers must take it upon themselves to ensure the financial responsibility of the manufacturers they represent. Indeed, Chiarello reports that retailers and distributors have already assumed that duty and have, if anything, become overzealous in their oversight of manufacturers' insurance. Chiarello claims that this oversight was prompted less by the collapse of bad actors like Leeds than by the collapse of more upstanding market participants like Reliance and Legion.[48] Since the collapse of Reliance, "all of the distributors will not accept" a manufacturer's certificate of insurance "from someone they do not know." Chiarello relates an anecdote in which a distributor questioned a certificate of insurance from the venerable gun manufacturer Browning, merely because Browning had "gone digital" and had sent its certificate in a format with which the distributor was unfamiliar.[49]

COMMERCIAL INSURERS AND GUN REGULATION BY INSURANCE

Selective Exclusion. Selective exclusion is the commercial liability insurance industry's main approach to the kinds of gun-related injuries that are the focus of gun control advocacy generally and the mass tort litigation in particular. There are two main parts to insurers' exclusion of gun violence risks. First, many insurers exclude products liability coverage from the liability insurance that they sell to businesses such as sporting goods stores, hunting clubs, rifle ranges, and gunsmiths (i.e., businesses other than manufacturers and distributors)[50] and, sometimes, even to manufacturers and distributors.[51] Second, all or most of the relatively few insurers that are willing to provide products liability coverage to manufacturers and distributors appear to have adopted in recent years an exclusion designed to eliminate coverage for mass tort gun litigation.[52]

We were able to obtain a copy of one such mass tort exclusion. The exclusion applies to any "industry liability claim," which is defined to include any class action, whether or not certified as such, and any claim brought by a municipality, interest group or other entity that has not itself been injured in a bodily way.[53] The clear intent of this exclusion is to eliminate any doubt about whether there is coverage for the current round of gun-related mass tort litigation. For example, the omission of property damage as a coverage trigger is not accidental. The small contribution of municipal property damage (e.g., bullet holes in police cruisers) to the overall costs of gun violence has occasionally become an important battleground. Gun manufacturers challenge the municipalities' standing to sue for what the manufacturers claim is an indirect injury, derivative of injuries to third parties. The municipalities cite, inter alia, their own property damage as proof that they have suffered direct injury and thus have standing.[54]

Even without the mass tort or products liability exclusions, some liability insurers have argued that the municipal litigation is not covered. To date, there are only two published opinions, one favoring the insurance companies and one favoring a manufacturer, and both of these opinions rest on unusual circumstances that may limit their precedental value.[55] The coverage litigation continues, and there are substantial arguments on both sides, suggesting that manufacturers and distributors cannot count on coverage even under the old forms.[56]

Gatekeeping.   Insurers have the opportunity to act as gatekeepers when insurance is a necessity. Distributors apparently regularly require that manufacturers provide evidence of product liability insurance coverage before they will agree to distribute the manufacturers' guns, and some retailers may as well.[57] Thus, manufacturers who are unable to purchase product liability coverage will not have access to those distributors or retailers. The "sleazy insurance" problem complicates this picture, however, because manufacturers that are unable to get access to reliable insurance coverage may nevertheless be able to obtain a certificate of insurance that would satisfy an unsophisticated risk manager. While we are not in a position to evaluate the extent of this problem, a recent, somewhat impressionistic study of insurance fraud by the sociologist Robert Tillman provides support for the claim that it exists.[58]

Other gatekeeping opportunities are presented when sporting goods stores, gunsmiths, and other gun-related businesses that rent commercial space are obligated under their lease agreements to purchase liability insurance. (Insurance clauses are a standard feature in commercial leases.) Whether the liability insurance that these gun-related businesses obtain in fact provides comprehensive coverage against gun-related risks is doubtful in the current insurance environment (because of the selective exclusion approach, addressed earlier). Nevertheless, the insurance would provide coverage against the ordinary liability risks that are likely to motivate commercial landlords to require that their tenants be insured.

Prevention. As noted previously, *Best's Underwriting Guide* contains many prevention-related suggestions for underwriters of businesses with gun risks, but those suggestions largely concern fire and crime risks. In the relatively few instances in which the suggestions address bodily injury, the primary focus of concern is accidental injury on location, either by customers inspecting or using weapons or by employees working on them.[59]

Some exceptions appear in the entry for gunsmiths, which reflects a concern about liability relating to procedural irregularities in the sale of guns, improper instruction in the use of guns, and improper repair of guns. Under the heading for "general liability," underwriters are cautioned to inquire the following:

> Are special precautions taken to insure that only customers with legal permits are allowed to buy guns? Are all employees who sell guns aware of local and state laws regarding age, criminal record, mental health and waiting periods? Does the insured instruct buyers on the use of guns? What are the qualifications of the instructors and under what conditions are instructions given?

Under the heading for "products liability," underwriters are cautioned as follows:

> A serious exposure will exist relating to accidents arising from the improper repair of customers' guns. This may encompass faulty work or assembly, improper installation of parts, or use of substan-

dard parts. Improperly repaired guns can misfire and cause severe bodily injury to the user as well as others around the user.

We were unable to determine whether underwriters in fact ask the questions that Best suggests and, if the "wrong" answers are given, whether they deny applications. Assuming that they do, however, these prevention efforts are unlikely to address the intentional gun violence that is the main focus of this book. (The exception might be efforts directed at ensuring that policyholders comply with gun laws.) Instead, insurance industry prevention efforts are directed at minimizing "normal," accidental injuries associated with the legal use of guns—accidents in stores, explosions of powder and ammunition, and injuries from product malfunction.

Management of Loss Costs.   Management of loss costs is an important aspect of regulation by insurance generally, particularly because of the impact on the medical and legal professions, but there does not appear to be anything special about management of loss costs in the gun-injury context. For example, emergency room personnel have made great strides in the treatment of gun injuries, but those efforts do not appear to have been led by health insurance interests. Similarly, insurance law textbooks commonly feature cases involving gun-related injuries, but the cases are chosen because they nicely illustrate the difficulties involved in drawing lines between auto and homeowners' insurance and between intentional and unintentional injuries,[60] not because of a special focus in the insurance industry on defending gun-related injury cases.

Liability Limitation.   In response to the recent gun-related mass tort litigation, there have been legislative efforts in the states and Congress to limit liability. While insurance industry organizations appear to be supportive of at least some of these efforts, the insurance industry does not appear to be a driving force.[61] This situation contrasts with that of recent legislative efforts directed at limiting liability for asbestos-related injuries, environmental cleanups, and medical malpractice, in which insurance industry organizations are intensively and publicly involved. Although it is always difficult to provide persuasive causal explanations for inaction, the insurance industry's ability to avoid the mass tort litigation risk through selective exclusion is certainly a plausible explanation.

Conclusions and Implications

Although insurance may well be a form of governance, and insurance institutions governmental, the approach to government described here would hardly qualify as activist. Indeed, if we were to limit the use of the term *regulation* to the command and control approach epitomized by the Occupational Safety and Health Administration and by much of the work of the Environmental Protection Agency, then there is very little regulation by insurance of gun-related activities. As noted already, the guidelines from Best are directed primarily at preventing fire and theft and only secondarily at preventing the ordinary accidents that arise in the context of the legal sale and use of guns. The only guidelines that address the gun violence that is the target of the mass tort gun litigation are those that encourage underwriters to make sure that gun sellers follow the procedural requirements established by the applicable state and federal law.

Instead of command and control directives targeted at preventing and minimizing the costs of gun violence, what we find, instead, is selective exclusion. By excluding claims based on intentional harm, liability insurers have largely kept the costs of gun violence out from under the insurance umbrella. Where those costs have threatened to creep in—as in the municipal litigation—insurers have responded by leaving the market or by further selective exclusion.

By excluding gun violence, the insurance industry cannot fairly be accused of *knowingly* facilitating gun violence. Indeed, the historic, moral hazard justification for the most important exclusion—that for intentional harm—was first articulated precisely to protect insurers from similar accusations.[62] Yet, leaving gun violence outside the liability insurance umbrella may in fact promote gun violence by depriving the gun arena of a potentially powerful institutional force for the prevention of harm. Unless liability insurance covers the costs of gun violence, there is no incentive for the liability insurance industry to use the regulatory tools that it has available.

A liability insurance industry responsible for paying millions of dollars in gun-related claims in any given year would have an incentive to learn more about gun violence and, if it determined that there were cost-effective prevention measures, to impose those prevention measures on insureds either through the underwriting process or through engagement with public regulators. In addition, depending on what the research revealed, owning a gun could lead to a premium surcharge, which could remove some guns from circulation. Moreover, as the conditional nature of this discussion suggests, insurance-funded researchers could function as "honest brokers" in the debates over the safety and costs of guns, much as they have in the field of auto and fire safety.

The liability insurance reform that would be most likely to bring gun violence under the liability insurance umbrella would be the elimination of the intentional harm exclusion in personal liability policies. While many people who use guns undoubtedly do not have homeowners' or renters' insurance, some do. Eliminating the intentional harm exclusion would promote the deterrence goals of tort law for the reasons just suggested, without, in our view, affecting the behavior of someone who is deciding whether to draw a gun.[63] Eliminating the intentional harm exclusion would also promote the compensation and retribution goals of tort law.[64] If there is an insurance company available to pay a claim, it is much more likely that a victim of gun violence will bring a tort action against the perpetrators (furthering the retribution goal) and collect the damages to which she or he is entitled under the law (furthering the compensation goal). Jennifer Wriggins has recently made similar observations in the domestic violence context.[65]

As noted earlier, insurers have extended the selective exclusion approach to gun violence by adopting an "industry liability" exclusion when the municipal litigation threatened to bring gun violence under the liability insurance umbrella. This has become standard procedure in the mass tort context. Almost as soon as any manufacturer becomes the subject of mass tort litigation, insurers adopt product-specific exclusions that preclude any new coverage for the mass tort claims. In effect, liability insurers offer manufacturers one set of policy limits per product; after that, liability for the product is treated as a "known loss" that cannot be insured. This reality should temper whatever enthusiasm remains for mass tort litigation as a loss-spreading device.

On the other hand, the routine practice of adopting product-specific exclusions increases the power of tort litigation to force the withdrawal of a product from the market. The gun litigation failed in that regard, not because liability insurers came to the rescue of the manufacturers with promises of continuing protection (they did not) but rather because the manufacturers successfully repulsed the litigation (with some help from insurers under liability policies already sold). In considering whether mass tort litigation can force products off the market, it is important to keep in mind a fundamental difference between gun litigation and other products liability litigation. The gun litigation (like the tobacco litigation before it) had the goal of shutting down entire businesses. That goal prompts a very different response than litigation directed at a single product manufactured by a business that manufactures a variety of products. In the latter context, mass tort litigation and the accompanying withdrawal of insurance might well prompt the manufacturer to cut its losses, abandon the product, and move on, only to return the product to market if and when it prevails in the mass tort litigation.

Finally, the "sleazy insurance" problem highlights an important consequence of relying on insurance as regulation. When an individual or entity is motivated to buy insurance to get through the gate (and not primarily to obtain the risk-spreading and related benefits), we can't rely on the market alone to ensure that the resulting insurance will be high quality, because the person buying the insurance cares less about the quality of the insurance. As this suggests, the more we rely on private insurance to achieve social policy goals, the more we have to regulate insurance itself. Absent a government mandate, the liability insurance industry has little reason to take on gun violence. If we force insurers to provide insurance that they don't want to provide and force consumers to purchase insurance that they don't want to buy, we will need an administrative enforcement mechanism to ensure that insurers really provide and consumers really purchase that insurance.

CHAPTER 13

Gun Litigation & the Constitution

BRANNON P. DENNING

For all of the discussion about litigation against the firearms industry, and the academic commentary concerning the meaning of the Second Amendment generated in the past decade, the question of whether there is a constitutional dimension to gun litigation has received surprisingly little scholarly attention.[1] Assuming that raising constitutional questions about this litigation is not a frivolous endeavor,[2] I hope that this chapter will help fill a gap in the literature. What sorts of constitutional issues are implicated by civil lawsuits against firearms manufacturers and distributors? The obvious one involves the Second Amendment. To the extent that one believes, as I do, that the amendment guarantees an individual right to private firearms ownership, could the Second Amendment limit gun control by lawsuit as it might limit gun control measures initiated by Congress or state legislatures? The first part of this chapter critically analyzes this question using as a point of departure the argument put forth by Dave Kopel and Richard Gardiner that the First Amendment case *New York Times v. Sullivan*[3] furnishes a precedent for restricting civil lawsuits against gun manufacturers.

The second part of the chapter then raises another constitutional question: Do the lawsuits brought by cities and municipalities violate the dormant Commerce Clause doctrine (DCCD)? The DCCD is the set of self-executing limitations the judiciary has inferred from the Constitution's grant of power over interstate commerce to Congress that prohibit states from discriminating or otherwise burdening commerce among the states.[4] In addition to prohibiting protectionism and discrimination against out-of-state commerce,[5] the DCCD also prevents states from legislating "extraterritorially"[6] or imposing a burden on interstate commerce that is "clearly excessive" when measured against "putative local benefits."[7] This part examines whether lawsuits that, for example, seek to alter nationwide advertising and distribution practices or that seek alteration in product design are vulnerable to challenge under the DCCD.

The Second Amendment and Gun Litigation

In 1964, the United States Supreme Court held that the First Amendment's guarantee of a free press placed constitutional limits on the enforcement of state libel law. Dave Kopel and Richard Gardiner have argued that the reasoning of *Sullivan* ought to be extended to gun litigation and constitutional limits be placed on suits against gun manufacturers.[8] In this section, I examine that argument critically and ask whether Kopel and Gardiner's proposed analogy—offered prior to the initiation of the latest round of suits—is stronger in light of cities' and counties' involvement.

New York Times v. Sullivan *and the Constitutional Limits on Common Law Libel Suits*

In 1960, the *New York Times* ran an ad paid for by prominent civil rights leaders seeking financial support for Dr. Martin Luther King's efforts to combat segregation in the South.[9] The ad itself contained a few errors of fact in its references to events that had occurred in Alabama, though it did not specifically name any public officials in its text. State officials who claimed that they were libeled by the ad demanded a retraction from the *Times*. When none was forthcoming, they sued. One was awarded five hundred thousand dollars by an Alabama jury, which the state supreme court upheld.

The *Times* appealed the award, and the U.S. Supreme Court held Alabama libel law "constitutionally deficient for failure to provide the safeguards for freedom of speech and of the press that are required by the

First and Fourteenth Amendments in a libel action brought by a public official against critics of his official conduct."[10] For good measure, the Court also held that the evidence presented at trial was "constitutionally insufficient" to support a jury verdict.

The Court first concluded that the state court's application of Alabama libel law constituted "state action" for purposes of the Fourteenth Amendment and that the First Amendment applied though the statement was a commercial advertisement. Justice Brennan located at the core of the First Amendment's guarantee of a free press and of free speech the right to "uninhibited, robust, and wide-open" debate on public issues that may even include "vehement, caustic, and sometimes unpleasantly sharp attacks on government and public officials." The *Times* ad was unquestionably "an expression of grievance and protest on one of the major public issues of our time" and "would seem clearly to qualify for the constitutional protection." The question was whether the portions that were false deprived the ad of that protection.

Brennan concluded that the inaccuracies in the ad could not strip the *Times* of the First Amendment's protections if "the freedoms of expression are to have the 'breathing space' that they 'need . . . to survive.'" Nor was injury to official reputation sufficient to overcome the constitutional interest in promoting robust debate on public issues. And if neither falsity nor injury to reputation alone was sufficient to remove the First Amendment's "constitutional shield from criticism of official conduct," then "the combination of the two elements is no less inadequate." Analogizing the Alabama civil law of libel to the law of seditious libel criminalized in the 1798 Alien and Sedition Acts, Brennan wrote that "[w]hat a State may not constitutionally bring about by means of a criminal statute is likewise beyond the reach of its civil law of libel." That truth was a defense was of no consequence because "would-be critics of official conduct may be deterred from voicing their criticism . . . because of doubt whether it can be proved in court or fear of the expense of having to do so."

Brennan wrote that "[t]he constitutional guarantees require . . . a federal rule that prohibits a public official from recovering damages for a defamatory falsehood relating to his official conduct unless he proves that the statement was made with 'actual malice'—that is, with knowledge that it was false or with reckless disregard of whether it was false or not."

The Argument for Extending Sullivan *to Gun Litigation*

Kopel and Gardiner have argued that *Sullivan* should be extended to tort suits against firearms manufacturers on the theory that such suits could have a chilling effect on the exercise of Second Amendment rights by driving gun manufacturers out of business, thereby depriving citizens of the firearms necessary to exercise their Second Amendment rights.[11] In this subsection, I summarize their argument and discuss the strength of the proposed analogy in the following subsections.

First, Kopel and Gardiner argue that the First and Second Amendments both guarantee individual rights and that, like the First Amendment, the Second Amendment should be applied to the states through the Fourteenth Amendment. They review the legal theories behind the lawsuits filed against gun manufacturers circa 1995, concluding that, while the suits were largely unsuccessful, they nevertheless harmed manufacturers, who either went bankrupt as a result of defending the litigation or who simply left the business, unwilling to bear the costs necessary to defend similar suits.

Kopel and Gardiner then lay out the parallels between the libel suits at issue in *Sullivan* and the tort suits against gun manufacturers. In addition to the kinship they see between the First and Second Amendments as guarantors of important individual rights, they also argue that inferring constitutional limits on tort suits involving those guarantees is essential to their full exercise, given the official immunities available to public officials. According to *Sullivan,* the fact that public officials are entitled to immunity from suit arising out of the discharge of official duties (even if mistakes occur) means that sometimes the only way to call those officials to account is by criticizing them in the press.[12] To permit those same officials to insulate themselves from criticism by threatening libel suits for any erroneous information—no matter how trivial—seemed to the Court to effectively place those officials beyond all criticism.[13] Similarly, since public officials are generally immune from suit for failing to protect citizens from crime, even if the failure was attributable to negligence,[14] Kopel and Gardiner argue that "it would be highly inappropriate for the government, through the courts, to make it economically impossible for persons to own handguns for self-defense. . . . [T]he government's courts certainly should not let themselves become a vehicle that deprives people of the tools with which to protect themselves."[15] They argue that the financial burden on gun manufacturers occasioned by suits or threats of suits "is sufficient to compel a Constitutional remedy for the Second Amendment" analogous to that which the Court provided the First Amendment in *Sullivan*.

Finally, they claim that "the legal assault on the exercise of Second Amendment rights in the 1990s is far more consciously developed and carefully planned than the assault on First Amendment rights in the 1960s." They noted that law clinics specializing in firearms litigation were established at a number of law schools and that suits were being brought "in jurisdictions such as San Francisco and New York City which are notorious for their antipathy to Second Amendment rights" just as "libel suits were brought in plaintiff-friendly, speech-hostile venues such as Montgomery, Alabama" in *Sullivan*. "If the facts of the 1960s," they conclude, "were sufficient to necessitate the Supreme Court to take action in [*Sullivan*] to protect the First Amendment, the facts of the 1990s are more than sufficient to mandate judicial action to protect the Second Amendment." To that end, they propose that "a person injured through the criminal use of a firearm" would be prohibited "from recovering damages against the non-criminal manufacturer and seller, unless he proved that the firearm was transferred by the defendant with knowledge or reckless disregard that the firearm was to be used criminally."

Is the Analogy to Sullivan *Valid?*

Only one manufacturer has offered Kopel and Gardiner's theory as a defense against suits by private litigants or by municipalities.[16] Despite the superficial appeal of the analogy, a number of factors make it unlikely that appeals to *Sullivan* will succeed as a *legal* strategy. However, there is reason to believe that Kopel and Gardiner's analogy has a definite *political* appeal to legislators considering limiting municipal suits.

First,[17] federal courts generally (if, in my view, mistakenly)[18] do not subscribe to an individual rights reading of the Second Amendment. Moreover, the Second Amendment has never been applied to the states through the Fourteenth Amendment,[19] despite convincing arguments that it should be.[20] Until the state of the law changes, analogies to *Sullivan* would founder on the objection that the Second Amendment neither guarantees an individual right nor binds the states through the Fourteenth Amendment. But the potency of the analogy to *Sullivan* may not be appreciably enhanced even were courts more accepting of the individual rights interpretation and willing to bind states to that interpretation.

Consider table 1, which compares *Sullivan* to Kopel and Gardiner's formulation of an analogous tort immunity rule to be applied to firearms litigation.

Kopel and Gardiner's analogy to *Sullivan* falls short in several respects. First, the proper analogy for the constitutional limits on libel suits by *private* citizens (as opposed to public officials) is found not in *Sullivan* but rather in later cases that relaxed the *Sullivan* rule for suits brought by nonpublic figures. Second, Kopel and Gardiner's analogy depends upon questionable characterizations of the core meaning of the two amendments and of the threat to that core posed by lawsuits against gun makers. Third, the general failure of the suits against gun manufacturers by crime victims suggests that institutional safeguards absent in *Sullivan* are providing sufficient protections for defendants and that a constitutional rule is unnecessary. Recent suits against manufacturers filed by cities, moreover, do not rehabilitate the analogy to *Sullivan*.

TABLE 1. Comparison of *Sullivan* Rule with Kopel and Gardiner's Formulation

Sullivan Rule	Kopel and Gardiner Article
In libel suits by public official	In tort suits by private citizens
Against news media	Against gun manufacturers and distributors
Regarding matter of public concern	For criminal misuse of firearm
First Amendment requires	Second Amendment requires
No liability unless false statements made with knowledge or reckless disregard of falsity	No liability unless manufacturer or distributor intentionally or recklessly made gun available to criminal
Because at core of the First Amendment is the right of citizens to criticize public officials	Because at core of the Second Amendment is the right of citizens to obtain firearms for self-defense against crime committed by other private citizens

*Libel Standards Post-*Sullivan

In the paradigm tort case described in Kopel and Gardiner's article, private plaintiffs bring suit against a manufacturer for harm caused by either the manufacturer's product or the use to which that product was put. Stated in those terms—litigation between private parties—then the facts of *Sullivan,* where a *public official* sued a newspaper for publishing erroneous information about the official's discharge of public duties, no longer look apposite. The proper analogy, it seems, is found in the Court's post-*Sullivan* cases.[21]

In *Gertz v. Robert Welch, Inc.,*[22] the Court rejected an attempt by the John Birch Society to invoke *Sullivan'*s actual malice rule to shield it from damages awarded in a libel suit filed by a lawyer against the society. Gertz was the subject of an article in a Birch periodical accusing him of being part of a communist-inspired conspiracy to harass the police based on a suit Gertz had filed.

Rejecting the society's claim of constitutional immunity from suit, the Court concluded that the justifications for the rule in *Sullivan*—including the need to hold public officials to account and the availability of other avenues of redress to defamed public officials—did not apply in the case of a private individual, and therefore *Sullivan* itself did not control. It then held that "so long as they do not impose liability without fault, the States may define for themselves the appropriate standard of liability for a publisher or broadcaster of defamatory falsehood injurious to a private individual." While the Court barred strict liability in libel claims, which had been the rule at common law, it permitted a negligence standard to be applied in these cases, though the Court made clear that *Sullivan'*s actual malice rule had to be applied when plaintiffs sought punitive damages.

A plurality of the Court further loosened constitutional restrictions on libel suits by private parties in *Dun & Bradstreet, Inc. v. Greenmoss Builders, Inc.*[23] At issue was Dun & Bradstreet's liability for erroneously (and negligently) reporting to its subscribers that Greenmoss Builders had filed for bankruptcy. Dun & Bradstreet appealed a state court verdict against it ($350,000 in actual and punitive damages), claiming that *Gertz* prohibited the imposition of punitive damages without a demonstration that it had acted with actual malice. A plurality declined to apply *Gertz* because the defamatory statements involved "no issue of public concern." Justice Powell's opinion stressed that the First Amendment interest in protecting Dun & Bradstreet from the consequences of its negligently prepared credit statement was less important than the state's interest in compensating plaintiffs harmed by defamatory statements and its interest in providing for presumed or punitive damages on evidence that would not satisfy *Sullivan*'s actual malice standard.

In light of *Gertz* and *Dun & Bradstreet*, then, Kopel and Gardiner's analogy seems to have been formulated incorrectly. The proper analogy to the sort of suits Kopel and Gardiner describe—suits of private manufacturers and sellers by private victims of violent crime for negligent sales or negligent distribution—is not *Sullivan* but rather *Gertz* or *Dun & Bradstreet*. Even assuming that a private lawsuit can be deemed a matter of public concern, *Gertz* would permit private plaintiffs to collect actual damages from defendants under a negligence standard, without requiring proof of actual malice. If such suits are *not* matters of public concern—and I think a strong argument could be made that they are not—then punitive damages are available as well.

Are There Analogous Constitutional Interests?

The success of Kopel and Gardiner's proposed analogy, however, does not turn on characterizations of whether firearms litigation is a matter of "public concern" or whether the parties are public or private figures but rather turns on the interests being protected. Are the constitutional interests protected by the First and Second Amendments analogous and their values commensurate?

Sullivan was explicit in locating the immunity in the core of the First Amendment's protection of political speech—particularly speech criticizing the actions of elected officials.[24] The Court explained that without a constitutional rule limiting libel suits the *Times* and similarly situated parties would be forced to choose between risking financial ruin and reporting material critical of public officials. The possibility of huge jury verdicts like the one in *Sullivan* would mean that newspapers would be extremely cautious not only in accepting advertisements commenting on public events, like the ad at issue, but also in their own reporting. This would have a "chilling effect" on free speech. *Sullivan* thus provided a constitutional shield against a potential threat to individual liberty by a government seeking to squelch debate about its policies. A critic of the government is free to voice those criticisms (even if they are erroneous or factually inaccurate) without fear that government officials can retaliate through the tort system.

Kopel and Gardiner argue that the right to armed self-defense is at the core of the Second Amendment. This interest might be seen as analogous to the First Amendment rights protected in *Sullivan*, but the strong form of this argument—which is not clearly made by Kopel and Gardiner—is unlikely to have much appeal to federal judges. One might characterize the purpose of the Second Amendment as guaranteeing a check on governmental power to oppress individual citizens by preventing government from denying those citizens the means to oppose the government with force.[25] More often, however, the argument is made that permitting individuals to arm allows them to resist the unlawful activities of other private citizens, not those of the government. But the defense-against-crime rationale for the Second Amendment does not so clearly implicate the interest protected by *Sullivan*—protection from governmental power—unless one argues that, by depriving citizens of the ability to engage in self-defense, individuals are thus made subordinate to the government.[26] But even at one remove, the argument that citizens need arms to defend themselves against governmental power is unlikely to resonate with judges, though these arguments seem to have more purchase with some legislators.

Further, it remains unclear whether tort suits for negligent manufacture or distribution seriously threaten the ability of citizens either to resist a tyrannical government or to engage in less revolutionary forms of self-defense against crime. Kopel and Gardiner note that some firearms manufacturers have been forced out of business because of litigation, but only a few.[27] Even if the mere prospect of *some* liability is sufficient to cause some manufacturers to shutter their doors, it is difficult to believe that all such manufacturers would follow suit. If every firearms manufacturer in existence were to cease operations tomorrow, the inventory of firearms (estimated to be between 200 and 250 million) presently in existence would not be reduced.[28] Even if the price of remaining guns would rise—possibly endangering widespread availability of relatively inexpensive guns—there is little evidence to suggest that the cost of gun ownership would be prohibitive, whereas unchecked use of libel actions would very quickly have driven papers like the *Times* into bankruptcy.

Moreover, the fact that the present suits are brought under theories of negligence (with regard to marketing and distribution) that require proof of duty, breach of that duty, and harm to plaintiffs proximately caused by the breach of legal duty provides another distinction between past and present gun suits and the strict liability that attached to libel under the Alabama law struck down in *Sullivan*. Unlike newspaper editors, who would be forced, on pain of a large libel judgment, to *guarantee* the truth of everything printed in their publication, by proceeding on a negligence standard, plaintiffs have largely foregone any attempt to place distributors and manufacturers in the position to guarantee that the guns they manufacture and sell never end up in the hands of criminals.

Gun Litigation and the Operation of Institutional Checks

It is important to emphasize the factual differences between *Sullivan* and the gun suits that Kopel and Gardiner discuss. Evidence exists that courts are functioning and that the legal process has not been entirely commandeered by those wishing to disarm America or even to drive gun manufacturers completely out of business. In fact, despite the plethora of suits, few manufacturers have been bankrupted by damage awards. Further, the primary theory of liability employed now is negligence, not strict liability. As the numerous dismissals suggest, plaintiffs are having trouble surmounting the legal hurdles that exist in proving their negligent distribution and marketing cases.

Legislatures have also shown a willingness to exercise a political check on these lawsuits through the passage of legislation restricting the ability of cities to bring such lawsuits or prohibiting them altogether.[29] A similar bill nearly passed in the U.S. Congress.[30] Thus, I think it beyond cavil that gun manufacturers have more friends in the states than the *New York Times* had in the South at the time *Sullivan* was decided.

Do State and Municipal Lawsuits Strengthen the Sullivan *Analogy?*

Kopel and Gardiner wrote prior to the recent wave of municipal lawsuits against gun manufacturers. Since public officials are initiating these recent suits, is Kopel and Gardiner's analogy more viable now than perhaps it was when they first proposed it? On the one hand, involvement by indisputably public officials gives some weight to the argument that the industry needs a corresponding immunity to counter official immunity shielding municipalities from liability for failing to prevent crime to particular victims. If cities can litigate firearms out of existence, then citizens are left with no means to protect themselves from crime and no avenue of redress should the police negligently fail to protect them.

Yet problems with the analogy still exist. First, it is not clear that the protection-from-crime rationale is persuasive with regard to some of the claims—such as defective design and negligent marketing—that have been brought by municipalities. In fact, those claims are the ones that cities claim will actually aid in crime reduction. Second, the new suits sound in negligence, not strict liability; cities are not asking gun dealers and manufacturers to guarantee that their products will not be used in criminal acts. Third, most of the suits seek only actual damages (though the amounts that might be proven would be substantial, especially if cities can demonstrate how much they pay to prevent gun crime or to deal with its aftermath and can require manufacturers to reimburse them for those costs associated with the alleged wrongdoing). Perhaps most important, the suits by cities are aimed not at gun ownership or armed self-defense, per se, but rather at the secondary effects of allegedly negligent sales of those products. To further borrow from First Amendment doctrine, the cities' suits might be characterized as seeking to ameliorate the harmful secondary effects of gun sales, not striking at the right to keep and bear arms itself.[31] Cities might argue that, as long as they are not trying to suppress *all* gun ownership and as long as the suits still leave open "ample alternative channels" either for self-defense or for law-abiding citizens to obtain a gun for protection, there should be no constitutional bar to them.

Is Sullivan's *Extension to Gun Litigation Desirable?*

Despite its surface appeal, Kopel and Gardiner's *Sullivan* analogy fails on a technical level because of the numerous differences between the cases and the two types of suits. At a more general level, however, it seems undesirable to seek *Sullivan*'s transplant from its First Amendment context and to ignore the important civil rights context in which it was originally decided. In the forty years since *Sullivan*, courts have wrestled to apply it in a variety of factual circumstances. The Court has intervened on a number of occasions since, to almost no one's satisfaction. If courts have such difficulty striking the balance between the right of tort victims to receive compensation from their injury and the right of states to use tort law to deter wrongful conduct on the one hand and the First Amendment rights of defendants on the other hand, do we want to introduce those difficulties into an area in which the constitutional right in question is so contested? Moreover, with courts dismissing suits and legislatures barring suits in some cases, the need for a constitutional check on this litigation—at least of the sort imposed by *Sullivan*—is not self-evident.

The Political Value of the Sullivan Analogy

The role legislatures have played in limiting these suits in a number of states raises a final point that is worth making. A growing number of constitutional scholars have urged that opportunity be given by courts to our elected officials to interpret and enforce the Constitution. Some scholars have even suggested that, when given the opportunity, elected officials are more reliable guarantors of liberty than are courts. I submit that legislative protection of the Second Amendment is, in part, what is motivating state legislators to rein in municipalities that filed suit against gun manufacturers and is what motivated members of Congress to support the bill to immunize gun manufacturers from similar suits. If so, then the foregoing analysis is too legalistic. If there is an instinctive appeal to the notion that the right to keep and bear arms is threatened by litigation that could bankrupt firearms manufacturers, and legislators are acting to protect the right by banning or restricting such suits, then my quibbles with the analogy are somewhat beside the point. State legislators' (and perhaps Congress's) actions here are testaments to the power of the analogy,[32] though a court might have substantial problems translating the analogy into workable judicial doctrine and perhaps should not even try.

Gun Litigation and the Dormant Commerce Clause Doctrine

My conclusion that the Second Amendment is not likely to affect the *judicial* analysis of the latest wave of gun litigation does not mean that *no* plausible constitutional argument could be made to courts regarding the suits. In this section I will outline one of the most promising alternative arguments—that municipal suits violate the so-called dormant Commerce Clause doctrine (DCCD). I will briefly describe the doctrine itself, sketch the strands of the doctrine that speak to the litigation most directly, and then address the obstacles to the successful deployment of such arguments.

The Dormant Commerce Clause Doctrine: A Primer

The U.S. Supreme Court has long held that the delegation of power over interstate commerce by the Constitution to Congress implicitly restricted states' power to regulate that same commerce.[33] After considerable doctrinal evolution, the scope of the DCCD can be briefly stated.

First, states may not discriminate against interstate commerce, through either regulation or taxation, unless the discrimination is for a "legitimate" purpose (i.e., one that is not protectionist) *and* there are no less discriminatory means by which the state could effectuate its purpose.[34] Second, this antidiscrimination principle extends to state statutes that discriminate in their purpose or effects as well as those that discriminate on their face.[35] Third, discriminatory regulations passed at the local level, which may also affect in-state as well as out-of-state commercial actors, are nevertheless subject to strict scrutiny under the DCCD.[36] Fourth, the Court has held that a state may not "project" its legislation into another state or seek to effectively regulate economic activity that takes place beyond its borders. As the Court has put it, a state may not, consistent with the DCCD, regulate "extraterritorially," though the scope of this principle and its future are uncertain. Sometimes the Court has included in its statement of extraterritoriality principles a rule that extraterritorial state legislation may include that which, if all states passed similar laws, would subject interstate economic actors to inconsistent and possibly conflicting regulatory regimes.[37] Finally, even statutes that are neutral on their face and in their effects may be struck down if, on balance, the burdens they impose on interstate commerce clearly exceed the local benefits they purport to confer,[38] though this is, as the formulation suggests, a more deferential standard.

How Municipal Litigation May Be Vulnerable to DCCD Challenges

Assuming that tort litigation, particularly that brought by states and municipalities, constitutes state action that could trigger the DCCD—an assumption that is strongly suggested by the Supreme Court in other contexts[39]—what sorts of arguments might be formulated under the doctrine? Three come to mind: (1) that this litigation has discriminatory effects or is otherwise motivated by an improper purpose; (2) that it seeks to project state regulatory policies into other states and to regulate economic activity that occurs beyond the state's borders; and (3) that, even in the absence of improper motives or demonstrable discriminatory effects, the benefits of the litigation are clearly exceeded by the possible burdens on interstate commerce. I will look first at how firearms manufacturers have cast their DCCD arguments. Subsequent sections discuss how those claims were treated by courts and whether—despite their being rejected in the overwhelming majority of cases—the DCCD may yet have a role to play in the litigation against the firearms industry.

DCCD Claims Raised by the Industry

Initially, the industry unsuccessfully sought removal of the suits from state to federal court, invoking the DCCD as one way in which the suits "arose under" federal law, a condition necessary to secure removal.[40] In state courts, manufacturers have also made an extremely broad preemption argument: congressional power to regulate the manufacture and sale of firearms under its "affirmative" Commerce Clause power was, in essence, an exclusive power that, even in the absence of federal legislation, preempted the state suits.[41] By far, however, the most common allegation was that the cities' suits—insofar as they seek broad injunctive relief mandating changes to gun design, distribution, and marketing practices by manufacturers—would inevitably have impermissible extraterritorial effects.[42] Gun manufacturers not only cited Supreme Court cases striking down state legislation regulating activity taking place in other states[43] but also cited language from the U.S. Supreme Court's 1996 *BMW v. Gore* decision,[44] which applied DCCD principles to restrict state common law remedies in tort suits, though it is commonly understood primarily as a due process case.

Because the *BMW* case forms the basis for the manufacturers' arguments that the cities' suits violate the DCCD, a brief review of that case and its holding is in order. A civil suit was filed in Alabama state court against BMW by a doctor who discovered that his "new" BMW had suffered minor damage during shipment and had been repainted. BMW had a nationwide policy not to disclose minor repairs if the cost of repair was less than 3 percent of the cost of the car. The jury held BMW liable for nondisclosure and awarded Gore four thousand dollars in compensatory damages plus four million dollars in punitive damages, which was computed based on the total number of cars in the same condition sold nationwide.

The Supreme Court reversed the punitive damage award, concluding primarily that the award violated the Due Process Clause of the Fourteenth Amendment. However, its opinion also mentioned the DCCD, specifically the Court's extraterritoriality cases.[45] Justice Stevens wrote that, "while we do not doubt that Congress has ample authority to enact such a policy for the entire Nation [imposing affirmative disclosure obligations on sellers of new cars], it is clear that no single State could do so, or even impose its own policy choice on neighboring states."[46] States "may not impose economic sanctions on violators of [their] laws with the intent of changing the tortfeasors' lawful conduct in other States."

In a footnote, Stevens said that it was of no importance that the state regulation came in the form of a jury verdict. "State power," he wrote (citing *Sullivan*), "may be exercised as much by a jury's application of a state rule of law in a civil lawsuit as by a statute." Stevens concluded, "Alabama does not have the power . . . to punish BMW for conduct that was lawful where it occurred and that had no impact on Alabama or its residents. Nor may Alabama impose sanctions on BMW in order to deter conduct that is lawful in other jurisdictions."

Relying heavily on *BMW v. Gore*'s apparent application of the DCCD's extraterritoriality principles to state tort claims, manufacturers argue that these lawsuits seek to alter (or inescapably affect) otherwise legal design, distribution, and marketing decisions and practices in other states and are thus barred by the DCCD.[47]

Treatment of DCCD Claims by Courts

Resort to DCCD arguments has not been a successful strategy for gun manufacturers. Courts have rejected claims that the mere existence of potential federal authority over the manufacturing and marketing of firearms preempts the cities' suits.[48] In addition, federal courts regularly granted plaintiffs' motion to remand cases to state courts following defendants' motion for removal. The courts noted that, while the principles of the DCCD might operate as a *defense* to remedies, if any, granted to the plaintiffs under state law, they were insufficient grounds for removal.[49]

Further, courts—especially state courts, understandably—have expressed considerable skepticism about gun manufacturers' arguments that extraterritoriality principles limit state tort law. Courts argue that, *BMW* notwithstanding, the "applicability of the dormant commerce clause to causes of action under state law is unsettled"[50] and that the "standard for analysis under the Commerce Clause has its focus on positive law—statutes or regulations."[51] Other courts have held that *BMW* and its DCCD principles would only become relevant to the question of the type and scope of remedies and cannot form the basis for a motion to dismiss on the pleadings.[52] Even when courts assume that *BMW* is applicable to the cities' suits, they often turn the language of that decision back on the defendants by concluding that the alleged conduct *did* "directly affect" residents of the plaintiff cities, that the suits seek only compensatory damages, and that they are not intended solely to deter lawful conduct in other states.[53] Rarely, though, do courts provide extensive analysis or elaborate justification for their conclusions.

Only two courts have cited the DCCD as a reason for dismissing the suits against firearms manufacturers. However, in one of those cases, the court merely recited the defendants' allegations "that the City's lawsuit, in violation of the Commerce Clause, seeks to regulate the lawful conduct of the defendants outside Gary's borders, in their production, distribution, and sales practices" and concluded, with no accompanying analysis, that "the City's proposed claim and relief inevitably have an unconstitutional and extraterritorial effect."[54] That decision was later overturned by the Indiana Supreme Court, which first expressed doubts about the characterization of *BMW* as a DCCD case,[55] then concluded that the burdens on interstate commerce were likely outweighed by the city's interest in controlling illegal conduct, or, if they were, such a finding would "turn on factual issues resolved at this pleading stage in favor of the plaintiffs."[56] This decision is discussed in more detail later.

The other case, in which a District of Columbia Superior Court judge dismissed the District's suit, is somewhat different than the other cities' suits because the District had passed a statute imposing strict liability on gun manufacturers for harm resulting from the discharge of certain firearms in the District.[57] The court concluded that "the Act does and was meant to restrict commercial behavior beyond the borders of the District of Columbia." The scope of the District's statute was such that "there is no way of avoiding liability under the Act without going out of business altogether or at least implementing a substantial overhaul of the entire set of relationships with suppliers, distributors, etc." These effects, the judge concluded, offended the "clear prohibitions against the attempts of local legislatures to regulate commercial activities beyond their borders."[58]

Other courts merely take for granted the lack of protectionist or discriminatory purpose of the suits and apply the deferential balancing test. They often conclude (again with little analysis) that whatever burdens on interstate commerce arise from the successful prosecution of these suits would be exceeded by the benefits to the local population from a reduction in gun violence.[59]

Are Suits Vulnerable to DCCD Attack?

Given the novelty of the cities' suits, which has in turn spurred defendants to offer somewhat novel defenses, it is not surprising that many judges have found themselves at sea in sorting through the claims and defenses offered by each side. None of the cases that address DCCD arguments has done a particularly good job in offering reasoned analysis for accepting or rejecting those arguments. This may, in part, be the fault of defendants who, according to one judge, "rather than seriously litigating these claims . . . are attempting to preserve them for later use."[60]

It may also reflect the unfamiliarity of state judges with these sorts of constitutional claims—since most DCCD cases are litigated in federal courts—the extreme discomfort with the broader implications of applying the DCCD to state tort law, or both. The important question of how the Constitution affects the fairly recent phenomenon of regulation by litigation is not one that has received much scholarly treatment. This may account for the trouble that judges have had assessing the constitutional arguments offered by the parties. Space prohibits extensive consideration of that important question, but I hope that what follows may provide a framework for further inquiry with respect to the applicability of the DCCD.

First, there is no reason to presume that tort suits should be immune from DCCD scrutiny, particularly when, like these suits, they have an undeniable regulatory purpose and are brought by governmental entities.[61] At the very least, the principles of the DCCD—which prohibit not only discriminatory or protectionist legislation by states but also one state legislating, de facto, for other states—should restrict the availability of certain types of remedies, be they excessive punitive damages (as in *BMW*) or far-reaching injunctive relief (as is sought in gun suits). The fact that cities are exercising their police powers to protect the welfare of their citizens provides no automatic immunity from DCCD scrutiny.[62]

But saying that tort suits like those against firearms manufacturers should not be immune from the DCCD says nothing about the level of scrutiny that ought to be employed. As noted earlier, the DCCD subjects state laws either to strict scrutiny or to a more deferential standard of review balancing costs and benefits.[63] Not only are laws or regulations that *discriminate* against interstate commerce subject to the more searching review, but laws that regulate "extraterritorially" are subject to strict scrutiny as well.[64]

While the Court has recently hinted it might limit the scope of extraterritoriality principles,[65] prior cases (including *BMW v. Gore*) suggest that the principles have broad application. In considering whether cities' suits against gun manufacturers violate the DCCD, I will focus on extraterritoriality, since (1) that is the strongest argument and (2) it is the argument that has been consistently and forcefully advocated by manufacturers resisting these suits. I will initially elaborate on this first point and then explain how extraterritoriality might aid manufacturers in avoiding some of the more extreme remedies sought, should any of the remaining suits result in a victory for the plaintiffs.

Extraterritoriality is the only species of DCCD argument on which manufacturers have a hope of prevailing. The cities' suits are not motivated by protectionism. There are few (if any) manufacturers in the cities that have filed suit; there does not appear to be an effort to discriminate against out-of-state or out-of-city gun manufacturers. Nor would any local industries likely benefit from suits that might have the effect of banning the import of guns (most of the cities suing, like Chicago, already have strict gun bans in place). While defendants could claim that, whatever the motivation, the suits have a discriminatory effect since only out-of-state commercial actors would feel the pinch, discriminatory effects cases require a well-developed factual record of the sort generally not present in many of the cases in which the DCCD has been raised by defendants.

The industry could make the argument (and has done so in a few cases)[66] that—issues of protectionism or discrimination aside—the burdens on interstate commerce of these suits far exceed the putative local benefits. This kind of balancing test, however, also requires an extensive factual record and leaves tremendous discretion to judges, who are usually inclined to find that the benefits (assuming there is evidence to support their existence) are not "clearly exceeded" by the burdens on interstate commerce, as the deferential balancing test commands.[67]

Extraterritoriality, on the other hand, requires neither proof of intent to discriminate nor proof of discriminatory effects. Nor does it prescribe a deferential balancing test. The Supreme Court recently synthesized its extraterritoriality decisions and extrapolated the following propositions: (1) a state may not apply its laws to activity that takes place outside the state's borders; (2) statutes with such effects are invalid, regardless of whether the extraterritorial reach was intended by the legislature; (3) in assessing extraterritorial effects, courts should consider how state laws interact with similar laws in other states that exist or might exist, with a view toward avoiding inconsistent regulatory regimes; and (4) states may not force out-of-state merchants to seek in-state regulatory approval before undertaking transactions in other states.[68]

Given the injunctive relief sought in most of the lawsuits—including court-mandated changes to marketing, distribution, and design practices that would affect not only the plaintiff city but also other cities and states in the country—and the apparent focus of extraterritoriality on ensuring that state regulatory power is aimed at those problems that are "local" and that admit of local solution, in contrast to those for which a uniform national solution is appropriate,[69] this branch of the DCCD seems to be the most apposite. The viability of this approach is confirmed when one examines each of *Healy v. The Beer Institute*'s four elements of extraterritoriality in light of the recent round of municipal-led litigation.

Unlike some other extraterritoriality cases,[70] the suits here do not involve attempts to regulate or set in-state prices by reference to prices charged elsewhere for the same goods. However, since most of the cities' suits demand extensive alterations to marketing and distribution practices claimed to have deleterious effects within the suing cities,[71] and since most of those decisions would be made by out-of-state manufacturers, extraterritoriality principles seem to limit—if not bar—a court in State A to enjoin economic or commercial activity in State B, even if that activity has effects in State A. An apt analogy would be a state court injunction addressed to an out-of-state power plant to cease operations that send pollution across its borders into the state in which the court is located. To the extent that the DCCD prohibits courts from imposing that sort of remedy, the far-reaching injunctive relief sought by many municipal plaintiffs could be similarly barred. Implicit in these restrictions is that remedies for such conduct, if any, should come from Congress, which can address such problems with national regulations binding on the states.

Then consider that the various state courts hearing the remaining suits would prescribe different, possibly conflicting, injunctions. That possibility raises precisely *The Beer Institute*'s other concern: that interstate commercial actors not be subject to a riot of diverse regulations that might restrict them from operating at all. In all likelihood, were manufacturers to stay in business, they would simply choose the most restrictive regulation and comply with it. That state's regulation would become a de facto national standard, thus projecting its regulatory policy into other states. At the very least, losing manufacturers might be subject to conflicting injunctions, with one requiring, say, personalized technology and another requiring child-protection devices.[72]

Finally, there is that thread of the extraterritoriality concept mentioned earlier barring an interstate commercial actor from being required to seek regulatory approval in one state for undertaking a transaction occurring in another. Unless one is persuaded that judicial relief granted in a tort suit is simply not covered by the DCCD, the injunctive relief sought in the cases—particularly alterations to distribution and marketing practices—would hold the potential to require just that sort of approval. Presumably manufacturers subject to various injunctions prescribing the incorporation of safety devices into gun design, or the manner in which guns can be distributed or marketed, would have to seek modification of those injunctions should a particular type of safety device prove unworkable or should the market dictate the need to change marketing or distribution practices set in the injunction. This seems well within the scope of *The Beer Institute*'s description of the DCCD's prohibition. Moreover, as a *practical* matter, the mixed success of *federal* courts overseeing school desegregation and prison reform should make plaintiffs think twice about the desirability of delegating the regulation of the firearms industry to a half dozen or more *state* courts.[73]

Nevertheless, state courts remain quite skeptical that these suits, which apply state tort law, implicate the DCCD at all, as a recent decision by the Indiana Supreme Court demonstrates.[74] The City of Gary, Indiana, filed public nuisance, negligent marketing and distribution, and negligent design claims against several gun manufacturers and sought both compensatory and punitive damages and injunctive relief. First, the court rejected reliance on *BMW*, concluding that it was not a DCCD case. The court then rejected the defendants' argument that "the City's relief would require manufacturers to change their distribution methods nationwide, and therefore constitutes extraterritorial regulation which violates the Commerce Clause." The city, the court wrote, did "seek to change how handguns are distributed, but only those handguns that are sold in and around Gary . . . Imposing liability for negligent, reckless, or intentional facilitation of violations of [state law governing sales to felons] that cause harm within the local jurisdiction does no more than state tort law has historically done." All the manufacturers need do, the court explained, was to "comply with existing state and federal laws governing gun distribution." The court repeatedly stressed that "all the requested relief can be accomplished at a local level" and the availability of "more tailored forms of local relief limited to local impact." If the local benefits of Gary's suit imposed burdens on interstate commerce that required balancing, the court concluded, such a claim "would turn

on factual issues resolved at this pleading stage in favor of the plaintiff.
... [W]hether there are less restrictive means and proof of the degree of
harm alleviated remain issues for trial. They do not justify dismissal of
the claim on Commerce Clause grounds."

There are problems with the Indiana court's analysis—prime among
them is that, while the court cites one extraterritoriality decision,[75] it
ignores other extraterritoriality decisions, such as *The Beer Institute*,
where the Court attempted to synthesize its various cases into a set of
principles. Had it done so, it could not have maintained its position that,
because some of the relief requested by Gary applied *only* to "local"
activities in and around Gary, there was no extraterritoriality problem.
The proper inquiry, according to the Supreme Court, is whether there
would be extraterritorial effects as a practical matter and what might
happen if all jurisdictions followed Gary's example. One claim made by
the city was for deceptive advertising: Gary claimed that guns were marketed as providing protection for occupants when the opposite is true
and that such advertising has harmed residents of Gary. Presumably
injunctive relief would be sought prohibiting such advertisements. Were
the court to award such relief, how could that relief be "limited to local
impact"? Would the manufacturers have to ensure that no advertisements, wherever run, would be seen by Gary's residents? Manufacturers
might have to stop making such claims at all, in which case Gary's regulation would constitute a de facto national standard, or it would have to
take extraordinary steps to insulate the residents of Gary from seeing
such ads, which could be quite costly. Likewise, forcing changes in distribution practices for guns sold "around Gary," including out of state,
would similarly extend the state court's regulatory power into other
jurisdictions, which seems to be what the Court's extraterritoriality
jurisprudence prohibits.

Noting that states are free to establish their own standards for product
liability, absent federal preemption, the Court saw "no qualitative difference between recognition of the negligence and nuisance claims the City
asserts as to handguns and restrictions on any other product deemed
dangerous"; it also perceived "no difference between local requirements
designed to make the product itself more safe [i.e., state products liability law] and requirements that its distribution be conducted consonant
with public intent."

Since the DCCD is a form of federal constitutional preemption, the court simply begs the question of whether the aspects of the DCCD also apply to state tort claims or remedies state law offers. There may be no difference between products liability law and injunctive relief sought, but the points raised previously merely raise further questions about state tort law and whether constitutional doctrines have anything to say about its regulatory effects on products with national markets. Perhaps the Indiana high court's assumption, shared by many commentators, ought to be examined more closely.

Pursuing extraterritoriality arguments, as the Indiana Supreme Court's decision demonstrates, is by no means a sure win for the gun industry. For one thing, the Court itself may have signaled that it regards its extraterritoriality decisions as confined to state laws requiring goods sold in-state to be no more expensive than goods sold elsewhere.[76] Moreover, extraterritoriality as a constitutional concept has come in for some rather harsh criticism of late. Jack Goldsmith and Alan Sykes, for example, have criticized the Court's "overbroad extraterritoriality dicta,"[77] noting that "[t]here is nothing unusual about non-uniform regulations in our federal system. States are allowed to make their own regulatory judgments about scores of issues." Different standards for liability among state tort systems is one example they give. That "states may promulgate different substantive regulations of the same activity," they posit, "cannot possibly be the touchstone for illegality under the dormant Commerce Clause." Their characterization of the DCCD restricting state tort law as a reductio ad absurdum is understandable: limiting the tort law of the fifty states through the DCCD would be nothing short of revolutionary, which explains state courts' eagerness to deny the DCCD's applicability and federal courts' desire to push off consideration until the merits of the suits are resolved. Nevertheless, if the DCCD's extraterritoriality principles are taken at face value and read in conjunction with *BMW*, then the DCCD will have to be addressed sooner or later.

Goldsmith and Sykes advocate substituting the rulelike formulations set forth in cases like *The Beer Institute* with an explicit balancing test that measures the costs of compliance with diverse state regulatory regimes against the benefits to the state regulating the cross-border externalities (like gun distribution) that are harming the citizens of the regulating state. Were courts to abandon *The Beer Institute* approach for something akin to Goldsmith and Sykes's proposal, manufacturers might have a more difficult time compiling the sort of factual record necessary to demonstrate that "non-uniform state regulations might impose compliance costs that are so severe that they counsel against permitting the states to regulate a particular subject matter" or that they "may become subject to different regulations to such an extent that compliance becomes effectively impossible if they are to engage in interstate commerce."

Despite Supreme Court hints and academic criticism, though, the extraterritoriality prong of the DCCD remains a viable defense against some of the relief requested, while *BMW v. Gore* could prevent the imposition of ruinous punitive damage awards (whether large compensatory awards are similarly limited is not clear)[78] if the industry can demonstrate an intent to punish for nationwide conduct. The bad news for manufacturers, however, is that the opportunity to deploy these arguments effectively will come only after they have *lost* on a host of legal issues—issues of duty, breach, causation, and public nuisance.

NOTES

INTRODUCTION

1. Richard J. Bonnie and Bernard Guyer, "Injury as a Field of Public Health: Achievements and Controversies," *Journal of Law, Medicine, and Ethics* 30 (2002): 267–69.

2. Windle Turley and James E. Rooks Jr., *Firearms Litigation* (New York: Shepard's-McGraw-Hill, 1988), 12.

3. See, e.g., Garen J. Wintemute, "The Future of Firearm Violence Prevention: Building on Success," *Journal of the American Medical Association* 282, no. 5 (1999): 476; Susan DeFrancesco, "Children and Guns," *Pace Law Review* 19 (1999): 278–84.

4. Wintemute, "Future," 475–77.

5. For a recent survey of this public health approach to gun violence, see David Hemenway, *Private Guns, Public Health* (Ann Arbor: University of Michigan Press, 2004).

6. Turley and Rooks, *Firearms Litigation*, 12; Walter K. Olson, *The Rule of Lawyers: How the New Litigation Elite Threatens America's Rule of Law* (New York: St. Martin's, 2003), 101–2.

7. DeFrancesco, "Children and Guns," 282–83.

8. See chapters 5, 6, 7, 8, and 10 of this book.

9. Richard E. Kaye, Annotation, "Products Liability: Firearms, Ammunition, and Chemical Weapons," *American Law Reports*, 5th ser., 96 (2003), §2a.

10. George L. Blum, Annotation, "Firearm or Ammunition Manufacturer or Seller's Liability for Injuries Caused to Another by Use of Gun in Committing Crime," *American Law Reports*, 5th ser., 88 (2003), §6a.

11. As of November 2004, the only unreversed jury verdict in favor of plaintiffs, based on defective design, is *Maxfield v. Bryco Arms*, Index # 841-636 (Sup. Ct. CA., Alameda County 2003). Jury verdicts in favor of plaintiffs that

were overturned on appeal include *Hamilton v. Beretta U.S.A. Corp.*, 727 N.Y.S.2d 7 (2001) (manufacturer liability), and *Grunow v. Valor Corp. of Florida*, No. CL 00-9657 (Fla. Cir. Ct., Palm Beach County Jan. 27, 2003) (distributor liability).

12. *Johnson v. Bull's Eye Shooter Supply*, a case arising out of a widely publicized sniper shooting in Washington, DC, was settled for the limit of the manufacturer's insurance policy without any admission of liability. See Fox Butterfield, "Sniper Victims in Settlement with Gun Maker and Dealer," *New York Times*, Sept. 10, 2004, A10. Claims brought by several California municipalities against the gun industry resulted in a settlement with gun distributors in which they agreed to voluntary restrictions on marketing. See Jean Guccione, "Dealers, Firms Accept Curbs, Settle Gun Suits," *Los Angeles Times*, Aug. 22, 2003, 3. *Matthieu v. Beretta*, involving a design defect claim, ended in a monetary settlement for an undisclosed amount. See http://www.gunlawsuits.org/docket/casestatus.php?RecordNo=51 (last accessed Nov. 2004).

13. Restatement (Second) Torts §519 (1977).

14. For examples, see Timothy D. Lytton, "Tort Claims against Gun Manufacturers for Crime-Related Injuries: Defining a Suitable Role for the Tort System in Regulating the Firearms Industry," *Missouri Law Review* 65 (2000): 6n16, 8–10.

15. Some courts have also held that the doctrine of strict liability for abnormally dangerous activities is limited to abnormally dangerous uses of land. See Lytton, "Tort Claims," 8–9.

16. *Kelley v. R.G. Industries*, 497 A.2d 1143 (Md. 1985).

17. Monica Fennell, "Missing the Mark in Maryland: How Poor Drafting and Implementation Vitiated a Model State Gun Control Law," *Hamline Journal of Public Law and Policy* 13 (1992): 43–49.

18. Howard L. Siegel, "Winning without Precedent: Kelley v. R.G. Industries," *Litigation* 14, no. 4 (1988): 32–34.

19. Ibid., 34. Appeal to the Supreme Court of Maryland occurred prior to any trial in the case and was initiated by the Federal District Court, which certified questions to the Supreme Court in order to clarify questions of state law.

20. Restatement (Second) Torts §401A (1977); Restatement (Third) Products Liability §2 (2001).

21. For examples, see Lytton, "Tort Claims," 6n17, 10–21.

22. W. Keeton, D. Dobbs, R. Keeton, and D. Owens, *Prosser and Keeton on Torts*, 5th ed. (St. Paul, MN: West, 1984).

23. For examples, see Lytton, "Tort Claims," 11n51.

24. *Patterson v. Rohm Gesellschaft*, 608 F. Supp. 1206, 1211 (N.D. Tex. 1987).

25. Restatement (Third) Torts Products Liability §2(b) (2001).

26. See, e.g., *Dix v. Beretta*, No. 750681:9 (Cal. Super. Ct., Alameda

County, Aug. 2, 2004) (discussed in *Andrews Litigation Reporter*, vol. 6, Aug. 2004, at 3).

27. See, e.g., Petition in *Morial v. Smith & Wesson Corp.*, No. 98-18578 (Civ. Dist. Ct. Parish of Orleans 1998). Personalization, or "smart gun," technology includes equipping guns with microchips that would allow a gun to fire only upon recognition of the fingerprints of an authorized user or with sensors that would allow a gun to fire only when held by a person wearing a special ring or lapel pin. Anne Eisenberg, "Smart Guns Can Check Identities before Firing," *New York Times*, Sept. 10, 1998, 63; Leslie Wayne, "'Smart' Guns Proving Not to Be a Quick Fix," *New York Times*, June 15, 1999, A24.

28. See, e.g., *Dix v. Beretta*.

29. Gary Kleck, "Guns Aren't Ready to Be Smart," *New York Times*, March 11, 2000, A15; Olson, *The Rule of Lawyers*, 113, 123–24; Peter H. Brown and Daniel G. Abel, *Outgunned: Up against the NRA* (New York: Free Press, 2003), 64–65.

30. *Dix v. Beretta* (jury verdict in favor of defendants); *Maxfield v. Bryco Arms*, Index # 841-636 (Sup. Ct. CA., Alameda County 2003) (jury verdict in favor of plaintiff).

31. See, e.g., *Bloxham v. Glock Inc.*, 53 P.3d 196 (Ariz. Ct. App. 2002).

32. Trial Transcript of Feb. 3, 1999, *Hamilton v. Accu-Tek*, 62 F. Supp. 2d 802 (No. CV-95-0049) (E.D.N.Y. 1999), 3829–37, 3908–9; Sporting Arms and Ammunition Manufacturers' Institute, *Non-Fiction Writer's Guide: A Writer's Resource to Firearms and Ammunition* (1998), 12.

33. Keeton et al., *Prosser and Keeton*, §56.

34. Ibid.

35. *Riordan v. International Armament Corp.*, 477 N.E. 2d 1293, 1295 (Ill. App. Ct. 1985).

36. *First Commercial Trust Co. v. Lorcin Engineering, Inc.*, 900 S.W.2d 202, 203 (Ark. 1995).

37. *Hamilton v. Beretta*, 727 N.Y.S. 2d 7 (2001).

38. For a more detailed analysis of these claims, see Lytton, "Tort Claims," 34.

39. In a special verdict, the jury found fifteen of the twenty-five defendant manufacturers negligent, found that the negligence of nine of them was a proximate cause of harm to the plaintiffs, and assessed damages against three of the nine. *Hamilton v. Beretta*, at 10–11. The rest of this paragraph draws on pp. 15–16 of the court's opinion.

40. *Merrill v. Navegar*, 110 Cal. Rptr. 2d 370 (Cal. 2001). All references to this case can be found at this citation.

41. For the view that plaintiffs have misconstrued these advertising claims, see Randy E. Barnett and Don B. Kates, "Under Fire: The New Consensus on the Second Amendment," *Emory Law Journal* 45 (1996): 1139, 1197.

42. *Cal. Civ. Code* §1714.4 (repealed). For further analysis of the repeal, see my discussion in chapter 6.

43. See, e.g., *Bloxham v. Glock Inc.*, 53 P.3d 196 (Ariz. Ct. App. 2002); *Lemongello v. Will Co., Inc.*, No. 02-C-2952 (W. Va. Cir. Ct. Kanawha County 2003).

44. For example, *Bloxham* (dismissed) and *Ileto v. Glock, Inc.*, 349 F.3d 1191 (9th Cir. 2003) (pending).

45. Restatement (Second) Torts §821B (1977).

46. *City of Chicago v. Beretta*, 2004 Ill. LEXIS 1665 at 64-5 (Ill. 2004).

47. See *City of Philadelphia v. Beretta*, 126 F. Supp. 2d 882, 902 (E.D. Pa. 2000).

48. *People ex rel. Spitzer v. Sturm, Ruger & Co., Inc.*, 761 N.Y.S.2d 192, 201 (1st Dept. 2003).

49. *City of Gary, Ind. ex rel King v. Smith & Wesson Corp.*, 94 F. Supp. 2d 947 (N.D. Ind. 2000).

50. *People ex rel. Spitzer*, 761 N.Y.S.2d at 208 (Rosenberger, J., dissenting).

51. *NAACP v. AcuSport Corp.*, 271 F. Supp. 2d 435 (E.D.N.Y. 2003).

52. *City of New York v. Beretta USA Corp.*, No. 00CV 3641 [JBW] [CLP], 2004 WL 764959 (E.D.N.Y. Apr. 12, 2004).

53. *Ileto v. Glock, Inc.*, 349 F.3d 1191 (9th Cir. 2003), *cert. denied*, 125 S.Ct. 865 (2005).

54. See, e.g., Complaint, *City of Bridgeport v. Smith & Wesson*, No. CV-99-036-1279 (Conn. Super. Ct. 1999) (filed Jan. 27, 1999), 18; Complaint, *California v. Arcadia Mach. & Tool, Inc.*, No. BC210894 (Cal. Super. Ct. Los Angeles 1999) (filed May 25, 1999), 34.

55. See, e.g., *Ganim v. Smith & Wesson*, 780 A.2d 98 (Conn. 2001); *Arcadia*, No. BC210894; *Gary ex rel. King v. Smith & Wesson Corp.*, 2003 WL 23010035 (Ind.) (Dec. 23, 2003); *City of Boston v. Smith & Wesson Corp.*, 2000 WL 1473568 (Mass. Super. Jul. 13, 2000).

56. On the so-called remoteness doctrine, see Victor E. Schwartz, "The Remoteness Doctrine: A Rational Limit on Tort Law," *Cornell Journal of Law & Public Policy* 8 (1999): 421.

57. *Ganim v. Smith & Wesson*, 26 Conn. L. Rptr. 39, 40 (Conn. Super. Ct. 1999), *aff'd* 780 A.2d 98 (Conn. 2001) (dismissing the City of Bridgeport suit).

58. See, e.g., *City of Philadelphia v. Beretta*, 126 F. Supp. 2d 882, 894, 895 (E.D. Pa. 2000), *aff'd on other grounds*, 277 F.3d 415 (3d Cir. 2002).

59. Keeton et al., *Prosser and Keeton*, §42.

60. See, e.g., *City of Philadelphia v. Beretta*.

61. See Timothy D. Lytton, "Should Government Be Allowed to Recover the Costs of Public Services from Tortfeasors? Tort Subsidies, the Limits of Loss Spreading, and the Free Public Services Doctrine," *Tulane Law Review* 76 (2002): 727 (discussing the doctrine); see also at 776–77. For more recent examples, see *City of Gary, Ind. ex rel King v. Smith & Wesson Corp.*, 94 F. Supp. 2d 947 (N.D. Ind. 2000).

62. See Lytton, "Free Public Services Doctrine," 776–77.

63. Franklin Zimring and Gordon Hawkins, *Crime Is Not the Problem: Lethal Violence in America* (New York: Oxford University Press, 1997), 2.

64. Shannon Frattaroli and Stephen P. Teret, "Why Firearm Injury Surveillance?" *American Journal of Preventative Medicine* 15, 3d supp. (1998): 2–5.

65. Andrew W. Molchan, "Industry Insights," *American Firearms Industry* (February 1993): 74.

CHAPTER 1

1. National Center for Injury Control and Prevention, Web-Based Injury Statistics Query and Reporting System, http://www.cdc.gov/ncipc/wisqars/default.htm (hereinafter WISCARS).

2. P. J. Cook, B. A. Lawrence, J. Ludwig, and T. R. Miller, "The Medical Costs of Gunshot Injuries in the United States," *Journal of the American Medical Association* 282, no. 5 (1999): 447–54.

3. G. J. Wintemute, "Firearms as a Cause of Death in the United States, 1920–1982," *Journal of Trauma* 27, no. 5 (1997): 532–36.

4. S. P. Baker, S. P. Teret, and P. E. Dietz, "Firearms and the Public Health," *Journal of Public Health Policy* 1 (1980): 224–29.

5. S. P. Baker, B. O'Neill, M. J. Ginsberg, and G. Li, *The Injury Fact Book* (New York: Oxford University Press, 1992).

6. National Center for Injury Control and Prevention, WISCARS.

7. L. S. Robertson, "Automobile Safety Regulations and Death Reductions in the United States," *American Journal of Public Health* 71, no. 8 (1981): 818–22.

8. Baker, Teret, and Dietz, "Firearms and the Public Health," 4.

9. For example, S. P. Teret and G. J. Wintemute, "Policies to Prevent Firearm Injuries," *Health Affairs* 12, no. 4 (winter 1993): 96–108.

10. U.S. Department of Health, Education, and Welfare, *Healthy People: The Surgeon General's Report on Health Promotion and Disease Prevention* (Washington, DC: Government Printing Office, 1979).

11. J. A. Mercy and V. N. Houk, "Firearm Injuries: A Call for Science," *New England Journal of Medicine* 319, no. 19 (1988): 1283–85.

12. D. B. Kates, H. E. Schaffer, J. K. Lattimer, G. B. Murray, and Edwin H. Cassem, "Guns and Public Health: Epidemic of Violence or Pandemic of Propaganda?" *Tennessee Law Review* 62 (1995): 513, 522.

13. B. Thompson, "Trigger Points: The Evangelists of 'Injury Control' Believe That Scientific Knowledge and Public Health Activism Can Break America's Cycle of Firearms Mayhem. But Can They Survive the Treacherous Politics of Gun Control?" *Washington Post Magazine*, March 29, 1998, W12.

14. Only 30 percent of the gun deaths included in the CDC's 2000 data specify whether the gun involved was a long gun or a handgun. For 70 percent of those deaths, this basic information is recorded as unknown or not specified. See

United States Department of Health and Human Services, Centers for Disease Control and Prevention, National Center for Health Statistics, Office of Analysis, Epidemiology, and Health Promotion, *Compressed Mortality File.*

15. A. M. Minino, E. Arias, K. D. Kochanek, S. L. Murphy, and B. L. Smith, "Deaths: Final Data for 2000," *National Vital Statistics Reports* 50, no. 15 (2002): 1–120.

16. P. J. Cook and J. Ludwig, "The Costs of Gun Violence against Children," *Future of Children* 12, no. 2 (2002): 87–99.

17. E. D. Shenassa, S. N. Katlin, and S. L. Buka, "Lethality of Firearms Relative to Other Suicide Methods: A Population-Based Study," *Journal of Epidemiology and Community Health* 57 (2003): 120–24.

18. R. S. Spicer and T. R. Miller, "Suicide Acts in 8 States: Incidence and Case Fatality Rates by Demographics and Method," *American Journal of Public Health* 90, no. 12 (2000): 1885–91.

19. A. Blumstein, *Youth Violence, Guns, and Illicit Drug Markets* (Washington, DC: U.S. Department of Justice, National Institute of Justice, Research Preview, 1996).

20. This section is based on P. J. Cook and J. Ludwig, *Gun Violence: The Real Costs* (New York: Oxford University Press, 2000); Cook and Ludwig, "Costs of Gun Violence."

21. Public Law 94-284, § 3(e), *U.S. Statutes at Large* 90 (1976): 504; S. P. Teret and P. L. Culross, "Product-Oriented Approaches to Reducing Youth Gun Violence," *The Future of Children* 12, no. 2 (2002): 119–31.

22. For example, see "Beretta Announces Position Concerning 'Smart Gun' Technology," National Rifle Association web site, formerly available at http://www.nraila.org/NewsCenter.asp?FormMode=Detail&ID=1027&i= View.

23. J. S. Vernick, M. O'Brien, L. M. Hepburn, S. B. Johnson, et al., "Unintentional and Undetermined Firearm Related Deaths: A Preventable Death Analysis for Three Safety Devices," *Injury Prevention* 9 (2003): 307–11.

24. J. S. Vernick, Z. F. Meisel, S. P. Teret, J. S. Milne, and S. W. Hargarten, "'I Didn't Know the Gun Was Loaded': An Examination of Two Safety Devices That Can Reduce the Risk of Unintentional Firearm Injuries," *Journal of Public Health Policy* 20, no. 4 (1999): 427–40.

25. Ibid.

26. Vernick et al., "'I Didn't Know the Gun Was Loaded'"; J. S. Milne, S. W. Hargarten, A. L. Kellermann, and G. J. Wintemute, "Effect of Current Federal Regulations on Handgun Safety Features," *Annals of Emergency Medicine* 41, no. 1 (2003): 1–9.

27. Vernick et al., "Unintentional and Undetermined Firearm Related Deaths."

28. S. P. Teret and N. L. Lewin, "Policy and Technology for Safer Guns: An Update," *Annals of Emergency Medicine* 41, no. 1 (2003): 32–34.

29. Taurus International Manufacturing web site, formerly available at http://www.taurususa.com/PDF2002/security.pdf.

30. Cook and Ludwig, *Gun Violence.*

31. P. J. Cook and J. A. Leitzel, "'Perversity, Futility, Jeopardy': An Economic Analysis of the Attack on Gun Control," *Law and Contemporary Problems* 59, no. 1 (1996): 91–118.

32. Bureau of Alcohol, Tobacco, and Firearms, *Firearms Commerce in the United States* (Washington, DC: Department of the Treasury, 2001–2).

33. Bureau of Alcohol, Tobacco and Firearms, *Commerce in Firearms in the United States* (Washington, DC: U.S. Department of the Treasury, 2000).

34. J. Wachtel, "Sources of Crime Guns in Los Angeles, California," *International Journal of Police Strategies and Management* 21, no. 2 (1998): 220–39; C. S. Koper, "Federal Legislation and Gun Markets: How Much Have Recent Reforms of the Federal Firearms Licensing System Reduced Criminal Gun Suppliers?" *Criminology and Public Policy* 1, no. 2 (2002): 151–78; Bureau of Alcohol, Tobacco and Firearms, *Commerce in Firearms in the United States* (2000).

35. S. B. Sorenson and K. A. Vittes, "Buying a Handgun for Someone Else: Firearm Dealer Willingness to Sell," *Injury Prevention* 9 (2003): 147–50.

36. Bureau of Alcohol, Tobacco, and Firearms, *Commerce in Firearms in the United States* (2000). For refutation of the argument that gun dealers who sell more guns will have more crime guns traced back to them so the number of traces is not a good indicator of corrupt or negligent dealer activity see G. J. Wintemute, "Relationship between Illegal Use of Handguns and Handgun Sales Volume," *Journal of the American Medical Association* 284, no. 5 (2000): 566–67.

37. Bureau of Alcohol, Tobacco, and Firearms, *Following the Gun: Enforcing Federal Laws against Firearms Traffickers* (Washington, DC: U.S. Department of the Treasury, 2000).

38. D. W. Webster, J. S. Vernick, and L. M. Hepburn, "Effects of Maryland's Law Banning 'Saturday Night Special' Handguns on Homicides," *American Journal of Epidemiology* 155, no. 5 (2002): 406–12.

39. C. S. Koper and J. A. Roth, "The Impact of the 1994 Federal Assault Weapon Ban on Gun Violence Outcomes: An Assessment of Multiple Outcome Measures and Some Lessons for Policy Evaluation," *Journal of Quantitative Criminology* 17, no. 1 (2001): 33–80.

40. D. C. Grossman, D. T. Reay, and S. A. Baker, "Self-inflicted and Unintentional Firearm Injuries among Children and Adolescents: The Source of the Firearm," *Archives of Pediatric and Adolescent Medicine* 153 (1999): 875–78.

41. T. W. Smith, *2001 National Gun Policy Survey of the National Opinion Research Center: Research Findings* (Chicago: University of Chicago, 2001).

42. Bureau of Alcohol, Tobacco, and Firearms, *Following the Gun;* idem, *Commerce in Firearms in the United States* (2000).

43. D. S. Weil and R. C. Knox, "Effects of Limiting Handgun Purchases on Interstate Transfer of Firearms," *Journal of the American Medical Association* 275, no. 22 (1996): 1759–61.

44. M. A. Wright, G. J. Wintemute, and F. P. Rivara, "Effectiveness of Denial of Handgun Purchase to Persons Believed to Be at High Risk for Firearm Violence," *American Journal of Public Health* 89, no. 1 (1999): 88–90.

45. G. J. Wintemute, M. A. Wright, C. M. Drake, and J. J. Beaumont,

"Subsequent Criminal Activity among Violent Misdemeanants Who Seek to Purchase Handguns: Risk Factors and Effectiveness of Denying Handgun Purchase," *Journal of the American Medical Association* 285, no. 5 (2001): 1019–26.

46. P. J. Cook, S. Molliconi, and T. B. Cole, "Regulating Gun Markets," *Journal of Criminal Law and Criminology* 86 (1995): 59–91.

47. J. B. Jacobs, *Can Gun Control Work?* (New York: Oxford University Press, 2002).

48. D. W. Webster, J. S. Vernick, and L. M. Hepburn, "Relationship between Licensing, Registration, and Other Gun Sales Laws and the Source State of Crime Guns," *Injury Prevention* 7 (2001): 184–89.

49. Bureau of Alcohol, Tobacco, and Firearms, *Commerce in Firearms in the United States* (2000). The information in the following two paragraphs is drawn from this report and the subsequent 2001–2002 report as well as U.S. General Accounting Office (2000), Gun Control: Improving the National Instant Criminal Background Check System: Statement of Laurie E. Ekstrand, GAO/T-GGD-00-163.

50. Personal communication with Gregory T. Gundlach, JD, PhD, MBA, professor of marketing, Coggin College of Business, University of North Florida.

51. D. W. Webster and M. Starnes, "Reexamining the Association between Child Access Prevention Gun Laws and Unintentional Shooting Deaths of Children," *Pediatrics* 106, no. 6 (2000): 1466–69.

52. P. J. Cook and J. Ludwig, *Guns in American: Results of a Comprehensive National Survey on Firearms Ownership and Use, Summary Report* (Washington, DC: Police Foundation, 1996).

53. M. A. Schuster, T. M. Franke, A. M. Bastian, S. Sor, S. and N. Halfon, "Firearm Storage Patterns in U.S. Homes with Children," *American Journal of Public Health* 90, no. 4 (2000): 588–94.

54. D. Azrael, M. Miller, and D. Hemenway, "Are Household Firearms Stored Safely? It Depends on Whom You Ask," *Pediatrics* 106, no. 3 (2000): 1–6.

55. See, e.g., P. J. Cook and J. Ludwig, *Guns in American: National Survey on Private Ownership and Use of Firearms* (Washington, DC: U.S. Department of Justice, National Institute of Justice, Research in Brief, NCJ 165476, 1997); D. Hemenway, S. J. Solnick, and D. R. Azrael, "Firearm Training and Storage," *Journal of the American Medical Association* 273, no. 1 (1995): 46–50.

56. T. Coyne-Beasley, V. J. Schoenbach, and R. M. Johnson, "'Love Our kids, Lock Your Guns': A Community-Based Firearm Safety Counseling and Gun Lock Distribution Program," *Archives of Pediatrics and Adolescent Medicine* 155 (2001): 659–64.

57. Cook and Ludwig, *Guns in America;* Hemenway, Solnick, and Azrael, "Firearm Training and Storage"; D. S. Weil and D. Hemenway, "Loaded Guns in the Home: Analysis of a National Random Survey of Gun Owners," *Journal of the American Medical Association* 267, no. 22 (1992): 3033–37.

58. D. J. Wiebe, "Firearms in U.S. Homes as a Risk Factor for Unintentional Gunshot Fatality," *Accident Analysis and Prevention* 35 (2003): 711–16.

59. D. J. Wiebe, "Homicide and Suicide Risks Associated with Firearms in

the Home: A National Case-Control Study," *Annals of Emergency Medicine* 41, no. 6 (2003): 771–82.

60. A. L. Kellermann, F. P. Rivara, N. B. Rushforth, J. G. Banton, et al., "Gun Ownership as a Risk Factor for Homicide in the Home," *New England Journal of Medicine* 329, no. 15 (1993): 1084–91; J. E. Bailey, A. L. Kellermann, G. W. Somes, J. G. Banton, et al., "Risk Factors for Violent Death of Women in the Home," *Archives of Internal Medicine* 157 (1997): 777–82; A. L. Kellermann, F. P. Rivara, G. Somes, D. T. Reay, et al., "Suicide in the Home in Relation to Gun Ownership," *New England Journal of Medicine* 327, no. 7 (1992): 467–72.

61. K. M. Grassel, G. J. Wintemute, M. A. Wright, and M. P. Romero, "Association between Handgun Purchase and Mortality from Firearm Injury," *Injury Prevention* 9 (2003): 48–52; G. J. Wintemute, C. A. Parham, J. J. Beaumont, M. Wright, M. and C. Drake, "Mortality among Recent Purchasers of Handguns," *New England Journal of Medicine* 341, no. 21 (1999): 1583–89.

62. D. W. Webster, M. E. H. Wilson, A. K. Duggan, and L. C. Pakula, "Parents' Beliefs about Preventing Gun Injuries to Children," *Pediatrics* 89 (1992): 908–14.

63. M. M. Farah, H. K. Simon, and A. L. Kellermann, "Firearms in the Home: Parental Perceptions," *Pediatrics* 104, no. 5 (1999): 1059–63.

64. M. S. Hardy, F. D. Armstrong, B. L. Martin, and K. N. Strawn, "A Firearm Safety Program for Children: They Just Can't Say No," *Developmental and Behavioral Pediatrics* 17, no. 4 (1996): 216–21; Webster et al., *supra* n. 62.

65. Hardy, Armstrong, Martin, and Strawn, "A Firearm Safety Program for Children."

66. M. S. Hardy, "Teaching Firearm Safety to Children: Failure of a Program," *Developmental and Behavioral Pediatrics* 23, no. 2 (2002): 71–76.

67. M. B. Himle, R. G. Miltenberger, B. J. Gatheridge, and C. A. Flessner, "An Evaluation of Two Procedures for Training Skills to Prevent Gun Play in Children," *Pediatrics* 113, no. 1 (2004): 70–77.

68. G. A. Jackman, M. M. Farah, A. L. Kellermann, and H. K. Simon, "Seeing Is Believing: What Do Boys Do When They Find a Real Gun?" *Pediatrics* 107, no. 6 (2001): 1247–50.

69. G. J. Wintemute, S. P. Teret, J. F. Kraus, M. A. Wright, and G. Bradfield, "When Children Shoot Children: 88 Unintended Deaths in California," *Journal of the American Medical Association* 257, no. 22 (1987): 3107–9.

70. Grossman, Reay, and Baker, "Self-inflicted and Unintentional Firearm Injuries."

71. N. Sinauer, J. L. Annest, and J. A. Mercy, "Unintentional, Nonfatal Firearm-Related Injuries: A Preventable Public Health Burden," *Journal of the American Medical Association* 275, no. 22 (1996): 1740–43.

72. S. Shah, R. E. Hoffman, L. Wake, and W. M. Marine, "Adolescent Suicide and Household Access to Firearms in Colorado: Results of a Case-Control Study," *Journal of Adolescent Health* 26 (2000): 157–63; D. A. Brent, J. A. Per-

per, G. Mortiz, M. Baugher, et al., "Firearms and Adolescent Suicide: A Community Case-Control Study," *American Journal of Diseases of Children* 147 (1993): 1066–71; D. A. Brent, J. A. Perper, C. J. Allman, G. M. Moritz, et al., "The Presence and Accessibility of Firearms in the Homes of Adolescent Suicides: A Case-Control Study," *Journal of the American Medical Association* 266, no. 21 (1991): 2989–95.

73. American Academy of Child and Adolescent Psychiatry, "Practice Parameter for the Assessment and Treatment of Children and Adolescents with Suicidal Behavior," *Journal of the American Academy of Child and Adolescent Psychiatry* 40, no. 7 (2001): 24S–51S.

74. A. L. Berman and R. H. Schwartz, "Suicide Attempts among Adolescent Drug Users," *American Journal of Diseases of Children* 144 (1990): 310–14.

75. See D. A. Brent, M. Baugher, B. Birmaher, D. J. Kolko, and J. Bridge, "Compliance with Recommendations to Remove Firearms in Families Participating in a Clinical Trial for Adolescent Depression," *Journal of the American Academy of Child and Adolescent Psychiatry* 39, no. 10 (2000): 1220–26. M. J. P. Kruesi, J. Grossman, J. M. Pennington, P. J. Woodward, et al., "Suicide and Violence Prevention: Parent Education in the Emergency Room," *Journal of the American Academy of Child and Adolescent Psychiatry* 38, no. 3 (1999): 250–55.

76. J. R. Lott Jr., *More Guns, Less Crime* (Chicago: University of Chicago Press, 1998).

77. See, e.g., I. Ayers and J. J. Donohue III, "Shooting Down the 'More Guns, Less Crime' Hypothesis," *Stanford Law Review* 55 (2003): 1193.

78. M. Miller, D. Azrael, and D. Hemenway, "Rates of Household Firearm Ownership and Homicide across U.S. Regions and States, 1988–1997," *American Journal of Public Health* 92, no. 12 (2002): 1988–93; M. Miller, D. Azrael, and D. Hemenway, "Household Firearm Ownership and Suicide Rates in the United States," *Epidemiology* 13 (2002): 517–24.

79. *Motor Vehicle Mfr. Ass'n of the U. S. v. State Farm Mut. Auto. Ins. Co.,* 463 U.S. 29, 49 (1983).

80. S. P. Teret, "Litigating for the Public's Health," *American Journal of Public Health* 76, no. 8 (1986): 1027–29.

CHAPTER 2

The author wishes to thank C. B. Kates, Gary Kleck (School of Criminology, Florida State University), Gloria Main (History, University of Colorado), Gary Mauser (Fraser Institute, Simon Fraser University, Canada), Robert Weisberg (Law, Stanford University), and all the authors in this book, especially Timothy Lytton (Law, Albany Law School), for their helpful advice. Of course, for errors of fact or interpretation, I alone am responsible.

1. For 1946 figures see Gary Kleck, *Targeting Guns: Firearms and Their Control* (New York: Aldine, 1997), 96–97, 262–63. The 2000 firearms density figures were provided me by Professor Kleck. The murder rate figures for 2000 are from Arialdi M. Minino, Elizabeth Arias, Kenneth D. Kochaneki, Sherry L.

Murphy, and Betty L. Smith, *Deaths: Final Data for 2000*, *National Vital Statistics Reports* 50, no. 15 (Washington, DC: CDC, 2002). Incidentally, the 2001 murder rate was slightly lower (6.06), not counting the September 11 terrorist-caused deaths.

2. Kleck, *Targeting Guns*, 18; see also Lawrence Southwick, "Do Guns Cause Crime? Does Crime Cause Guns? A Granger Test," *Atlantic Economic Journal* 25 (1997): 256.

3. See note 1.

4. See, e.g., John R. Lott, *The Bias against Guns* (Washington, DC: Regnery, 2003); Gary A. Mauser and Dennis Maki, "An Evaluation of the 1977 Canadian Firearms Legislation: Robbery Involving a Firearm," *Applied Economics* 35 (2003): 423–36; James B. Jacobs, *Can Gun Control Work?* (Oxford: Oxford University Press, 2002); Joyce Lee Malcolm, *Guns and Violence: The English Experience* (Boston: Harvard University Press, 2002), chaps. 5–8; Jeffrey A. Miron, "Violence, Guns, and Drugs: A Cross-Country Analysis," *Journal of Law and Economics* 44 (2001): 615; David B. Kopel, "Treating Guns Like Consumer Products," *University of Pennsylvania Law Review* 148 (2000): 1213; John R. Lott, *More Guns, Less Crime*, 2d ed. (Chicago: University of Chicago Press, 2000); Kleck, *Targeting Guns;* Chester L. Britt, Gary Kleck, and David J. Bordua, "A Reassessment of the D.C. Gun Law: Some Cautionary Notes on the Use of Interrupted Time Series Designs for Policy Impact Assessment," *Law and Society Review* 30 (1996): 61–379; Joseph Sheley and James Wright, *In the Line of Fire: Youth, Guns and Violence in Urban America* (New York: Aldine, 1995), 151; Samuel Walker, *Sense and Nonsense about Crime and Drugs* (New York: Wadsworth, 1994), chaps. 10 and 13; David B. Kopel, *The Samurai, the Mountie, and the Cowboy* (Buffalo, NY: Prometheus, 1992); Hans Toch and Alan Lizotte, "Research and Policy: The Case of Gun Control" in *Psychology and Social Policy*, ed. P. Suedfeld and P. Tetlock (New York: Hemisphere Publications, 1990); Gary A. Mauser and Richard Holmes, "Evaluating the 1977 Canadian Firearms Control Legislation: An Econometric Approach," *Evaluation Review* 16 (1993): 603; Brandon Centerwall, "Homicide and the Prevalence of Handguns: Canada and the United States, 1976 to 1980," *American Journal of Epidemiology* 134 (1991): 1245–65; James D. Wright and Peter Rossi, *Armed and Dangerous: A Survey of Felons and Their Firearms* (New York: Aldine, 1986); Alan Lizotte, "The Costs of Using Gun Control to Reduce Homicide," *Bulletin of the New York Academy of Medicine* 62 (1986): 539; James D. Wright, Peter Rossi, and Kathleen Daly, *Under the Gun: Weapons, Crime, and Violence in the United States* (New York: Aldine, 1983); John Kaplan, "The Wisdom of Gun Prohibition," *Annals of the American Academy of Political and Social Sciences* 455 (1981): 11; Raymond Kessler, "Enforcement Problems of Gun Control: A Victimless Crimes Analysis," *Criminal Law Bulletin* 16 (1980): 131.

5. *First Reports Evaluating the Effectiveness of Strategies for Preventing Violence: Firearms Laws* (Washington, DC: CDC, 2003), http://www.cdc.gov/mmwr/preview/mmwrhtml/rr5214a2.htm.

6. See note 1.

7. George Newton and Franklin Zimring, *Firearms and Violence in Ameri-*

can Life (Washington, DC: Government Printing Office, 1970), 6; Don B. Kates and Daniel D. Polsby, "Long Term Non-Relationship of Firearm Availability to Homicide," *Homicide Studies* 4 (2000): 185–201.

8. Kleck, *Targeting Guns*, chap. 3.

9. Compare *Vital Statistics Report* for 2000 to *Vital Statistics Report* for 1991.

10. William A. Pridemore, "Using Newly Available Homicide Data to Debunk Two Myths about Violence in an International Context: A Research Note," *Homicide Studies* 5 (2001): 267–75, figures kindly supplied me by Prof. Pridemore; Miron, "Violence, Guns, and Drugs," 625; Randy E. Barnett and Don B. Kates, "Under Fire: The New Consensus on the Second Amendment," *Emory Law Journal* 45 (1996): 1139, 1239.

11. Quoting, respectively, Kleck, *Targeting Guns*, 254; Abstract to Martin Killias, John van Kesteren, and Martin Rindlisbacher, "Guns, Violent Crime, and Suicide in 21 Countries," *Canadian Journal of Criminology* 43 (2001): 429–48; see also Malcolm, *Guns and Violence*, 204; Philip C. Stenning, "Gun Control—A Critique of Current Policy," *Policy Options* 15 (1994): 15.

12. Quoting Newton and Zimring, *Firearms and Violence*, chap. 11; see, e.g., E. G. Krug et al., "Firearm-Related Deaths in the United States and 35 Other High- and Upper-Middle-Income Countries," *International Journal of Epidemiology* 27 (1998): 214–21.

13. See studies discussed in Kleck, *Targeting Guns*, chap. 8; Jacobs, *Can Gun Control Work?* 119–21.

14. Barnett and Kates, "Under Fire," 1236–42.

15. Malcolm, *Guns and Violence*, 209, 219.

16. John van Kesteren et al., *Criminal Victimization in 17 Industrialised Countries: Key Findings from the 2000 International Crime Victimization Surveys* (Feb. 23, 2001), http://www.minjust.nl:8080/b_organ/wodc/reports/ob187i.htm.

17. Franklin Zimring and Gordon Hawkins, *Crime Is Not the Problem: Lethal Violence in America* (New York: Oxford University Press, 1997).

18. "Homicides Jump to Record Levels," *West Australian*, March 4, 2003.

19. See discussion in Gary Kleck and Don B. Kates, *Armed: New Perspectives on Gun Control* (Buffalo, NY: Prometheus, 2001), 20–22, and further supporting references therein.

20. Delbert S. Elliott, "Life Threatening Violence Is Primarily a Crime Problem: A Focus on Prevention," *Colorado Law Review* 69 (1998): 1081–98.

21. David Kennedy and Anthony A. Braga, "Homicide in Minneapolis: Research for Problem Solving," *Homicide Studies* 2 (1998): 263, 269.

22. References for this paragraph are from Kleck and Kates, *Armed*, 20–22, and Wade Myers and Kerrilyn Scott, "Psychotic and Conduct Disorder Symptoms in Juvenile Murderers," *Homicide Studies* 2 (1998): 161–63.

23. Kleck, *Targeting Guns*, 236.

24. Murray A. Straus, "Domestic Violence and Homicide Antecedents," *Bulletin of the New York Academy of Medicine* 62 (1986): 446, 454.

25. Linda Langford, Nancy Isaac, and Sandra Adams, "Criminal and Restraining Order Histories of Intimate Partner-Related Homicide Offenders in Massachusetts, 1991–95," in *Varieties of Criminal Homicide*, ed. Paul Blackman, Vanessa Leggett, Brittawni Olson, and John P. Davis (Quantico, VA: FBI Academy Behavioral Science Unit, 2000).

26. See the review of laws in Jacobs, *Can Gun Control Work?* chap. 2.

27. Lott, *The Bias against Guns*, 6–8, 18–27, 64–66; Barnett and Kates, "Under Fire," 1239–40.

28. Barnett and Kates, "Under Fire," 1255–59 (quoting Betty Friedan and, to the same effect, Garry Wills, Ramsey Clark, and other activists and groups supporting handgun or all-gun bans).

29. Quoting then Handgun Control Inc. chairman Nelson "Pete" Shields, *Guns Don't Die, People Do* (New York: Arbor House, 1981), 124–25, emphasis added. To the same effect, see Franklin Zimring and James Zuehl, "Victim Injury and Death in Urban Robbery: A Chicago Study," *Journal of Legal Studies* 15 (1986): 1, 37–38; Matthew Yeager, *How Well Does the Handgun Protect You and Your Family?* (Handgun Control Staff of the U.S. Conference of Mayors, 1976).

30. Kleck and Kates, *Armed*, 288–93.

31. Jacobs, *Can Gun Control Work?* 14.

32. Kleck and Kates, *Armed*, 16 (quoting Marvin E. Wolfgang). Studies paralleling Kleck's include Lawrence Southwick, "Self-Defense with Guns: The Consequences," *Journal of Criminal Justice*, 28 (2000): 351–70; and Gary Mauser, "Armed Self Defense: The Canadian Case," *Journal of Criminal Justice* 24 (1996): 393–406.

33. See, e.g., Philip J. Cook and Jens Ludwig, "Defensive Gun Uses: New Evidence from a National Survey," *Journal of Quantitative Criminology* 14 (1998): 111–31; David Hemenway, "Survey Research and Self-defense Gun Use: An Explanation of Extreme Overestimates," *Journal of Criminal Law and Criminology* 87 (1997): 1443–44.

34. See note 29.

35. Colin Loftin and Ellen J. MacKenzie, "Building National Estimates of Violent Victimization," unpublished National Research Council paper, cited in Kleck and Kates, *Armed*, 247.

36. James B. Jacobs, "The Regulation of Personal Chemical Weapons: Some Anomalies in American Weapons Law," *University of Dayton Law Review* 15 (1989): 141; Massad Ayoob, *In the Gravest Extreme* (Concord, NH: Police Bookshelf, 1980).

37. Sheley and Wright, *In the Line of Fire*, 63; Wright and Rossi, *Armed and Dangerous*, 151; Philip J. Cook, "The Effect of Gun Availability on Robbery and Robbery-Murder: A Cross Section Study of 50 Cities," *Policy Studies Review Annual* 3 (1979): 776–78.

38. See discussion in Kleck and Kates, *Armed*, 17–18.

39. Franklin Zimring and Gordon Hawkins, "Concealed Handgun Permits:

The Case of the Counterfeit Deterrent," in *The Responsive Community* (Washington, DC: Center for Policy Research, 1997); Albert W. Altschuler, "Two Guns, Four Guns, Six Guns, More: Does Arming the Public Reduce Crime?" *Valparaiso University Law Review* 31 (1997): 309; Ian Ayres and John J. Donohue, "Shooting Down the 'More Guns, Less Crime' Hypothesis," *Stanford Law Review* 55 (2003): 1193.

40. Lott, *More Guns, Less Crime*, 128–58; Lott, *The Bias against Guns*, appendix 1.

41. See the seven articles printed in the *Journal of Law and Economics* 44 (October 1991). Ayres and Donohue, in "Shooting Down," vehemently disagree, but analyses by two other scholars dismiss this as a result of misevaluation, asserting that when the Ayres and Donohue results are correctly evaluated they further support Lott. See Florenz Plassman and John Whitley, "Confirming 'More Guns, Less Crime,'" *Stanford Law Review* 55 (2003): 1313.

42. See note 4.

43. For an updated version of this 1995 article, see Kleck and Kates, *Armed*, chap. 2.

44. See Kleck and Kates, *Armed*, 32–35 and the references given therein.

45. Ibid.

46. Douglas J. Wiebe, "Guns in the Home: Risky Business," *Leonard Davis Institute of Health Economics Issue Brief* 8 (2003). Compare the numerous contrary studies that are not cited, including David B. Kopel, "Lawyers, Guns and Burglars," *Arizona Law Review* 43 (2001): 346–67; Gary Kleck and Marc Gertz, "Armed Resistance to Crime: The Prevalence and Nature of Self-defense with a Gun," *Journal of Criminal Law and Criminology* 86 (1995): 150–87; Don B. Kates, "The Value of Civilian Arms Possession as Deterrent to Crime or Defense against Crime," *American Journal of Criminal Law* 18 (1991): 113; Gary Kleck, "Crime Control through the Use of Force in the Private Sector," *Social Problems* 35 (1988): 1.

47. Compare Wiebe, "Guns in the Home: Risky Business," to the following studies it fails to cite: Lott, *The Bias against Guns*, chap. 3; Kleck, *Targeting Guns*, chap. 7; Southwick, "Do Guns Cause Crime?"; Gary Kleck and E. Britt Patterson, "The Impact of Gun Control and Gun Ownership Levels on Violence Rates," *Journal of Quantitative Criminology* 9 (1993): 249–88; David McDowall, "Gun Availability and Robbery Rates: A Panel Study of Large U.S. Cities, 1974–1978," *Law and Policy* 8 (1986): 135–48; Joseph P. Magaddino and Marshall H. Medoff, "An Empirical Analysis of Federal and State Firearm Control Laws," in *Firearms and Violence: Issues of Public Policy*, ed. D. Kates (Cambridge, MA: Ballinger, 1984), 225–58; Gary Kleck, "The Relationship between Gun Ownership Levels and Rates of Violence in the United States," in *Firearms and Violence*, ed. Kates, 99–135.

48. Kleck and Kates, *Armed*, 38–40, 47, discussing false citations in the following Sloan et al. articles: "Firearms Regulations and Rates of Suicide: A

Comparison of Two Metropolitan Areas," *New England Journal of Medicine* 322 (1990): 369–73; "Handgun Regulations, Crime, Assaults and Homicide: A Tale of Two Cities," *New England Journal of Medicine* 319 (1988): 1256–62.

49. See comment in Daniel D. Polsby, "Firearms Costs, Firearms Benefits and the Limits of Knowledge," *Journal of Criminal Law and Criminology* 86 (1995): 207, 210–11; Arthur L. Kellermann et al., "Gun Ownership as a Risk Factor for Homicide in the Home," *New England Journal of Medicine* 329 (1993): 1084–91; and "Protection or Peril? An Analysis of Firearm-Related Deaths in the Home," *New England Journal of Medicine* 314 (1986): 1557–60.

50. Kleck and Kates, *Armed*, 48–53.

51. See Garen J. Wintemute, "Closing the Gap between Research and Policy: Firearms," *Injury Prevention Network Newsletter* (winter 1989–90): 21; D. A. Brent and J. A. Perper, "Reply," *Journal of the American Medical Association* 267 (1992): 3026–27.

52. Gary Mauser, "Gun Control in the United States," *Criminal Law Forum* 3 (1992): 147–59.

53. See Kleck and Kates, *Armed*, 52.

54. See, e.g., Diane Schetky, "Children and Handguns: A Public Health Concern," *American Journal of Diseases of Children* 139 (1985): 229, 230 (of eleven footnotes, four are to anti-gun lobby publications, none of their affiliations being revealed); National Committee for Injury Prevention and Control, *Meeting the Challenge* (Oxford: Oxford University Press, 1989), 3 (reiterating "facts" from a report by National Coalition to Ban Handguns without identifying it as such); see also examples cited in Kleck and Kates, *Armed*, chap. 2, nn. 11, 13.

55. See, e.g., John Sloan et al., "Correspondence," *New England Journal of Medicine* 323 (1990): 136 ("Coming from an official spokesman for the National Rifle Association, Blackman's invective is no surprise. . . . We understand [his] need to attack this paper; it is what he is paid to do"). For other examples see Kleck and Kates, *Armed*, chap. 2, nn. 7, 8, 28, 29, 33.

56. Quoted in Kleck and Kates, *Armed*, 84.

57. Gary Kleck, "BATF Gun Trace Data and the Role of Organized Gun Trafficking in Supplying Guns to Criminals," *St. Louis University Public Law Review* 18 (1999): 23–45.

58. Newton and Zimring, *Firearms and Violence* (Ammunition might have to be replaced every twenty-five years or so, but no great amount of it is needed to use a gun in crime).

59. Sheley and Wright, *In the Line of Fire*, 150–52; Wright, Rossi, and Daly, *Under the Gun*, 137–38. For detailed discussion see Don B. Kates, "Handgun Banning in Light of the Prohibition Experience" in *Firearms and Violence*, ed. Kates.

60. See, e.g., "Illegal Guns Flourish in the Trigger-Happy Philippines," *Taipei Times*, Dec. 8, 2003, http://www.taipeitimes.com/News/world/archives/2003/12/08/2003078798 (makers of cottage-manufactured guns sell .38 revolvers for $27; submachine guns for up to $215).

61. Darius Bazargan, "Balkan Gun Traffickers Target UK," BBC, Dec. 5, 2003, http://news.bbc.co.uk/1/hi/programmes/correspondent/3256318.stm.

62. "Britain's Police Chief Calls for Gun Crackdown," Reuters News America Wire Service, Aug. 1, 1994; M. L. Friedland, "Gun Control: The Options," *Criminal Law Quarterly* 18 (1975–76): 29, 34–35.

63. See note 16.

64. See "Gun Crime Growing 'Like Cancer,'" BBC, May 21, 2003, http://news.bbc.co.uk/2/hi/uk_news/england/3043701.stm; "Guns, Crack, and Child Porn—UK's Growing Crimes," Reuters, July 22, 2002.

65. Paul Bendis and Steven Balkin, "A Look at Gun Control Enforcement," *Journal of Police Science and Administration* 7 (1979): 438–48.

66. Discussion by career ATF agent-turned-criminologist William J. Vizzard, *Shots in the Dark: The Policy, Politics, and Symbolism of Gun Control* (Lanham, MD: Rowman and Littlefield, 2000), 167–69.

67. Lawrence W. Sherman et al., *The Kansas City Gun Experiment* (Washington, DC: National Institute of Justice Research in Brief, 1995).

68. Ibid., 165.

69. Jacobs, *Can Gun Control Work?* 120 (author's emphasis); Lott, *The Bias against Guns*, 229–32.

70. Under California law, for instance, the potential penalty for robbery is nine years plus a one-year enhancement if a gun was used. *Cal. Penal Code* §§ 215, 12022 (West 2004).

71. Gary Kleck, "Guns and Violence: A Summary of the Field," *Social Pathology* 1 (1995): 34.

CHAPTER 3

1. Ruth Schwartz Cohen, *A Social History of American Technology* (New York: Oxford University Press, 1997), 78–82; David A. Hounshell, *From the American System to Mass Production, 1800–1932* (Baltimore, MD: Johns Hopkins University Press, 1984).

2. Hounshell, *From the American System to Mass Production*, 322.

3. Ibid., xvi, 263–67, 322–30.

4. Robert Ricker (lawyer, former industry lobbyist, and association executive), interview by author, July 22, 2003.

5. There are nine types of Federal Firearms Licenses: Type 01, "Dealer in firearms other than destructive devices"; Type 02, "Pawnbroker in firearms other than destructive devices"; Type 03, "Collector of curios and relics"; Type 06, "Manufacturer of ammunition for firearms other than ammunition for destructive devices or armor piercing ammunition"; Type 07, "Manufacturer of firearms other than destructive devices"; Type 08, "Importer of firearms/ammunition other than destructive devices or armor piercing ammu-

nition"; Type 09, "Dealer in destructive devices"; Type 10, "Manufacturer of destructive devices, ammunition for destructive devices, or armor piercing ammunition"; and Type 11, "Importer of destructive devices, ammunition for destructive devices, or armor piercing ammunition." Bureau of Alcohol, Tobacco, and Firearms, *Types of Federal Firearms License*, formerly available at http://atf.treas.gov/firearms/nlc/ffl/ffl_types.htm.

6. Bureau of Alcohol, Tobacco and Firearms, *Frequently Asked Questions: Licensing*, formerly available at http://www.atf.treas.gov/firearms/nlc/ffl/faqs_lic.htm.

7. See "Wholesale dealer in liquors," 27 C.F.R. § 194.24 (2002); "Wholesale dealer in beer," 27 C.F.R. § 194.26.

8. Department of the Treasury, Bureau of Alcohol, Tobacco, and Firearms, "General Questions (A2), Who can get a license?" in *ATF Online: Federal Firearms Regulations Reference Guide*, formerly available at http://www.atf.gov/pub/fire-explo_pub/2000_ref.htm.

9. U. S. Treasury Department, U.S. Department of Justice, National Institute of Justice, *Guns in America: National Survey on Private Ownership and Use of Firearms* (Washington, DC, 1997), 6–7.

10. Robert Ricker, interview by author, July 22, 2003.

11. See Daniel J. Boorstin, *The Americans: The Colonial Experience* (New York: Vintage, 1958), chaps. 53, 54.

12. U.S. Department of the Treasury, Bureau of Alcohol, Tobacco, and Firearms, *Crime Gun Trace Reports (1999): National Report*, ix, ixn1 (Washington, DC).

13. See also William J. Vizzard, *Shots in the Dark: The Policy, Politics, and Symbolism of Gun Control* (Lanham, MD: Rowman and Littlefield, 2000), 23 (estimating that "the current number of guns in the United States most likely exceeds 220 million and grows at a rate of about 4 million per year").

14. U.S. Census Bureau, "Your Gateway to Census 2000," http://www .census.gov/main/www/cen2000.html.

15. *Small Arms Survey 2003: Development Denied*, http://www.small armssurvey.org/publications/yb_2003.htm. The Small Arms Survey is an independent research project located at the Graduate Institute of International Studies, Geneva, Switzerland, http://www.smallarmssurvey.org.

16. U.S. Department of Justice, *Guns in America*, 1–3, exhibit 2.

17. Ibid., 2.

18. *Small Arms Survey 2003*.

19. "The Industry White Papers: Expert Intelligence on the State of the Industry; the Future of the Gun Industry," *Shooting Industry*, July 1993, 40.

20. U.S. Department of the Treasury, *Commerce in Firearms in the United States* (Washington, DC), 5.

21. U.S. Department of Commerce, Economics and Statistics Administration, U.S. Census Bureau, *Small Arms Manufacturing 1997*, (Washington, DC), table 1.

22. U.S. Census Bureau, *1997 Economic Census: Comparative Statistics for United States,* http://www.census.gov/epcd/ec97sic/E97SUSD.HTM.

23. U.S. Department of Commerce, Economics, and Statistics Administration, U.S. Census Bureau, *Small Arms Ammunition Manufacturing 1997,* (Washington, DC), table 1.

24. U.S. Census Bureau, *1997 Economic Census.*

25. U.S. Department of the Treasury, *Commerce in Firearms in the United States,* table C.3, Federal Firearms Licensees Total, FY 1975–1999.

26. Computed by author from data in U.S. Bureau of Alcohol, Tobacco, and Firearms, *Annual Firearms Manufacturing and Export Report: 2000* (Washington, DC).

27. U.S. Department of the Treasury, *Commerce in Firearms in the United States,* 6, fig. 1. Unless otherwise noted, this report is the source of the information presented in the following four paragraphs.

28. Ibid., 11–17; U.S. General Accounting Office, *Federal Firearms Licensees: Various Factors Have Contributed to the Decline in the Number of Dealers,* March 1996 (Washington, DC).

29. U.S. Department of the Treasury, *Commerce in Firearms in the United States,* table C.3, Federal Firearms Licensees Total, FY 1975–999.

30. "Distributors' Products and Business Requirements," *Shooting Industry,* December 2002, 156.

31. See Merritt Roe Smith, "The Craft Origins of Production, 1798–1816," in *Harpers Ferry Armory and the New Technology: The Challenge of Change* (Ithaca: Cornell University Press, 1977), 52–68.

32. National Park Service, *History of the Springfield Armory,* http://www.nps.gov/spar/history.html.

33. Roe Smith, *Harpers Ferry Armory,* 28.

34. Schwartz Cohen, *A Social History of American Technology,* 78–82; Hounshell, *From the American System to Mass Production,* 28.

35. Hounshell, *From the American System to Mass Production,* 25–28; Schwartz Cohen, *A Social History of American Technology,* 80.

36. Hounshell, *From the American System to Mass Production,* 31.

37. Ibid., 40–41; Schwartz Cohen, *A Social History of American Technology,* 81.

38. Hounshell, *From the American System to Mass Production,* 45; Schwartz Cohen, *A Social History of American Technology,* 81.

39. Hounshell, *From the American System to Mass Production,* 45–46.

40. Dean K. Boorman, *The History of Colt Firearms* (New York: Lyons, 2001), 36–37.

41. Colt's Manufacturing Co., Inc., "Colt History," http:www.colt.com/CMCI/history.asp; Boorman, *History of Colt Firearms,* 44–45.

42. Boorman, *History of Colt Firearms,* 15.

43. Colt's Manufacturing, "Colt History."

44. Dean K. Boorman, *The History of Smith & Wesson Firearms* (Guilford, CT: Lyons Press, 2002), 18–19.

45. Sturm, Ruger and Co., Inc., "A Brief History of Sturm, Ruger and Company, Inc.," http://www.ruger-firearms.com, accessed February 1998.

46. Garen Wintemute, *Ring of Fire: The Handgun Makers of Southern California* (Sacramento, CA: Violence Prevention Research Program, 1994).

47. Ibid., x.

48. See, e.g., "In the Market for Guns, the Customers Aren't Coming Back for More," *Wall Street Journal,* October 26, 1999, A1.

49. Andrew W. Molchan, "Industry Insights," *American Firearms Industry,* February 1993, 74.

50. See U.S. Department of the Treasury, Bureau of Alcohol, Tobacco, and Firearms, *Civilian Firearms—Domestic Production, Importation and Exportation* (Washington, DC).

51. Department of the Treasury, *Commerce in Firearms in the United States,* 6–7.

52. "Top 10 Gun Trends of the Decade! Handguns," *Guns and Ammo,* September 1989, 38.

53. "Trends in Law Enforcement Handguns," *American Guardian,* July 1999, 33 ("How was downsizing accomplished? One major contribution was materials.").

54. See, e.g., "Handguns Today: Autoloaders," in *Gun Digest 2000,* 54th ann. ed. (1999): 117 ("As the concealed-carry movement grows across the country, the demand for small but powerful handguns grows.").

55. Bob Rogers, "Headache Cure #2000," *Shooting Sports Retailer,* January 1997, 6.

56. See, e.g., Jack Lewis, *The Gun Digest Book of Assault Weapons,* 3d ed. (Northbrook, IL: DBI Books, 1993), 41 ("one could not afford to waste even one round climbing over their heads when you were hosing them down").

57. "Calico M-100 Rifle," *American Rifleman,* January 1987, 60–61.

58. See, e.g., "A Tale of Two Fifties; 0.50-calibre Sniper Rifles Gain Popularity," *International Defense Review,* June 1, 1994, 67.

59. "The Internet Pathology Laboratory: Firearms Tutorial," Department of Pathology, University of Utah, http://www.medlib.med.utah.edu/webpath/TUTORIAL/guns/GUNINTRO.html, accessed August 30, 1999.

60. "The Miami Shootout: What Really Happened!" *Handguns,* August 1999, 66, 80.

61. D. B. Dean and K. D. Powley, "Comparative Performance of 9mm Parabellum, .38 Special and .40 Smith & Wesson Ammunition in Ballistic Gelatin," *Wound Ballistics Review* 2, no. 3 (1996): 9.

62. Ammunition expert Evan Marshall, quoted in "Anatomy of a Bullet Wound," *Los Angeles Times,* January 14, 1990, E1.

63. G. J. Wintemute, "The Relationship between Firearm Design and

Firearm Violence," *Journal of the American Medical Association* 275, no. 22 (1996): 1749 ("Reports from major cities document a contemporaneous increase in the overall severity of firearm-related injuries. The transition from revolvers to pistols is considered a key factor by many observers.").

64. A. Westrick, "Body Armor Facts: Protecting the Protectors," *Law and Order*, July 2001, 131, 132.

65. *"Officer Down": Assault Weapons and the War on Law Enforcement* (Washington, DC: Violence Policy Center, 2003).

66. U.S. Bureau of Alcohol, Tobacco, and Firearms, *Frequently Asked Questions: Licensing*. Formerly available at http://www.atf.gov/firearms/nlc/ffl/faqs_lic.htm.

67. U.S. Department of the Treasury, *Commerce in Firearms in the United States*, table C.5, "Firearms Licensees and Compliance Inspection, FY 1969–1999," A-21; U.S. General Accounting Office, *Federal Firearms Licensees*.

68. U.S. Department of the Treasury, *Commerce in Firearms in the United States*, table C.6, "Actions on Federal Firearms Licenses, FY 1975–999," A22.

69. See "Gun Dealer's License Revoked," *Seattle Post-Intelligencer*, July 2, 2003, B1.

70. Ibid.; "Despite Violations, U.S. Let Gun Shop in Sniper Case Stay Open, Records Show," *New York Times*, December 9, 2002, A1.

71. "Retracing a Trail: The Weapon," *New York Times*, October 29, 2002, A28.

72. Transcript, testimony of Robert Ricker, *NAACP v. AcuSport., Inc.*, CV 99-7037 (E.D.N.Y.) April 7, 2003, 1255.

73. U.S. Department of the Treasury, Bureau of Alcohol, Tobacco and Firearms, *Following the Gun: Enforcing Federal Laws against Firearms Traffickers* (Washington, DC, 2000), 10.

74. Ibid., 15.

75. Ibid., 41.

76. Ibid.

77. U.S. Departments of Justice and Treasury, *Gun Shows: Brady Checks and Crime Gun Traces*, January 1999, 4 (Washington, DC).

CHAPTER 4

1. Don B. Kates and Gary Kleck, *The Great American Gun Debate: Essays on Firearms and Violence* (San Francisco: Pacific Research Institute for Public Policy, 1997).

2. For a sampling of work, from a variety of disciplines, addressing the cultural groundings of gun control attitudes (both pro and con), see Jan E. Dizard, Robert M. Muth, and Stephen P. Andrews, "Introduction: Guns Made Us Free—Now What?" in *Guns in America: A Reader*, ed. Jan E. Dizard,

Robert M. Muth, and Stephen P. Andrews (New York: New York University Press, 1999); Dan M. Kahan, "The Secret Ambition of Deterrence," *Harvard Law Review* 113 (1999): 413; Gary Kleck, "Crime, Culture Conflict, and the Sources of Support for Gun Control," *American Behavioral Scientist* 4 (1996): 39; Richard Slotkin, *Gunfighter Nation: The Myth of the Frontier in Twentieth-Century America* (Norman: University of Oklahoma Press, 1998).

3. See Elke Weber, "The Utility of Measuring and Modeling Perceived Risk," in *Choice, Decision, and Measurement*, ed. A. A. J. Marley (Mahwah, NJ: Lawrence Erlbaum, 1997).

4. See Richard H. Pildes and Cass R. Sunstein, "Reinventing the Regulatory State," *University of Chicago Law Review* 62 (1995): 1.

5. See generally Karl Dake, "Orienting Dispositions in the Perception of Risk," *Journal of Cross-Cultural Psychology* 22 (1991); Mary Douglas and Aaron Wildavsky, *Risk and Culture* (Berkeley: University of California Press, 1982).

6. For an influential statement of this view, see Stephen G. Breyer, *Breaking the Vicious Circle: Toward Effective Risk Regulation, The Oliver Wendell Holmes Lectures, 1992* (Cambridge, MA: Harvard University Press, 1993).

7. See generally Richard L. Revesz, "Environmental Regulation, Cost-Benefit Analysis, and the Discounting of Human Lives," *Columbia Law Review* 99 (1999): 341.

8. See Mary Douglas, *Risk Acceptability According to the Social Sciences* (New York: Russell Sage Foundation, 1985), 59–60.

9. Joseph R. Gusfield, "The Social Symbolism of Smoking and Health," in *Smoking Policy: Law, Politics, and Culture*, ed. Robert L. Rabin and Stephen D. Sugarman (London: Oxford University Press on Demand, 1993), 49.

10. See generally Douglas and Wildavsky, *Risk and Culture*.

11. See Pildes and Sunstein, "Reinventing the Regulatory State," 38, 51–52.

12. See ibid., 51–52.

13. See generally Dake, "Orienting Dispositions in the Perception of Risk"; Douglas and Wildavsky, *Risk and Culture;* Wildavsky and Dake, "Theories of Risk Perception: Who Fears What and Why?" *Daedalus* 112 (1990): 41–60.

14. See Dake, "Orienting Dispositions in the Perception of Risk," 66–78.

15. See Leon Festinger, *A Theory of Cognitive Dissonance* (Evanston, IL: Row, 1957).

16. See Paul Slovic, "Trust, Emotion, Sex, Politics, and Science: Surveying the Risk-Assessment Battlefield," in *The Perception of Risk* (London: Earthscan, 2000), 404–5; George A. Akerlof and William T. Dickens, "The Economic Consequences of Cognitive Dissonance," *American Economic Review* (1982).

17. David K. Sherman and Geoffrey L. Cohen, "Accepting Threatening Information: Self-Affirmation and the Reduction of Defensive Biases," *Current Directions in Psychological Science* 4 (2002): 119–20. See also Roy F. Baumeister and Mark R. Leary, "The Need to Belong: Desire for Interpersonal Attachments as a Fundamental Human Motivation," *Psychological Bulletin* 117 (1995): 504.

18. See generally Slovic, "Trust, Emotion, Sex, Politics, and Science," 405–9.

19. Indeed, even individuals who *are* in a position to evaluate complex data for themselves are subject to such influences. Slovic, for example, reports experimental data showing that variation among professional toxicologists on persuasiveness of animal-carcinogen studies is explained by differences in cultural orientation. Ibid. See also Jonathan J. Kohler, "The Influence of Prior Beliefs on Scientific Judgments," *Organizational Behavior and Human Decision Processes* 56 (1993).

20. See Sushil Bikhchandani, David Hirshleifer, and Ivo Welch, "A Theory of Fads, Fashion, Custom, and Cultural Change as Informational Cascades," *Journal of Political Economy* 100, no. 5 (1992); D. Kabraman, *Modeling Facts, Culture, and Cognition in the Gun Debate* (New Haven: Yale University Press, 2003).

21. Douglas and Wildavsky, *Risk and Culture*, 81, 189.

22. B. Bruce-Briggs, "The Great American Gun War," *Public Interest* (fall 1976): 61. See also Tonso, *Gun and Society: The Social and Existential Roots of the American Attachment to Firearms* (University Press of America, 1982); James D. Wright, Peter H. Rossi, and Kathleen Daly, *Under the Gun: Weapons, Crime, and Violence in America* (New York: Aldine de Gruyter, 1983); James D. Wright, "Ten Essential Observations on Guns in America," *Society*, March–April 1995, 68; Richard Slotkin, *Gunfighter Nation*. For an excellent ethnographic account of this feature of the pro-gun culture, see Abigail Kohn, *Shooters: Myths and Realities of America's Gun Cultures* (New York: Oxford University Press, 2004).

23. See H. Taylor Buckner, "Sex and Guns: Is Gun Control Male Control?" Manuscript on file with the Harvard Law School Library.

24. See Lee Kennett and James La Verne Anderson, *The Gun in America: The Origins of a National Dilemma* (Westport, CT: Greenwood, 1975), 223–25, 231.

25. Hofstadter, "America as a Gun Culture," *American Heritage* (1970): 84.

26. Don B. Kates Jr., "Public Opinion: The Effects of Extremist Discourse on the Gun Debate," in *The Great American Gun Debate*, ed. Kates and Kleck (quoting Gary Wills, internal quotation marks omitted).

27. Dan M. Kahan and Donald Braman, "More Statistics, Less Persuasion: A Cultural Theory of Gun-Risk Perceptions," *University of Pennsylvania Law Review* 151 (2003): 1291.

28. Cf. David Hemenway, *Book Review*, formerly available at http://www.hsph.harvard.edu/faculty/hemenway/book.html.

29. Lindsay Boyer, "Who Needs Guns?" *New York Times*, June 19, 1999. (Focus Group: Women Supporters of Gun Control, conducted April 23, 2003. "I also don't want to live in a society where you have a gun, and you have a gun, and you have a gun." On file with authors.)

30. See Robert J. Spitzer, *The Politics of Gun Control* (New York: Chatham House, 1995), 25–26, 49. (Focus Group: Male Opponents of Gun Control, recorded April 24, 2003. "[The framers of the Constitution] gave us the right to be able to have free conversation. They gave us a gun to be able to protect that conversation. When that is gone, it's over.")

31. See Kahan, "The Secret Ambition of Deterrence," 452.

32. See Chris Mooney, "Double Barreled Double Standards," *Mother Jones*, October 13, 2003, http://www.motherjones.com/news/feature/2003/10/we_590_01.html (quoting Yale law professor Ian Ayres: "A lot of people would say, thank God Lott is still in the academy, but [I say] thank God he's not at my school."); John Lott, http://groups.google.com/groups?selm=23fa92fe.0209230650.202e3526%40posting._google.com (accessed Sept. 23, 2002) (written under pseudonym "Mary Rosh").

33. Cf. John R. Lott Jr., *More Guns, Less Crime: Understanding Crime and Gun Control Laws*, 2d ed. (Chicago: University of Chicago Press, 2000); Ayres, 2003 #1394 (critiquing Lott's study); and John R. Lott Jr., http://johnrlott.tripod.com (critiquing Ayres and Donohue's critique of his work).

34. Restatement (Third) Products Liability §2(b) (1998).

35. See John R. Lott, *The Bias against Guns* (Lanham, MD: Regnery, 2003).

36. Ian Ayres and John J. Donohue III, "Shooting Down the 'More Guns, Less Crime' Hypothesis," *Stanford Law Review* 55 (2003): 1193 (arguing that the effect is mixed but often decreases crime).

37. Philip Cook and Jens Ludwig, "Litigation as Regulation: Firearms," in *Regulation through Litigation*, ed. W. Kip Viscusi (Washington, DC: AEI-Brookings Joint Center for Regulatory Studies, 2002), 82.

38. See Richard Brooks, *In the Crossfire between Litigating Liability and Legislating Immunity* (New Haven: forthcoming, 2003).

39. See Cook and Ludwig, "Litigation as Regulation," 75.

40. See Guido Calabresi, *The Cost of Accidents* (New Haven: Yale University Press, 1970), 143–50 ("the point of tort law is to internalize externalities").

41. See *Losee v. Buchanan*, 51 N.Y. 476, 484–85 (1873). See also Note, "Absolute Liability for Ammunition Manufacturers," *Harvard Law Review* 108 (1995): 1679, 1684–88.

42. Cf. Brooks, *In the Crossfire* ("No one is quite sure at what point the costs of gun regulation will exceed the benefits.").

43. Nancy Pennington and Reid Hastie, "A Cognitive Theory of Juror Decision Making: The Story Model," *Cardozo Law Review* 13 (1991): 520–29.

44. See Neil Vidmar and Shari Seidman Diamond, "Juries and Expert Evidence," *Brooklyn Law Review* 61 (2001): 1121, 1138 ("The Story Model is widely accepted as a general description of how jurors process information and reach their decisions.").

45. Ibid.

46. See Vicki L. Smith, "Prototypes in the Courtroom: Lay Representations

of Legal Concepts," *Journal of Personality and Social Psychology* 61 (1991) (showing that jurors follow socially constructed prototypes, not legal definitions in assessing evidence).

47. Nancy Pennington and Reid Hastie, "Explanation-Based Decision Making: The Effects of Memory Structure on Judgment," *Journal of Experimental Psychology: Learning, Memory, and Cognition* 14 (1988),

48. See Reid Hastie, "The Role of 'Stories' in Civil Jury Judgments," *University of Michigan Journal of Law Reform* 32 (1999): 227. See Sherry S. Diamond and J. D. Casper, "Blindfolding the Jury to Verdict Consequences: Damages, Experts, and the Civil Jury," *Law and Society Review* 26 (1992): 513. See also Sherry Diamond, "Scientific Jury Selection: What Social Scientists Know and Do Not Know," *Judicature* 73 (1990): 178–83.

49. See Nelson Graves, "Firearms on School Property a Bad Idea," *Daily News Leader*, June 13, 2003.

50. John R. Lott Jr., "Keep Schools Safe—Arm the Teachers," *Record*, July 16, 2003.

51. Tom W. Smith, *1999 National Gun Policy Survey of the National Opinion Research Center: Research Findings* (Chicago: National Organization for Research, University of Chicago, 2000).

52. See Neil Feigenson, *Legal Blame: How Jurors Think and Talk about Accidents* (Washington, DC: American Psychological Association, 2000), 14; see also Gerold Mikula, Klaus R. Scherer, and Ursula Athenstaedt, "The Role of Injustice in the Elicitation of Differential Emotional Reactions," *Personality and Social Psychology Bulletin* 24 (1998).

53. See generally Norman Finkel, *Commonsense Justice: Jurors' Notions of the Law* (Cambridge, MA: Harvard University Press, 1995).

54. Feigenson, *Legal Blame*, 103.

55. See Keith J. Holyoak and Dan Simon, "Bidirectional Reasoning in Decision Making by Constraint Satisfaction," *Journal of Experimental Psychology* 128 (1999): 3; Dan Simon, Quan Lien B. Pham, and Keith J. Holyoak, "The Emergence of Coherence over the Course of Decisionmaking," *Journal of Experimental Psychology* 27 (2001): 1250; Dan Simon, "A Third View of the Black Box: Coherence Based Reasoning in Law," *University of Chicago Law Review* 71 (2004): 511.

56. Mark D. Alicke, "Culpable Causation," *Journal of Personality and Social Psychology* 63, no. 3 (1992): 368–70.

57. Vidmar and Diamond, "Juries and Expert Evidence," 1135–36, 1139.

58. See ibid., 1139.

59. See ibid.

60. 62 F. Supp.2d 802 (E.D.N.Y. 1999), *vacated*, 264 F.3d 21 (2d Cir. 2001).

61. Vanessa O'Connell and Paul M. Barrett, "Open Season: How a Jury Placed the Firearms Industry on the Legal Defensive," *Wall Street Journal*, Feb. 16, 1999, A1. This article is the source for the remainder of this paragraph.

62. Ibid.

63. Ibid.

64. Ibid.

65. Ibid.

66. *Hamilton v. Beretta U.S.A. Corp.*, 264 F.3d 21 (2nd Cir. 2001).

67. 271 F. Supp. 2d 435, 466 E.D.N.Y. (2003).

68. See *La. Rev. Stat. Ann.* art. 40 § 1799 (West 2003); *Morial v. Smith & Wesson Corp.* 785 So. 2d 1 (2001) (upholding the Louisiana Statute as constitutional).

69. See James Davidson Hunter, *Culture Wars: The Struggle to Define America* (New York: Basic Books, 1991), 320–21. Cf. Guido Calabresi, *Ideals, Beliefs, Attitudes, and the Law: Private Law Perspectives on a Public Law Problem*, 1st ed, Frank W. Abrams Lectures (Syracuse, NY: Syracuse University Press, 1985).

70. Compare Glendon, *Abortion and Divorce in Western Law*.

71. Margery Eagan, "Rally Proves Gun Lovers Are Still Out There," *Boston Herald*, May 18, 1999, 4. See also Richard Cohen, "The Tame West," *Washington Post*, July 15, 1999, A25; Ted Flickinger, "Dodge City," *Pittsburgh Post-Gazette*, June 1, 1999, A10; Perry Young, "We Are All to Blame," *Chapel Hill Herald*, April 24, 1999, 4.

72. Norman W. Nielsen, letter to the editor, *Los Angeles Times*, April 30, 1999, B6. See also Robert Reno, "NRA Aims but Shoots Self in Foot," *Newsday*, May 9, 1999, 5H (sign at gun control rally: "Gun owners have penis envy.").

73. See Charlton Heston, "The Second Amendment: America's First Freedom," in *Guns in America: A Reader*, ed. Jan E. Dizard, Robert M. Muth, and Stephen P. Andrews (New York: New York University Press, 1999); David Keim, "NRA Chief Proves Big Draw at Vote Freedom First Rally," *Knoxville News-Sentinel*, Nov. 2, 2000, A1.

CHAPTER 5

1. *Hamilton v. Accu-Tek*, 62 F. Supp. 2d 802 (E.D.N.Y. 1999), *vacated*, *Hamilton v. Beretta U.S.A. Corp.*, 264 F.3d 21 (2d Cir. 2001).

2. Bob Van Voris, "Gun Cases Use Tobacco Know-How: New Orleans, Chicago Lead the Charge," *National Law Journal* 21, no. 15 (1998).

3. David Kairys, "A Philadelphia Story," *Legal Affairs*, May–June 2003, 63–67.

4. Ibid.; Paul M. Barrett, "The Big Bang: Evolution of a Cause," *Wall Street Journal*, October 21, 1999.

5. Kairys, "A Philadelphia Story," 66.

6. Barrett, "The Big Bang."

7. Kairys, "A Philadelphia Story," 63–67; Barrett, "The Big Bang."

8. "Philadelphia Mayor Ed Rendell Offers Ways to Prevent Handgun Violence," U.S. Conference of Mayors, June 1998, formerly available at http://www.usmayors.org/uscm/reno-live/sunday.htm.

9. Fox Butterfield, "Chicago Is Suing over Guns from Suburbs," *New York Times*, Nov. 13, 1998, sec. A, final edition.

10. David Barstow, "A Chicago Story of Guns, Gangs, and Self-Defense: To Destroy or Defend," *St. Petersburg Times*, January 3, 1999.

11. Linnet Myers, "Go Ahead . . . Make Her Day: With Her Direct Approach and Quiet Confidence, Chicago Lawyer Anne Kimball Gives Gunmakers a Powerful Weapon," *Chicago Tribune Magazine*, May 2, 1999, 12.

12. Barstow, "A Chicago Story of Guns, Gangs, and Self-Defense."

13. Myers, "Go Ahead . . . Make Her Day," 12.

14. Kairys, "A Philadelphia Story," 63–67; Myers, "Go Ahead . . . Make Her Day," 12.

15. "Following in Tobacco's Footsteps: Three Cities Take Aim at Gun Manufacturers," *Products Liability Law and Strategy*, Dec. 17, 1998, 6.

16. Complaint, *City of Chicago v. Beretta U.S.A. Corp.*, No. 98-CH15596 (Ill. Cir. Ct. Cook County) (Filed Nov. 12, 1998).

17. Van Voris, "Gun Cases Use Tobacco Know-How."

18. Peter Harry Brown and Daniel G. Abel, *Outgunned: Up against the NRA* (New York: Free Press, 2003), 14; Marcia Coyle, "Runners-Up," *National Law Journal*, December 26, 1994, C11; Gregory Roberts, "Wendell's New War: Wendell Gauthier Has Made Millions for Victims of Fire, Plane Crashes, and Explosions. Now He's Taking on the $100 Billion Tobacco Industry," *Times-Picayune* (New Orleans, LA), May 29, 1994.

19. Peter Pringle, *Cornered: Big Tobacco at the Bar of Justice* (New York: Henry Holt and Company, 1998), 7.

20. Douglas McCollam, "Long Shot," *American Lawyer*, June 1999, 86.

21. *Castano v. American Tobacco Co.*, 84 F.3d 734 (5thCir. 1996).

22. McCollam, "Long Shot," 86.

23. Brown and Abel, *Outgunned*, 17.

24. Peter J. Boyer, "Big Guns," *New Yorker*, May 17, 1999, 53.

25. Brown and Abel, *Outgunned*, 10.

26. Ibid., 18.

27. Boyer, "Big Guns," 54–67.

28. Brown and Abel, *Outgunned*, 1–4.

29. Van Voris, "Gun Cases Use Tobacco Know-How."

30. Complaint, *Morial v. Smith & Wesson Corp.*, No. 98-18578 (Civ. Dist. Ct. Parish of Orleans) (Filed Oct. 31 1998).

31. Complaint, *City of Chicago v. Beretta U.S.A. Corp.*, No. 98-CH15596 (Ill. Cir. Ct. Cook County) (Filed Nov. 12, 1998); Kairys, "A Philadelphia Story," 63–67.

32. "Following in Tobacco's Footsteps."

33. Complaint, *Ganim v. Smith & Wesson Corp.*, No. CV99-036-1279 (Conn. Super. Ct.) (Filed Jan. 27, 1999).

34. Complaint, *Penellas v. Arms Tech., Inc.*, No. 99-01941 (Fla. Cir. Ct. 11th Jud. Cir.) (Filed Jan. 27, 1999).

35. Brown and Abel, *Outgunned*, 37–38; see also Brady Center to Prevent Handgun Violence, Legal Action Project, "Liability Suits against Gun Manufacturers, Dealers, and Owners," http://www.gunlawsuits.org/docket/docket.php#pec.

36. Brown and Abel, *Outgunned*, 291.

37. Ibid., 151.

38. Barrett, "The Big Bang."

39. Paul M. Barrett, "HUD May Join Assault on Gun Makers," *Wall Street Journal*, July 28, 1999; John Riley, "Cuomo's Stepping Stone/HUD Position Was a Platform for His Political Career," *Newsday*, August 23, 2001.

40. Eric Lipton, "Duel for the Limelight: A Special Report: Behind Gun Deal, 2 Ambitious Democrats Wrestle for the Credit," *New York Times*, April 3, 2000.

41. Rick Valliere, "Boston Drops Suit against Gun Industry," *BNA Product Liability Daily*, April 11, 2002.

42. Gregory Korte, "Drop Gun Suit, City Advised," *Cincinnati Enquirer*, April 30, 2003.

43. Steven Harras, "Cincinnati Drops Suit against Gun Industry," *BNA Product Liability Daily*, May 22, 2003.

44. *Spence v. Glock*, 227 F.3d 308, 316 (5th Cir 2000); *Hamilton v. Accu-Tek*, 935 F. Supp. 1307, 1332 (E.D.N.Y. 1996).

45. Barrett, "The Big Bang" (quoting David Kairys).

46. Walter K. Olson, *The Rule of Lawyers: How the New Litigation Elite Threatens America's Rule of Law* (New York: St. Martin's, 2003), 102, 108.

47. Ibid., 105.

48. Michael I. Krauss, "Regulation Masquerading as Judgment: Chaos Masquerading as Tort Law," *Mississippi Law Journal* 71 (2001): 631, 656.

49. Barrett, "The Big Bang."

50. Brown and Abel, *Outgunned*, 6; Fox Butterfield, "Results in Tobacco Litigation Spur Cities to File Gun Suits," *New York Times*, Dec. 24, 1998.

51. Brown and Abel, *Outgunned*, 6.

52. Ibid., 288–89.

53. Ibid., 74.

54. Matt Labash, "Lawyers, Guns, and Money," *Weekly Standard*, February 1, 1999, 25.

CHAPTER 6

1. See Karl von Clausewitz, *On War*, trans. J. J. Graham (Harmondsworth: Penguin, 1968).

2. Wendell Gauthier, quoted in Peter H. Brown and Daniel G. Abel, *Outgunned: Up against the NRA* (New York: Free Press, 2003), 10.

3. Elisa Barnes, quoted in Walter K. Olson, *The Rule of Lawyers: How the New Litigation Elite Threatens America's Rule of Law* (New York: St. Martin's, 2003), 101.

4. On capture theory, see James Q. Wilson, *The Politics of Regulation* (New York: Basic Books, 1980), 357–94; Jerry L. Mashaw and David L. Harfst, *The Struggle for Auto Safety* (Boston: Harvard University Press, 1990), 16–19.

5. This paragraph draws heavily on Robert J. Spitzer, *The Politics of Gun Control*, 2d ed. (New York: Chatham House, 1998), 103–5 (discussing the 1934, 1938, and 1968 acts), 74, 80–81 (discussing the CPSC exemption), 69–89 (discussing NRA lobbying power), and 110–14 (discussing the 1986 act); Osha Gray Davidson, *Under Fire: The NRA and the Battle for Gun Control*, exp. ed. (Iowa City: University of Iowa Press, 1998), generally (discussing NRA lobbying power), 137 (NRA influence at the state level).

6. James B. Jacobs, *Can Gun Control Work?* (New York: Oxford University Press, 2002), 51.

7. This membership figure is from Richard Robinson, Tennessee field representative for the NRA, quoted in Owen Schroeder, "Movement Afoot to Form Local NRA Committee," *Leaf-Chronicle*, Jan. 12, 2003, 7B. Davidson, *Under Fire*, 306, puts the figure lower at 2.7 million members in 1998, a figure that may include deceased lifetime members. See also Spitzer, *Gun Control*, 70. 2002 contribution figures are from the State of Pennsylvania's Department of State web site, formerly available at http://web.dos.state.pa.us/perl/charities/dsf/creapat.cgi. A copy of this information is currently on file with the author. 2000 election contribution figures based on NRA Political Victory Fund financial reports filed with the Federal Election Commission and available at http://www.tray.com. A copy of this information is on file with the author.

8. This membership figure is from Geneva Overholser, "Staying on Target; With Plans for Theme Restaurant on Times Square, the NRA Continues to Lack Common Sense," *Chicago Tribune*, May 31, 2000, 23 (citing 500,000 Handgun Control, Inc., members). See also Spitzer, *Gun Control*, 90. 2002 contribution figures are from the State of Pennsylvania's Department of State web site, formerly available at http://web.dos.state.pa.us/perl/charities/dsf/creapat .cgi. A copy of this information is currently on file with the author.

9. Davidson, *Under Fire*, 65–66.

10. Ibid., 80.

11. Spitzer, *Gun Control*, 80–81.

12. Davidson, *Under Fire*, 93.

13. This paragraph and the next draw heavily on ibid., 232.

14. Jacobs, *Can Gun Control Work?* 48–52; Stephen P. Teret et al., "Support for New Policies to Regulate Firearms," *New England Journal of Medicine* 339 (1998): 813.

15. Brown, *Outgunned*, 5.

16. Davidson, *Under Fire*, 53–78.

17. The rest of this paragraph draws heavily on Peter H. Schuck, *The Limits of Law: Essays on Democratic Governance* (Boulder, CO: Westview, 2000), 204–50.

18. William N. Eskridge, Philip P. Frickey, and Elizabeth Garrett, *Cases and Materials on Legislation: Statutes and the Creation of Public Policy*, 3d ed. (St. Paul, MN: West, 2001), 66–69.

19. Ibid., 66; McNollGast, "Legislative Intent: The Use of Positive Political Theory in Statutory Interpretation," *Law and Contemporary Problems* 57 (1994): 3.

20. Figures from the Library of Congress's "Thomas" web site, http://thomas.loc.gov/bss/d107/d107laws.html.

21. New York State Legislative Bill Drafting, "Preface," *2001 Legislative Digest* (Albany: New York State Legislative Bill Drafting, 2002).

22. Michael Walzer, *Spheres of Justice* (New York: Basic Books, 1983), 10, 20.

23. Davidson, *Gun Control*, 64–65.

24. Brown, *Outgunned*, 10.

25. Douglas McCollam, "Long Shot," *American Lawyer*, June 1999 (quoted in Olson, *Rule of Lawyers*, 95, and Brown, *Outgunned*, 17).

26. Olson, *Rule of Lawyers*, 77–78, 226–29, 263–92.

27. Philip J. Cook and Jens Ludwig, "Litigation as Regulation: Firearms," in *Regulation through Litigation*, ed. W. Kip Viscusi (Washington, DC: AEI-Brookings Joint Center for Regulatory Studies, 2002), 93.

28. See Stephen C. Yeazell, *Civil Procedure*, 5th ed. (New York: Aspen, 2000), chap. 7 (discussing the history of the discovery process and its modern functions).

29. The "settlement value" of tort claims is calculated in precisely this manner.

30. See Lynn Mather, "Theorizing about Trial Courts: Lawyers, Policy-making, and Tobacco Litigation," *Law and Social Inquiry* 23 (1998): 897, 918–25 (on the use of tobacco litigation to frame the legislative and public debate over tobacco regulation).

31. Deborah Stone, *Policy Paradox: The Art of Political Decision Making* (New York: Norton, 1988), 248.

32. *Morial v. Smith & Wesson*, 785 So. 2d 1, 11 (2001).

33. *Sturm, Ruger and Co. v. City of Atlanta*, 560 S.E.2d 525 (Ga. Ct. App. 2002); *Mayor of Detroit v. Arms Tech.*, 669 N.W.2d 845 (Mich. App. 2003).

34. HR 1036, §§ 2(a)(1), 2(a)(6) 108th Cong., 2d Sess. (2003).

35. Ibid., § 2(a)(6).

36. *Protection of Lawful Commerce in Arms Act*, HR 181, HR 1036, 108th Cong., 1st sess., *Congressional Record*, April 9, 2003, H2944–2950.

37. Monica Fennel, "Missing the Mark in Maryland: How Poor Drafting and Implementation Vitiated a Model State Gun Control Law," *Hamline Journal of Public Law and Policy* 13 (1992): 43–45.

38. John Fowler, "Will a Repeal of Gun Manufacturer Immunity from Civil Suits Untie the Hands of the Judiciary?" *McGeorge Law Review* 34 (2003): 339, 347–49.

39. *Kelley v. R.G. Industries*, 497 A.2d 1143, 1151 (1985).

40. *Md. Ann. Code* art. 27 §§ 36I-J (Bender, 2002).

41. Sarah Koenig, "Elich Clarifies Gun Panel Remark," *Baltimore Sun*, Sept. 18, 2002, 1B; Fennell, "Missing the Mark," 48.

42. *Merrill v. Navegar*, 110 Cal. Rptr. 2d 370, 373 (2001).

43. See Fowler, "Repeal of Gun Manufacturer Immunity," 347–49.

44. See Anthony J. Sebok and John C. P. Goldberg, *The Coming Tort Reform Juggernaut: Are There Constitutional Limits on How Much the President and Congress Can Do in This Area?* Findlaw's Writ: Legal Commentary, http://writ.news.findlaw.com/sebok/20030519.html.

CHAPTER 7

1. Deborah Hensler, "The New Social Policy Torts: Litigation as a Legislative Strategy—Some Preliminary Thoughts on a New Research Project," *DePaul Law Review* 51 (winter 2001): 498.

2. Lawrence S. Greenwald and Cynthia A. Shay, "Municipalities' Suits against Gun Manufacturers—Legal Folly," *Journal of Health Care Law and Policy* 4 (2000): 14–15.

3. See Jon S. Vernick and Stephen P. Teret, "A Public Health Approach to Regulating Firearms as Consumer Products," *University of Pennsylvania Law Review* 148 (2000): 1193–246.

4. Richard A. Nagareda, "In the Aftermath of the Mass Tort Class Action," *Georgetown Law Journal* 85 (1996): 296.

5. The leading exposition of this position remains David Rosenberg, "The Causal Connection in Mass Exposure Cases: A 'Public Law' Vision of the Tort System," *Harvard Law Review* 97 (1984): 851–929.

6. See Hanoch P. Dagan and James J. White, "Government, Citizens, and Injurious Industries," *New York University Law Review* 75 (2000): 354–428.

7. See Michael I. Krauss, Regulation, "Masquerading as Judgment: Chaos Masquerading as Tort Law," *Mississippi Law Journal* 71 (winter 2001): 656; H. Sterling Burnett, "Suing Gun Manufacturers: Hazardous to Our Health," *Texas Review of Law and Politics* 5 (spring 2001): 441.

8. See David A. Dana, "Public Interest and Private Lawyers: Toward a Normative Evaluation of Parens Patriae Litigation by Contingency Fee," *DePaul Law Review* 51 (winter 2001): 323.

9. See Erichson, chapter 5, this volume.

10. The web site of the Brady Center to Prevent Gun Violence provides updates on the status of public entity lawsuits against the gun industry. See http://www.gunlawsuits.org/docket/docket.php#pec (last accessed Nov. 17, 2004).

11. See Vanessa O'Connell and Paul M. Barrett, "As Lawsuits Falter, a Big Gun Maker Retools Its Image," *Wall Street Journal*, Oct. 16, 2002, A1.

12. See Richard A. Nagareda, "Outrageous Fortune and the Criminalization of Mass Torts," *Michigan Law Review* 96 (1998): 1121–98.

13. Ibid., 1137–43.

14. Joseph Sanders, *Bendectin on Trial* (Ann Arbor: University of Michigan Press, 1998), 131–32.

15. See John C. P. Goldberg and Benjamin C. Zipursky, "Cause for Concern: A Comment on the Twerski-Sebok Plan for Administering Negligent Marketing Claims against Gun Manufacturers," *Connecticut Law Review* 32 (summer 2000): 1411–23.

16. See Timothy D. Lytton, "Should Government Be Allowed to Recover the Costs of Public Services from Tortfeasors? Tort Subsidies, the Limits of Loss Spreading, and the Free Public Services Doctrine," *Tulane Law Review* 76 (2002): 727–81.

17. For excellent intellectual histories of tort law in the United States, see G. Edward White, *Tort Law in America: An Intellectual History* (New York: Oxford University Press, 2003); John C. P. Goldberg, "Twentieth Century Tort Theory," *Georgetown Law Journal* 91 (2003): 513–83.

18. John C. P. Goldberg, "Unloved: Tort in the Modern Legal Academy," *Vanderbilt Law Review* 55 (2002): 1510–11.

19. See Oliver Wendell Holmes Jr., *The Common Law* (Boston: Little, Brown and Company, 1881).

20. Leon Green, "Tort Law Public Law in Disguise (Part I)," *Texas Law Review* 38 (1959): 1.

21. William L. Prosser, *Handbook on the Law of Torts* (St. Paul, MN: West, 1941), 15. I am grateful to John Goldberg for pointing me to this telling passage from Prosser.

22. See generally Guido Calabresi, *The Costs of Accidents* (New Haven: Yale University Press, 1970); see also ibid., 135–43.

23. Michael L. Wells, "Scientific Policymaking and the Torts Revolution: The Revenge of the Ordinary Observer," *Georgia Law Review* 26 (spring 1992): 727.

24. See, e.g., Jules Coleman, *Risks and Wrongs* (New York: Cambridge University Press, 1992); Ernest J. Weinrib, *The Idea of Private Law* (Cambridge, MA: Harvard University Press, 1995); Arthur Ripstein, *Equality, Responsibility, and the Law* (New York: Cambridge University Press, 1999).

25. See Barry E. Adler, Jules Coleman, and Arthur Ripstein, "Lawyers, Guns, and Money," *Cornell Journal of Law and Public Policy* 10 (fall 2000): 154–58.

26. Ibid., 158–59.

27. Gary T. Schwartz, "Cigarette Litigation's Offspring: Assessing Tort Issues Related to Guns, Alcohol, and Other Controversial Products in Light of the Tobacco Wars," *Pepperdine Law Review* 27 (2000): 754.

28. Ronald Reagan, *Public Papers of the Presidents of the United States: Ronald Reagan 1981*, vol. 1 (Washington, DC: Government Printing Office, 1982).

29. William J. Clinton, *Public Papers of the Presidents of the United States: William J. Clinton 1996*, vol. 1 (Washington, DC: Government Printing Office, 1997), 79.

30. See Colin Camerer, Samuel Issacharoff, George Loewenstein, Ted O'Donoghue, and Matthew Rabin, "Regulation for Conservatives: Behavioral Economics and the Case for 'Asymmetric Paternalism,'" *University of Pennsylvania Law Review* 151 (2003): 1211–54; Christine Jolls, Cass R. Sunstein, and Richard Thayer, "A Behavioral Approach to Law and Economics," *Stanford Law Review* 50 (1998): 1471–550.

31. See Stephen G. Breyer, *Breaking the Vicious Circle* (Cambridge, MA: Harvard University Press, 1993).

32. See Lisa Heinzerling, "Regulatory Costs of Mythic Proportions," *Yale Law Journal* 107 (1998): 1981–2070.

33. 3 C.F.R. 127 (1981).

34. Lisa Schultz Bressman, "Beyond Accountability: Arbitrariness and Legitimacy in the Administrative State," *New York University Law Review* 78 (2003): 487.

35. 3 C.F.R. 638 (1993).

36. See Elena Kagan, "Presidential Administration," *Harvard Law Review* 114 (June 2001): 2290–99.

37. 3 C.F.R. 204 (2002).

38. See Brent W. Landau, "State Bans on City Gun Lawsuits," *Harvard Journal on Legislation* 37 (summer 2000): 623–38; see also Lytton, chapter 6, this volume.

39. *Daubert v. Merrell Dow Pharmaceuticals, Inc.*, 509 U.S. 579, 597 (1993).

40. *Daubert*, 509 U.S. at 583.

41. Ibid., 590.

42. *General Elec. Co. v. Joiner*, 522 U.S. 136, 146 (1997).

43. *Kumho Tire Co., Ltd. v. Carmichael*, 526 U.S. 137, 152 (1999).

44. See David Faigman, David Kaye, Michael Saks, and Joseph Sanders, eds., *Modern Scientific Evidence* (St. Paul, MN: West, 2002).

45. See Donald G. Gifford, "Public Nuisance as a Mass Products Liability Tort," *University of Cincinnati Law Review* 71 (spring 2003): 741–837; see also Note, "Developments in the Law—The Paths of Civil Litigation," *Harvard Law Review* 113 (2000): 1752–875.

46. See Robert L. Rabin, "Enabling Torts," *DePaul Law Review* 49 (winter 1999): 435–53.

47. Michael D. Green, D. Michal Freedman, and Leon Gordis, "Reference Guide on Epidemiology," in Federal Judicial Center, *Reference Manual on Scientific Evidence* (Washington, DC: Lexis, 2000), 348–49.

48. Ibid., 340–45.

49. See David W. Robertson, "The Common Sense of Cause in Fact," *Texas Law Review* 75 (1997): 1770.

50. Aaron Twerski and Anthony J. Sebok, "Liability without Cause? Further Ruminations on Cause-in-Fact as Applied to Handgun Liability," *Connecticut Law Review* 32 (summer 2000): 1403.

51. *NAACP v. AcuSport, Inc.*, 271 F. Supp. 2d 435, 513–15 (E.D.N.Y. 2003).

52. See *Sterling v. Velsicol Chem. Corp.*, 855 F.2d 1188, 1200 (6th Cir. 1988).

53. The song appears on Tom Lehrer, *That Was the Year That Was*, reprise compact disc 6179.

54. *City of Erie v. Pap's A.M.*, 529 U.S. 277, 291 (2000) (O'Connor, J., plurality opinion).

55. *Morrison v. Olson*, 487 U.S. 654 (1988).

56. Ibid., 730 (Scalia, J., dissenting).

CHAPTER 8

1. Much of the description of the tobacco problem and tobacco control policy efforts draws from Robert Rabin and Stephen Sugarman, eds., *Regulating Tobacco* (New York: Oxford University Press, 2001); Robert Rabin and Stephen Sugarman, eds., *Smoking Policy* (Oxford: Oxford University Press on Demand, 1993); the many reports on smoking from the U.S. surgeon general (see http://www.cdc.gov/tobacco/), and the author's personal experience in the tobacco control movement.

2. Much of the description of the gun problem and gun control policy efforts draws from other chapters in this book; James B. Jacobs, *Can Gun Control Work?* (New York: Oxford University Press, 2002); J. Ludwig and P. Cook, eds., *Evaluating Gun Policy* (Washington, DC: Brookings Institute, 2002); Philip J. Cook and Jens Ludwig, "Litigation as Regulation: Firearms," in *Regulation through Litigation*, ed. W. Kip Viscusi (Washington, DC:

AEI-Brookings Joint Center for Regulatory Studies, 2002); Gary Kleck, *Targeting Guns* (New York: Aldine, 1997); Brady Campaign to Prevent Gun Violence (http://www.bradycampaign.org/); Violence Policy Center (http://www.vpc.org/); "First Reports Evaluating the Effectiveness of Strategies for Preventing Violence: Firearms Laws from the Task Force on Community Preventive Services" (http://www.cdc.gov/mmwr/preview/mmwrhtml/rr5214a2.htm).

3. Franklin E. Zimring and Jeffrey Fagan, "The Search for Causes in an Era of Crime Declines: Some Lessons from the Study of New York City Homicide," *Crime and Delinquency* 46 (2000): 446; Jeffrey Fagan, Franklin E. Zimring, and June Kim, "Declining Homicide in New York City: A Tale of Two Trends," *Journal of Criminal Law and Criminology* 88 (1998): 1277.

4. Much of the description of tobacco litigation draws from Stephen D. Sugarman, "Book Reviews," *Journal of Policy Analysis and Management* 22 (2003): 712; Stephen D. Sugarman, "Review of W. Kip Viscusi, *Smoke-filled Rooms: A Postmortem on the Tobacco Deal*" *Law and Politics Book Review* 13 (January 2003): 1; Stephen D. Sugarman, "Mixed Results from Recent United States Tobacco Litigation," *Tort Law Review* 10 (2002): 94; Stephen D. Sugarman, "The Smoking War and the Role of Tort Law," in *The Law of Obligations: Essays in Celebration of John Fleming*, ed. P. Cane and J. Stapleton (Gloustershire: Clarendon, 1998).

5. Restatement (Third) Torts: Products Liability §2(b) (1998).

6. Restatement (Second) Torts § 402A, comment i (1965).

7. Restatement (Third) Torts: Products Liability § 2, comment e (1998).

8. Restatement (Third) Torts: Liability for Physical Harm (Basic Principles), Tentative Draft No. 1 (2001) § 20.

9. *Kelley v. R.G. Industries, Inc.*, 497 A.2d 1143 (Md. 1985).

10. *Md. Code Ann.* art. 27 § 36-I.

11. Jim Hughes, "Punitive-Award Limits Awaiting Legal Bellwether," *Denver Post*, January 12, 2004.

12. *Carter v. Brown & Williamson Tobacco Corp.*, 778 So. 2d 932 (2000); V. Wakefield, "Patience, Persistence Pay Off for Man Who Beat Big Tobacco," *Florida Times Union*, March 9, 2001.

13. "Ex-Smoker's Estate Receives Settlement," *Associated Press*, August 28, 2003, previously available at http://www.ajc.com/news/content/news/ap/ap-story.html/National/AP.V0808.AP-Smokers-Trial.htm.

14. G. Winter, "Jury Awards $5.5 Million in a Secondhand Smoke Case," *New York Times*, June 20, 2002.

15. *Engle v. R. J. Reynolds Tobacco Corp.*, No. 94-08273 CA-22 (Fla. Civ. Ct., Nov. 6, 2000).

16. Barry Meier, "Huge Award for Smokers Is Voided by Appeals Court," *New York Times*, May 22, 2003.

17. Susan Finch, "Jurors Gives Split Tobacco Verdict," *Times Picayune*, July 29, 2003.

18. Myron Levin, "Tobacco Giant, in a Shift, Pays Victim," *Los Angeles Times*, October 2, 2003.

19. "Federal Appeals Court Upholds Dismissal of Damage Claims in HMO Lawsuit," Philip Morris Press Release, September 16, 2003.

20. Myron Levin, "Philip Morris Loses Lawsuit," *Los Angeles Times*, March 22, 2003.

21. For a more optimistic appraisal, see R. Daynard, "Why Tobacco Litigation?" *Tobacco Control* 12 (2003): 1.

22. See, e.g., Stanton A. Glantz, John Slade, Lisa A. Bero, Peter Hanaver, and Deborah E. Barnes. *The Cigarette Papers* (Berkeley: University of California Press, 1996).

23. Much of the description of gun litigation draws from other chapters in this book and Peter Harry Brown and Daniel G. Abel, *Outgunned: Up against the NRA* (New York: Free Press, 2003).

CHAPTER 9

1. At the symposium of this volume's contributors, a lively discussion occurred concerning whether it is accurate or useful to refer to the gun control plaintiffs as a collective "they." Those contributors who advocate strict controls emphasized the absence of any unified grand strategy similar to that of the NAACP Legal Defense and Education Fund during the civil rights movement. Indeed, these advocates pointed to many differences—with respect to litigation goals, liability theories, public education strategies, and other factors—among gun control groups and even within the relatively well-coordinated coalition of municipalities suing the industry. Other contributors, while acknowledging these differences, insisted that the many points of agreement and cooperation among gun control groups justify the use of the shorthand "they."

2. See Kahan, Braman, and Gastil, chapter 4, this volume.

3. See Robert L. Rabin, "The Third Wave of Tobacco Tort Litigation," in *Regulating Tobacco*, ed. Robert Rabin and Stephen D. Sugarman (Oxford: Oxford University Press on Demand, 2001), 176–206.

4. I am unaware of any significant gun control tort litigation in Europe. This is certainly not because of an absence of firearms in private hands there. According to a United Nations study released in July 2003, there are an estimated 67 million privately owned firearms in the European Union states, or roughly seventeen guns per one hundred people, with almost double that rate in France and Germany. This compares with between eighty-three and ninety-six guns per one hundred people in the United States. Daniel B. Schneider, "Firearms in Europe," *New York Times*, July 10, 2003, A6. See also "Switzerland and the Gun," *BBC News*, Sept. 27, 2001, http://news.bbc.co.uk/1/hi/world/europe/1566715.stm.

5. See, e.g., Gregory Korte, "Drop Gun Suit, City Advised," *Cincinnati Enquirer,* Apr. 30, 2003, available at 2003 WL 55041752 (firm representing city says it spent $425,000 in billable hours and $136,000 in expenses in unsuccessful suit); John Tierney, "A New Push to Grant Gun Industry Immunity from Suits," *New York Times,* Apr. 4, 2003, A12 (trade association says litigation has cost industry more than $100 million in legal fees).

6. See Wagner, chapter 11, this volume; see also *Johnson v. Bulls Eye Shooter Supply,* 2003 WL 21639244 (Wash. Super. Ct. June 27, 2003); *City of Chicago v. Beretta,* 2004 Ill. LEXIS 1665 (Ill. 2004).

7. Kahan, Braman, and Gastil, in chapter 4 of this volume, argue, based on other conflicts over culturally divisive issues, that a response of this kind is readily predictable.

8. Fox Butterfield, "Lawsuits Lead Gun Maker to File for Bankruptcy," *New York Times,* June 24, 1999, A14 (Davis Industries).

9. Mike Allen, "Colt to Curtail Sale of Handguns," *New York Times,* Oct. 11, 1999, A1.

10. See http://www.gunlawsuits.org/docket/smithandwesson.php.

11. See, e.g., Brent W. Landau, "State Bans on City Gun Lawsuits," *Harvard Journal on Legislation* 37 (2000): 623, 626.

12. See Douglas C. Bice and David D. Hemley, "The Market for New Handguns: An Empirical Investigation," *Journal of Law and Economics* 45 (2002): 251.

13. Wendy Wagner, in chapter 11 of this volume, discusses this new information.

14. See William Glaberson, "Gun Makers Repel Lawsuit by N.A.A.C.P.," *New York Times,* July 22, 2003, B1.

15. Philip Cook and Jens Ludwig, "Litigation as Regulation: Firearms," in *Regulation through Litigation,* ed. W. Kip Viscusi (Washington, DC: AEI-Brookings Joint Center for Regulatory Studies, 2002), 91.

16. See, e.g., James B. Jacobs, *Can Gun Control Work?* (New York: Oxford University Press, 2002).

17. I recognize, of course, that tort adjudication is one form of risk regulation. See Peter H. Schuck, "Comment: Regulation, Litigation, and Science," in *Regulation through Litigation,* ed. Viscusi, 178–81. For the present purpose, however, I use "risk regulation" to refer to nonjudicial regulatory techniques.

18. Henry M. Hart Jr. and Albert M. Sacks, *The Legal Process: Basic Problems in the Making and Application of Law* (Westbury, NY: Foundation Press, 1958); cf. Akhil Reed Amar, "Law Story," *Harvard Law Review* 102 (1989): 688 (critiquing the legal process theory generally).

19. See, e.g., Isaac Ehrlich and Richard Posner, "An Economic Analysis of Legal Rulemaking," *Journal of Legal Studies* 3 (1974): 257; Rogers M. Smith, "Political Jurisprudence, the 'New Institutionalism,' and the Future of Public Law," *American Political Science Review* 82 (1988): 89.

20. Neil K. Komesar, *Imperfect Alternatives: Choosing Institutions in Law,*

Economics, and Public Policy (Chicago: University of Chicago Press, 1994); see also Peter H. Schuck, *The Limits of Law: Essays on Democratic Governance* (St. Paul, MN: Westview, 2000), 420.

21. Courts may also need to address institutional competence issues when they engage in statutory interpretation requiring them to decide whether the legislature did, or the court should, decide the legal question at issue.

22. Peter H. Schuck, *Suing Government: Citizen Remedies for Official Wrongs* (New Haven: Yale University Press, 1983), 178.

23. See, e.g., Donald L. Horowitz, *The Courts and Social Policy* (Washington, DC: Brookings Institute, 1977); Ross Sandler and David Schoenbrod, *Government by Decree: What Happens When Courts Run Government* (New Haven: Yale University Press, 2003); sources cited in Schuck, *The Limits of Law*, 466n103.

24. See, e.g., Komesar, *Imperfect Alternatives;* Peter H. Schuck, *Diversity in America: Keeping Government at a Safe Distance* (Cambridge, MA: Belknap, 2003), chap. 8; Schuck, *The Limits of Law*, chap. 13.

25. The discussion of these criteria draws, sometimes verbatim, on Schuck, *The Limits of Law*, chap. 13, especially pt. II.

26. Substitute weapons are highly likely. Kates, chapter 2, this volume; see also Jim Yardley, "Rat Poison: Murder Weapon of Choice in Rural China," *New York Times*, Nov. 17, 2003, A3.

27. When, as is usually the case, more than one institution contributes to the policy system for managing a particular social problem, the question becomes, How can the resources of those institutions best be combined and coordinated?

28. The discussion that follows draws, sometimes verbatim, on Schuck, *The Limits of Law*, 350–51.

29. See generally Jacobs, *Can Gun Control Work?* chap. 2.

30. See Erichson, chapter 5, this volume.

31. See Wagner, chapter 11, this volume.

32. See generally Guido Calabresi and Alvin Klevorick, "Four Tests for Liability in Torts," *Journal of Legal Studies* 14 (1985): 585.

33. See George L. Priest and Benjamin Klein, "The Selection of Disputes for Litigation," *Journal of Legal Studies* 13 (1984): 1; cf. Theodore Eisenberg, "Litigation Models and Trial Outcomes in Civil Rights and Prisoner Cases," *Georgetown Law Journal* 77 (1989): 1567; Donald Wittman, "Is the Selection of Cases for Trial Biased?" *Journal of Legal Studies* 14 (1985): 185.

34. An exception might occur in some states if plaintiffs manage to reach the punitive damages stage and the state's punitive damage rules permit introduction of such ability-to-pay evidence.

35. Kahan, Braman, and Gastil, in chapter 4, while emphasizing cultural conflicts, are also concerned with what I call political information. They claim—erroneously or too broadly, in my view—that the politics of gun control is what they call the politics of "avoidance" rather than of "advertence" in that it fails to recognize and confront the symbolic or cultural dimension of

political conflict. See generally chapter 4. In truth, however, much political activity entails the self-conscious manipulation and exploitation of precisely these symbolic or cultural meanings. The politics of gun control is no exception.

36. The rest of this paragraph draws heavily on Schuck, *The Limits of Law*, 225–26.

37. *Kelley v. R.G. Industries, Inc.*, 497 A.2d 1143 (Md.1985).

38. See *Cal. Civ. Code* § 1714 (repealed) (abrogating holdings of *Coulter v. Superior Court*, 21 Cal. 3d 144 (1978); *Bernhard v. Harrah's Club*, 16 Cal. 3d 313 (1976); *Vesely v. Sager*, 5 Cal. 3d 153 (1971)).

39. See Jacobs, *Can Gun Control Work?* 42 and 233n15 (discussing annual sales rates).

40. Ibid., 51–52.

41. See Charles C. Sipos, Note, "The Disappearing Settlement: The Contractual Regulation of Smith & Wesson Firearms," *Vanderbilt Law Review* 55 (2002): 1297, 1303.

42. James A. Henderson Jr. and Aaron D. Twerski, "Closing the American Products Liability Frontier: The Rejection of Liability without Defect," *New York University Law Review* 66 (1991): 1263, 1310–11 (explaining the propensity of excessive liability to produce black markets).

43. Jacobs, *Can Gun Control Work?* 165.

44. See Steven Croley, "Public Interested Regulation," *Florida State University Law Review* 28 (2000): 7.

45. Jacobs, *Can Gun Control Work?* 38–39. I am extrapolating from the 1999 data that Jacobs presents in his tables 3.1 and 3.2 estimating the annual growth in the gun stock.

46. *Lawrence v. Texas*, 123 S. Ct. 2472, 2484 (2003).

47. This information may come from many sources, including feedback from judicial decisions interpreting or enforcing the regulatory policy.

48. The rest of this paragraph draws heavily on Peter H. Schuck, "The New Judicial Ideology of Tort Law," in *New Directions in Liability Law*, ed. W. Olson (Montpelier, VT: Capital City Press, 1988).

49. See Jacobs, *Can Gun Control Work?* 51, table 3.4.

50. Ibid., 50.

51. See Lytton, chapter 6, this volume.

52. See Kahan, Braman, and Gastil, chapter 4, this volume.

53. Schuck, *The Limits of Law*, 319–20.

54. See generally, Jacobs, *Can Gun Control Work?*

55. Centers for Disease Control and Prevention, "First Reports Evaluating the Effectiveness of Strategies for Preventing Violence: Early Childhood Home Visitation and Firearms Laws," *Morbidity and Mortality Weekly Report* 52, no. RR-14 (2003): 18, http://www.cdc.gov/mmwr/PDF/rr/rr5214.pdf.

56. See, e.g., David A. Harris, "Superman's X-Ray Vision and the Fourth Amendment: The New Gun Detection Technology," *Temple Law Review* 69 (1996): 1; Laura B. Riley, "Concealed Weapon Detectors and the Fourth

Amendment: The Constitutionality of Remote Sense-Enhanced Searches," *UCLA Law Review* 45 (1997): 281; Christopher Slobogin, "Technologically Assisted Physical Surveillance: The American Bar Association's Tentative Draft Standards," *Harvard Journal of Law and Technology* 10 (1997): 383.

CHAPTER 10

1. For examples, see Walter Olson, *The Rule of Lawyers: How the New Litigation Elite Threatens America's Rule of Law* (New York: St. Martin's, 2003), 94–98, 306–14; Michael Krauss, *Fire and Smoke: Government Lawsuits and the Rule of Law* (Oakland, CA: Independent Institute, 2000); Anne Giddings Kimball and Sarah L. Olson, "Municipal Firearms Litigation: Ill Conceived from Any Angle," *Connecticut Law Review* 32 (2000): 1301–3; Jeff Reh, "Social Issue Litigation and the Route around Democracy," *Harvard Journal on Legislation* 37 (2000): 515–20; Phillip D. Oliver, "Rejecting the Whipping-Boy Approach to Tort Law: Well-Made Handguns Are Not Defective Products," *University of Arkansas at Little Rock Law Journal* 14 (1991): 5; Catherine Crier, *The Case against Lawyers* (New York: Broadway Books, 2002), 4.

2. Peter H. Schuck, "The New Judicial Ideology of Tort Law," in *New Directions in Liability Law*, ed. Walter Olson (Montpelier, VT: Academy of Political Science, 1988), 15; Peter H. Schuck, *The Limits of Law* (St. Paul, MN: Westview, 2000), 363–64; Peter H. Schuck, chapter 9, this volume.

3. W. Kip Viscusi, "Overview," in *Regulation through Litigation*, ed. W. Kip Viscusi (Washington, DC: AEI-Brookings Joint Center for Regulatory Studies, 2002), 2.

4. Douglas McCollam, "Long Shot," *American Lawyer*, June 1999 (interview with plaintiffs' lawyer Wendell Gauthier); Andrew J. McClurg, "Strict Liability for Handgun Manufacturers: A Reply to Professor Oliver," *University of Arkansas at Little Rock Law Journal* 14 (1991): 516–17; Carl Bogus, *Why Lawsuits Are Good for America* (New York: New York University Press, 2001), 8–9, 211–12, 219–20.

5. David Rosenberg, "The Regulatory Advantage of Class Action," in *Regulation through Litigation*, ed. Viscusi, 244–304.

6. For a thoughtful discussion of tort law's role in complementing legislative and agency regulation, see Robert L. Rabin, Keynote Paper, "Reassessing Regulatory Compliance," *Georgetown Law Journal* 88 (2000): 2049, 2060–84. See also Peter D. Jacobson and Kenneth E. Warner, "Litigation and Public Health Policy Making: The Case of Tobacco Control," *Journal of Health Politics, Policy, and Law* 24, no. 4 (1999): 769–804; Charles Fried and David Rosenberg, *Making Tort Law: What Should Be Done and Who Should Do It?* (Washington, DC: AEI Press, 2003), 78–103.

7. The Bureau of Alcohol, Tobacco, Firearms and Explosives has issued

an opinion that the Gun Control Act does not control the sale of firearms parts, except for frames or receivers, silencer parts, certain machine gun parts, and large-capacity ammunition feeding devices. Department of the Treasury, Bureau of Alcohol, Tobacco, and Firearms, *Federal Firearms Regulations Reference Guide* (Washington, DC: ATF P 5300.4) (10–95), 104, question (A6).

8. For a discussion of this unreported case, see Timothy D. Lytton, "Halberstam v. Daniel and the Uncertain Future of Negligent Marketing Claims against Firearms Manufacturers," *Brooklyn Law Review* 64 (1998): 681.

9. Title 41, 18 U.S.C. §921(a)(29)(B) (2003).

10. The trial judge rejected the plaintiffs' negligence per se claim based on violation of federal law, refusing to adjudicate the question of whether the defendant's gun kit was covered by the statutory definition of a firearm, which included "any combination of parts from which a firearm . . . can be assembled." See Lytton, "Halberstam v. Daniel," 687.

11. It is also possible, as indicated by the statutory language cited in note 7, that Congress did indeed intend to regulate gun kits.

12. 33 P.3d 638 (N.M. Ct. App. 2001), *cert. denied, Smith v. Bryco Arms*, 34 P.3d 610 (N.M. October 17, 2001).

13. *Bryco Arms*, 33 P.3d at 643.

14. Ibid.

15. *Consumer Products Safety Act*, Public Law 92-573 § 2, *U.S. Statutes at Large* 86 (1972):1207, *codified as* 15 U.S.C. §2074 (2003).

16. For a recent U.S. Supreme Court articulation of this principle, see *Sprietsma v. Mercury Marine*, 537 U.S. 51 (2002).

17. See *City of Chicago v. Beretta*, 2004 Ill. LEXIS 1665 at *64–65 (Ill. 2004).

18. For a more detailed discussion, see Timothy D. Lytton, "Tort Claims against Gun Manufacturers for Crime-Related Injuries: Defining a Suitable Role for the Tort System in Regulating the Firearms Industry," *Missouri Law Review* 65 (2000): 42–45. See also Allen Rostron, "Beyond Market Share Liability: A Theory of Proportional Share Liability for Nonfungible Products," *UCLA Law Review* 52 (2004): 151.

19. See *Hymowitz v. Eli Lilly*, 73 N.Y.2d 487 (1989), *cert. denied sub. nom. Rexall Drug Co. v. Tigue*, 493 U.S. 444 (1989).

20. For example, see Schuck, "New Judicial Ideology"; Olson, *Rule of Lawyers*, 94–98, 306–14; Krauss, *Fire and Smoke;* Reh, "Social Issue Litigation," 515–20; Oliver, "Rejecting the Whipping-Boy Approach"; Crier, *The Case against Lawyers*, 4.

21. Complaint, *City of Chicago v. Beretta*, No. 98 CH 015596, 72 (Cir. Ct. Cook County 2002).

22. See Schuck, "New Judicial Ideology," 16.

23. Peter H. Brown and Daniel G. Abel, *Outgunned: Up against the NRA* (New York: Free Press, 2003), 172–92; Olson, *Rule of Lawyers*, 123.

24. Brown, *Outgunned*, 193–234; Olson, *Rule of Lawyers*, 126–27; Timothy

D. Lytton, "Lawsuits against the Gun Industry: A Comparative Institutional Analysis," *Connecticut Law Review* 32 (2000): 1247, 1259–66.

25. See Brady Center to Prevent Gun Violence, Legal Action Project, *Reforming the Gun Industry: California,* http://www.gunlawsuits.org/docket/cities/cityview.php?RecordNo=13.

26. For further discussion, see Charles C. Sipos, "The Disappearing Settlement: The Contractual Regulation of Smith & Wesson Firearms," *Vanderbilt Law Review* 55 (2002): 1297.

27. Rabin, "Reassessing Regulatory Compliance," 2061–70; Wendy Wagner, Symposium Article, "Rough Justice and the Attorney General Litigation," *Georgia Law Review* 33 (1999): 935.

28. For example, see the affidavit of Robert I. Hass, former senior vice president of marketing and sales at Smith & Wesson, quoted in David Kairys, "Legal Claims of Cities against the Manufacturers of Handguns," *Temple Law Review* 71 (1998): 1, 7; testimony of Robert Ricker, former NRA lobbyist and former president of the American Shooting Sports Council, summarized in *NAACP v. AcuSport Corp.,* 210 F.R.D. 446, 450–453 (2002).

29. "Percentage of Firearms Licensees Inspected," BATFE web site, http://www.atf.treas.gov/pub/gen_pub/2000annrpt_html/goals.htm; *Firearms Owner's Protection Act,* 18 U.S.C. §923(g)(1)(B)(ii)(I) (2003).

30. Rabin, "Reassessing Regulatory Compliance," 2084.

31. *MacPherson v. Buick Motor Co.,* 271 N.Y. 382 (1916); *Greenman v. Yuba Power Prod., Inc.,* 59 Cal. 2d 57 (1963).

32. See James A. Henderson Jr., "MacPherson v. Buick Motor Company: Simplifying the Facts while Reshaping the Law," in *Torts Stories,* ed. Robert L. Rabin and Stephen D. Sugarman (New York: Foundation Press, 2003), 59–63.

33. *O'Brien v. Muskin Corp.,* 463 A.2d 298 (1983); *Kelley v. R.G. Industries,* 497 A.2d 1143 (1985).

CHAPTER 11

1. Violence Policy Center, "Litigation against the Gun Industry" (table of litigation), http://www.vpc.org/litigate.htm; Peter D. Jacobson and Soheil Soliman, "Litigation as Public Health Policy: Theory or Reality?" *Journal of Law, Medicine, and Ethics* 30 (2002): 224, 233.

2. Timothy D. Lytton, introduction, this volume.

3. Peter Harry Brown and David Abel, *Outgunned: Up against the NRA* (New York: Free Press, 2003), 216–20.

4. Richard A. Epstein, "Implications for Legal Reform," in *Regulation through Litigation,* ed. W. Kip Viscusi (Washington, DC: AEI-Brookings Joint Center for Regulatory Studies, 2002), 325; Peter H. Schuck, "The New Judicial

Ideology of Tort Law," in *New Directions in Liability Law,* ed. Walter Olson (Montpelier, VT: Capital City Press, 1988), 4–17.

5. Kenneth S. Abraham, *The Forms and Functions of Tort Law* (Westbury, CT: Foundation Press, 2002), 14–20.

6. W. Page Keeton, Dan B. Dobbs, Robert E. Keeton, and David G. Owen, *Prosser and Keeton on the Law of Torts* (St. Paul, MN: West, 1984), 3.

7. Ibid.

8. Walter Olson, "Big Guns," *Reason,* Oct. 1999, 60; Peter H. Schuck, "Benched," *Washington Monthly,* Dec. 2000, 35.

9. Tracy R. Lewis, "Protecting the Environment When Costs and Benefits Are Privately Known," *RAND Journal of Economics* 27 (1996): 819, 826–31.

10. Neil K. Komesar, *Imperfect Alternatives: Choosing Institutions in Law, Economics, and Public Policy* (Chicago: University of Chicago Press, 1994), 7.

11. Constance A. Nathanson, "Social Movements as Catalysts for Policy Change: The Case of Smoking and Guns," *Journal of Health Politics, Policy, and Law* 24 (1999): 421, 422.

12. Ibid., 477, 479.

13. Wendy Wagner, "Commons Ignorance: Why the Environmental Laws Have Failed Us," *Duke Law Journal* 53 (2004): 1601.

14. See, e.g., Robert Vaughn, "Consumer Access to Product Safety Information and the Future of the Freedom of Information Act," *Admin. Law Journal* 5 (1991): 673.

15. Paul Brodeur, *Outrageous Misconduct: The Asbestos Industry on Trial* (New York: Pantheon, 1985).

16. Morton Mintz, *At Any Cost: Corporate Greed, Women, and the Dalkon Shield* (New York: Pantheon, 1985).

17. *Bichler v. Eli Lilly and Co.,* 436 N.E.2d 182, 185 (N.Y. 1982).

18. Gary Markowitz and David Rosner, *Deceit and Denial: The Deadly Politics of Industrial Pollution* (Berkeley: University of California Press, 2002).

19. *West v. Johnson and Johnson Prods., Inc.,* 220 Cal. Rptr. 437, 442–43 (Cal. Ct. App. 1985).

20. Joseph Sanders, "The Bendectin Litigation: A Case Study in the Life Cycle of Mass Torts," *Hastings Law Journal* 43 (1992) 301, 321.

21. Joni Hersch, "Breast Implants: Regulation, Litigation, and Science," in *Regulation through Litigation,* ed. Viscusi, 143–44.

22. Robert Rabin, "The Third Wave of Tobacco Litigation," in *Regulating Tobacco,* ed. Robert L. Rabin and Stephen D. Sugarman (New York: Oxford University Press, 2001), 197.

23. See, e.g., Howard M. Erichson, chapter 5, this volume.

24. See, e.g., Fed. R. Civ. P. 11, 12(b)(6); Model Rules of Prof'l Conduct R. 3-1.

25. Phillip J. Cook and Jens Ludwig, "Litigation as Regulation: Firearms," in *Regulation through Litigation,* ed. Viscusi, 67, 89.

26. Peter H. Schuck, "Mass Torts: An Institutional Evolutionist Perspective," *Cornell Law Review* 80 (1995): 941, 969–73.

27. Lytton, introduction, this volume; Lytton, chapter 6, this volume.

28. See generally Lytton, chapter 6, this volume (describing the Maryland litigation).

29. Cook and Ludwig, "Litigation as Regulation: Firearms," 68.

30. See Harvard Injury Control Center's National Violent Injury Statistics System, http://www.hsph.harvard.edu/hicrc/nviss/.

31. Division of Behavioral and Social Sciences and Education, National Research Council, National Academy of Science, *Firearms and Violence: What Do We Know?* (Washington, DC: National Academy Press, forthcoming 2004).

32. Gary Kleck and Don Kates, *Armed: New Perspectives on Gun Control* (Buffalo, NY: Prometheus, 2001), 155; Mark Duggan, "More Guns, More Crime," *Journal of Political Economy* 109 (2001): 1086.

33. Memorandum from Steven M. Silwa, CEO and president of Colt, to Zilkha Capital Partners et al., June 28, 1999, "iColt Offering Memorandum Draft," 27, http://www.gunlawsuits.org/pdf/docket/041803.pdf. Later in the memorandum, Colt discusses seven prototype "safe guns" under development in 1999, five of which had patents pending with anticipated release dates from 2000 through 2006. Ibid, 34.

34. Tom Diaz, *Making a Killing: The Business of Guns in America* (New York: New Press, 1999), 15.

35. Brown and Abel, *Outgunned*, 127, 140–43, 155, 195, 205, 276–80.

36. Brady Center to Prevent Gun Violence, *Smoking Guns: Exposing the Gun Industry's Complicity in the Illegal Gun Market* (Washington, DC: Brady Center to Prevent Gun Violence, 2003), 2. See Gary Gordon, "Insurers and Manufacturers Succeeded in Sealing Asbestos Records," *Star Tribune*, Dec. 28, 2003, formerly available at http://www.startribune.com/stories/484/4288864.html (discussing "gag" settlements).

37. Diaz, *Making a Killing*, 5.

38. Brady Center, "Special Interest Rider Makes Crime Gun Data Secret," Feb. 13, 2003, www.bradycampaign.org/press/release.asp?Record=451.

39. Cook and Ludwig, "Litigation as Regulation: Firearms," 74n23.

40. Brady Center, *Smoking Guns*, 34; Cook and Ludwig, "Litigation as Regulation: Firearms," 82–83.

41. *NAACP v. AcuSport, Inc.*, 271 F.Supp. 2d 435, 503 (E.D.N.Y. 2003). Unless otherwise indicated, all references to this case are found at this citation.

42. Public Law 94-284, § 3(e), *U.S. Statutes at Large* 90 (1976): 504.

43. *National Firearms Act of 1934*, 26 U.S.C. §§5801 et seq.; *Crime Control Act of 1994*, 42 U.S.C. § 13701 et seq. See also BATFE, "Firearms Laws in the United States," http://www.atf.treas.gov/field/columbus/press/gunlaws.htm.

44. Cook and Ludwig, "Litigation as Regulation: Firearms," 71.

45. Brown and Abel, *Outgunned*, 91–103.

46. Diaz, *Making a Killing*, 55.

47. *The Gun Control Act of 1968*, 18 U.S.C. § 921 et seq.

48. *McClure-Volkmer Act of 1986* or *Firearm Owners' Protection Act of 1986*, Public Law 99-308, *U.S. Statutes at Large* 100 (1986): 449, sec. 103(1).

49. Ibid. at sec. 103(6).

50. *NAACP v. AcuSport, Inc.*, 271 F.Supp. 2d 435, 521–22 (E.D.N.Y. 2003).

51. BATFE, *Operation Snapshot* (Washington, DC: Government Printing Office, 1993); BATFE, *Operation Snapshot: An Analysis of the Retail Regulated Firearms Industry* (Washington, DC: Government Printing Office, 1998).

52. William H. Rodgers, *Environmental Law* (St. Paul, MN: West, 1994), 39–42.

53. Ibid.

54. S. P. Baker, B. O'Neill, M. J. Ginsburg, and G. Li, *The Injury Fact Book* (New York: Oxford University Press, 1992).

55. David Hemenway, Editorial, "Regulation of Firearms," *New England Journal of Medicine* 339 (1998): 843.

56. Nathanson, "Social Movements," 463, 465–66.

57. Ibid., 474.

58. Brown and Abel, *Outgunned*, 258.

59. See Diaz, *Making a Killing*, 65–66 (discussing some of these smaller organizations).

60. Robert Spitzer, *The Politics of Gun Control* (Chatham, NJ: Chatham House, 1998).

61. Douglas S. Weil and David Hemenway, "I Am the NRA: An Analysis of a National Random Sample of Gun Owners," *Violence and Victims* 8 (1993): 353; Douglas S. Weil and David Hemenway, "Reply to Commentary: A Response to Kleck," *Violence and Victims* 8 (1993): 377.

62. Weil and Hemenway, "I Am the NRA," 363.

63. Brady Center, *Smoking Guns*, 31 (citing National Shooting Sports Foundation [NSSF] survey documents produced in litigation).

64. Ibid., 361; "Vote on Lawsuit Preemption Could Be Near," formerly available at http://www.nraila.org/LegislativeUpdate.asp?FormMode=DetailandID=804; Brown and Abel, *Outgunned*, 213–24.

65. This is reinforced by NRA defender Gary Kleck's own apparent obliviousness to these positions. Weil and Hemenway, "Reply to Commentary," 379–81.

66. Compare tables 1 and 2 in ibid., 378, 382. It is also possible that this majority is the least active in NRA leadership and meetings since they are the most complacent about the prospect of greater legal controls. Ibid., 361 (less than 10 percent of the members eligible to vote in 1992, for example, returned their ballots).

67. Nathanson, "Social Movements," 473.

68. Brady Center, *Smoking Guns*, 20 (citing Riker deposition).

69. Diaz, *Making a Killing*, 53–60; Nathanson, "Social Movements," 455.

70. Ronald G. Shaiko, *Voices and Echoes for the Environment: Public Interest Representation in the 1990s and Beyond* (New York: Columbia University Press, 1999), 152, 161, 165, 173.

71. Jim Leitzel, Comment, in Viscusi, *Regulation through Litigation*, 99.

72. *NAACP v. AcuSport, Inc.*, 271 F.Supp. 2d 435, 521–22 (E.D.N.Y. 2003); Silwa, Colt Memorandum, 27–28, 31.

73. Leitzel, Comment, 101.

74. Diaz, *Making a Killing*, part II; see also chap. 10 (focusing on public relations tactics of the gun industry).

75. Brady Center, *Smoking Guns*, part 2.

76. Philip J. Hilts, *Smokescreen: The Truth behind the Tobacco Industry Cover-Up* (Reading, MA: Addison-Wesley, 1996), 17, 46.

77. Rebecca Dresser, Wendy Wagner, and Paul Giannelli, "Breast Implants Revisited: Beyond Science on Trial," *Wisconsin Law Review* 1997 (1997): 705, 743–44.

78. Brady Center, *Smoking Guns*, 15–16.

79. Brown and Abel, *Outgunned*, 298; "Pushing the Envelope: Smith & Wesson Settlement with Cities and Counties Suing the Gun Industry," formerly available at www.gunsuits.org.

80. Brown and Abel, *Outgunned*, 66–67, 157–58; Fox Butterfield, "Lawsuits Lead Gun Maker to File for Bankruptcy," *New York Times*, June 24, 1999, A14.

81. In 1997, total small arms shipments were only $1.2 billion. U.S. Department of the Treasury, Bureau of Alcohol, Tobacco, and Firearms, *Commerce in Firearms in the United States* (Washington, DC: Government Printing Office, 2000).

82. Brown and Abel, *Outgunned*, 73.

83. Lytton, chapter 6, this volume.

84. Brown and Abel, *Outgunned*, 216–20.

85. See, e.g., Marcia Angell, *Science on Trial: The Clash of Medical Evidence and the Law in the Breast Implant Case* (New York: W.W. Norton, 1996).

86. See Rachana Bhowmik, "Aiming for Accountability: How City Lawsuits Can Help Reform an Irresponsible Gun Industry," *Journal of Law and Policy* 11 (2002): 67, 127–34; see also Lietzel, Comment, 95–96, 98.

87. Barbara Vobejda, "Colt to Discontinue Cheaper Handguns," *Washington Post*, Oct. 12, 1999, E1.

88. Brady Center, *Smoking Guns*, 15.

89. William Hermann, "Safety Reigns at Yearly Las Vegas Gun Show," *Arizona Republic*, Jan. 19, 2000.

90. National Association of Firearms Retailers, "Don't Lie for the Other Guy," formerly available at http://www.nafr.org/DontLie/index.html. See also Brady Center, *Smoking Guns*, 9.

91. Carol Vinzant, "Gun Victims' Silver Bullet? The New Secret Weapon in Gun Litigation," http://slate.msn.com/?id=2075714.

92. See Steven Shavell, "The Optimal Structure of Law Enforcement," in *A Reader on Regulation*, ed. Robert Baldwin (London: Oxford University Press, 1998), 307.

93. William M. Sage, "Regulating through Information: Disclosure Laws and American Health Care," *Columbia Law Review* 99 (1999): 1701; Bradley

Karkkainen, "Information as Environmental Regulation: TRI and Performance Benchmarking, Precursor to a New Paradigm?" *Georgetown Law Journal* 89 (2001): 257.

94. W. Kip Viscusi, "Overview," in *Regulation through Litigation*, ed. Viscusi, 1.

95. Stephen P. Teret et al., "Support for New Policies to Regulate Firearms: Results of Two National Surveys," *New England Journal of Medicine* 339 (1998): 813–14.

96. Weil and Hemenway, "I Am the NRA," table 3, 360.

97. See Nathanson, "Social Movements," 440; Spitzer, *Politics of Gun Control*, 118; Jens Ludwig and Philip J. Cook, "The Benefits of Reducing Gun Violence: Evidence from Contingent-Valuation Survey Data," *Journal of Risk and Uncertainty* 22 (2001): 207.

98. Brady Center, *Smoking Guns*, 18 (quoting Riker deposition).

99. Brady Center, "Gun Dealers, Distributors Agree to Reform to Curb Illegal Market in California," http://www.bradycampaign.com/press/release.asp?Record=503.

100. As of September 13, 2003, no information on this settlement could be located on either the NRA or NSSF web sites.

101. Jim Wasserman, "Assembly Passes Requiring Gun Design Changes," *ContraCosta Times*, Sept. 5, 2003, http://www.bayarea.com/mld/cctimes/news/6697952.htm.

102. Dresser, Wagner, and Giannelli, "Breast Implants Revisited," 744.

103. Lytton, chapter 6, this volume; see also Daniel LeDuc, "Shooting for a Safer Deadly Weapon; Gunmakers, Lawmakers Look to High-Tech Locks and Personalized Pistols," *Washington Post*, Feb. 28, 2000, A1. Similar regulatory developments occurred in New Jersey and Massachusetts. *Mass. Gen. Laws* chap.140 § 131K (2003).

104. The day the legislation was passed, the NRA posted the development on its web site with a single, explanatory sentence: "The California Assembly passed a bill Sept. 4 requiring new safety designs in semi-automatic handguns sold in the state after 2006 and 2007. 'It's really simple why we're doing this. We're doing this because the (Democratic) majority doesn't like guns,' said Assemblyman Ray Haynes, R-Temecula," *NRA News Center*, Sept. 5, 2003 (posted on web site on Sept. 7, 2003; no longer available on Sept. 8, and legislation received no coverage on Sept. 8).

CHAPTER 12

The authors thank Laura Nigro for significant assistance in fieldwork.

1. See Richard Ericson, Aaron Doyle, and Dean Barry, *Insurance as Governance* (Toronto: University of Toronto Press, 2003); Richard Ericson and

Aaron Doyle, *Uncertain Business: Risk, Insurance, and the Limits of Knowledge* (Toronto: University of Toronto Press, 2004); Tom Baker, "Risk, Insurance, and the Social Construction of Responsibility," in *Embracing Risk: The Changing Culture of Insurance and Responsibility*, ed. Tom Baker and Jonathan Simon (Chicago: University of Chicago Press, 2002).

2. An Acte concerninge matters of Assurances, amongste Merchantes, 1601, 43 Eliz., c. 12 (Eng.).

3. See *Fla. Stat.* ch. 458.320 (2003) (medical malpractice insurance); see also *Fla. Admin. Code Ann.* r. 62-730.170(2)(a) (2003) (insurance for hazardous waste transporters).

4. Carol Heimer, "Insuring More, Ensuring Less: The Costs and Benefits of Private Regulation through Insurance," in *Embracing Risk*, ed. Baker and Simon, 116.

5. See generally George M. Cohen, "Legal Malpractice Insurance and Loss Prevention: A Comparative Analysis of Economic Institutions," *Connecticut Insurance Law Journal* 4 (1997–98): 305.

6. See Tom Baker, "Containing the Promise of Insurance: Adverse Selection and Risk Classification," in *Risk and Morality*, ed. Richard V. Ericson and Aaron Doyle (Toronto: University of Toronto Press, 2003).

7. See Richard V. Ericson and Kevin D. Haggerty, "The Policing of Risk," in *Embracing Risk*, ed. Baker and Simon, 238 (describing how police departments collect information in a manner that is designed to be useful to insurance companies).

8. Tom Baker, "Blood Money, New Money, and the Moral Economy of Tort Law in Action," *Law and Society Review* 35 (2001): 275–320.

9. A decision to exclude selective risks from the liability insurance pool does not mean that there are no means to socialize the losses that result. For business activities, shareholders and creditors will absorb some of the loss, and, to the extent that victims have first-party insurance, the losses will be spread through those insurance pools.

10. Cf. Marc Galanter, "Why the 'Haves' Come out Ahead: Speculations on the Limits of Legal Change," in *In Litigation: Do the "Haves" Still Come Out Ahead?*" ed. Herbert M. Kritzer and Susan S. Silbey (Stanford, CA: Stanford Law and Politics, 2003), 13.

11. Our assumption, however, is that life insurance companies have not in fact tested the effect of gun ownership one way or the other. Cf. Brian J. Glenn, "The Shifting Rhetoric of Insurance Denial," *Law and Society Review* 37 (2000): 779.

12. Insurance Services Office, Inc., "Homeowners 3—Special Form" in *Personal Risk Management and Insurance* (Dallas: International Risk Management Institute, 2001), 17. See *State Farm Fire and Cas. Co. v. Morgan*, 2003 WL 1796004 (7th Cir. 2003) (declaring no obligation for an insurer to defend a policyholder against criminal charges of reckless homicide involving the use of a gun); *N.C. Farm Bureau Mut. Ins. Co. v. Mizell*, 530 S.E.2d 93 (N.C. Ct. App.

2000) (exempting insurer from its obligation to defend policyholder claiming that the use of his gun was solely for self-defense); see also *Auto-Owners Ins. Co. v. Harrington*, 565 N.W.2d 839 (Mich. 1997); *Chapman by Ricciardi v. Wis. Physicians Serv. Ins. Corp.*, 523 N.W.2d 152 (Wis. Ct. App. 1994).

13. See Tom Baker, *Insurance Law and Policy: Cases, Materials, and Problems* (New York: Aspen, 2003), 498–505; *American Family Mut. Ins. Co. v. White*, 65 P.3d 449 (Ariz. Ct. App. 2003).

14. Baker, *Insurance Law and Policy*, 498–505. But see *Safeco Ins. Co. v. Robert S.*, 26 Cal 4th 758 (2001) (declining to apply an exclusion for "illegal acts").

15. Standard homeowners' and renters' policies contain a special $2,500 limit "for loss by theft of firearms or related equipment." Insurance Services Office, Inc., "Homeowners 3—Special Form," 3–4. Applicants can purchase additional theft coverage through an "increased special limits of liability" endorsement. Ibid., 13.E.212–13. Firearms losses arising out of perils other than theft are covered up to the insured's limit of coverage for personal property.

We were able to determine the underwriting policies of three of the five largest residential insurance carriers in the United States (State Farm, Allstate, and Travelers). In combination, these three companies wrote $12.5 billion in homeowners' premiums in 2000, representing 36.7 percent of the market. See Insurance Information Institute, *The Fact Book 2002* (New York: Insurance Information Institute, 2002), 61. In underwriting a residential package policy, none of the three asks whether the applicant has a gun, except to the extent that the agent is attempting to inquire whether the applicant will need additional first-party property coverage for the guns. See David Tideman, counsel, State Farm Insurance Cos., telephone interview with author, June 19, 2003 ("I don't think that we actually mandate that the information be communicated to us. Of course, if some extreme situation, like the keeping of an arsenal, came to the attention of the local agent, we might take some underwriting action on that."). State Farm's web site confirms that questions about gun ownership are the exception rather than the rule. While the site does not yet quote homeowners' insurance online, it does quote renters' insurance, and it will produce a quote on both property and liability insurance without any inquiry into the gun habits of the prospective insured. State Farm Ins. Cos., "Renters Rate Quote," http://www.statefarm.com/quote/renters.htm (accessed June 24, 2003). Allstate's and Travelers's underwriting policies appear to be similar. See Marissa Quiles, media relations, Allstate Insurance Co., e-mail to author, May 29, 2003 (Allstate does not ask a prospective insured if she owns or keeps guns, "except to the extent the agent is attempting to determine whether the policyholder will need additional property coverage for the firearms."); Travelers Property Casualty Corp., "Homeowners E-Quote General Insurance Information," http://www.travelerspc.com/personal/equote/homecondrent/HCR_gen eral.cfm (accessed June 19, 2003) and "Homeowners E-Quote Information about Your Valuable Items," http://www.travelerspc.com/personal/ equote/homecondrent/HCR_valuables.cfm (accessed June 19, 2003) (indicating that Travelers does not ask its prospective insureds whether they own guns, except in the context of scheduled personal property insurance).

16. Evidently one gun rights group has concluded that State Farm is unfairly reluctant to insure gun owners and has publicized the charge. "State Farm Frowns on Guns," *Conservative Monitor* http://www.conservativemoni tor.com/news/2001020.shtml. The NRA carried a brief description of the incident on its web site. See National Rifle Association, "State Farm Insolence," formerly available at http://www.nrahq.org/publications/tag/gijoe.asp (describing State Farm's failure to offer adequate gun coverage to a homeowner).

17. Nor, in our view, is it anti-gun to ask people whether they own guns in order to evaluate whether gun ownership increases or reduces the risk of liability or property insurance claims. Thus, an insurance company should be able to conduct internal research through the policy renewal process in order to evaluate whether a gun in the home increases or decreases the risk of injury or property loss.

18. See Brady Campaign to Prevent Gun Violence, "Firearm Facts," http://www.bradycampaign.org/facts/research/firefacts.asp. We extrapolate that there were 2,598 fatal and nonfatal gun injuries in that year. By contrast, in 1996 there were 3,552,907 motor vehicle injuries and fatalities. National Highway Traffic Safety Administration, *Report to Congress: The Effect of Increased Speed Limits in the Post-NMSL Era* (Washington, DC: National Highway Traffic Safety Administration, 1998), 15.

19. From a public health perspective, the more effective insurance-based strategy may well be to persuade insurers to offer discounts for gun locks and smart guns as a way to reduce crime losses (and to reduce the flow of stolen guns into the hands of criminals). Of course, the kind of person who purchases a gun lock or a smart gun may well be the kind of person who is less likely to have a gun stolen in the first place. Although this "propitious selection" would not undercut the utility of discounts to insurers, it would reduce the public health benefits of the discount. Cf. Peter Siegelman, "Adverse Selection in Insurance Markets: An Exaggerated Threat," *Yale Law Journal* 113 (2004): 1223.

20. International Risk Management Institute, Inc., *Classification Cross-Reference* (Dallas: International Risk Management Institute, 1999), 228. Information for the following two paragraphs draws on this publication.

21. A.M. Best Co., *Best's Underwriting Guide* (2003). This is not a public document. We obtained a copy from an underwriter on the condition that we not reveal the source. This information is used for much of the remainder of this section.

22. Cynthia Michener, media relations, Hartford Financial Services Group, e-mail to author, July 28, 2003.

23. Donna Choquette, underwriter, Safeco Property and Casualty Insurance Cos., interview with author, June 26, 2003.

24. Insurance Information Institute, *The Fact Book 2002*, 21.

25. John Badowski, managing director, National Association of Firearms Retailers, telephone interview with author, Aug. 11, 2003 (hereinafter Badowski interview).

26. Robert Chiarello, broker, Joseph Chiarello and Co., Inc., telephone interview with author, Aug. 7, 2003 (hereinafter Chiarello interview).

27. Badowski interview. We asked Badowski if retailers had attempted to solve their insurance availability problems by asking the manufacturers they represent for vendors' protective liability endorsements—in other words, if the retailers were solving their insurance problems by transferring them to the manufacturer. Badowski says that the business sophistication of gun dealers varies greatly—some are sizable concerns with their own risk management departments, and others are small mom-and-pop operations with little insurance savvy—and consequently awareness of that technique is spotty. Badowski confirmed that some retailers have indeed approached the problem that way, but he had no sense of how common it was. He said that he did not perceive the practice to be widespread.

28. See generally Scott E. Harrington, *Tort Liability, Insurance Rates, and the Insurance Cycle*, in Richard J. Herring and Robert L. Litern, Brookings-Wharton Paper on Financial Services (Washington, DC: Brookings Institute, 2004) (describing the phases of underwriting cycles); Sean M. Fitzpatrick, "Fear Is the Key: A Behavioral Guide to Underwriting Cycles," *Connecticut Insurance Law Journal*, 10:255–75 (2004). At some point in the 2000–2001 period, the commercial property casualty insurance market entered a "hard" phase that continued through early 2004.

29. A.M. Best Co., *Best's Underwriting Guide*.

30. Ibid.

31. One reader suggested that the higher hazard rating for sporting goods stores might reflect the fact that they are less competent at selling guns. While that may be the case, the fact that sporting goods stores carry the same hazard index for liability risks whether they sell guns or not (see text at note 20) suggests that gun risks are not a significant component of liability risks for sporting goods stores.

32. A.M. Best Co., *Best's Underwriting Guide*.

33. See Northland Insurance Company, "Hunting Club Liability Application" (2002).

34. "Hunt Clubs Quick Application for General Liability Insurance," formerly available at http://www.locktonrisk.com/nrains/huntclubsapp.asp.

35. "Rifle Clubs Quick Application for General Liability Insurance," formerly available at http://www.locktonrisk.com/nrains/rifleclubsapp.asp.

36. Chiarello interview.

37. Sporting Activities Insurance Ltd., "Your Ally in Risk Management," http://www.sail-bm.com/yairm.htm (accessed August 2, 2004).

38. Sporting Activities Insurance Ltd., "Defending an Industry under Attack," http://www.sail-bm.com/daiua.htm.

39. Tom McDermott, telephone interview with author, Aug. 11, 2003 (hereinafter McDermott interview).

40. Chiarello interview.

41. Joseph Chiarello and Co., Inc., "Application for Sporting Firearms Business Insurance" (2002).

42. Joseph Chiarello and Co., Inc., "Application for Products Liability Insurance" (2003).

43. Carol Vinzant, "Gun Victims' Silver Bullet? The New Secret Weapon in Gun Litigation," *Slate*, Dec. 18, 2002, http://slate.msn.com/id/2075714/.

44. Davis's prior carrier had charged $285,000 a year with a self-insured retention of $25,000 per claim; Leeds and London charged Davis only $75,000 a year for the same coverage. McDermott interview.

45. Ibid. See also Sharon Walsh, "Insurers Put Pressure on Gun Industry," *Washington Post*, Nov. 26, 1999, sec. A.

46. See Robert Tillman, *Global Pirates: Fraud in the Offshore Insurance Industry* (Boston: Northeastern University Press, 2002).

47. McDermott interview.

48. See Phil Zinkewicz, "'The Perfect Storm': As in the Movie, Are Conditions Right for State Guaranty Funds to Get Horrendously Hit?" *Rough Notes*, Dec. 2002, http://www.roughnotes.com/rnmagazine/2002/december02/12p66.htm.

49. Chiarello interview.

50. Ibid. See Michele Lawler, underwriter, Carpenter Insurance Group, letter to Laura Nigro, research assistant, University of Connecticut School of Law, June 11, 2003 (describing endorsements for many other risks, including asbestos and terrorism but excluding guns).

51. See *Beretta U.S.A. Corp. v. Federal Ins. Co.*, 17 Fed.Appx. 250, 252 (4th Cir. 2001) (holding that the insurer was not obligated to defend Beretta in twelve municipal lawsuits because the policy did not provide products liability coverage).

52. Chiarello interview; see also Phil Zinkewicz, "United Coastal Rides High through Turbulent Seas," *Rough Notes*, Oct. 2001, http://www.roughnotes.com/rnmag/october01/10p64.htm. Even SAIL has adopted a new mass tort exclusion in more recent policies, however. Chiarello interview.

53. Lexington Insurance Co., *Industry Liability Claims Exclusion* (2002).

54. See, e.g., *Ganim v. Smith & Wesson Corp.*, 780 A.2d 98, 129 (Conn. 2001).

55. *Ellett Bros., Inc. v. U.S. Fid. and Guar. Co.*, 275 F.3d 384 (4th Cir. 2001), *cert. denied* 537 U.S. 818 (2002) (holding that "the term 'damages' as used in the [USF and G policy], does mean legal damages only, and therefore does not extend to claims for equitable relief"). The types of claims brought in the California suits differ from the types of claims brought elsewhere, though, and consequently the result of this suit may not have broad applicability. At the time, the California legislature barred California municipalities from bringing the

most common claim—the claim that "negligent marketing" of guns caused direct monetary damage to municipalities in the form of increased policing and health costs—and consequently their prayers for relief were composed entirely of equitable remedies. See former *Cal. Civ. Code* § 1714.4 (repealed). See *SIG Arms Inc. v. Employers Ins. of Wasau*, 122 F. Supp. 2d 255 (D. N.H. 2000) (granting declaratory judgment for gun manufacturer against its insurer—in a case involving the scope of the insurer's defense requirement under the policy—because of the breadth of the policy regarding defense coverage).

56. See, e.g., Walter J. Andrews and Michael J. Levine, "Is There Insurance Coverage for Lawsuits against the Firearm Industry?" *Nevada Law Journal* 2 (2002): 533; Steven M. Levy and Mary Kay Lacey, "Are Sales of Dangerous Products Such as Guns 'Accidents' for Purposes of Liability Insurance Coverage?" *A.L.I.-A.B.A. Continuing Education* (2000) (available on Westlaw at SE64 ALI-ABA 1085).

57. Chiarello interview; McDermott interview. See also Sharon Walsh, "Insurers Put Pressure on Gun Industry," *Washington Post*, Nov. 26, 1999, sec. A.

58. Tillman, *Global Pirates*.

59. See, e.g., entry for "sporting goods stores" under "general liability":

The sale of guns and ammunition presents the most serious exposure. This is more typical of general line stores than specialty stores; specialty shops, such as gunsmiths or hunting shops, may carry a full line of firearms. The potential for injury is severe, and all firearms should be secured in display cases. Customers should not have unsupervised access to guns. Additionally, all firearms must be displayed unloaded and kept separate from ammunition at all times. See Gunsmiths for more information. (A.M. Best Co., *Best's Underwriting Guide*)

60. See, e.g., Baker, *Insurance Law and Policy*, 492.

61. See Robert Hartwig Sr., *Liability Trends, Issues, and Jury Verdicts: Impact on Insurance Liability and Excess Casualty Markets* (New York: Insurance Information Institute, October 2002). See also Robert Hartwig, senior vice president and chief economist, Insurance Information Institute, e-mail to author, September 3, 2003.

62. See Tom Baker, "On the Genealogy of Moral Hazard," *Texas Law Review* 75 (1996): 255.

63. Nevertheless, we recognize that others may not be so ready to dismiss moral hazard concerns. The answer to those concerns need not be the intentional harm exclusion, however, because there exists a much more effective approach to addressing that concern. Instead of excluding intentional harm claims, liability insurance contracts could cover those claims but authorize the insurer to subrogate against the responsible insured for the limited purpose of recovering damages paid in satisfaction of claims based on that harm. Cf.

Ambassador Ins. Co. v. Montes, 388 A.2d 603 (1978) (holding that a liability insurance company that paid an intentional tort claim may subrogate against its insured.). See Baker, *Insurance Law and Policy*, 488n3 (discussing the legislative and/or administrative actions necessary for the elimination of internal harm exclusions).

64. Although compensation is no longer a favored goal of liability among many tort law scholars (e.g., Shavell), it remains a fundamental purpose of tort law as articulated by lawmakers. See, e.g., *Lodge v. Arett Sales Corp.*, 1994 WL 421428 (Conn. 1998). Cf. John Fleming, "The Collateral Source Rule and Loss Allocation in Tort Law," *California Law Review* 54 (1966): 1549 (suggesting that tort liability will and should become only a secondary source of compensation "to the extent that the cost of compensation has not been met by another source"). See also Tom Baker, "Reconsidering Insurance for Punitive Damages," *Wisconsin Law Review* 1998 (1998): 101–30.

65. Jennifer Wriggins, "Domestic Violence Torts," *Southern California Law Review* 75 (2001): 121.

CHAPTER 13

1. See generally Andrew J. McClurg, David B. Kopel, and Brannon P. Denning, eds., *Gun Control and Gun Rights: A Reader and Guide* (New York: New York University Press, 2002), chap. 4; Symposium, "Guns and Liability in America," *Connecticut Law Review* 32 (2000): 1159; David B. Kopel and Richard E. Gardiner, "The Sullivan Principles: Protecting the Second Amendment from Civil Abuse," *Seton Hall Legislative Journal* 19 (1995): 737; Jerry J. Phillips, "The Relation of Constitutional and Tort Law to Gun Injuries and Deaths in the United States," *Connecticut Law Review* 32 (2000): 1337; William L. McCoskey, Note, "The Right of the People to Keep and Bear Arms Shall Not Be Litigated Away: Constitutional Implications of Municipal Lawsuits against the Gun Industry," *Indiana Law Journal* 77 (2002): 873.

2. McCoskey, "The Right of the People to Keep and Bear Arms," 875n17.

3. *New York Times v. Sullivan*, 376 U.S. 254 (1964).

4. See generally Boris I. Bittker, *Bittker on the Regulation of Interstate and Foreign Commerce* (New York: Aspen Law and Business, 1999 and 2005 Supp.), chap. 6.

5. Ibid., § 6.06.

6. See, e.g., *Healy v. Beer Institute, Inc.*, 491 U.S. 324 (1989).

7. See, e.g., *Pike v. Bruce Church, Inc.*, 397 U.S. 137 (1970).

8. Kopel and Gardiner, "The Sullivan Principles."

9. See Lucas A. Powe Jr., *The Warren Court and American Politics* (Cambridge, MA: Harvard University Press, 2000), 304–7.

10. *New York Times v. Sullivan*, 376 U.S. 254, 264 (1964) (footnote omitted). Unless otherwise indicated, all references to *New York Times v. Sullivan* are from this citation, and all quotes can be found within this citation.

11. Kopel and Gardiner, "The Sullivan Principles." All references to Kopel and Gardiner in this section are drawn from this source.

12. *New York Times v. Sullivan*, 376 U.S. 254, 282 (1964).

13. Ibid.

14. See, e.g., *Warren v. District of Columbia*, 444 A.2d 1, 3 (D.C. 1981) ("[A] fundamental principle [of American law is] that a government and its agents are under no general duty to provide public services, such as police protection, to any particular individual citizen.").

15. Kopel and Gardiner, "The Sullivan Principles," 748.

16. See *NAACP v. AcuSport, Inc.*, 271 F.Supp.2d 435 (E.D.N.Y. 2003).

17. I suppose that one might argue, initially, that *Sullivan* was a mistaken decision and that it should certainly not be extended to other areas. See Richard A. Epstein, "Was New York Times v. Sullivan Wrong?" *University of Chicago Law Review* 53 (1986): 782 (suggesting that it was).

18. See, e.g., Brannon P. Denning, "Gun Shy: The Second Amendment as an 'Underenforced Constitutional Norm,'" *Harvard Journal of Law and Public Policy* 21 (1998): 719; Brannon P. Denning, "Can the Simple Cite Be Trusted? Lower Court Interpretation of United States v. Miller and the Second Amendment," *Cumberland Law Review* 26 (1996): 961.

19. See *Presser v. Illinois*, 116 U.S. 252 (1886).

20. See, e.g., Akhil Reed Amar, *The Bill of Rights: Creation and Reconstruction* (New Haven: Yale University Press, 1998).

21. See Daniel A. Farber, *The First Amendment*, 2d ed. (New York: Foundation Press, 2003), 86–91 (summarizing the post-Sullivan cases and the questions they have raised).

22. *Gertz v. Robert Welch, Inc.*, 418 U.S. 323 (1974). Unless otherwise noted, the remainder of this section draws on the Court's opinion in this case.

23. *Dun & Bradstreet, Inc. v. Greenmoss Builders, Inc.*, 472 U.S. 749 (1985). This case is summarized in the remaining part of this section. All quotes are available at this citation.

24. See note 17 and the accompanying text in the chapter.

25. David G. Browne, "Treating the Pen and the Sword as Constitutional Equals: How and Why the Supreme Court Should Apply Its First Amendment Expertise to the Great Second Amendment Debate," *William and Mary Law Review* 44 (2003): 2287, 2293.

26. Don B. Kates Jr., "The Second Amendment and the Ideology of Self-Protection," *Constitutional Commentary* 9 (1992): 87.

27. See Kopel and Gardiner, "The Sullivan Principles," 769 (using one business example).

28. See McClurg, Kopel and Denning, *Gun Control and Gun Rights*.

29. See Brady Center to Prevent Gun Violence, *Lawsuit Preemption Statutes*, http://www.gunlawsuits.org/docket/cities/preemption.asp.

30. See H.R. 1036, 108th Cong., 2d sess.

31. See, e.g., *City of Renton v. Playtime Theaters, Inc.*, 475 U.S. 41 (1986); see also *City of Erie v. Pap's A.M.*, 529 U.S. 277 (2000).

32. See, e.g., "Editorial, Criminals, Not Gun Makers, Should Pay the Price for Misuse," *Charleston [WV] Gazette and Daily Mail*, April 4, 2003, 4A, available at 2003 WL 5455611 (arguing that suits against gun manufacturers threaten Second Amendment rights); Paul Craig Roberts, "Gun Control: The Criminal Lobby," *Washington Times*, April 26, 2003, A10, available at 2003 WL 7710129 ("All that is required for a small wealthy elite to destroy the Second Amendment is a gullible jury and a judge who permits a class action suit to expropriate the powers of legislators."); see also Press Release, "Foley Pushes Ban on Frivolous Lawsuits against Gun Manufacturers," April 9, 2003, available at 2003 WL 11709826 (touting Representative Mark Foley [R-FL]'s support for H.R. 1036; accusing those opposing the bill immunizing manufacturers of opposing Second Amendment rights); James G. Lakely and Stephen Dinan, "Democrats Eye Filibuster on Gun Bill," *Washington Times*, May 14, 2003, A4, available at 2003 WL 7711278 (quoting sponsor of H.R. 1036 as saying that "'[t]he antigun lobby is continually coming up with things to go against our Second Amendment rights and to bring in trial lawyers and litigation against law-abiding citizens. We think that's outrageous, and that's what this bill is intended to stop.'").

33. See, e.g., *Willson v. Black Bird Creek Marsh Co.*, 27 U.S. (2 Pet.) 245, 252 (1829); *Camps Newfound/Owatonna v. Harrison*, 520 U.S. 564, 575, 581 (1997).

34. See, e.g., *Hughes v. Oklahoma*, 441 U.S. 322, 336 (1979). See *C & A Carbone, Inc. v. Clarkstown*, 511 U.S. 383, 413 (1994).

35. See *Healy v. Beer Institute, Inc.*, 491 U.S. 324, 336–37 (1989).

36. See *Pike v. Bruce Church, Inc.*, 397 U.S. 137, 142 (1970).

37. See, e.g., *BMW v. Gore*, 517 U.S. 559, 572 n.17 (1996); *New York Times v. Sullivan*, 376 U.S. 254, 265 (1964).

38. See, e.g., *White v. Smith & Wesson*, 97 F. Supp. 2d 816, 829–30 (N.D. Ohio 2000); *City of Gary, Ind. ex rel King v. Smith & Wesson Corp.*, 94 F. Supp. 2d 947, 949–51 (N.D. Ind. 2000); *Camden v. Beretta U.S.A. Corp.*, 81 F. Supp. 2d 541, 547–49 (D.N.J. 2000); *Boston v. Smith & Wesson Corp.*, 66 F. Supp. 2d 246, 249–50 (D. Mass. 1999); see also James Fleming Jr., Geoffrey C. Hazard Jr., and John Leubsdorf, *Civil Procedure*, 5th ed. (New York: Foundation Press, 2001), §§ 2.25–2.26, 2.31 (discussing requirements for "arising under" jurisdiction and for removal).

39. See, e.g., *NAACP v. AcuSport, Inc.*, 271 F.Supp.2d 435 (E.D.N.Y. 2003); *Gary*, 94 F. Supp. 2d at 949–51.

40. See *AcuSport, Inc.*, 271 F. Supp. 2d at 435; *White*, 97 F. Supp.2d at 829–30; *Camden County Bd. Freeholders*, 123 F. Supp.2d at 253–55; *Camden*, 81

F. Supp.2d at 547–49; *Boston*, 66 F. Supp. 2d at 246; *Cincinnati v. Beretta U.S.A. Corp.*, 768 N.E.2d1136, 1150 (Ohio, 2002); *District of Columbia v. Beretta U.S.A Corp.*, 2002 WL 31811717, at *43–45; *Gary ex rel. King v. Smith & Wesson Corp.*, 2001 WL 333111 (Ind. Ct. App.) (Jan. 11, 2001) (unpublished), at *6, *rev'd* 2003 WL 23010035 (Ind.) (Dec. 23, 2003). See also Allen Rostron, "The Supreme Court, the Gun Industry, and the Misguided Revival of Strict Territorial Limits on the Reach of State Law," *Michigan State University-Detroit College of Law Review* 2003 (2003): 115, 151–56.

41. See notes 69–74 and the accompanying text in the chapter.

42. 517 U.S. 559 (1996). Unless otherwise noted, references to this case and quotes from this case are all available at this citation.

43. Ibid., 571–72.

44. *BMW v. Gore*, 517 U.S. 559, 571 (1996) (footnote omitted).

45. The citation to DCCD as well as the discussion of damages as "economic sanctions" strongly suggests, contrary to a recent assertion of the Indiana Supreme Court—see *Gary ex rel. King v. Smith & Wesson, Corp.*, 2003 WL 23010035 (Ind.) (Dec. 23, 2003)—that *BMW* involves the DCCD to some extent. The *Gary* court wrote that "we think *BMW* is a due process case, not a Commerce Clause case." Ibid., *9.

46. *BMW*, 517 U.S. at 572n17.

47. See notes 43–47 and the accompanying text in the chapter.

48. See *NAACP v. AcuSport, Inc.*, 271 F.Supp.2d 435, 463 (E.D.N.Y. 2003) (rejecting arguments that the dormant Commerce Clause doctrine preempts state lawsuits); *City of Gary*, 94 F. Supp.2d at 949–51 ("Defendant's deduction that if the Commerce Clause empowers Congress to regulate interstate commerce, then the Commerce Clause itself, even in the absence of Congressional regulation, must also have preemptive effect, is a faulty syllogism. . . . [T]he Commerce Clause itself does not wholly preempt state regulation of interstate commerce to any extent."); *Camden v. Beretta U.S.A. Corp.*, 81 F. Supp. 2d 541, 547–49 (D.N.J. 2000) ("[S]imply because a state law or claim may have an effect on interstate commerce does not mean that such law is precluded by the Commerce Clause."); see also *Sills v. Smith & Wesson Corp.*, 2000 WL 33113806 (Del. Super. Ct.) (Dec. 1, 2000), at *8 (unpublished) ("[D]efendants do not even allege in passing that federal preemption applies to the handgun industry.").

49. See *City of Gary*, 94 F. Supp.2d 947 at 951 ("The defendants' arguments that Gary's action violates the Commerce Clause . . . is a defense, not a basis for removal as an exception to the well-pleaded complaint rule."); *Camden*, 81 F. Supp.2d at 547–49; *Boston v. Smith & Wesson Corp.*, 66 F. Supp. 2d 246, 249–50 (D. Mass. 1999); see also James, Hazard, and Leubsdorf, *Civil Procedure*, § 2.31, at 156 ("an action based on state law may not be removed to federal court on the ground that the defendant has a defense of counterclaim that rests on federal law," footnote omitted).

50. *Camden County Bd. of Chosen Freeholders v . Beretta U.S.A. Corp.*, 273 F.3d 536 (3d Cir.2001); see also *City of Boston*, 2000 WL 1473568, at *11 ("The

applicability of the Commerce Clause to causes of action under state tort and contract law is unsettled.").

51. *City of Boston*, 2000 WL 1473568, at *11.

52. *Camden County Bd. Freeholders*, 123 F. Supp.2d at 255; *City of Boston*, 2000 WL 1473568, at *13–14; see also *Boston*, 66 F. Supp.2d at 49–50 (conceding that "the Commerce Clause may affect the measure of plaintiffs' relief should plaintiffs prove successful in their suit"); *Camden*, 81 F. Supp.2d at 547–49.

53. See *White v. Smith & Wesson*, 97 F. Supp. 2d 816, 829–30 (N.D. Ohio 2000); *Cincinnati v. Beretta U.S.A. Corp.*, 768 N.E.2d 1136, 1150 (Ohio 2002); *Boston*, 2000 WL 1473568, at *13–14.

54. *City of Gary*, 2001 WL 333111, at *6.

55. *City of Gary v. Smith & Wesson Co.*, 2003 WL 23010035 (Ind.) (Dec. 23, 2003), at *9 ("[W]e think *BMW* is a due process case, not a Commerce Clause case."). Cf. *Ileto v. Glock, Inc.*, 349 F.3d 1191, 1217 (9th Cir. 2003) (treating *BMW* as a DCCD case but nevertheless concluding that it did not prohibit suit for negligence and nuisance claims).

56. *City of Gary*, 2003 WL 23010025 at *10.

57. *District of Columbia v. Beretta U.S.A. Corp.*, 2002 WL 31811717 (D.C. Super. Ct.) (Dec. 16, 2002), at *44 (discussing the D.C. Strict Liability Act, which "confers strict liability for all damages that flow from the discharge of such weapons inside the District, without regard to any allegation of proof or 'fault'"). Unless otherwise noted, references to this case and quotes from this case are all available at this citation.

58. The court also expressed doubt as to the true "non-discriminatory" nature of the ordinance and whether it would even pass muster under *Pike* balancing. See ibid., *45

59. *NAACP v. AcuSport, Inc.*, 271 F.Supp.2d 435, 465 (E.D.N.Y. 2003) at *18 ("The Commerce Clause furnishes no defense under the circumstances of the instant case to conduct occurring inside and outside the state that causes a public nuisance within the state; any burden placed on interstate commerce is far outweighed by the substantial positive effect on the New York public's health and safety that more scrupulous supervision of the sale of their handguns by gun manufacturers and distributors would have."); see also *Camden County Bd. Freeholders*, 123 F. Supp.2d at 254–55; see also *Ileto v. Glock, Inc.*, 349 F.3d 1191, 1217 (9th Cir. 2003). But see note 62.

60. *Sills v. Smith & Wesson Corp.*, 2000 WL 33113806 (Del. Super. Ct.) (Dec. 1, 2000), at *8 (unpublished).

61. See, e.g., *Geier v. American Honda Motor Co., Inc.*, 529 U.S. 861 (2000) (holding that state tort claim preempted for defective design preempted by federal law); *Cipollone v. Liggett Group, Inc.*, 505 U.S. 504 (1992) (assuming that congressional statutes could preempt state tort law claims).

62. See, e.g., *Morgan v. Virginia*, 328 U.S. 373, 380 (1946) (noting that state may not avoid the DCCD "by simply invoking the convenient apologetics of the police power," internal quotations omitted).

63. See notes 37–41 and the accompanying text in the chapter.

64. See, e.g., *Healy v. Beer Institute, Inc.,* 491 U.S. 324, 336–37 (1989); Erwin Chemerinsky, *Constitutional Law: Principles and Policies,* 2d ed. (New York: Aspen Law and Business, 2002), 422–23.

65. *Pharm. Research and Mf. of America v. Walsh,* 538 U.S. 644 (2003) (refusing to strike down state program funding prescription drug benefit for its citizens with rebates charged drug manufacturers providing drugs for state Medicaid program).

66. *Ileto v. Glock, Inc.,* 349 F.3d 1191, 1216–17 (9th Cir. 2003).

67. *Pike v. Bruce Church, Inc.,* 397 U.S. 137, 142 (1970); see also *Ileto,* 349 F.3d at 1217.

68. *Healy v. Beer Institute,* 491 U.S. 324, 336–37 (1989) (footnotes and citations omitted).

69. Cf. *Cooley v. Bd. Wardens,* 53 U.S. (12 How.) 298, 319 (1851) ("Whatever subjects of . . . are in their nature national, or admit only of one uniform system, or plan of regulation, may justly be said to be of such a nature as to require exclusive legislation by Congress.").

70. *Healy v. Beer Institute,* 491 U.S. 324, 326–31 (1989) (describing Connecticut's "price-affirmation" statute for beer sales).

71. See Brady Center to Prevent Gun Violence, Legal Action Project, "Theories in Lawsuits Brought by Cities and Counties Against the Gun Industry," available at http://www.gunlawsuits.org/docket/cities/theories.php (last accessed Nov. 29, 2004).

72. There is another problem here: federal consumer product safety legislation, to the chagrin of gun control advocates, specifically *exempts* guns from its provisions. See 15 U.S.C. § 2052(a)(1)(E) (2002). This raises the real possibility that—insofar as that choice is indicative of congressional desire to leave safety aspects of firearms *unregulated*—its choice preempts states (and state courts) from undertaking to regulate in its stead.

73. See Neal Devins, "I Love You Big Brother," *California Law Review* 87 (1999): 1283.

74. *City of Gary ex rel. King v. Smith & Wesson, Corp.,* 2003 WL 23010035 (Ind.) (Dec. 23, 2003). Unless otherwise noted, references to this case and quotes from this case are all available at this citation.

75. Ibid. (citing *Edgar v. MITE Corp.,* 457 U.S. 624 (1982)).

76. *Pharm. Research and Mf. of America v. Walsh,* 123 S. Ct. 1855, 1870–71 (2003).

77. Jack L. Goldsmith and Alan O. Sykes, "The Internet and the Dormant Commerce Clause," *Yale Law Journal* 110 (2001): 785, 806. All of the following quotations to Goldsmith and Sykes are taken from this article.

78. See *Ileto v. Glock Inc.,* 349 F.3d 1191, 1217 (9th Cir. 2003) (distinguishing, in the Ninth Circuit, *BMW* on the ground that "plaintiffs [had] abandoned all requests for injunctive relief and economic sanctions in the form of punitive damages to protect the rights of citizens from other states").

CONTRIBUTORS

Tom Baker is the Connecticut Mutual Professor of Law at the Insurance Law Center of the University of Connecticut. He is an alumnus of both Harvard University and Harvard University School of Law. Professor Baker has published several legal articles, is the coauthor of *Embracing Risk: The Changing Culture of Insurance and Responsibility*, and is the author of *Insurance Law and Policy*.

Donald Braman is currently studying law at Yale Law School. He received his PhD in anthropology from Yale University prior to attending law school. Mr. Braman has published on a variety of subjects and recently completed a book on the effects of incarceration on inmates' families, entitled *Doing Time on the Outside*.

Brannon P. Denning is Associate Professor at the Cumberland School of Law at Samford University. Professor Denning received his BA from the University of the South, his JD from the University of Tennessee School of Law, and his LLM from Yale Law School. He has published many articles dealing with constitutional issues, served as the editor of *Gun Control and Gun Rights: A Reader and a Guide*, and continues to collaborate on updates to *Bittker on the Regulation of Interstate Commerce and Foreign Commerce*.

Tom Diaz is a senior policy analyst at the Violence Policy Center. He received his BA from the University of Florida and his JD from Georgetown University Law Center. The author of many studies on firearms and gun violence, Mr. Diaz is also the author of *On the Front Lines: Making Gun Interdiction Work*—written for the Law Enforcement Division of the Brady Center to Prevent Handgun Violence—and *Making a Killing: The Business of Guns in America.*

Howard M. Erichson is Professor of Law at Seton Hall University School of Law. He earned his BA from Harvard University and his JD from the New York University School of Law. His publications include multiple articles regarding mass tort law and the forthcoming *American College of Trial Lawyers Mass Tort Litigation Manual,* for which he is a reporter.

Thomas O. Farrish is a research assistant to Professor Tom Baker at the University of Connecticut.

Shannon Frattaroli is an Assistant Scientist at the Health Policy and Management Department of the Johns Hopkins Bloomberg School of Public Health and is affiliated with the Center for Injury Research and Policy and the Center for Gun Research and Policy at Johns Hopkins University. Ms. Frattaroli received her BA from UCLA, her MPH from the Johns Hopkins School of Public Health, and her PhD from Johns Hopkins University. Her publications primarily concentrate on gun violence and policy.

John Gastil is Associate Professor of communications at the University of Washington. He received his BA from Swarthmore College and his PhD from the University of Wisconsin-Madison. Professor Gastil is the author of two books, *Democracy in Small Groups* and *By Popular Demand: Revitalizing Representative Democracy through Deliberate Elections.*

Dan M. Kahan is the Elizabeth K. Dollard Professor of Law at Yale Law School. He received his BA from Middlebury College and his JD from Harvard Law School. Professor Kahan's publications include *Urgent Times: Policing and Rights in Inner-City Communities,* of which he is a coauthor.

Don B. Kates is a civil liberties lawyer, criminologist, and retired professor. He is a graduate of Reed College and Yale Law School. A prolific author on civil liberties and violence issues, Mr. Kates is the editor of *Firearms and Violence: Issues of Public Policy,* the coauthor of *Armed:*

New Perspectives on Gun Control and *The Great American Gun Debate: Essays on Firearms and Violence,* and the author of *Restricting Handguns.*

Timothy D. Lytton is Professor of Law at Albany Law School, where he teaches torts, legislation, constitutional law, alternative dispute resolution, and jurisprudence. He holds BA and JD degrees from Yale University and is the author of scholarly articles on civil litigation and the philosophy of law.

Julie Samia Mair is Assistant Scientist at the Health Policy and Management Department of the Johns Hopkins Bloomberg School of Public Health. She received her BA from Smith College, her JD from the University of Pennsylvania, and her MPH from the Johns Hopkins School of Public Health. Professor Mair is the author of numerous articles.

Richard A. Nagareda is Professor of Law at Vanderbilt University Law School. He earned his AB from Stanford University and his JD from the University of Chicago School of Law. Professor Nagareda has published articles on mass tort litigation and evidence.

Peter H. Schuck is the Simeon E. Baldwin Professor of Law at Yale Law School and is Visiting Professor at New York University School of Law. He received his BA from Cornell University, his JD from Harvard Law School, his LLM from New York University School of Law, and his MA from Harvard University. He is the author and editor of books on topics ranging from administrative law to tort law to citizenship; his most recent work is *Diversity in America: Keeping the Government at a Safe Distance.*

Stephen D. Sugarman is the Agnes Roddy Robb Professor of Law at the University of California at Berkeley School of Law, Boalt Hall. He earned both his BS and JD from Northwestern University. He is the author and coauthor of over ten books focusing on a broad segment of legal issues.

Stephen Teret is Director of the Center for Law and the Public's Health at the Johns Hopkins Bloomberg School of Public Health and is professor at both the Center for Gun Policy and Research and the Center for Injury Research and Policy. Professor Teret received his BA from St. Lawrence University, his JD from Brooklyn Law School, and his MPH from the Johns Hopkins School of Public Health. He is the author of many articles on violence and injury prevention.

Wendy Wagner is Professor of Law at the University of Texas School of Law. She received her BA from Hanover College and both her master's degree in environmental science and her JD from Yale University. Professor Wagner is the author of numerous articles and book chapters. She is also the author of the white papers "Enforcement against Concentrations of Toxic Pollutions in Texas" and "Legal Aspects of Regulatory Use of Environmental Modeling."

TABLE OF CASES

INDEX